Workers and Capital

Workers and Capital

Mario Tronti

Translated by David Broder

VERSO

London • New York

This book has been translated thanks to a translation grant awarded by the
Italian Ministry of Foreign Affairs and International Cooperation.
Questo libro è stato tradotto grazie ad un contributo alla traduzione assegnato dal
Ministero degli Affari Esteri e della Cooperazione Internazionale italiano.

The translation of this book has been funded by SEPS
SEGRETARIO EUROPEO PER LE PUBBLICAZIONI SCIENTIFICHE

SEGRETARIATO EUROPEO PER LE PUBBLICAZIONI SCIENTIFICHE

Via Val d'Aposa 7 – 40123 Bologna – Italy
seps@seps.it – www.seps.it

This English-language edition published by Verso 2019
Published in Italian as Operai e capitale by Einaudi in 1966 and 1971,
   republished by DeriveApprodi in 2006 and 2013
Translation © David Broder 2019

1 3 5 7 9 10 8 6 4 2

Verso
UK: 6 Meard Street, London W1F 0EG
US: 20 Jay Street, Suite 1010, Brooklyn, NY 11201
versobooks.com

Verso is the imprint of New Left Books

ISBN-13: 978-1-78873-040-2
ISBN-13: 978-1-78873-039-6 (HARDBACK)
ISBN-13: 978-1-78873-041-9 (UK EBK)
ISBN-13: 978-1-78873-042-6 (US EBK)

British Library Cataloguing in Publication Data
A catalogue record for this book is available from the British Library

Library of Congress Cataloging-in-Publication Data
A catalog record for this book is available from the Library of Congress

Typeset in Minion by Hewer Text UK Ltd, Edinburgh
Printed and bound by CPI Group (UK) Ltd, Croydon CR0 4YY

Contents

Foreword

Steve Wright

The publication of an English-language edition of Mario Tronti's 1966 classic *Operai e capitale* has been long awaited. One or two complete chapters have appeared in the past, together with some fragments; more recently, other sections of the book have appeared online. Now, thanks to David Broder's fine translation, a complete version of the book's second edition of 1971 is available. English-language readers who had previously encountered *Workers and Capital* only in part, or else as refracted through second hand commentary, are finally in a position to judge for themselves the value of Tronti's most famous text.

Initially published in 1966, *Operai e capitale* is the first book produced by the political tendency known as *operaismo* (literally 'workerism', although arguments continue as to whether that is a useful rendering of the word in English). Many such books followed over the next fifteen years, and some of these too would be best sellers. None, however, could match the shiver of recognition and excitement that Tronti's volume evoked within a large part of Italy's generation of 1968. At a time when the likes of Marcuse and Mao were as popular there as elsewhere in the West, *Workers and Capital* stood out amongst the local outpourings of revolutionary thought. In truth, for many Italian radical circles of the time, the book was treated as nothing less than a bible – above all by the group Potere Operaio, which briefly brought together a significant proportion of the country's workerists, in pursuit of what Brecht once called 'the simple thing / So difficult to achieve'.

As with other political tendencies, *operaismo* did not emerge one morning fully formed and complete. Instead, its central precepts were developed over the course of the early 1960s, during which its advocates slowly differentiated themselves amongst a range of perspectives critical of the postwar practices of the mainstream left in Italy. United by a common belief that the leadership of the local Communist (PCI) and Socialist (PSI) parties did not understand the recent massive changes in working-class composition and politics, these various dissenters offered very different solutions to this conundrum. Amongst them, the worker-ists insisted that 'a Marxian purification of Marx' was indispensable for understanding and organising class conflict. So far, so usual: what made the *operaisti* less typical (although not unique) was an equal insistence that this task could only be achieved through an encounter between Marx's critique of political economy and the realities of workplace power relations in contemporary Italy.

Tronti was born into a Roman working-class family in 1931. As secretary of the university PCI branch, he was one of the many party members who protested against the USSR's invasion of revolutionary Hungary. Not long afterwards, Tronti began to make a name for himself as a talented if unconventional writer on Marx's mature work, influenced in this by Galvano della Volpe. The latter was then unusual as a Communist intellectual who read Marx closely: Tronti's early work went further, and turned Marx into a goad to be used against the Communist party's tutelary saint Antonio Gramsci. Criticising what he saw as the profoundly idealist outlook of the Gramsci championed by the Communist party, Tronti argued that 'If philosophy coincides with good sense, we must distrust philosophy.'[1] Unlike Gramsci, Tronti did not hail any 'revolutions

---

1 What followed was the paradoxical story of a general defeat, punctuated by illusory small-scale victories. Thus it went until the end of the 1980s, when we were all forced to understand where history had ended up going. The leadership of the PCI suffered, in a subordinate mode, the same fate as the ruling classes of the country. Modernisation required a passing of the baton from the generations of war and resistance to the generations of peace and development. The movements of 1968 supplied new personnel for this handover. What happened in the party was what happened in the circles of power: a new political class was not born; rather, in its place, a new administrative class emerged, always managerial, at the levels of both government and opposition. The whole Berlinguer leadership – as much with the

against *Capital*; rather, he sought 'to engage with Marx not in his own time, but in our own. *Capital* should be judged on the basis of *the capitalism of today*.' And the capitalism of the early 1960s was one through which Italian society was subjected to massive change: in the first place, an unprecedented industrial development underpinned by internal migration to the country's North, swelling in turn the population of cities like Milan and Turin. Faced with such changes, the country's official labour movement seemed to Tronti and his closest associates to be ill-equipped to understand the processes in tow, let alone to formulate appropriate class strategies in response.

By the late 1950s, Tronti and his immediate associates had been drawn into the national network of young militants then being assembled by Raniero Panzieri. A dissident Socialist from an older generation, Panzieri shared the scepticism of Tronti and others as to the ability of the main left-wing parties to develop a class politics adequate to a rapidly changing Italy. Recalling their time working together around the iconic journal *Quaderni Rossi* (Red Notebooks), Tronti would later write that, for all the differences in their outlook, Panzieri deserved to be remembered as someone who 'had anticipated the 1960s', a decade that in Italy culminated not only in an imposing student movement, but also in a wave of mass workers struggles that challenged the unions

---

historic compromise as with its alternative – proved to be nothing more than a tumultuous period of defence, which lined up *il popolo comunista* to contain and slow the neobourgeois flood. But, at that point, there was little else that could be done. In the last act of the tragedy, the Communist Party was rechristened as the Democratic Party of the Left. This was followed by the farce, when even the word 'party' disappeared, under pressure from antipolitical populism. There were no more barriers. Just the flood.

From the 1980s onwards, neoliberal capitalist restoration sapped the workers' capacity for opposition. With the breaking of the weakest link in the anticapitalist chain – the Soviet state – there was no longer any way to block the returning hegemonic power from taking absolute command. The newly declared dominance of capital was not just economic but social, political and cultural. It was at once theoretical and ideological, a combination of intellectual and mass common sense. Yet it's worth stressing one final fact: for as long as the postcapitalist horizon remained open, the struggle to introduce elements of social justice within capitalism achieved some success. Once the revolutionary project was defeated, the reformist programme became impossible, too. In this sense, the latest form of neoliberal capitalism may prove ironically similar to the final forms of state socialism: incapable of reform.

Mario Tronti, 'Some Questions Around Gramsci's Marxism', translated by Andrew Anastasi, *Viewpoint* 2016 [1958].

and the parties of the mainstream left as much as it challenged capital itself.[2]

Like Lukács's *History and Class Consciousness*, *Workers and Capital* is a collection of essays composed over a period of years. Most had previously appeared in a range of left-wing journals across the first half of the 1960s – primarily *Quaderni Rossi* and *Classe Operaia* (Working Class), the review that Tronti and others began publishing in 1964. As a consequence, the evolution of many of the book's key themes can be traced within and across its very pages. For that reason, reading the book by beginning with its introduction can be a little deceiving, given that 'A course of action' was in fact the last section written for its first edition. While Tronti seems not to have revamped any of the individual components of his book, the manner in which his introduction frames the essays that follow cast the latter in a new light, as does his decision to select particular writings from *Classe Operaia* and treat them as part of one composite treatise. The texts that predate that journal – grouped together in the book's initial section as 'First hypotheses' – set the scene for what is to follow, arguing not only that 'working-class struggle has always objectively functioned as a dynamic moment of capitalist development', but drawing the conclusion that 'The bourgeois state machine today must today be broken within the capitalist factory'. Still, it will take the opening sentences of the first essay of the book's second section ('Lenin in England' – also the editorial of *Classe Operaia*'s first issue) for *operaismo* to be ushered into being through what has since been called Tronti's 'Copernican revolution': 'At the level of socially-developed capital, capitalist development is subordinate to working-class struggles.'

Operai e capitale is written in a clear and elegant Italian that somehow manages to combine passion with the laconic. It is a style that many later imitators have tried (and usually failed) to mimic. And, for all the talk in its pages of 'caution', the line of argument presented is a bold and confident one. If what was required was 'the theoretical rebirth of the working-class viewpoint', that goal only made sense in pursuit of one goal: 'give us the party in Italy, and we will overthrow all Europe!' Although Tronti once wrote apologetically to the publisher Giulio Enaudi about the book's 'biblical' language, there is no doubt as to *Workers and*

---

    2 Mario Tronti, 'Testimonianza', in Paolo Ferrero, ed, *Raniero Panzieri. Un uomo di frontiera*, Milan: Edizioni Punto Rosso, 2005, 238.

Capital's prophetic tone, which Broder's translation captures ably. Reviewing the book in 1967 for the Communist Party cultural weekly *Rinascita*, Adalberto Minucci – then one of Tronti's fiercest opponents within the PCI – made no effort to hide his contempt for the book's 'subtle theological discussions … totally impermeable to an effective relationship with reality'.[3] Yet, in doing so, Minucci largely missed the point. As Riccardo Bellofiore and Massimiliano Tomba have argued instead,

> When Mario Tronti, in 'Lenin in England', read workers' passivity, non-collaboration with unions, standoffishness, and refusal as 'organised passivity', 'planned non-collaboration', 'polemical standoffishness', and 'political refusal', he was on the one hand preparing new lenses with which to read new working class behaviours, and seeking on the other new modalities of reading marked by a strongly performative value. Tronti did not intend to produce an objective reading of reality, but rather of the effects on that reality.[4]

Or, as Tronti himself later wrote, 'the writing of a "political thinker" ' can only be 'a speaking for the purpose of producing an effect'.[5]

The centrepiece of *Workers and Capital* is 'Marx, Labour-Power, Working Class' – by far the book's longest essay (more than half the original book), and the only one not to have been published in a journal before *Operai e capitale*'s appearance. This chapter has been called 'perhaps the most analytical text ever written by Tronti',[6] and it is certainly different in important ways from others in the volume. Divided into fourteen sections, Tronti's argument builds relentlessly in tracing the course by which the commodity labour-power might transform itself into a revolutionary class 'within and against' the capital relation.

---

3   Adalberto Minucci, 'Il marxista dimezzato. Su un libro di Mario Tronti: Operai e capitale', *Rinascita* 12, 1967, available at operaviva.info.

4   Riccardo Bellofiore and Massimiliano Tomba, 'Afterword to the Italian Edition', in Steve Wright, *Storming Heaven: Class Composition and Struggle in Italian Autonomist Marxism*, London: Pluto Press 2017, 238.

5   Mario Tronti, 'Politica e destino', in Mario Tronti, et al., *Politica e destino*, Rome: Luca Sossella Editore 2006, 11.

6   Matteo Cavalleri, Michele Filippini and Jamila M.H. Mascat, 'Introduzione', in Mario Tronti, *Il demone della politica. Antologia di scritti 1958–2015*, Bologna: Il Mulino, 2017, 20.

The essay begins with a discussion of how Marx's notion of the unique-
ness of that commodity – first and foremost, the twofold nature of its
labour within capitalist production – was developed over time. If part of
that development occurred through the appropriation and critique of
earlier thinkers (not only Hegel, but Ricardo perhaps even more so),
Tronti asserts the importance for Marx of learning from the class struggle of his time. As a consequence, Tronti wants to reread the German's
classic pamphlets on revolution in 1848, holding that, whatever their
other failings,

> they have a clear-sightedness in foreseeing future developments such
> as only class hatred could provide. And in these writings, we see for
> the first time the overlapping and conjugation of the abstract concept
> of labour and the concrete reality of the worker.[7]

Some of the influences on Tronti's perspectives as set out in 'Marx,
Labour-Power, Working Class' are clear enough – Lukács, for example,
is explicitly cited in the essay, if only in passing, and we also know that
the early workerists were familiar with texts by the likes of Boggs and
Dunaveyskya. But, if Lukács had insisted that only the proletariat could
make sense of capitalist society, if Boggs had prophesied an impending
'workless society', and if Dunaveyskya had traced the ways in which
working class struggle had acted to force along capitalist development,
'Marx, Labour-Power, Working Class' represents an extremely ambi-
tious attempt to combine and move beyond these insights. The essay
ends by presenting two separate if parallel understandings of political
struggle needed to challenge capital – the refusal of work that springs
from the very nature of the capital relation, and the urgency of the party
that requires a Lenin for its success. If the precise contours of the way
forward are left hanging, it is also true that the central pivot remains the
party, understood as 'the organisation of what already exists within the
class, but which the class alone cannot succeed in organising'.

Whilst *Workers and Capital* is unquestionably the foundational text
of *operaismo*, it is worth noting nonetheless what is absent from the
book. Like many others, I believe the theme of class composition to be
workerism's most original contribution. What overt discussion of class

---

7 This volume, 150–1.

composition exists in its pages, however, really only appears in the long essay on Marx, and even this is limited in terms of any exploration of method or analysis. In a similar fashion, there is no examination of the 'mass worker' forged within the mass production that underpinned the consumer durables sector – another crucial political touchstone of workerism by the late 1960s, when this subject was widely heralded as the preeminent revolutionary actor. Instead, the first edition of the book closes with an admission that, if 'The abolition of work by the working class and the violent destruction of capital are one and the same', no one had yet addressed 'the most obscure aspect of the whole process: … *what has happened within the working class since Marx.*' In a similar way, a reader looking for examples of *operaismo*'s direct engagement with concrete struggles in concrete workplaces and communities of the period is similarly obliged to turn elsewhere: to the sometimes meandering, but always rich accounts offered by Romano Alquati, or even to novels such as Nanni Balestrini's *We Want Everything.* Nor, despite all the talk of moving 'from factory to society', is there any analysis (or even acknowledgement) of what today is called the realm of social reproduction. And yet, for all its apparent abstractness in parts, *Workers and Capital* still managed to resonate across the 1960s and 1970s with a large number of militants in Italy, inspiring in them a commitment to class self-organisation. If Sergio Bologna is to be believed, this is because Tronti's words were able 'to provide a synthesis for the thousands of cues transmitted through everyday experience and contact with a working class then in the process of stirring itself'.[8]

Since multiple pathways could and were read into *Workers and Capital* by those who heeded the book's call to action in the 1960s and 1970s, the directions that various *operaisti* came to follow in its wake were often diverse (think of the whole suite of practices and analyses that are commonly folded into the slogan 'Wages for Housework'). One suspects that Tronti may have been almost embarrassed by what many other workerists made of his writings – especially the young hotheads who would join Antonio Negri first in Potere Operaio, and then in and around the movement of Autonomia Operaia. For Tronti, in contrast, *operaismo* ended with the 1960s, which closed off one set of political

---

8 Sergio Bologna, *Ceti medi senza futuro? Scritti, appunti sul lavoro e altro,* Rome: DeriveApprodi, 2007, 259.

problems whilst simultaneously opening new ones. Seen in this light, if many of the arguments set out in the book's 1971 postscript can be said to build upon what Tronti had written previously, they do so in a manner that in turn lays down the foundation for his subsequent perspective of 'the autonomy of the political', with its focus upon the 'political-institutional' dimension of the capitalist state form.[9] Indeed, the course subsequently chosen by Tronti is already hinted at in the final words of his postscript to the second edition, which calls for 'never-yet-seen techniques allowing the working class to make political use of the capitalist economic machine'. Having returned his focus to the PCI as the most appropriate vehicle for this project, Tronti's own notes introducing the second edition are brief, even curt, suggesting that he was now keen to move on from these earlier explorations: 'The "next errors" will not be of this same type.' As for how useful *Workers and Capital* might still prove on this score, that is a task best left to a new generation of readers.

---

9 Cavalleri, et al., 'Introduction', 22; see also Chapter 5 of Franco Milanesi, *Nel novecento. Storia, teoria, politica nel pensiero di Mario Tronti*, Milan: Mimesis, 2014.

Introduction

A Course of Action

We should start with a note of caution. Even all this is still just the 'prologue in Heaven'. Here, we are not presenting research that has already been signed and sealed. Let's leave the little schemas up to the great improvisers. Let's leave intricate but blind analyses up to the pedants. We're interested in all that has the power to grow and develop. We're interested in getting the message across that today this power lies almost exclusively in the hands of *working-class thought*. *Almost* exclusively, for while the capitalists' theoretical viewpoint on their own society has today entered its decadent phase, this does not mean that bourgeois thought is dead. The bosses' science is now condemned to its long twilight, but there will continue to be some flashes of practical thought that still strike us now and then. The quicker the working-class point of view advances, the sooner history's condemnation of bourgeois thought will be complete. In this, then, lies one of our political tasks for today: we need, through the march of research, of experiments and experiences, of discoveries, to recreate the sense, the form of a path, and to give this path the form of a *process*. The thing that the capitalist side will soon be unable to grasp on the terrain of the class struggle is not the concept of science itself, but the concept of the development of science. If a *partial* thought, a class thought, sets in motion the mechanism of its own creative growth, then this fact alone will deny space to the development of any other scientific point of view on society. The blows it deals push this other viewpoint back into mere self-repetition, leaving it no other possibility than to contemplate the dogmas of its own tradition. This is what happened historically after Marx, when capital's theories once again got the upper hand. The margins for the development of working-class thought were cut back to the minimum and almost disappeared. It took the Leninist initiative, making a practical break at a determinate point, for the theoretical brain of the contemporary world to be delivered back into revolutionary hands. That was one moment. As everyone knows, after that moment it was only capital that proved able to grasp the scientific significance of the October Revolution. Hence the long lethargy of our own thought. The relationship between the two classes is such that whoever has the initiative wins. On the terrain of science, as on the terrain of practice, the strength of either side is inversely proportional to the other: if one grows and develops, the other stays put and thus slips backward. The theoretical rebirth of the working-class viewpoint is necessary today even just to meet the needs of the struggle. If we want to start going forward again, then we need to immobilise the enemy, the better to be able to strike him. The working class today is so mature that it will not accept political adventures on the terrain of material confrontations. That is true in fact as in principle. But, happily, on the terrain of the theoretical struggle, all the conditions seem to be imposing a new spirit of adventurous discovery on the class. Faced with bourgeois thought in its feeble old age, perhaps only now can the working-class point of view enjoy the fertile season of its own vibrant youth. To do this, it must violently break with its own immediate past. It must reject the traditional figure that has been officially attributed to it and surprise the class enemy with its sense of initiative, making a sudden, unpredicted, uncontrollable theoretical advance. And it is worth making our own partial contribution to this new genre, to this modern form of political work.

Rightly, we are asked: by what route do we propose to do this? By what means? For now, let's do without any discourse on method. We'll try not to give anyone the opportunity to dodge the hard, practical contents of working-class research by dwelling on the fine methodological forms of the social sciences. The relationship to be established with these latter is no different from the one which we could entertain with the world of human knowledge accumulated thus far and which all comes together in that set of technical knowledges necessary to grasping the objective functioning of present-day society. All of us, together, must come to use so-called 'culture' like one would use a hammer and a nail to hang a picture. For our part, we are doing it already. Of course, major feats are pulled off in sudden leaps. And the discoveries that really count often break the thread of continuity. And they are recognised as such precisely because these ideas of simple men seem like madness to the bearers of science. In this sense, Marx's place has not been fully appreciated, not even where this would have been easiest, on the terrain of theoretical thought alone. Every day we are hearing about Copernican revolutions by individuals who have pushed their desks from one corner of the room to the other. But, in the case of Marx – who overturned a social knowledge that had lasted for millennia – we only go so far as to say that he turned Hegel's dialectic upside down. Yet there is no lack of examples, contemporary to Marx, of a similar purely critical reversal of the perspective adopted by a millennia-old science. Can all of Marx possibly be reduced to the banality of a first-grader's sum, adding Feuerbach's materialism to Hegel's conception of history? What of the discovery of non-Euclidean geometry, which, from Gauss to Lobachevsky to Bolyai to Riemann, made the indivisibility of the axiom nothing less than a plurality of hypotheses? What of the discovery of the concept of 'field' in the terrain of electrical science, which, from Faraday to Maxwell and Hertz, exploded all of mechanistic physics for the first time? Do these not seem rather closer to the sense, the spirit, the scope of Marx's discoveries? Does not the new framing of space-time introduced by relativity take its cue from those revolutionary theories, just as the Leninist October set off, on its path, from the pages of *Capital*? But you can see this. Any intellectual who has read more than ten books – other than the ones required for school – is quite prepared to consider Lenin a dead dog when it comes to the field of science. Yet whoever looks at society and wants to understand its laws can do this without reference to Lenin only as much as whoever wants to understand natural processes could today do so without Einstein. There is no mystery in this. Here we are not talking about some indivisible human spirit that makes the same advance in every field. It is something rather more serious than that. It is that unifying power that provides capital's structures their dominance over the entire world and which can, in turn, be dominated only by the working class's labour. Marx credited Benjamin Franklin, that man of the New World, with the first conscious analysis of exchange-value as labour-time and thus the first conscious reduction of value to labour.

And it had also been Franklin who conceived of electrical phenomena as something produced by a single very fine substance that pervaded the entire universe. Before the bourgeois side constituted itself as a class under the pressure of the working class, on more than one occasion the bourgeois brain did find the strength to unite multiple given experiences under a single concept. Subsequently, the immediate needs of the struggle quite rightly began to command the production of ideas itself. The era of analysis, the age of the social division of intellectual labour, had begun. And no longer did anyone now know something about everything. Which poses the question: is a new synthesis possible? Or necessary?

Bourgeois science is pregnant with ideology just as the capitalist production relation is pregnant with the class struggle. From the viewpoint of capital's interest, it is ideology that lays the basis for science; for this reason, it founds it as a generalising social science. What had earlier been a discourse on humanity, and on the world, society and the state, increasingly becomes a mechanism objectively functional to the economic machine, as the level of struggle rises. Today's social science is like the production apparatus of modern society: everyone is within it and uses it, but only the bosses draw the profits. You cannot smash it apart – we are told – without pitching mankind back into barbarism. As a first objection, we might ask who said that human civilisation is indeed capital's dearest concern. And modern workers know of very different ways of defeating capital, beyond the prehistoric cry, 'Let's break the machines!' In short, big industry and its science are not the prize for whoever wins the class struggle. They are the battlefield itself. And so long as the enemy occupies that field, we must spray it with bullets, without crying over the roses that get destroyed along the way. Today a great new season of theoretical discoveries is possible only from the working-class point of view – difficult as that is to admit for those who fear it. The possibility, the capacity for synthesis, lies wholly in working-class hands. And there is a simple reason for that. For today the synthesis can only be a unilateral one, it can only be a consciously *class* science, the science of a class. If we base ourselves on capital, the whole can be understood only from the perspective of the part. Knowledge is connected to the struggle. Whoever has true hatred has truly understood. That is why the working class can know everything of capital, grasp the whole thing: simply because it is capital, it is the enemy of

everything and even itself. Despite this fact, capitalists face an unsur-
mountable limit to their knowledge of their own society, precisely
because they have to defend and preserve it. And the workers can know
everything, but sometimes it is instead impressive how little they know
of their own selves. To set oneself on the side of the totality – humanity,
society, the state – leads only to a partial analysis, leads us to grasp only
detached parts and leads us to lose scientific oversight over the whole.
Bourgeois thought has condemned itself to this every time that it has
uncritically accepted its own ideology. And working-class thought has
condemned itself to this fragmentary view every time that it has swallowed the bourgeois ideology of the general interest. There have been
moments in which the individual capitalist's crude practice has, conven-
iently enough, covered up for his class's awesome theoretical void and
rendered it harmless. In other moments, the collective capitalist has
responded decisively to the impulse of the direct interests of the bosses,
as expressed from below. On those occasions, there was a leap forward
in the development of the body of bourgeois science itself. Lord Keynes
is a splendid example of his. Through the deadly class conflicts of our
epoch, though not by any other means, the great bourgeois consciousness of the contemporary period – this critical, destructive consciousness – has at times had moments of lucid, totalising awareness of the
present conditions of human social relations. This is the story of a few
outstanding individuals – classic ones, in the tragic sense – from Mahler
to Musil. In kickstarting the development of working-class thought, we
must evaluate anew the active site of creative labour and do so by starting again from the beginning.

This demands that we get the mechanism of *discovery* moving again.
But such a mechanism can only be in the grip of those who have long
adopted a correct political stance toward the social object. That is, a
stance simultaneously both *within* and *against* society, a partial view
that theoretically grasps the totality precisely as a struggle to destroy this
totality in practice, a vital moment in all that exists and thus an absolute
power of decision over its survival. And this, indeed, is the condition of
workers as a class, faced with capital as a social relation. A new synthesis
from the working-class side, firmly grasped in its hands, will tear all
possibility of science from the hands of the bosses. The more necessary
it becomes for the working-class point of view to launch a great new
theoretical initiative, the more impossible it becomes for the capitalist

side to take such an initiative. Whoever is on our side can rest easy, then. If you see us abandoning the fossilised forest of vulgar Marxism, this is not because we want to run around the stadiums of contemporary bourgeois thought. When Marx criticised the high points of capitalist development, many took him for a reactionary, for he was turning his nose up at the last word in modern history. Marx's reply was simple and unambiguous: we are against constitutionalism, but that does not mean that we are for absolutism; we are against the present society, but that does not mean that we are for the world of the past. Some today criticise us for the contradiction of mounting a working-class critique of the workers' movement; but Marx's reply equally well answers that objection. We are against the present organisation of struggle and research, but that does not mean that we take the practical and theoretical solutions of the past as our model. Saying no to today's socialism does not mean having to say yes to yesterday's capitalism. Lenin said, 'when it comes to philosophy, I am one of those who search'. In philosophy today, there is nothing left to search for. But when it comes to the problems that concern us, from the perspective of unleashing the decisive struggle against the power of capital, there are unknown worlds that are waiting to be explored. The fate of those who sought another route to India and ended up discovering other continents is very similar to our own present manner of proceeding. For this reason, it is fair enough that the seeds of the new have not yet grown to the maturity of a fruit-bearing plant. It is important to recognise the force of what is being born. If it is alive, it will grow. You cannot criticise someone who is still continuing their research for what they have not yet found. Faraday discovered induced currents – the induction relation between magnets, current and the electric field. Someone asked him: what is this discovery useful for? His reply – what is a child useful for? Whitehead comments that once this 'child' had grown up to become a man, it constituted the basis for all modern applications of electricity.

The research work on this small body of hypotheses – born in Italy in the 1960s, not by accident – now finds itself at a delicate, decisive turning point. This research has set down some of its theoretical premises, which are only apparently abstract; it has attempted some political experiments of its own, which, in reality, have necessarily been rough and primitive; it has thus arrived at an initial heap of conclusions – once again, theoretical ones – in which, half concretely, half fantastically, it is possible to find the germ of new laws of action. And now we need to present all of this *en bloc*. The whole thing needs to be put to the test, in public, before we can go any further. The chronological succession of the texts purports to represent a logical development of our argument itself. But that may not be the case. There may be errors, within the nooks and crannies of our accumulated thoughts and experiences, which are difficult to see from the inside but easy to uncover from an external standpoint. If that is the case, we need to identify and correct these errors – and do it together. A discourse that takes itself as its own foundation runs the lethal risk of checking itself only by the yardstick of the formal logical continuity between its own successive stages. Rather, we need to choose the point at which we can consciously succeed in breaking this logic. It is not enough, then, to lower theoretical hypotheses down into lived experience in order to see if they function in practice. The hypotheses themselves need to be negated through exhaustive political work that prepares the terrain for their real verification. Only once the ground is prepared politically can these hypotheses operate materially, factually, in practice.

But this is a complex line of argument, and perhaps we ought to express it rather more straightforwardly. What do Marx, Lenin and past working-class experience mean for us? Different things to what they mean for others, no doubt. And that is quite right. Others, everyone, found therein the very things we think we should not be looking for: a new intellectual grasp on the world, thus providing a new orientation for one's studies; a new life science, and thus the ability to go calmly about choosing a place for ourselves in society; and a new consciousness of history. This latter is the worst and most dangerous thing of all, for it means putting a rubber stamp on the deed that places the worker's lost human essence back in their own hands. This essence is but a bequest granted by the dying boss and for good reason it is rejected and disdained by living labour. But we should not be looking for just anything. Rather, we should be searching for some things over others. This is the only useful approach to take. That is also how one travels in the world of classics. In so doing, we will find stones along the road more precious than the gold in the mines: bearings to orient us in the day-to-day class struggle, crude weapons for the offensive against the domineering boss, without any decorative embellishments or any illustrious values. In so doing, we find a mounting succession of practical criteria for working-class political action; each criterion is consciously adopted, one after another, and each level of action is subjectively raised above the last.

All this has the aim of inverting the subaltern nature of the demands advanced by the working class, depicting them as a force that threatens dominion over all of society. This means tearing the direction and control of the class struggle from the brain of capital and putting it once and for all in the fists of the workers. This succession, this path of struggle, this political growth of our class, starts out from Marx's *oeuvre* and passes by way of Lenin's initiative. Its development leaps forward in decisive moments of practical experience that have a directly working-class character. And it does not stop here: it goes *beyond* all this. And we, too, must be able to go beyond this, with an attitude toward this process that half foresees the future and half monitors the present – in part anticipating, in part following. *Anticipating* means thinking, seeing many things in one, seeing them in development, watching everything with theoretical eyes and from the point of view of our own class. *Following* means acting, moving at the real level of social relations, measuring the material state of the present forces, grasping the moment in the here and now to snatch the initiative in the struggle. Broad strategic anticipations of capitalist development are certainly needed, then, but they are needed precisely as limit-concepts within which we can pin down the tendencies of the objective movement of things. We should never confuse these anticipations with the real situation and never take them as an unescapable destiny for the world to which we must then conform. In certain moments, the possibility of getting a sense of the struggle – and of organisation – lies exactly in the ability to foresee capital's objective path and its needs within the terms of this path. We must thwart the fulfilment of these necessities and thus block capital's development, pitching it into crisis before – sometimes long before – it has achieved the ideal conditions that we have ourselves contemplated. Similarly, the modes of concrete action, the true and proper laws of tactics, are certainly also indispensable. But they are indispensable precisely as functions that must serve, must be made to serve, an overall perspective which entirely stands beyond these laws. We must never isolate these laws from one another or confuse them with long-term objectives, and we must never present them as something autonomous, as if they were themselves the whole battlefield, themselves the ultimate purpose.

This theoretical vigilance, by which the working class is continuously forced to abide, is pertinent precisely because it is sometimes necessary to break the chain of historical happenings, which so often present themselves anew in too similar a guise. It is necessary to judge these experiences afresh and select only some of them as models, in light of the latest developments, the latest foresights, the latest discoveries. When we run back through the history of workers' struggles and look into the eyes of those who headed and represented them, we can really see how these dualisms – anticipating and following, foresight and oversight, clear ideas and the will to action, wisdom and ability, far-sightedness and concreteness – have always appeared divorced from or even dispersed across different figures. This condition is death for the theoretical viewpoint of the working class. As for its political action, this condition is what explains the miserable life of the official workers' movement today. In this sense, the situation is grave, and the words in a book will certainly not be enough to change that. Such a volume may contain an element of truth only on condition that it is written in full awareness that we are doing something rather dreadful. If, in order to be able to act, we first need to write, then our level of struggle must be very backward indeed. Words, however you choose them, always strike you as something bourgeois. But that is how things are. In an enemy society, we cannot freely choose the means we use to fight it. And the weapons of proletarian revolt have always been taken from the bosses' arsenals.

The research must therefore keep going forward, in this form and with this consciousness. And as it proceeds beyond each confine, its task will become much more complex, more difficult and more strenuous. Up till this point, we could work with the fabric of the classics, adding some embellishments of our own. But from here on out, a new cloth must be woven, cut and sewn into the expanded horizons of today's workers' struggles. After Marx, no one has known anything new about the working class. It still remains an unknown continent. We know that it exists, of course, because we've all heard it being talked about, and anyone can read all manner of fabulous tales about it. But no one can say: I saw, I understood. A few sociologists have tried to demonstrate that it no longer really exists: the capitalist has sacked it because it didn't know how to do its job. How is the working class composed, internally? How does it function within capital? How does it work, how does it struggle? In what sense does it tacitly accept the system, and in what form does it strategically refute it? These are the key issues, and there are just as many questions. In the coming years we will have to know our theory as well as history, history as well as theory. Like Brecht's Galileo, we will try to advance inch by inch. 'Before we assume they are spots – which is what would suit us best – we should assume that they are fried fish'.

With a 'demanding and fruitful gaze', developing our own 'external eye', we will observe the flickering lamp of the class struggle today; the greater our amazement as we surprise ourselves watching its flickering, the closer we will be to discovering its laws. In our research thus far, we very much kept in mind this lesson on method, and it led us to discover things that had not been visible to the naked eye. And all of this is negligible compared to all of the things that we could have discovered proceeding along this route. It serves only to introduce our discourse, and even here, we may be mistaken. Yet it is difficult to deny the sense that today, lying open ahead of us, there is a path toward a new type of Marxist research and, likewise, that the dogmatic long night of working-class thought is coming to an end. Indeed, the ocean of possible discoveries has become so stormy that we need great powers of self-control to navigate it without putting all the old analytical instruments out of use. We have to keep our eyes rigorously fixed on our object of observation, without backing away from it and over a long period. And this object is present-day society, the society of capital, its two classes, the struggle between these classes, their histories and the prognoses for their development. To whoever asks what will come after, we can only respond: we do not know yet. This is a problem that we have to *arrive at*, not one we can *start out from*, and we have not yet reached our destination. This is one of the reasons why, in this whole discourse, the future seems not to exist. Indeed, none of what stands in front of us today is the future. And to base the model for a future society on the analysis of present-day society is a bourgeois ideological vice, an inheritance that only oppressed plebs and vanguard intellectuals can adopt as their own. This is the fanfare at the front of a march or a reward for bowing and scraping, with the promise that the world of the righteous awaits in the afterlife. No worker who is fighting against a boss is going to ask, 'And then what?' The fight against the boss is everything. The organisation of this struggle is everything. This constitutes a whole world. And we agree: the whole world needs tearing down. But who told you that the mere will to *overthrow* power – a will organised as a ruling class – is not enough to tear it down?

On one side stands the working *class*, on the other capitalist *society*: that is how the class struggle is plotted out today. It is not true that this shifts the relationship of forces in capital's favour. No, the opposite is true. For this is the only way in which the working class can acquire strength for itself and indeed recognise its strength, as the only living, active, productive element of society, as the hinge of social relations, as the fundamental articulation of economic development and thus a class that potentially already holds in its fists political domination over the present. The revolutionary process through which this domination is realised may also include some stages when the forward motion is forced to leap across a few phases. But at the apex of development, when power has been ripped out of the capitalists' hands, there comes a tough period in which the workers exercise political dictatorship over the whole society – and that phase that cannot be jumped across. This is the greatest future that we can see on the horizon, the one we want to see. As an objective for struggle, this will do us just fine. As a way of organising the struggle, it serves our purposes. Nothing more can be said. For us today, prophesies on the new world, on the new humanity, on the new human community, look as foul as apologias for a shameful past. No, the problem today is not a matter of envisioning what ought to replace the old world; we are still facing the issue of how to tear it down. So, it remains essential to know that old world, its direction and logic, its operational forces and many struggles. What concerns us, then, is not a matter of elaborating the argument in this vein. We can anticipate a lot of this concrete future, which also needs doing. This, indeed, is the recovery of the importance of theory. But at this point, a real question is posed that demands a real answer. And a real answer is anything but easy to provide. The young comrade who rightly wants a struggle against a living enemy immediately asks a very apposite question: what, in the meantime, are the margins of practical activity? What are actions most suited to tracking and remaining vigilant in the present? And how can this active presence over things today be connected and reconciled with theoretical discoveries on new continents? This decade (the 1960s) in Italy will never be sufficiently considered in its positive aspect. A fortunate combination of conditions – directly capitalist and directly working-class ones – has opened up a process in which revolutionary forces are growing, as they go through a decisively important turning point. These years have been rich in experiences. And the thing with experiences – when they are indeed new in type, when they break with the present officialdom and tradition – is that some people have them, make them happen, while others do not. This is not a dividing line, though. Those who have not experimented with the new experiences have repeated old ones, in a critical fashion; indeed, that is how each person can make forward steps when young. Here there is a wisdom difficult to practise, because at first it exists only embryonically and we gain it only once the opportunity has passed: namely, the wisdom of carrying out objective political work with the – even murky – consciousness that we are building up an experience only for ourselves, a function of the hypotheses built up in our heads, so that we can test and develop them. An experiment of this nature never seems to leave any trace. In reality, what does remain is the fundamental premise for doing everything: that is, the maturation both of a discourse that offers perspective and of the subjective forces that can begin to make it operational. The practical turning point must contain all of these dimensions. The level reached by discourse, the maturation of the forces that can carry it forward, the miraculously favourable class situation in Italy, demand that in this moment we no longer attempt practical experiences that serve theoretical discovery; they demand a political labour of deeds, a creative labour that seeks to deploy strength and the ability to achieve concrete results, material advances. We should know in advance: this political labour will be entirely beyond our theoretical horizon. And it must always be beyond it, every time that we again try to begin a revolutionary process, preparing the conditions, gathering the forces and organising the party. Yes, that's right: organising the party. There are moments in which all problems can and should be reduced to this problem alone. These are highly advanced moments of the class struggle, and we ought not always go and look for them at the points where capital has ripened most or where capitalism is at its weakest. Here, too, with the courage of discovery, outside of the theoretical schemas which someone may have been growing in their own garden, we need to know how to find the place, the point where a chain of circumstances has left a single knot to unravel for the thread of the revolutionary movement to resume its onward march: the knot of the party, the conquest of organisation. It can never be repeated enough that to foresee capital's development does not mean submitting to its iron laws: rather, it means forcing it to take a certain road, waiting in ambush at some point with weapons more powerful than iron, where we can attack and smash it. Too many today believe that the history of the workers' movement in the most advanced countries is a fatal destiny for us which we will not be able to escape. But isn't knowing what is about to happen useful precisely for those who want to stop it happening – for finding the ways, the forms, the forces to make sure it doesn't happen? What other point would it have? To give us tomorrow's horoscope, perhaps? The history of modern social democracy, of modern working-class reformism, is still all to be written, and this will require a lot of work. But, politically speaking, its fundamental processes are evident enough. No one can deny that the victory of social democracy is a defeat for the working class. It can likewise be taken for granted that this defeat ought not be blamed on the workers themselves – and yet you will find few prepared to admit as much. We can understand why. If the workers have not directly made errors themselves, then these errors must be attributed to the workers' leaders. If it was not the class, in its necessarily spontaneous action, that misread the signs of the fight against social democracy, then the misreading instead lies at the door of those who ought to have functioned as the organisers, also including – in our view – authentic workers' leaders and proven revolutionaries. In this vein, we today need a profound and concise critique of all the positions of the historical left wing of the international workers' movement, which ought to be charged not with having blocked social democracy's onward march, but rather with having aided it. The first Bolshevik response ought to be implicated in this critique, too. Certainly, it was no chance thing that when the communist movement did win at certain points, the left's positions toward it committed the same errors as always. The right's positions were not demolished but simply turned on their head. When the right made day-to-day tactics into a long-term strategy, the left responded by making long-term strategy into a day-to-day tactic. It opposed the false realism of practice with phony abstract theorisations. In rejecting the popular movement, it closed itself down in the isolation of the group. The historic parties of the workers' movement have had an easy time because to their left there have always been (and still are) Zarathustra-type blowhards who go around promising to tear down the world but wouldn't be able to tell you how to brush the dust off their ancient sacred texts. In the meantime, the workers learned that neither the brutality of compromise with the enemy nor the response provided by moral-force Chartism concerned them, their interests and their class war. These workers had themselves taken on leading the insurrection, when it came to hand-to-hand combat with the reformist perspective that then seemed so invincible, precisely because it had already won in other, much more advanced countries. It is true, in that case, that together with the workers at the head of the insurrection there was also Lenin. And Lenin, alone among all the leaders of the revolution in Europe, had always remained faithful to an elementary principle of subversive praxis, to what was, for him, a commandment for all practice: never leave the party in the hands of those already in charge. He had understood, through his work and his study, that even for the Russia of that time, the knot that had to be unravelled was the party. Whether within or outside the party, whether in the majority or in the minority, without ruling out any means that served the ultimate purpose, the party struggle and the open struggle for the leadership of the organisation is the red thread that runs through Lenin's life and works and led both to the reckoning of 1917. And then, by one of those miracles that are, in fact, only miracles for those who do not know the laws of action, at the right moment the party happened to be in the right hands. '6 November is too early, 8 November is too late': this watchword, which would long remain the model for any revolutionary decision, became possible at precisely that point, with those forces and for those objectives. We think that the model provided by Lenin's initiative is a lesson that we still need to learn. We ought to attend this same school each day; it is there that we will grow, it is there that we will prepare ourselves, until we manage to read things directly without the foul mediation of books, until we are able to violently reshape reality without the cowardice of the ponderous intellectual. In this way, we will learn that tactics are not written on the Tables of the Law once and for all time: rather, they are an invention to be made each day, a harmony with real things and at the same time a freedom from any preconceived ideas. They are a kind of productive imagination that alone serves to make thought work amid the facts; they are the real leap to be made, if only for those who know what needs doing.

If you know how to look for them, in this book you will find a series of changes in the way in which we consider this problem. And it is only right that they remain there to see; this shows how these advances were made over time. There is no static equilibrium between political work and theoretical discoveries; there is a relationship-in-movement that makes the one serve the other according to the needs of the moment. Today, there seem to be no doubts as to the need to dump all discovery, out of the urgent need to resume practical activity in the correct way. The coming years in Italy will be decisive – everyone can feel it. Few have understood, though, that they will be decisive not just for Italy, but likewise for international capital. To consider the Italian class situation 'normal' or fatally doomed to follow the normal path of the countries that went before us in modern history is the typical error of pure strategy, and this view in itself represents a troubling display of a lack of political sensibility. Indeed, here is a living example of the way in which on the basis of leftist positions one can turn the official line of the workers' movement on its head without touching its true contents, which, for us, are always given by the relationship concretely established within the working class's level of political development and with its degree of organisation. In this sense, if anyone today imagines that the answer to every question that faces us is to be found in the United States, because Marx told us that man explains the ape and not the other way around, this is but a form of theoretical orthodoxy that itself naively contributes to the mishmash that is today's vulgar Marxism, in which the only thing that you will never find is the working-class initiative in the class struggle in a determinate time and place. To see the underdeveloped countries as being at the epicentre of the revolution, simply because Lenin said that the chain will be broken at the weakest link, is a way of being practically concrete that also coincides with what is perhaps the highest form of contemporary opportunism, so theoretically illiterate as to be unable to tell which part of the paper tiger is the head and which is the tail. The point at which, through a combination of historical factors, the working class's degree of political development has advanced beyond the economic level of capitalist development still today remains the most favourable site for the opening up of a revolutionary process in the short term. On that condition, here we are talking about the working class and capitalist development in the scientific sense of two social classes in an era in which they have already reached maturity. The thesis that today the chain must be broken not where capital is weakest, but rather where the working class is strongest, is indeed very dear to us;

even where the argumentation to back up this thesis is still insufficient, it ought to be granted particular attention. A lot of things can derive from this, like the 'mean value theorem' – the possibility of taking one point that is itself in movement and using it to grasp what lies ahead as the tendency of things, and what lies in the past as a passive inheritance. There is good reason why Italy today offers ideal terrain for working-class theoretical research, if we start from here, and with this concreteness, in order to look out on the world of capital. Precisely because it is in the middle of capitalist development in its international extension, the Italian class situation, still today favourable to workers, can become a moment for the subjective unification of different and opposed levels of struggle. If it is true that it is urgent, and perhaps a precondition for everything else, that we put international revolutionary strategy back on its feet, we should understand that this cannot be done so long as we continue to play with the child's atlas invented by bourgeois political geography, which, for its own didactic convenience, is divided into the First, Second and Third Worlds. It is high time we began to distinguish between the different degrees, levels and successive determinations of capitalist contradictions, without each time confusing them for an alternative to the system. Capitalist society is made in such a way that it can only allow for one single alternative, the directly working-class one. All the rest are the very contradictions that feed capital, and without which it could not live. It would certainly do so rather less if it knew how. But it often knows it only *post-festum*, always after the critical moment has passed. This is a good thing for us. From the working-class point of view, capital's contradictions should neither be rejected nor resolved but only utilised. But making use of these contradictions also demands that we exacerbate them, even when they present themselves as ideals of socialism and they proceed under the banners of labour. The task of theory is to reconstruct the chain of contradictions, to connect it again and to grasp it anew, by way of the class's collective thought, as our enemy's single development process – hence the need for a strategic renaissance of the international workers' movement. At the same time, we must start again from a determinate level, or point, of development, to set a concrete revolutionary process in motion again, indeed on its own legs – this is the task of practice, this is the prodigious rediscovery of the world of tactics, which the class situation in Italy each day compels us to mount. It would be wrong to maintain that the international web of the most developed capital is now so dense, even at the institutional level, that it would not allow a hole to show up at any point. Never overestimate the enemy, never take a subordinate position toward it and never give up the initiative in the struggle. Precisely because the web is getting denser, to force a rupture at some point means bringing together at this same point all the forces that want to break the web as a whole.

Every further link between the various parts of capital is a further channel of communication between the diverse constituents of the working class. Every deal among capitalists presupposes and recommences, despite itself, a process of working-class unification. And it does not even take much thinking. If the Italian working class today had a new and high-level experience of political organisation, this would represent a powerful spark, a subversive drive, a model of the revolutionary path, for both the advanced capitalist countries and the ones whose capitalism is most backward; even a minimum of practical intuition, the feeling of class instinct, today sets this reality directly before our eyes. Again, here, you ought not ask right away: what will the party be like? There are some who have already begun to consider this word too corrupt for us to go on using it. And perhaps they are right. But we have not yet gone this far, and for now we do not want to. In the sky of theoretical discoveries, it is only right to fly on the wings of an intelligent fantasy. But, on the terrain of practice, and when we are addressing the most difficult problem of all – the question of organisation – we ought to proceed carefully, with humility and due caution, speaking everyday prose. Yes, we need to jump from one form to the other, but we should do this without losing anything of the positive potential of the real experiences built up through decades of tough struggle. It may seem strange – it isn't. But when we speak of the party, this is the only time in which we feel like the old generation. To put that better: this is the moment in which we look at all the other problems with the consciousness of a transitional generation, compelled to anticipate the future using means from the past. We should, then, be talking about a party struggle to conquer organisation; a Leninist tactic within a strategic research project of a new type; and a revolutionary process at one point that can set the mechanism of the international revolution in motion again. Faced with the question of 'what is to be done', one possible answer has arisen – that all of us spend the next few years working guided by a single orientation: give us the party in Italy and we will overthrow all of Europe!

Only recently has this answer arisen. In a capitalist society, the slow and imperceptible path of historical development is a mad rush of ephemeral political moments. We have to know how to position ourselves among these moments and how to grasp each of them, and all those that follow, if indeed we want to lay hold of the thread that ties them together and which must itself be broken. These are not the old historic opportunities for which one waits on the street corner. Nor is this a matter of restoring the continuity between events, as if they were all equal to one another, and none of them marked a break with the past. We need to understand that it is precisely this phenomenon that takes away the general character of the eras of history and makes each into the field of action for a determinate struggle. Discovering the necessities of capital's development and inverting them so that they become the working class's opportunities for subversion; these are the two elementary tasks of theory and practice, of science and politics, of strategy and tactics. We know that these, too, are all old words – however, we cannot substitute them so long as we have not grasped them afresh with new meanings. We cannot take the terrible last decades of the workers' movement and the whole post-Leninist phase only as a *nihil negativum* to which we make polemical reference as we seek to define the future limits of our action. Subjectively, however, some results have remained. It is up to us to draw the lessons that can be used precisely in the future struggle. The division of the party from the class and of the class from the party has entailed another division, the one between people and the objective perspectives that they represent, between revolutionaries, on the one hand, and the revolutionary process, on the other, to the point of making them into two opposed worlds that today do not meet or understand one another. Those who wanted to fight within the party's internal structures have not in fact done so, for want of imagining a general perspective truly different than the official one. Likewise, those seeking this alternative did not in fact find it, because they did not preoccupy themselves with maintaining real relationships with – and possibilities of leadership over – the bulk of the movement. These errors should not be repeated. Never throw yourself into a practical struggle without theoretical weapons. Never set yourself to building perspectives while remaining distant from the masses. The reformists will today likely need to go and fight them on their terrain, but with an army of new revolutionary ideas, with the baggage of historical knowledge of their movements, with such clarity of foresight on the final outcome of the struggle and such control over its internal passageways and such awareness of its transient contradictions as to stupefy the traditional world of politics itself, with all its naïve erudition. Tactics and strategy: in the world of things, keep them objectively divided and never confuse or equate them, because once they have been made identical they impede action; in subjective terms, though, in our heads, in our own person, keep them united, and here never separate them, because once they are separated, they destroy people, cutting them in two, making them into this grey shadow to which the party leader is today reduced. What seems to be the tragic side of today's situation – that we cannot do right away what we plan to do tomorrow – is the reality of the class struggle, when those struggling find themselves beyond the level of organisation achieved and want and demand that this primary condition be imposed so that they can then move to the decisive attack. And it is not enough just to recognise this. For once it has been recognised, it ought to be taken as a positive fact, a necessary period that has to be lived all the way through, which compels us to mount great subjective development, prolongs the time in which we prepare our forces and makes these forces both deeper and clearer. Thus, the more one-sided we are, the more whole we are; the more we are political realists, the more we are high-level theorists: the more we are merely human, the more we are complex mediations of the working-class interest. And all of this the other way around, too, in a circle of continual collective growth. They have already told us that there is nothing universally human in all that we propose. And they are right. Indeed, here there is nothing of the bourgeoisie's particular interest. Have you ever seen a working-class struggle with a platform of generically human demands? There is nothing more limited and partial, nothing less universal in the bourgeois sense, than the struggle which workers wage on the factory floor against their direct boss. It is precisely for this reason that we manage to add together these struggles across society, to tie them together in a perspective, to unite them in organisation. And we will thus have the world's destinies in our hands, for we will have conquered the most powerful weapon thus far imaginable, the power of decision over the movements of capital. This, indeed, is the point we need to reach. Anything that does not serve this end should be abandoned. It is worth giving a hand to carry whatever is strictly necessary, the essentials for the journey. Likewise, it is possible that a pause

A Course of Action

along the way,[1] at who knows what moment, may become necessary. Perhaps even right away. From the prologue in heaven to the adventures on earth, this passage has not yet proven to be imminent. The whole way of seeing, here presented, is not only itself provisional; in the world of things, it is one that still seems possible. So, let's measure it against the other possibilities. Let's see if it has grown enough to defend itself and to go on the attack. Let's test what strength it has. Certainly, the working class today is no longer the young comrade 'who wanted the right thing but acted in the wrong way'. It has now reached the age of a mature adult, the stage in which one sometimes prefers not to act rather than make a mistake. The agitators thus find themselves using a language which sometimes isn't best suited to the present situation. And yet once we have established the need to change the world, we have no need to depart from or change the Brechtian line of conduct suggested by the 'control choir':

It takes a lot of things to change the world:
Anger and tenacity. Science and indignation.
The quick initiative, the long reflection,
The cold patience, and the infinite perseverance,
The understanding of the particular case, and the
understanding of the ensemble,
Only the lessons of reality can teach us to transform reality.

September 1966

---

1 Tronti describes this as a 'sosta sul ponte', literally a 'pause on the bridge', here referring to the title of Lucio d'Ambra's 1936 novel.

Note on this Edition

Here the text of the First Edition is reproduced without any changes. The date we have put at the end of each text forbids any posthumous replacement of words or concepts. For its part, time – even if a short time – has already done justice to its own past: this naïve and sentimental stretch of politics, here and there some summary execution of a living problem, and everywhere that late-romantic problem of formally posing things. The 'next errors' will not be of this type. The Postscript, which has its own date, gives an account of the subsequent course of this research: it is a list of problems that have not yet all been resolved, a programme of study for young forces whose minds are open to the discoveries of critical consciousness, a realistic becoming-aware of today's struggles, based on a new yardstick of political judgement on real workers' struggles of yesteryear. As for the rest: it's best to keep quiet on things we don't yet know what we should say about.

28 January 1971

First Hypotheses

Marx Yesterday and Today

'We cannot today refuse to accept the fundamental affirmations of Marxism any more than a serious physicist can be a non-Newtonian, indeed with the great difference that in the field of sociology numerous generations will have to pass before an Einstein can emerge. This figure will not arrive until Marx's work has borne all its historical fruit'. This was the conclusion that Rudolf Schlesinger reached after he had worked through all of Marx's thought as well as the whole historical period on which it left its mark. This conclusion is worth taking as a cue to throw together a few initial comments, *working hypotheses*, that will need further exploring and testing.

Let's set down one premise before anything else: namely, that a research project which wants to continue the discourse on the contemporary validity of the fundamental affirmations of Marxism has to engage with Marx not in his time, but in our own. *Capital* should be judged on the basis of *the capitalism of today*. Thus, all the ridiculous petty-bourgeois banalities asserting that Marx's work is both the product and explanation of a society of small-scale commodity production will finally fall away once and for all.

One of Marx's fundamental theses holds that on the social basis of capitalism, the historical process itself always realises a logical operation of abstraction, which strips the object of all casual and occasional elements, immediately subsumed by its contingent presence, in order then to discover and valorise its permanent and necessary aspects;

these very aspects designate it as a specific product of a historically determinate reality and thus make it relevant across this whole reality. The process of capitalist development itself takes charge of *simplifying* its own history and making its own "nature" ever *purer*, stripping it of all its inessential contradictions to uncover that *fundamental* contradiction that simultaneously both exposes and condemns it. In this sense, capitalist development is the *truth* of capitalism itself; in fact, only capitalist development brings to light the *secret* of capitalism. Expressed from the bourgeois point of view, this secret becomes the ultimate mystification of a capitalism *for all*; in other words, a capitalism that lies within everyone's reach. That is, this secret is the ultimate verification of capital and thus the *ideological* instrument of its indefinite stabilisation. The same secret seen from the working-class perspective, though, becomes the deepest scientific apprehension of the true *nature* of capitalism, through analysing the recent results of its own *history*; that is, it points out the greatest contradiction of capitalism and thus the *theoretical* instrument of its coming overthrow. If it is true that the decisive historic confrontation between the working class and capital must take place precisely here – on the basis of the most developed capitalism – it is also true that this is the same terrain on which the class struggle between working-class *theory* and bourgeois *ideologies* must also today be expressed.

This too is a fundamental thesis in Marx's thought: namely, that it is the most developed point which explains the most backward and not vice versa; that it is capital which explains ground rent and not the reverse. As such, the verification of a given thought should be achieved not on the social terrain which apparently produced it, but instead on that which subsequently surpassed it – for in reality, it was precisely the latter which did produce it. In his own work, Marx used Hegel to investigate not the backward situation of semi-feudal Germany but that of the most advanced developments of capitalist Europe; Marx similarly forced Ricardo to give an urgent answer to the problems that his own time posed to the author of *Capital* in his own time. Likewise, Marx today cannot eternally continue to settle scores with his old philosophical conscience. Rather, he must become embroiled in an active clash with the most modern reality of contemporary capitalism precisely in order to understand and destroy it. For this is the moment of verification, this is the working-class demand imposing itself. Not by chance, today, precisely when bourgeois thought is composing its existentialist novels about the 'alienation of the human essence', sitting enraptured before a few unfortunate lines in the 1844 Manuscripts, working-class thought instead returns to *Capital*, to a classic model of a scientific analysis of the present, in function of the revolutionary struggle which seeks to abolish and overcome this reality.

In one striking page in his book, Michaud finds the courage to put into words an idea which I believe to be very widespread – even if only as a confused sensation: he refers to 'the re-appearance in our own era of what is in some senses a pre-Marxist ideological situation'. But can we indeed say this? In what sense? The answer to these questions may cast a great deal of light on many areas that have remained in shadow.

Like any authentically revolutionary thought, Marx's is driven to destroy what already exists in order to build in its place something which does not yet prevail. So, Marx's thought has two sides which are distinct from one another yet also make up an organic whole. One is the 'ruthless criticism of all that exists', in Marx expressed as the discovery of the mystified procedure of bourgeois thought and thus as the theoretical demystification of capitalist ideologies. The other is the 'positive analysis of the present', which, with the maximum level of scientific understanding, brings the future alternative to our present. One is a *critique of bourgeois ideology*; the other is a *scientific analysis of capitalism*. These two moments in Marx's *oeuvre* can be understood as both logically divided and chronologically successive from the *Critique of Hegel's Philosophy of Right* to *Capital*. This does not at all mean that they *always* have to repeat this division and succession. When Marx himself looked at classical political economy and went back along the path which had already led him to discover certain general abstract relations through his analysis, he well knew that this path was not to be repeated. Rather, it was necessary to start out from these simple abstractions – the division of labour, money, value – in order again to reach the 'living whole': the population, the nation, the state, the world market. Thus, today, once we have reached the point of arrival of Marx's *oeuvre* – that is, *Capital* – we need to take it as our starting point; once we have arrived at the analysis of capitalism, it is this analysis from which we must build again. Now, research around certain determinate abstractions – alienated labour, the modifications that have taken place in the organic composition of capital, value in oligopolistic capitalism – should be the starting point for arriving at a new 'living whole': the people, democracy, the political state of neocapitalism, the international class struggle. Not by chance, this was also Lenin's path, from *The Development of Capitalism in Russia* to *The State and Revolution*. It is also not by chance that all bourgeois sociology and all reformist ideologies of the workers' movement follow the opposite path.

But all this is still not enough: even if we grasp the specific character which *the analysis of capitalism* should today assume, we also simultaneously need to grasp the specific character that the *critique of ideology* should assume. And, here, it is useful to start out from a precise presupposition, deploying one of those tendentious exaggerations which are a positive characteristic of Marx's own *science*, stimulants to new thought and to active intervention in the practical struggle. This presupposition is that *any ideology is always bourgeois*, because it is always the *mystified reflection* of the class struggle on the terrain of capitalism.

Marxism has been conceived as an "ideology" of the workers' movement. This is a fundamental error, since Marxism's starting point, its birth certificate, was always precisely the destruction of *all* ideology through the destructive critique of all *bourgeois* ideologies. A process of *ideological mystification* is only possible, indeed, on the basis of modern bourgeois society: it has always been and continues to be the *bourgeois* point of view regarding *bourgeois* society. And anyone who has looked at the opening pages of *Capital* even once can see that this is not a process of pure thought which the bourgeoisie consciously *chooses* in order to mask the *fact* of exploitation; rather, it is itself the real, objective process of exploitation. That is, it is itself the mechanism of capitalism's development, through all of its phases.

For this reason, the working class does not need an 'ideology' of its own. For its existence *as a class* – that is, its presence as a reality antagonistic to the entire system of capitalism, its *organisation* into a revolutionary class – does not link it to the mechanism of this development but make it independent of and counterposed to it. Rather, the more that capitalist development advances, the more the working class can make itself *autonomous of* capitalism; the more accomplished the system becomes, the more *the working class must become the greatest contradiction within the system*, to the point of making this system's survival impossible and rendering *possible* and thus *necessary* the revolutionary rupture which liquidates and transcends it.

Marx is not the *ideology* of the workers' movement but its *revolutionary theory*. This is a theory born as the critique of bourgeois ideologies and which must make this critique its daily bread – it must continue to be the 'ruthless criticism of all that exists'. A theory that came to constitute itself as the scientific analysis of capitalism and that must, at each moment, feed on this analysis, must at times identify with it when it needs to make up the lost ground and cover the gap, the distance, which has opened up between the development of things and the updating and verification of research and its tools. A theory which lives only in a function of the working class's revolutionary practice, one that provides weapons for its struggle, develops tools for its knowledge, and identifies and magnifies the objectives of its action. Marx has been and remains the *working-class* point of view regarding *bourgeois* society.

But if Marx's thought is the working class's revolutionary theory, if Marx is the *science of the proletariat*, on what basis and by what paths has at least one part of *Marxism* become a populist ideology, an arsenal of banal commonplaces to justify all possible compromises in the course of the class struggle? Here, the historian's task becomes enormous. Yet it is obvious that, if ideology is a part, a specific, historically determinate articulation of the very mechanism of capitalism's development, then the acceptance of this 'ideological' dimension – the construction of the ideology of the working class – can only mean that the workers' movement has itself become, as such, a part, a *passive* articulation of capitalist development. That is, it has undergone a process of integration into the system. This integration process can have various phases and levels, but it nonetheless has one single consequence in provoking different phases and different levels – that is, *different forms* – of that *reformist* practice which ends up today seeming, *in appearance*, implicit in the very concept of the working class. If ideology in general is always *bourgeois*, an ideology of the working class is always *reformist*: that is, it is the *mystified* mode through which its revolutionary function is *expressed* and at the same time *inverted*.

If this is true, it follows from this that the demystification process must today pass *through* Marxism itself, must express itself *also* as a process of the deideologisation of Marxism. Here, I am speaking of Marxism and not of Marx's *oeuvre*, for the discourse on this latter is rather different. There is, naturally, a work of critique *internal to* Marx's

own *oeuvre*, of separating out and selecting some of the main orienta-
tions therein. To be grasped and valorised are the points in which
scientific generalisation is exercised at the highest level; therefore, the
analysis of capitalism demonstrates the whole powerful sense of a
dynamic understanding of the system which identifies and assesses
fundamental tendencies that continually transform capitalism and
revolutionise it from within. On the other hand, those parts that
should be isolated and rejected are those in which this type of scientific generalisation seems not to have succeeded and where, as a result,
particular facts, a particular stage of the development of capitalism,
are immediately generalised, and thus end up putting on the vest,
becoming the allegorical figure of capitalism as a whole. This internal
criticism – which represents, in a certain sense, Marx's self-critique –
is something different from the work of demystifying certain Marxist
theories. This latter task regards not Marx's own *oeuvre*, but a certain
part of Marxism.

Today we are used to speaking about *vulgar Marxism* with some irony
and contempt: this, too, is something we learned from Marx. We already
know his judgement and attitude toward classical political economy,
with respect to what he himself called *vulgar economy*. The merit of classical political economy is the effort to reduce, through analysis, the
different forms of wealth to their intrinsic unity, stripping them of the
figures in which they coexist independently of one another. Classical
economics seeks to understand the intimate connection between facts,
liberating them from the multiplicity of phenomenal forms. In so doing,
even as it operates its own specific process of mystification, classical
economics is able to proceed hand in hand with the *real* development of
social antagonisms and thus with the objective level of class struggle
implicit within capitalist production. But within political economy,
there is – or, better, at a specific stage in its development, there appears
– an element which represents therein 'the simple reproduction of the
phenomenon' as its simple representation. And this is its *vulgar element*,
which, at a certain point, isolates itself from the rest as a *particular exposition of economics in general*. The more the real contradictions advance,
the more complex becomes their reproduction on the plane of thought,
the more difficult and laborious becomes their analysis at the scientific
level, then ever more does that vulgar element stand counterposed to all
this work as an autonomous element which substitutes for it in 'eclectic,

syncretic compendia'[1] vulgar economics and becomes increasingly *apologetic* and 'seeks to eliminate through chatter' all the contradictory thoughts through which real contradictions express themselves. When we read these pages from Marx and we think about vulgar Marxism, we are tempted to conclude that everything has been said already.

Yet another essential point needs adding. If it is true that mystification has today eaten into the very roots of Marxism and if it is true that there are objective reasons which led and continue to lead this vulgarisation process, then the most urgent task is that of identifying what those objective reasons are, of pinning down the primary material causes, not only to know them, but moreover to combat them. We need to be clear in this respect. This is not about a struggle at the simply theoretical level. This is not about opposing a neoscholasticism of *pure Marxists* against the old academy of *vulgar Marxists*. We must take the struggle to the real level, conceiving the theoretical task itself as a moment of the class struggle. Once we're convinced of the need for this, let's say, Marxian purification of Marxism; once we've regained the scientific level of the analysis of capitalism, which should today be applied to the whole complexity of international phenomena; once recovered and verified anew that *scientific unity* of Marx's thought, which expresses itself in the *organic* unity of economics and sociology, of political theory and practical struggle – from here, it is necessary to start again, or rather, from this point, we have to *make a jump* and return to finding the real forces which must guide this process, the objective causes which necessarily produce it, the material reasons which will once again make theory itself a *material force*.

Today, perhaps more than ever, the truth of the Leninist thesis jumps out in all its force: namely, there is no revolutionary *movement* without revolutionary *theory*. When we hear *everyone* talking about the need to see and understand the strategic perspective of the revolution beyond blind day-to-day tactics, we can understand the significance today of this *need for theory*. This need for theory concerns the full array of forces antagonistic to the capitalist system but also splits them at a decisive point, thereby contributing to keeping those forces divided – that is, insofar as theory could in any case contribute to make them united and homogeneous. Yet never has the opposite been as true as it is today: that

---

1 Marx and Engels Collected Works (hereafter MECW), Vol. 28, 5.

revolutionary theory is not possible without a revolutionary movement. Today's theorist should thus lend a hand to the whole practical work of rediscovering and reorganising the only authentically subversive forces which live within capitalism; they should once again become conscious of their existence and help to give a materially organised form to the revolutionary power objectively expressed in their existence. In the last instance, the process of demystifying Marxism is not possible without *workers' power*. Rather, workers' power – the *autonomous* organisation of the working class – is the *real* demystification process, since it is the *material* basis of revolution.

In this sense, the main polemical objective of today's Marx can no longer be *Vulgärökonomie*, not even in its present form as vulgar Marxism. For vulgar Marxism today has as both its presupposition and its result that it is the *Vulgärpolitik* of the workers' movement. It is this vulgar politics against which we must struggle. However, the modes of this battle ought to be chosen properly, and the task of contemporary Marxists cannot be limited to these same modes. There is an obvious principle in this, albeit one that has often been badly interpreted: namely, that the critique internal to the workers' movement should *always* express itself as an external struggle against the class enemy – thus, the internal critique of Marxism should express itself *first of all* as a struggle against bourgeois thought. The destructive criticism of all *neocapitalist* ideologies should today be the necessary starting point in order to arrive, once again, at the critique of all ideology, including *all* the reform-ist ideologies of the workers' movement. Yet we have seen that today the *analysis of capitalism* must, in a certain sense, precede the *critique of ideology*, in the sense that it should *provide its foundation*. We can say, therefore, that today the positive analysis of the present – that is, the elaboration of fundamental perspectives for the practical struggle and the rediscovery and reorganisation of the material forces which should carry this struggle forward – must necessarily precede and provide the foundation for the negative destruction of all *ideological* and *political* mystifications.

We can then conclude as follows: today's *ideological* situation is perhaps pre-Marxist, with the difference that the *theoretical* situation is perhaps pre-Leninist. By this I mean that the task today is not to set off again from *before Marx* or to resume the path from *after Lenin*. It is, perhaps, and I say this in a consciously provocative manner, to *again* make the jump from Marx to Lenin – to move from the analysis of contemporary capitalism to arrive at the elaboration of a *theory of the proletarian revolution on the basis of modern capitalism*. The working-class revolution – *with all of its tools* – should once again concretely become the minimum programme of the workers' movement. Already once before, the working class rediscovered Marx through Lenin: the result was the October Revolution. When this repeats itself, the death knells will sound – as Marx would say – for capitalism around the world.

January 1962

Factory and Society

At the end of the third section of *Capital*, Volume 1, after working through the production of absolute surplus-value, Marx returns to distinguish between the two faces of capitalist production and thus two points of view from which the capitalist form of the production of commodities can be considered: the labour process and the process of valorisation. In the first, the worker does not treat the means of production as capital but *consumes* the means of production as material for his productive activity; in the second, 'it is not the worker who uses the means of production, but the means of production which use the worker', and thus it is capital that *consumes* labour-power. It is true that, already in the labour process, capital develops into a *command over labour,* over labour-power and, therefore, over the worker; but only in the valorisation process does there develop a coercive relation, which compels the working class to surplus-labour and thus to the production of surplus-value. Capital manages to capture, it in its own way, the *unity* of the labour process with the process of valorisation; it is likewise all the more able to capture it as capitalist production develops and the more that the capitalist form of production becomes the master of all the other spheres of society, invading the entire web of social relations. Capital *poses* labour – as it is forced to do – as the creator of value, but then *sees* value – as it is forced to do – as the valorisation of itself. Capital sees the labour process *only* as a process of valorisation; it sees labour-power *only* as capital. It revolutionises the relation between living labour and dead labour, between the force that creates value and value itself; it is all the more able to do this as it can recuperate the whole social labour process within the process of capital valorisation, the more that it can integrate labour-power within capital.

In the bourgeois mystification of capitalist relations, these last two processes proceed hand in hand and in parallel, *both* appearing as objective and necessary. But they ought, instead, to be seen as distinct even in their unity, to the point of counterposing one another as contradictory processes which each, in turn, exclude the other; a material lever for the dissolution of capital, rooted in the decisive point of its system.

Anyone can see the procedure through which past labour is every day disguised by capital. This is the reason bourgeois economists are full of praise for the merit of such labour. In fact, it is this labour, as the means of labour, which collaborates once again in the living labour process; for this reason, the importance of labour is attributed to the *figure of capital* it assumes. In this case, the capitalist form of labour coincides with the means of production in which labour has objectified itself: to the point that 'the practical agents of capitalist production and their ideological word-spinners ... unable to think of the means of production separately from the antagonistic social mask they wear at present.'[1] Thus the labour of the past, like any natural force, provides a *free service* to capital; likewise, when it is invested and set in motion by living labour, it accumulates and reproduces itself *as capital* on an enlarged scale. It is more difficult to get any insight into the procedure through which living labour itself is completely caught and swallowed within this process, as a *necessary part* of its development. 'It is the natural property of living labour to keep old value in existence while it creates new' value.[2] For this reason, labour 'maintains and perpetuates an always increasing capital-value in an ever-renewed form,'[3] and all the more so the greater the growth in the efficiency, volume and value of its means of production – all the more so, the greater the accumulation which inevitably accompanies the development of its productive force. 'This natural power of labour appears as a power incorporated into capital for the latter's own

1 Karl Marx, *Capital*, Volume 1, translated by Ben Fowkes, London: Penguin, 1990, 757.
2 Ibid., 755.
3 Ibid.

self-preservation, just as the productive forces of social labour appear as inherent characteristics of capital, and just as the constant appropriation of surplus labour by the capitalists appears as the constant self-valorisation of capital'.[4]

The capitalist mode of production represents surplus-value and the value of labour-power to itself as 'aliquot parts of the total social capital'[5] and it is this which *hides* the specific character of the capitalist relation, 'the fact that variable capital is exchanged for living labour-power, and that the worker is accordingly excluded from the product'.[6] Insofar as all the developed forms of the capitalist process of production are forms of cooperation, the very development of capitalist production itself re-proposes and generalises the 'the false semblance of a relation of association, in which worker and capitalist divide the product in proportion to the different elements which they respectively contribute towards its formation'.[7] This is the basis upon which, at the surface level of bourgeois society, the workers' pay appears as the *price of labour*: a necessary or natural price which expresses in monetary terms the *value of labour*. Marx rightly says that the value of labour is an imaginary expression, an irrational definition, a phenomenal form of the substantial relation which is *the value of labour-power*. But what necessity lies behind this appearance? Is it a subjective choice to *hide* the substance of the real relation, or is it not rather the real manner of making the mechanism of this relation *function*? Exemplary in this regard is the manner in which the value and price of labour-power are presented in the transfigured form of the *wage*. The real movement of the *wage* appears to demonstrate that it is not the value of labour-power that is being paid, but rather the value of its function, the value of labour itself. For capitalist production, it is indispensable that labour-power presents itself as labour pure and simple and that the value of labour is paid in the form of the wage. Think of the second particularity of the form of the equivalent – when concrete labour becomes the phenomenal form of its opposite, of abstractly human labour. It is not concrete labour that, within the relation of value, possesses the general quality of being abstract human

---

4 Ibid., 755–6.
5 Ibid., 776.
6 Ibid., 670.
7 Ibid., 670–1.

labour. On the contrary, being human labour in the abstract is its own very nature; its being concrete labour is only the phenomenal or determinate form of the realisation of that nature. This total inversion is inevitable, for the labour represented in the product of labour *creates value* only to the degree in which it is abstract human labour, the expenditure of human labour-power. Is it not perhaps true that value 'transforms every product of labour into a social hieroglyphic'?[8] The *value of labour-power* expresses in the *wage* simultaneously both the capitalist form of the exploitation of labour and its bourgeois mystification; it gives us the *nature* of the capitalist relation of production, but *inverted*.

On this basis, *labour* becomes the necessary mediation for *labour-power* to transform into the wage: the condition for living labour to present itself *only* as variable capital and labour-power *only* as part of capital. Value, in which is represented the actually paid part of the working day, should appear, then, as the value or price of the labour day as a whole. More precisely, in the wage there disappears any trace of the division of the working day into necessary labour and surplus-labour. All of labour appears as paid labour; this distinguishes wage-labour from other historical forms of labour. The more that capitalist production (and the system of its forces of production) develops, the more the paid and unpaid parts of labour become inseparably confused. The various forms of wage payment are but discrete ways of expressing, at different levels, the constant nature of this process. We understand, then, 'the decisive importance of the transformation of the value and price of labour-power into the form of wages, or into the value and price of labour itself. All the notions of justice held by both the worker and the capitalist, all the mystifications of the capitalist mode of production, all capitalism's illusions about freedom, all the apologetic tricks of vulgar economics, have as their basis the form of appearance discussed above, which makes the actual relation invisible and indeed presents to the eye the precise opposite of that relation.'[9] In the history of the 'most varied forms' of the wage, we can chart a course following the whole development of capitalist production: the ever more complex internal unity established therein, between the labour process and the valorisation process, between labour and

---

8 Ibid., 167.
9 Ibid., 680.

labour-power, between the variable and the constant part of capital and, therefore, between labour-power and capital.

The wage is nothing other than wage-labour considered from another point of view. In the wage, labour's determinate character as an agent of production appears as a determination of distribution. The wage presupposes wage-labour, just as profit presupposes capital. 'These definite forms of distribution thus presuppose definite social characteristics of production conditions, and definite social relations of production agents'.[10] The wage provides an already-complete transcendance of 'the crude separation of production and distribution'.[11] The determinate manner in which we take part in production determines the particular forms of distribution. 'The relations and modes of distribution thus appear merely as the reverse aspect of the agents of production'.[12]

'The question as to how this form of distribution determining production itself relates to production obviously belongs to [the sphere of] production itself'.[13] The mediating moment between production and distribution, on the one hand, and between production and consumption, on the other, is *exchange*. In the first case, exchange is an act directly included in production; in the second case, it is entirely determined by production, if indeed it is true that exchange for consumption presupposes the division of labour, that private exchange presupposes private production, that a determinate intensity and expansion of exchange presupposes a determinate expansion and organisation of production. This is the basis on which the attempt to express an immediate identity between production and consumption has generally been made; that is, to the degree that there is indeed a consumptive production and a productive consumption. Or, we come to find a mutual dependence between them, with production as means for consumption and consumption as the goal of production. Finally, one can be presented as the realisation of the other and vice versa: consumption consumes the product, production produces consumption. But already Marx himself mocked the erudite socialists and the prosaic economists who played with this Hegelian identity of opposites. We only need add to this list the vulgar sociologists, who

---

10 Marx and Engels Collected Works (MECW), Vol. 37, 868.
11 MECW, Vol. 28, 25.
12 Ibid., 32.
13 Ibid., 34.

are also erudite and prosaic although they are not socialists or economists. Marx emphasises the 'important point here that production and consumption … appear in any case as moments of a process in which production is the actual point of departure and hence also the dominant moment … the act epitomising the entire process'. Production, distribution, exchange and consumption are *not* identical; they are 'all elements of a totality, differences within a unity'.[14] This unity is composed of an 'organic whole' and it is clear that the various moments within this whole initiate a reciprocal action. So, too, is production, *in its unilateral form*, determined by the other moments. But 'production is the dominant moment, both with regard to itself in the contradictory determination of production and with regard to the other moments'. It is from production that the process continually begins anew. 'A definite [mode of] production thus determines a definite [mode of] consumption, distribution, exchange and definite relations of these different moments to one another'. The need to invoke these basic concepts from Marx is itself fine evidence of the objective existence of too many 'Marxists' inclined to repeat 'the absurdity of those economists who treat production as an eternal truth and confine history to the domain of distribution'.[15]

If we consider capital directly in the production process, we must continually distinguish between two fundamental moments: the production of absolute surplus-value, where the relation of production appears in its simplest form and can immediately be captured either by the worker or by the capitalist; and the production of relative surplus-value – specifically, capitalist production, where we have at the same time the development of the social productive forces and their direct transfer from labour to capital. Only at this point, when all the social productive forces of labour appear as autonomous internal forces of capital, can we explain the whole process of circulation in all its richness. At this juncture, the realisation of surplus-value not only hides the specific conditions of its production; the realisation of surplus-value also *appears* as its effective creation. This appearance, too, is functional for the system.

Alongside labour-time is the time of circulation. The production of surplus-value receives new determinations in the process of circulation:

14   Ibid., 36.
15   Ibid., 34.

'Capital passes through the circuit of its metamorphoses. Finally, step-
ping beyond its inner organic life, so to say, it enters into relations with
outer life, into relations in which it is not capital and labour which
confront one another, but capital and capital in one case, and individuals, again simply as buyers and sellers, in the other'.[16] At this point, all
parts of capital appear equally as sources of excess value and, for this
reason, as the origin of profits. The extortion of surplus-labour loses its
character: its specific relation to surplus-value is obscured. This is why
the metamorphosis of the value of labour-power in the form of the wage
is so useful. The transformation of surplus-value into profit is effectively
determined both by the production process and by the process of circulation. But the mode of this transformation is nothing more than the
further development of the inverse relations which had already taken
place within the production process: when all of labour's *subjective*
productive forces of labour are presented as the *objective* productive
forces of capital. 'On the one hand, the value, or the past labour, which
dominates living labour, is incarnated in the capitalist. On the other
hand, the labourer appears as bare material labour-power, as a
commodity'.[17] Moreover, 'the actual process of production, as a unity of
the direct production process and the circulation process, gives rise to
new formations, in which the vein of internal connections is increasingly lost, the production relations are rendered independent of one
another, and the component values become ossified into forms independent of one another'.[18]

Already in analysing the simplest categories of the capitalist mode
of production, commodities and money, we can completely understand the mystification process which transforms social relations into
the properties of things themselves as well as the relation of production itself into a thing. In capital, and with the development of its
successive determinations, 'this inverted and cursed world' develops
and imposes itself ever further. At the basis of the capitalist mode of
production, the existence of the product as a commodity and of the
commodity as the product of capital implies 'the objectification of the
social features of production and the personification of the material

---

16   MECW, Vol. 37, 48.
17   Ibid., 49.
18   Ibid., 815.

foundations of production, which characterise the entire capitalist mode of production.[19] Not by chance, it is first in relative surplus-value, and then in the metamorphosis of surplus-value into profit, that the specifically capitalist mode of production sinks roots: a particular form of the development of the social productive forces of labour, which appear as the autonomous forces of capital counterposed to the worker, precisely because they are, in fact, a form of capital's dominion over the worker. 'Production for value and surplus value implies … the constantly operating tendency to reduce the labour time necessary for the production of a commodity, i.e., its value, below the actually prevailing social average. The pressure to reduce cost price to its minimum becomes the strongest lever for raising the social productive power of labour, which, however, appears here only as a continual increase in the productiveness of capital'.[20] We need only think of the capitalist's fanaticism in economising on the means of production, economising on the employment of constant capital and, at the same time, economising on labour.

'Just as capital has the tendency to reduce the direct employment of living labour to no more than the necessary labour, and always to cut down the labour required to produce a commodity by exploiting the social productive power of labour and thus to save a maximum of directly applied living labour, so it has also the tendency to employ this labour, reduced to a minimum, under the most economical conditions, i.e., to reduce to its minimum the value of the employed constant capital'.[21] An increase in the rate of profit derives not only from a more modern exploitation of the productivity of social labour employed in the production of constant capital, but also 'from the economizing of employing constant capital itself'. This economizing becomes possible only on the basis of the highest concentration of the means of production, which alone can give rise to their mass utilisation. As a result, 'They are commonly consumed in the process of production by the aggregate labourer, instead of being consumed in small fractions by a mass of labourers operating disconnectedly or, at best, directly cooperating on a

19 Ibid., 867.
20 Ibid.
21 Ibid., 90.

small scale'.[22] The means of production are now consumed in the production process, on the basis of a single criterion, by the collective worker – and no longer in the fractioned form by a mass of workers without reciprocal connections. Thus, 'the economy of production conditions found in large-scale production is essentially due to the fact that these conditions prevail as conditions of social, or socially combined, labour, and therefore as social conditions of labour … it originates quite as much from the social nature of labour, just as surplus value originates from the surplus labour of the individual labourer considered singly'.[23] Nonetheless, economizing on constant capital, on the employment of the conditions of production, as a specific instrument for pushing the rate of profit back up again, appears to the capitalist as an aspect wholly extraneous to the worker, 'appears more than any other inner power of labour as an inherent power of capital',[24] a property of the capitalist mode of production and thus a *function of the capitalist*. 'This conception is so much the less surprising since it appears to accord with fact, and since the relationship of capital actually conceals the inner connection behind the utter indifference, isolation, and estrangement in which they place the labourer vis-à-vis the conditions of realising his labour', to the point of creating 'the estrangement and indifference that arise between the labourer, the bearer of living labour, and the economical, i.e., rational and thrifty, use of the material conditions of his labour'.[25]

Thus, through labour's immediately social nature, the ever more exclusive domination of capital over the conditions of labour extends and deepens; through this domination, with the ever more rational employment of *all* the conditions of production, the capitalist exploitation of labour-power develops and *becomes more specific*. From this moment onward, the means of production are no longer simply an *objective property* of the capitalist, but a *subjective function* of capital. For precisely this reason, the worker who comes into confrontation with them in the production process recognises them only as use-values of production, instruments and material of labour; they again come to see the whole process of production as the simple labour process. The unity

---

22   Ibid., 82.
23   Ibid., 82–3.
24   Ibid., 88.
25   Ibid., 89.

of the labour process and the valorisation process remains in the hands of capital alone; from this point, the worker can understand the whole production process only through the mediation of capital; labour-power is no longer only *exploited* by the capitalist but *integrated* within capital.

The development of capitalism also entails the development of capitalist exploitation. This in turn entails the development of the class struggle, from factory legislation to the rupturing of the state. The struggle for the regulation of the working day sees the capitalist and the worker facing each other *still* as buyer and seller. The capitalist defends his right to buy surplus-labour, the worker the right to sell less of it. 'Right versus right ... between equal rights, force decides'. On one side, the power of the collective capitalist; on the other, that of the collective worker. It is through the mediation of legislation, through the intervention of the law, through the use of legal rights – which is to say, on the political terrain – that the contract of purchase and sale between the individual capitalist and isolated worker for the first time transforms into a relation of force between the capitalist and working classes. And it seems that this transition allows us to catch sight of the ideal terrain on which the general confrontation between the classes can alone unfold. Historically, at its birth, this is, in fact, how things were done. In order to evaluate the possible generalisation of this moment, we first have to understand the specific trait that distinguishes it: that is, the determinate way in which it functioned within a certain type of capitalist development. Not by chance, Marx brings in the chapter on the working day precisely when he is dealing with the passage from absolute surplus-value to relative surplus-value, from the capital that masters the labour process as it finds it to the capital that turns this labour itself upside down, until it has moulded it in its own image, in its own likeness. Historically, the struggle for the regulated working day is posed in the middle of this process. Given capital's natural impulse toward the extension of the working day, it is true that the workers, putting their heads together and through living force, *as a class*, secured a law from the state, a social barrier which stopped them from accepting slavery 'by means of a voluntary contract with capital'. The working-class struggle constrained the capitalist to change the *form* of his dominion. Thus, the pressure of labour-power is able to force capital to modify its own internal composition; it intervenes *within* capital as an essential component of capitalist development; it pushes capitalist production forward from within, to the point of driving it to penetrate all external relations of social life. What appears in the most advanced stage of development as a spontaneous function of the worker, separated from the conditions of labour and integrated into capital, appears at a more backward stage as the legal necessity of a social barrier that will prevent the exhaustion of labour-power and at the same time lay the foundation for its specifically capitalist exploitation. Political mediation assumes a specific place in each of these moments. It is not a given that the bourgeois political terrain must live eternally in the sky of capitalist society.

The transformations in the material mode of production and corresponding changes in the social relations between producers come to be considered 'outrages without measure, and then called forth, in opposition to this, social control, which legally limits, regulates, and makes uniform the working day and its pauses'.[26] All 'these highly detailed specifications, which regulate, with military uniformity, the times, the limits and the pauses of the work by the stroke of the clock, were by no means a product of the fantasy of Members of Parliament. They developed gradually out of circumstances as natural laws of the modern mode of production'.[27] Through experience the British parliament came to the understanding that 'a simple compulsory law is sufficient to enact away all the so-called impediments opposed by the nature of the process, to the restriction and regulation of the working day'.[28] The Factory Acts introduced in one branch of industry placed an absolute limit on the factory boss, making him remove any technical obstacles. The acts 'thus artificially ripen the material elements necessary for the conversion of the manufacturing system into the factory system, yet at the same time, because they make it necessary to lay out a greater amount of capital, they hasten the decline of the small masters, and the concentration of capital'.[29] In this sense, 'Factory legislation, that first conscious and methodical reaction of society against the spontaneously developed form of its production process, is, as we have seen, just as much the necessary product of large-scale industry as cotton yarn, self-actors and

---

26 *Capital*, Vol. 1, 412.
27 Ibid., 394–5.
28 Ibid., 607.
29 Ibid.

the electric telegraph'.[30] With the results of the various commissions of inquiry, with the violent intervention of the state, the collective capitalist seeks first to convince and then reaches the point of compelling the individual capitalist to conform to the general needs of capitalist social production. The exploitation of labour-power can take place *even* while economizing on labour, as the continuous increase in the constant part of capital goes hand in hand with the ever-increasing economy in the employment of constant capital itself. Only on this basis does the generalisation of capitalist production and its higher level development become possible. The clash between the classes on the political terrain, the political mediation of the class struggle, was *in this case* simultaneously the *result* of a certain grade of development and the *presupposition* for that development conquering an autonomous mechanism of its own – a mechanism that travelled very far, to the point of itself internally recuperating political mediation, the political terrain of the class struggle itself. 'If the general extension of factory legislation to all trades for the purpose of protecting the working class both in mind and body has become inevitable, on the other hand, as we have already pointed out, that extension hastens on the general conversion of numerous isolated small industries into a few combined industries carried on upon a large scale; it therefore accelerates the concentration of capital and the exclusive predominance of the factory system. It destroys both the ancient and the transitional forms behind which the dominion of capital is still partially hidden, and replaces them with a dominion which is direct and unconcealed. But by doing this it also generalises the direct struggle against its rule'.[31]

This should be taken before anything else as the arrival of a long historical process that set out from the production of absolute surplus-value and by necessity arrived at the production of relative surplus-value; from the forced lengthening of the working day to the *seemingly* spontaneous increase in the productive force of labour; from the pure and simple extension of the production process as a whole to its internal transformation, which leads to a continual revolutionisation of the labour process, in function of and ever more organically dependent on the valorisation process. What had earlier been an easily established

---

30   Ibid., 610.
31   Ibid., 635.

relation between the sphere of production and the other social spheres now becomes the much more complex relation between the transformations *internal* to the sphere of production and the transformations *internal* to the other spheres. It moreover becomes a much more *mediated*, more organic and more mystified relation – at once more self-evident and more hidden – between capitalist production and bourgeois society. The more the determinate relation of capitalist production takes charge of the social relation in general, the more it seems to disappear within this latter as a marginal particularity. The more that capitalist production deeply penetrates into and, by extension, invades the totality of social relations, the more society appears as a *totality* relative to production and production as a *particularity* relative to society. When the particular generalises or universalises itself, it *appears* to be represented by the general, by the universal. In the social relation of capitalist production, the generalisation of production expresses itself as the hypostatisation of society. When *specifically* capitalist production has already weaved the whole web of social relations, it itself emerges as a *generic* social relation. Likewise, the phenomenal forms reproduce themselves with immediate spontaneity, as the *commonplace forms of thought*: 'the substantial relation should be discovered by science'. If we limit ourselves to a purely *ideological* apprehension of this reality, we do nothing more than *reproduce* this reality as it presents itself, inverted in its appearance. If we want to understand the intimate material nexus of real relations, we need a scientifically penetrating theoretical effort which first of all strips the object –bourgeois society – of all its mystified, ideologised phenomenal forms, and then isolates and strikes at its hidden substance, which is the capitalist relation of production.

In his impressive *Development of Capitalism in Russia*, Lenin talks about large-scale mechanised industry. In this passage, he first establishes that the *scientific concept* of the factory does not at all correspond to the commonplace and common sense understanding of the word: 'In our official statistics, and in general in our literature, a factory is understood to be an industrial establishment of greater or smaller dimensions which employs a greater or smaller number of salaried workers. For Marx, conversely, large-scale machine industry (the factory) is understood solely as a certain level, precisely the most advanced level, of capitalism in industry'. He refers to the fourth section of *Capital* Volume 1 and especially to the passage from manufacture to big industry, where the scientific concept of the factory serves precisely to signal the 'forms and phases through which the development of capitalism in industry passes in a given country'. At a certain stage of capital's development, if it wants to lower the *value of labour-power*, it is inevitably compelled to increase the *productive power of labour*; it is forced to transform as much necessary labour as possible into surplus-labour. That is, it is forced to turn upside down all the technical and social conditions of the labour process, to revolutionise the mode of production from within. 'In capitalist production, economising on labour via the development of the productive force of labour does not have as its objective the shortening of the working day'. It has the sole objective of shortening the labour-time necessary for the production of labour-power and hence for the production of a determinate quantity of commodities. That is, the increase in the productive power of labour must first of all take over those branches of industry whose products determine the value of labour-power. But 'the value of a commodity is determined not only by the quantity of labour which gives it its final form, but also by the quantity of labour contained in the instruments by which it has been produced ... Hence, a fall in the value of labour-power is also brought about by an increase in the productivity of labour, and by a corresponding cheapening of commodities in those industries which supply the instruments of labour and the material for labour, i.e. the physical elements of constant capital which are required for producing the means of subsistence'.[32] If we understand this process not from the point of view of the individual capitalist, but from the point of view of capitalist society in its totality, then we see that *the general rate of surplus-labour* increases just as the value of labour-power decreases. 'Exceptionally productive labour acts as intensified labour'[33]; in other words, in the same periods of time it creates values higher than those created by the average social labour. Therefore, the capitalist who applies the most accomplished mode of production appropriates through surplus-labour a greater part of the working day than that appropriated by other capitalists in the same industry. 'He does as an individual what capital itself taken as a whole does when engaged in producing relative

32 Ibid., 432.
33 Ibid., 435.

surplus-value'.[34] The coercive law of competition operates in such a way
as to introduce and generalise the new mode of production; but competition itself, the external movement of capital, is nothing but another
way in which the 'scientific analysis of competition is possible only if we
can grasp the inner nature of capital, just as the apparent motions of the
heavenly bodies are intelligible only to someone who is acquainted with
their real motions, which are not perceptible to the senses'.[35] If it is to
remain positively untouched by this process, the general rate of surplus-
value needs at this point to continually reduce the value of labour-power,
to revolutionise the conditions of the labour process, and to generalise
and accelerate the mode of capitalist social production. This basic fact
would go on to make capitalism a formidable historical system in the
development of the social productive forces.

Capitalist development is organically linked to the production of
relative surplus-value. And relative surplus-value is organically linked to
all the vicissitudes *internal to* the process of capitalist production, to that
distinct and ever more complex unity between the labour process and
the valorisation process, between the upheavals in the conditions of
labour and the exploitation of labour-power, between the combination
of technical and social process, on the one hand, and capitalist despotism, on the other. The more that capitalist development advances, which
is to say, the greater the penetration and extension of the production of
relative surplus-value, the more necessarily production-distribution-
exchange-consumption form a complete circuit – that is, the relation
between capitalist production and society, between factory and society,
between society and state, becomes increasingly organic. At the highest
level of capitalist development, this social relation becomes a *moment* of
the relation of production, the whole of society becomes an *articulation*
of production, the whole society lives in function of the factory and the
factory extends its exclusive dominion over the whole society. It is on
this basis that the political state machine tends ever more to identify
with the figure of the *collective capitalist*; it increasingly becomes the
property of the capitalist mode of production and, therefore, a *function
of the capitalist*. The process of the unitary composition of capitalist
society, imposed by the specific development of its production, no

---

34 Ibid., 436.
35 Ibid., 433.

longer tolerates the existence of a political terrain even formally independent of the web of social relations. In a certain sense, it is true that
the political functions of the state are today beginning to be recuperated
within society, with the slight difference that this is the class society of
the capitalist mode of production. All of this, too, ought to be considered a *sectarian* reaction against those who see in the modern political
state the neutral terrain of the confrontation between capital and labour.
Marx uttered prophetic words which have never been surpassed in
Marxist *political* thought: 'It is not enough that the conditions of labour
are concentrated at one pole of society in the shape of capital, while at
the other pole are grouped masses of men who have nothing to sell but
their labour-power. Nor is it enough that they are compelled to sell
themselves voluntarily. The advance of capitalist production develops a
working class which by education, tradition and habit looks upon the
conditions of that mode of production as self-evident natural laws. The
organization of the capitalist process of production, once it is fully
developed, breaks down all resistance ... The silent compulsion of
economic relations sets the seal on the domination of the capitalist over
the worker. Direct extra-economic force is still of course used, but only
in exceptional cases. In the ordinary run of things, the worker can be left
to the "natural laws of production", i.e., it is possible to rely on his
dependence on capital, which springs from the conditions of production themselves, and is guaranteed in perpetuity by them.'[36]

But *one* of the instruments *functioning* within this process is precisely
the mystified relation which establishes itself, at a determinate level of
development, between capitalist production and bourgeois society,
between the relation of production and the social relation. This mystified relation is the *consequence* of the transformations that have taken
place in the heart of the social production relation as well as the *premise*
for this relation to be once again considered as a *natural law*. It is only
apparently paradoxical that when the factory is a particular fact – even
though an essential one – within society, it manages to maintain its
specific traits distinct from the total reality. Yet, when the factory extends
its control over the whole society – all of social production is turned into
industrial production – the specific traits of the factory are lost amid the
generic traits of society. When the whole society is reduced to the

36 Ibid., 899.

factory, the factory, as such, seems to disappear. This is the material basis, at a higher real level, on which the maximum ideological development of the bourgeois metamorphoses repeats and concludes. The highest level of development of capitalist production signals the deepest mystification of all bourgeois social relations. The real growing process of *proletarianisation* presents itself as a formal process of *tertiarisation*. The reduction of all forms of labour to industrial labour, of all types of labour to the commodity labour-power, presents itself as the extinction of labour-power itself as a commodity and thus as the depreciation of its value as a product. The payment of any price of labour in wages presents itself as the absolute negation of capitalist profit, as the absolute elimination of working-class surplus-labour. Capital, which decomposes and recomposes the labour process according to the growing necessities of its own valorisation process, now presents itself as society's objective potential, which self-organises and thus develops. The return of the state's political functions within the very structure of civil society presents itself as a contradiction between state and society, the ever-narrower functionality of politics and economics as a possible autonomy of the political terrain from economic relations. In a word, the concentration of capital and, simultaneously, the exclusive dominion of the factory regime – these two historic results of modern capitalism – are inverted: the first into the dissolution of capital as a determinate social relation, the second into the exclusion of the factory from the specific relation of production. For this reason, capital appears as the objective wealth of society in general and the factory as a particular mode of the production of 'social' capital. All this is how things seem to the crudely bourgeois outlook of the vulgar sociologist. When even the scholar is reduced to a wage-worker, then wage-labour reaches beyond the limits of scientific understanding, or better becomes the terrain of the exclusive application of the false bourgeois science called technology.

It is pointless to add that all of this has yet to occur, and we will only concern ourselves with it when it does indeed unfold. As Lenin put it, 'Whoever wants to represent any living phenomenon in its development should inevitably and necessarily confront the dilemma: advance the facts or stay behind'.

This is a methodological principle that ought to be deployed permanently – even when it forces us to adopt that fierce *unilateralism* which strikes so much fear into the moderate souls of so many 'professional revolutionaries'. Even more when this approach presents itself not – of course – as a whim of the mind, but as a real process of objective development, which is not to be *followed* but to be *anticipated*. No one wants us to forget the existence of a world external to production. Placing the accent on one part means recognising and insisting on the essential character of this part relative to the others – even more so when this particular element, *by its very nature*, generalises itself. The scientific *unilateralism* of the working-class point of view is not to be confused with a mystical *reductio ad unum*. Rather, the important thing is to look at distribution, exchange and consumption from the point of view of production. And, within production, to look at the labour process from the perspective of the valorisation process and the valorisation process from the viewpoint of the labour process; that is, to understand the organic unity of the production process, which then *provides the foundation for* the unity of production, distribution, exchange and consumption. The dynamic totality of this process can be understood through either the *partiality* of the collective capitalist, or that of the socially combined worker. But while the first presents it with all the despotic functionality of its conservative outer appearances, the second reveals it with all the liberatory force of its revolutionary development.

The social relation of capitalist production sees society as a *means* and production as an *end*: capitalism is production for production. The very *sociality* of production is nothing other than the *medium* for private appropriation. In this sense, on a capitalist basis the social relation is never *separate* from the production relation; the production relation becomes ever more identical with the *social relation of the factory*; likewise, the social relation of the factory acquires ever more directly *political* content. It is capitalist development itself which tends to subordinate every political relation to the social relation, every social relation to the production relation, every production relation to the relation of the factory – for only this then allows it to begin, from within the factory, the inverse path: that is, the capitalist's struggle to dismantle and recompose in his own image the antagonistic figure of the collective worker. Capital attacks labour on its very own terrain; only from within labour can capital disintegrate the collective worker and then integrate the isolated worker. No longer do we just have the means of production on the one hand and the worker on the other, but all the conditions of labour on the one hand and the worker who works on the other. Labour and labour-power are counterposed between themselves and yet both united *within* capital. At this point, the ideal for the most modern capitalism becomes that of recuperating the primitive relation of simple purchase-and-sale contracted between the individual capitalist and the isolated worker; however, while the former holds the social power of monopoly, the other is individually subordinated to the pay they get for their troubles. This *silent coercion by economic relations* itself seals the capitalist's dominion over the worker. The current factory legislation is the rationalisation of capitalist production. The constitution within the factory will sanction 'the exclusive predominance of the factory system'[37] over the whole society.

It is true: this 'generalizes the direct struggle' against this same predominance.[38] And indeed, by this point it is no longer simply *possible* but historically *necessary* to root the general struggle against the social system within the social relation of production; in other words, to pitch bourgeois society into crisis from within *capitalist production*. For the working class, it is essential once more to take, with all of its class consciousness, the path dictated by capitalist development: viewing the state from the point of view of society, society from the point of view of the factory and the factory from the point of view of the worker. Our task is to continually recompose the material figure of the collective worker against capital, which itself seeks to dismantle this figure; or, rather, with the objective of beginning to dismantle the inner nature of capital from within those potentially antagonistic parts of its own organic composition. To the capitalist who seeks to counterpose labour and labour-power within the collective worker, we respond by counterposing labour-power and capital within capital itself. At this point, capital attempts to dismantle the collective worker and the worker tries to dismantle capital; this is no longer a matter of right against right, decided by force, but directly force against force. This is the highest stage of the class struggle at the highest level of capitalist development.

The error of the old maximalism was to conceive of this counterposition, so to speak, *from the outside*: it saw the working class as being completely outside of capital and, as such, as its general antagonist

---

37 Ibid., 635.
38 Ibid.

– hence its own incapacity to reach any scientific understanding and the sterility of all practical struggle. But today we must say that, from the point of view of the worker, we should look directly not at the working-class condition, but at the situation of capital. Even in their own analysis, the worker should ascribe capital a privileged place, precisely the privilege which capital objectively possess within the system. And not only that: the working class should materially discover itself to be a *part* of capital if it wants to then counterpose the *whole* of capital to itself. It must recognise itself as a *particular element* of capital if it wants to then present itself as its *general* antagonist. The collective worker stands counterposed not only to the machine, as constant capital, but to labour-power itself, as variable capital. It has to reach the point of having as its enemy the whole of capital, including itself as a part of capital. Labour should see labour-power *as a commodity* as its enemy. It is on this basis that capitalism's need to *objectivise* in capital all the *subjective* potencies of labour can be transformed, on the worker's part, into a powerful understanding of capitalist exploitation. The attempt to integrate the working class within the system is what may provoke the decisive response – that of the rupture in the system, bringing the class struggle to its highest level. There is a point of development in which capitalism finds itself in this state of necessity; if that moment passes, then capital has won for a long period. Yet, if the *organised* working class were to succeed in breaking it even once on this terrain, then the model of working-class revolution in modern capitalism would have been born.

We have seen that the commodity labour-power is the properly active side of capital, the natural home of any capitalist dynamism. It is the protagonist not only of the expanded reproduction of the valorisation process, but also of the continual revolutionary upheavals of the labour process itself. Technological transformations are themselves dictated and imposed by changes in the value of labour-power. Cooperation, manufacturing and big industry are nothing more than particular methods of the production of relative surplus-value, different forms of economising labour, which in turn provoke growing changes in the organic composition of capital. Capital depends ever more on labour-power; it must therefore possess it ever more totally, just as it possesses the natural forces of its production; it must reduce the working class itself to a *natural force of society*. The more that capitalist development advances, the more that the collective capitalist has the need to see all labour

within capital: the more it needs to control all of the internal and external movements of labour-power; the more it is compelled to programme
the capital-labour relation in the long term, as the index of the stability
of the social system. When capital has conquered all of the territories
external to capitalist production, properly speaking, it begins its process
of internal colonisation; or when the circuit of bourgeois society is
finally complete – production, distribution, exchange and consumption
– we can say that there begins the true and proper process of *capitalist
development*. At this point, the process of the objective capitalisation of
subjective forces of labour is and must be accompanied by the process of
the material dissolution of the collective worker and thus of the worker
themself, as such. The worker is reduced to being property of the capitalist mode of production and is thus a *function of the capitalist*. On this
basis, it becomes vital for capitalism to integrate the working class within
the system; the working-class refusal of this integration impedes the
system's functioning. Therefore, only one alternative is left: either the
dynamic stabilisation of the system or working-class revolution.

Marx says that 'of all the instruments of production, the greatest
productive power is the revolutionary class itself'.[39] The process of capitalist production is already itself revolutionary: it keeps its productive
forces – including the conscious and living productive force, the working class – in continuous movement and operates incessant transformations therein. The development of the productive forces is capitalism's
'historic mission'. It is true that at the same time it *lays the foundations* of
its greatest contradiction: that is why the incessant development of the
productive forces cannot but provoke the incessant development of the
greatest productive force, the working class as revolutionary class. It is
this that should drive the collective worker consciously to value the
objectively revolutionary content of capitalist development, to the point
of forcing it to anticipate development if it does not want to be left
behind. For this reason, the working-class revolution does not have to
come *after*, when capitalism has already collapsed in a general catastrophe, nor can it come before, when capitalism has not even begun its
specific cycle of development. The revolution can and must take place
contemporaneously to that development; it must present itself as an
internal component of development and, at the same time, as its *internal*

---

39   MECW, Vol. 6, 212.

contradiction – just as labour-power can only set the entire capitalist society into crisis from *within capital*. Only the revolutionary development of the working class can render *efficient* and at the same time *self-evident* the fundamental contradiction between the productive forces and the social relations of production: without that development, the contradiction remains a *potential* and not *real* fact, a pure and simple *possibility*, as with the possibility of crises at the level of C – M – C. The level of the productive forces is not measured by the level of technological progress, but instead by the working class's degree of revolutionary consciousness. Or, better: the first is the capitalist's measure, conceiving the worker solely as a human appendage of his machines; the second is the organised workers' movement's measure. And it is precisely on this basis that it organises the process of rupture in that social relation which puts brakes on and cages around the revolutionary experience of the working class. In this sense, the contradiction between the level of the productive forces and the social relations of production is just the *external* expression of another contradiction that lives completely *internal to* the social relation of production: that is, the contradiction between the socialisation of the process of production and the private appropriation of the product, between the individual capitalist who attempts to decompose that sociality and the collective worker who *recomposes* it in more advanced fashion, between the bosses' attempt at *economic* integration and the *political* response of the working-class antagonism. We talk about these things for good reason, as this process is currently taking place in Italy and it does so out in the open. The alternative between capitalism and socialism will continue to be decided on this terrain for a long time. The political party of Italian capitalism seems to have understood this; the parties of the workers' movement have not.

It is not necessarily a question of eliminating all the other enduring contradictions – these are perhaps even more obvious to everyone and thus appear more essential to the comprehension of the whole. Instead, the important thing is to grasp the elementary principle that, at a determinate level of capitalist development, all the contradictions between the various parts of capital must express themselves in the fundamental contradiction between the working class and *the whole of* capitalism; only at this point does the *process* of the socialist revolution begin. To express all the contradictions of capitalism *through* the working class already means that *these* contradictions are irresolvable within capitalism itself – they thus point *beyond* the system which generates them. The working class *within* capitalism is the only *irresolvable* contradiction of capitalism – or, better, it becomes irresolvable the moment it *self-organises as a revolutionary class*. To be clear, this does not mean the organisation of the oppressed class or the defence of the toilers' interests, or its organisation as a governing class that manages capitalist interests, but its organisation as an antagonistic class: *the political self-government of the working class within the capitalist economic system*. If the formula of the "dual power" has any sense, this would be it. It is no longer a problem today if consciousness has to be brought to the worker *from the outside* and if it is the party that must do this. The solution already exists and is directly dictated by capitalism's development, by the capitalist production which has touched the limits of bourgeois society, by the factory which now imposes its exclusive dominion on the whole of society. Political consciousness must indeed be brought by the party, but from within the production process. No one today thinks that we can set a revolutionary process underway without the *political organisation* of the working class, without a *working-class party*. But too many still think that the party can direct the revolution even while remaining *cut off from the factory*, that political action begins where the relation of production ends and that the *general* struggle against the system is the same one which develops at the heights of the bourgeois state, which has in the meantime itself become the *particular* expression of capitalist production's social needs. Let us note that this is not a matter of giving up on the Leninist rupture in the state machine, as inevitably happens with all those who head down the democratic path. Rather, it is about founding this rupture in the state within society, founding the dissolution of society within the production process and founding the destruction of the production relation within the social relation of the factory. The bourgeois state machine today must today be broken within the capitalist factory.

Whether our analysis starts from *Capital* or from the actual level of capitalist development, it will arrive at the same conclusions. Still now we cannot say that these conclusions have been proven; rather, we have to start out from the beginning along another path and once again taste the meaning of this Marxian theory of capitalist development, which increasingly becomes the historical node of all other problems. We must do this in order to liberate this theory from all the ideological incrustations which have put part of the workers' movement to sleep in opportunist expectation of a catastrophic collapse, thus contributing to the integration of another part of the workers' movement into the autonomous mechanism of an indefinite stabilisation of the system. And we will do this as a follow-up to this line of argument.

Here it is enough that we have emphasised the primary necessity of getting back on *the most correct path*, be that for theoretical analysis or for practical struggle. Factory-society-state – this is the point at which scientific theory and subversive praxis, the *analysis of capitalism* and the *working-class revolution*, today coincide. This would alone suffice to confirm the correctness of this path. The 'scientific conception' of the factory today opens a way to the most complete comprehension of the present and, simultaneously, its most complete destruction. *Precisely for this reason* it is posed as the point of departure for the new construction, which must start out from the factory if it wants to grow the workers' state *entirely* within the socialist society's new relation of production.

1962

The Plan of Capital

At the beginning of the third section of Volume 2 of *Capital*, Marx distinguishes between the direct process of the production of capital and the total process of its reproduction. The former, we have seen, includes both the work process as well as the value-creation process. As we shall see, the latter includes both the process of consumption mediated by circulation and the process of the reproduction of capital itself. In the different forms assumed by capital within its cycle, and even more so in the different forms assumed by this cycle, the movement of individual capital proves to be *part* of the total movement of social capital. 'Each individual capital forms only a fraction of the total social capital, a fraction that has acquired independence and been endowed with individual life, so to speak, just as every individual capitalist is no more than an element of the capitalist class'.[1] Marx says that if we consider the annual function of social capital in terms of its results – that is, if we consider the annual commodity-product provided by society – we see that it includes both the *social* reproduction of capital and its *productive* and *individual* consumption. 'It thus includes the reproduction (i.e., maintenance) of the capitalist class and the working class, and hence too the reproduction of the capitalist character of the entire process of production',[2] meaning a simple reproduction on an invariant scale

---

1 Karl Marx, *Capital*, Vol. 2, translated by David Fernbach, London: Penguin, 1978, 427.
2 Ibid., 468.

which immediately presents itself as *part* of a more complex reproduction on an extended scale. It is thus a particular moment of and a real
factor for the accumulation of capital – that is, the accumulation no
longer of individual capital, but of social capital; the extended reproduction, therein, of the capitalist class on the one hand and of the working
class on the other. The process of the socialisation of capital is the specific
material base upon which is founded, at a certain level, the process of
the development of capitalism. The determinate formation of a capitalist
society presupposes the production of *social* capital as an already accomplished *historical* act which is already acknowledged as a *natural* fact.
The figure of the collective capitalist, a functionary of the total social
capital, is itself the product of a determinate degree of development of
capitalist production. Against this figure, as both its presupposition and
as its result, the total social labour as a class of organised workers – social
labour-power as a class – acquires an objective material existence. The
'plan' of capital emerges primarily from the need to make the working
class function *as such* within social capital. The growing socialisation of
the capitalist relation of production does not bring about the socialist
society, but only a growing working-class power within the capitalist
system.

Of the three forms in which the cyclic process of capital expresses
itself, the third form, the commodity-capital cycle (C' ... C'), is the
only one in which value-valorised capital appears as the starting point
for its valorisation. In the cycle of monetary capital and in that of
productive capital, the starting point is always the original value-
capital, which is yet to be valorised: the whole movement is only the
movement of the anticipated value-capital. C', on the other hand, as a
relation of capital, immediately implies both the cycle of value-capital
and the cycle of surplus-value, as well as that of a surplus-value already
in part spent as income and in part accumulated as capital. To set out
from C' means to set out from the overall commodity-product, as
commodity-capital: within this, individual consumption and productive consumption enter as conditions of the cycle; and if the productive
consumption takes place by the work of each individual capitalist, then
individual consumption immediately and only presents itself as a social
act. The transformation realised within this cycle concerns the magnitude of the value of capital: it is thus the result not of a formal shifting
of monetary capital within the process of circulation, but of a material

change of productive capital within the production process. The cycle C' ... C' presupposes other industrial capital within its own trajectory. But, as we have seen, its starting point is no longer only the originally anticipated value-capital, but the value-capital that has been valorised. Its movement 'in this way proclaims itself from the start as a total movement of industrial capital',[3] not only as 'a form of motion common to all individual industrial capitals, but at the same time as the form of motion of the sum of individual capitals, i.e. of the total social capital of the capitalist class'.[4]

Industrial capital is found simultaneously in all the different stages of its cycle and proceeds successively through the different functional forms presented by all three cycles. In fact, the total process is the unity of the three cycles; the total cycle is the real unity of the three forms. For this reason, in each single functional form of capital, the *total* cycle presents itself as that form's *specific* cycle. 'It is a necessary condition for the overall production process, in other words for the social capital, that it is at the same time a process of reproduction, and hence the circuit of each of its moments'.[5] One part of capital, as commodity-capital, always transforms into money; another, as monetary capital, transforms into productive capital; still another, as productive capital, transforms once again into commodity-capital. 'The constant presence of all three forms is mediated by the circuit of the total capital ... The forms are therefore fluid forms and their simultaneity is mediated by their succession'.[6] Insofar as it is self-valorising value, capital cannot but be a continuous movement, a cyclical process that passes through different stages and assumes different forms of development. 'The circuit of capital is a constant process of interruption; one stage is left behind, the next stage embarked upon; one form is cast aside, and the capital exists in another'.[7] Yet the continuity is 'the characteristic mark of capitalist production'. 'The continuity of the reproduction is at times more or less interrupted'.[8] When social capital as value undergoes a *revolution in value*, individual capital is always in danger of succumbing unless it proves able to adjust

---

3   Ibid., 177.
4   Ibid.
5   Ibid., 184.
6   Ibid.
7   Ibid., 182.
8   Ibid., 185.

to the conditions of this shift in value. 'The more acute and frequent these revolutions in value become, the more the movement of the independent value, acting with the force of an elemental natural process, prevails over the foresight and calculation of the individual capitalist'.[9] In this case, the mechanism of the cycle comes to a halt, production drops and the entire process of development is forced to stop: 'Every delay in the succession brings the coexistence into disarray[10] – hence the need to find a nexus between the cycles of individual capitals, understood as partial movements of the process of the reproduction of the total social capital. In fact, 'it is only in the unity of the three circuits that the continuity of the overall process is realized'. 'The total social capital always possesses this continuity, and its process always contains the continuity of the three circuits'. What happens to social capital is exactly what happens in 'a ramified factory system', where the process flows with maximum regularity and uniformity, where 'the product is continuously at the various stages of its formation, and in transition from one phase of production to another'.[11]

Let's go further. If we take capital as individual capital, the question of what natural form the commodity-product assumes proves to be wholly indifferent for our analysis. For here we are directly concerned with the process of value production and with the value of its products. This mode of exposition, however, appears purely formal as soon as we consider the total social capital and its value-product. The movement through which part of the products' value again transforms into capital while another part passes into individual consumption – both that of the capitalist and that of the working class – 'forms a movement within the value of the product itself' in the moment that the result of the total capital comes to be expressed in this value. Indeed, 'this movement is not only a replacement of value, but a replacement of materials, and is therefore conditioned not just by the mutual relations of the value components of the total social product but equally by their use-values, their material shape'.[12] The value reproduced in the means of production must be *at least* equal to the constant part of the value

---

9   Ibid.
10   Ibid., 183
11   Ibid.
12   Ibid., 470.

of social capital. So, for example, the part of the social working day that produces means of production produces nothing other than new constant capital; that is, it produces only a product designed to enter into productive consumption. Meanwhile, the part of the social working day which produces means of consumption produces nothing but new variable capital and new surplus-value. Or, better: it produces products in whose natural forms the value of variable capital and surplus-value are realised. *Each* of these two parts of the social working day produces and reproduces (and thus accumulates) the constant capital, variable capital and surplus-value of *both* main sections, namely those of the means of production and those of the means of consumption. The working day, which in the production of individual capital appeared immediately split between necessary labour and surplus-value, is only mystified in its realisation in the form of the wage. And it now appears, in the production of social capital, as actually divided between a constant and a variable part of capital: between the production-reproduction of the one and the production-reproduction of the other. Each of these parts includes both production and consumption, the means of production and means of consumption, productive consumption and individual consumption. Now the social working day functions directly within the process of the production of social capital; within this production process it produces, reproduces, and accumulates new capital, and it produces-reproduces and accumulates new labour-power. The division between necessary labour and surplus-labour does not at all disappear at this level; it is simply generalised – which is to say, *socialised* – in the total process of capitalist production. There is a social surplus-labour which is taken from the working class and which ends up socialising the very existence of surplus-value. But social surplus-value is nothing but the profit of social capital: it has nothing to do with the super-profits that the monopolies extract from all the pores of society. This is a process which has as both its material base and its final objective the maximal socialisation of capitalist production, of labour-power and thus of capital. 'In speaking of the social point of view, i.e. in considering the total social product, which includes both the reproduction of the social capital and individual consumption, it is necessary to avoid falling into the habits of bourgeois economics, as imitated by Proudhon, i.e. to avoid looking at things as if a society based on the capitalist mode of production lost its specific historical and economic character when considered *en bloc*, as a totality. This is not the case at all. What we have to deal with is the collective capitalist. The total capital appears as the share capital of all individual capitalists together'.[13]

Marx tells us that profit is nothing but surplus-value calculated in terms of social capital. In reality, surplus-value and profit are the same – they are quantitatively identical from the masses' point of view. Profit is the mystified form in which surplus-value *appears*, just as the wage is the mystified form in which the value of labour-power appears. It is only in surplus-value that the relation between capital and surplus-value is exposed: 'capital appears as a relation to itself'. Here, the organic difference between the constant and variable parts of capital itself disappears: surplus-value is simply faced with an indistinct total capital. And this process is already complete when the process of the production and circulation of capital, of the production and realisation of surplus-value is itself complete; that is, when extended reproduction is up and running and accumulation is therefore advancing. Yet there is a point *within* this process which allows its entire development to make a *leap* forward. This occurs when the whole of capitalist production comes to produce a general rate of profit and, consequently, an *average* profit. The fundamental idea of average profit is founded on the principle that 'the capital in each sphere of production must share *pro rata* to its magnitude in the total surplus-value squeezed out of the labourers by the total social capital; or, that every individual capital should be regarded merely as a part of the total social capital, and every capitalist as a shareholder in the total social enterprise'.[14] At this point, the profit that the single capitalist takes in is different from the surplus-value that they extort; profit and surplus-value are now in fact of different magnitudes. Only exceptionally or accidentally does the surplus-value effectively produced within a particular sphere of production coincide with the profit contained in the sales price of the commodity.

Already in the simple transformation of surplus-value into profit, 'the portion of the value of a commodity forming the profit' is distinguished 'from the portion forming its cost-price'. Thus, 'it is natural that the conception of value should elude the capitalist at this juncture so that

13   Ibid., 509.
14   MECW, Vol. 37, 207.

his profit appears to him as something outside the imminent value of the commodity'.[15]

This appearance receives confirmation and structure on the historical basis that corresponds to the profit of the average social capital when all capitals tend to realise, in the prices of the commodities that they produce, not the particular surplus-value that is produced directly, but the average social profit. That is, they seek to realise the price of production – and here, 'price of production' means cost price plus cost price multiplied by the average rate of profit $(k + kp')$. The price of production in fact *contains* the average profit. Only accidentally or exceptionally is the average profit determined by the unpaid labour absorbed in an individual sphere of production. As a rule, it is determined by the total exploitation of labour that is operated by the total capital. 'At a given degree of exploitation, the mark of surplus-value produced in a particular sphere of production is then more important for the aggregate average profit of social capital and thus for the capitalist class in general, than for the individual capitalist in any specific branch of production. It is of importance to the latter only in so far as the quantity of surplus-value produced in this branch helps to regulate the average profit.[16] But the capitalists – 'and therefore the economists, too', Marx tells us – do not account for this process in general, just as they do not take into account the particularity that 'in such crude and meaningful form we can glimpse that the value of commodities is determined by the labour contained in them'.[17]

To a given rate of labour exploitation, there corresponds a given level of capitalist development – and not vice versa. It is not the intensity of capital that measures the exploitation of the workers, but the determinate historical form of surplus-value that uncovers the ultimate social determination of surplus-value. On the basis of social capital, average profit is no longer simply the phenomenal and mystified form of social surplus-value, it is no longer only the ideological expression that serves to hide the exploitation of the working class behind the 'labour of capital'. The average profit of social capital is a historically determinate category which immediately follows on from an advanced process of the socialisation of capitalist production and immediately precedes the

---

15 Ibid., 167.
16 Ibid.
17 Ibid., 171.

further process of its development and relative stabilisation. It is, from
the outset, naturally implicit in the system of capital, yet it arrives
historically not as a peaceful and gradual passage from one phase of
capitalist development to the next but as a genuine and abrupt *leap*, full
of dangerous contradictions for the capitalist class and of miraculous
opportunities for the workers' movement. The history of the successive
determinations of capital – which is to say, the development of the
historical contradictions of capitalism – can offer, at many points and
different levels, the *possibility* of breaking the cyclical process through
which capitalist social relations are produced and reproduced. These
possibilities are not necessarily directly connected to periods of catastrophic crisis in the system: they can be directly connected to a growing phase of *development* which creates a positive upheaval in the whole
social fabric of production without presupposing that this latter is
owned and *organised* by the class of capitalists and without it being
made organically and internally functional to capitalist development.
We must not believe that capitalism and its functionaries have an absolute self-consciousness in all phases. Capital's self-consciousness is a
late acquisition of its maturity.

Lenin wrote that 'the idea of seeking salvation for the working class
in anything save the further development of capitalism is reactionary'.
The working class suffers more the insufficiencies of capitalist development than does capitalism itself. In fact, the bourgeois revolution offers
the greatest advantages to the proletariat: in a way, it is 'in the highest
degree advantageous to the proletariat'. The bourgeois revolution
continually reproduces itself within capitalist development; it is the
permanent form of expression of the growth of the productive forces,
the solidification of technological levels, the class tensions within the
relations of production, the system's growing expansion over all of society, and the consequent political struggle between capital's general
interest and the capitalists' particular interests. The bourgeoisie's politically moderate soul is committed, throughout the whole course of its
history, to giving a gradual and peaceful form to the continual revolutionary upheavals in its own economic mechanism. 'It is to the advantage of the bourgeoisie for the bourgeois revolution not to sweep away
all the remnants of the past too resolutely, but keep some of them, i.e.,
for this revolution not to be fully consistent, not complete, and not to
be determined and relentless. Social-Democrats often express this idea

somewhat differently by stating that the bourgeoisie betrays its own self, that the bourgeoisie betrays the cause of liberty, that the bourgeoisie is incapable of being consistently democratic'. At different levels, the proletariat is called to collaborate in development: at different levels, it must choose the specific form of its political refusal.

There is a point at which it is still the development of capitalist production *in itself* which can pitch the capitalist system into crisis. The working-class response can come so immediately as to provoke a high degree of class struggle and the beginning of a revolutionary process that goes beyond the system. In this case, the *taking off* of capitalist society can offer the historical opportunity for a revolution that is socialist in content – that is, if the workers' movement finds itself better *organised* politically than the bourgeoisie. But it would be a mistake to generalise this moment. It is of interest here only for the purposes of insisting that a revolutionary rupture in the capitalist system can occur at different levels of capitalism's development. That is, we cannot wait for the history of capitalism to *reach a conclusion* before beginning to organise the process of its dissolution.

The growing process of capitalist socialisation arrives at a point in which the production of capital must pose the task of constructing a specific type of social organisation. When capitalist production has generalised to the whole society – all social production has become the production of capital – only then, on this basis, does a genuinely capitalist society arise as a determinate historical fact. The social character of production has extended to such a point that the entire society now functions as a *moment* of production. The sociality of capitalist production can now entail a particular form of the socialisation of capital – the social organisation of capitalist production. This is the arrival point of a long historical process. Just as capitalist production presupposes the generalisation of simple mercantile production, which only capital, as a specific fact, is able to historically realise, so too does the formation of a capitalist society presuppose the generalisation of a specifically capitalist production that only *social capital* – and the *Gesamtprozess* of its production – is historically able to realise. Social capital – or, in other words the totality of the capitalists – is discernible from the individual capitalist, meaning the totality of the capitalists in any particular sphere of production. Here, social capital is not only the total capital of society, not simply the sum of individual capitals. It is the whole process of the socialisation of capitalist production; it is capital itself that emerges, at a certain level of its development, as a *social power*.

Even operating on the basis of individual capitals, capital is a social relation, and the capitalist individual, the single capitalist, is the personification of this relation. They are a function of their own capital and the direct expression of their private property. But on the basis of social capital, capital comes to represent all capitalists, and the single capitalist is reduced to an individual personification of this totality: the direct functionary no longer of their own capital but of the capitalist class. The management of the individual enterprise may still remain in the hands of managers. But its property is the property of capital – it *appears* as an objective aliquot part of the social wealth.

In fact, this social wealth now finds its private proprietor in the figure, itself historically determinate, of the collective capitalist. On the one hand, this latter is the supreme mediation and composition of all particular bourgeois interests, while on the other it is the direct representative, on capital's behalf, of the general social interest. The collective capitalist is the form assumed by the *power* that is in the hands of social capital – capitalist society's power over itself, capital's government of itself and therefore of the capitalist class, capitalism's maximum result and probably the final form of its existence. We should not take seriously the bourgeois brouhaha over state intervention in the economy: at a certain level of development, this apparent intervention is from the outside nothing more than a very advanced form of the economic mechanism's self-regulation or, in certain cases, it serves to set this type of mechanism back in motion at a higher level. Capitalist planning can itself be a particular moment within the development of capital; this specific general trait remains the objective historical existence of social capital.

'Under capitalist production it is not merely a matter of obtaining an equal mass of value in another form – be it that of money or some other commodity – for a mass of values thrown into circulation in the form of a commodity, but it is rather a matter of realising as much surplus-value, or profit, on capital advanced for production, as any other capital of the same magnitude, or *pro rata* to its magnitude in whichever line it is applied. It is, therefore, a matter, at least as a minimum of selling the commodities at prices which yield the average profit, i.e., of prices of production. In this form capital becomes conscious of itself as a social power in which every capitalist participates proportionally to his share in the total social capital'.[18] In these conditions, the particular interest of the individual capitalist, or of the capital in a determinate sphere of production, is reduced to the possibility of obtaining, through direct exploitation of its own workers, a particular gain, a profit higher than the average. It is practically reduced to the different figures of super-profit, to the various possible forms of extracting a supplementary surplus-value, to the different external movements inherent to the new 'mechanism' of oligopolistic competition. Individual enterprises, or entire 'privileged' productive activities, constantly tend, in a function that propels the whole system, to break the total social capital from within in order then to recompose it at a higher level. The struggle among capitalists continues, but now it functions directly within the development of capital. Given that 'the average rate of profit depends on the intensity of exploitation of the sum total of labour by the sum total of capital', 'the individual capitalist, as well as the capitalists as a whole, take direct part in the exploitation of the total working class by the total-ity of capital and in the degree of that exploitation, not only out of general class sympathy, but also for direct economic reasons'.[19] Thus, all individual capitalists – all the particular spheres of capital – are directly interested in the productivity of the social labour used by collective capital. In fact, both the mass of use-value in which the average profit expresses itself and the value of the total anticipated capital that deter-mines the profit rate are dependent on this productivity. Not by acci-dent, the development of labour's social productivity manifests itself in two ways: first in the grown absolute magnitude of the already accumu-lated productive capital, and second in the relative diminution of the part of living labour required for mass production. Hence the two organically complementary processes of the intensification of accumu-lation and the concentration of capital: 'a fall in the rate of profit again hastens the concentration of capital and its centralisation through expropriation of minor capitalists, the few direct producers who still have anything left to be expropriated. This accelerates accumulation with regard to mass, although the rate of accumulation falls with the rate

18   Ibid., 194.
19   Ibid., 195–6.

of profit'.[20] Concentration is the specific form in which expropriation is *now* expressed – the further separation between the conditions of labour and the producers. 'The labour of a capitalist stands altogether in inverse proportion to the size of his capital, i.e., to the degree in which he is a capitalist'.[21] But this division between the conditions of labour and the producers is precisely what constitutes the historical notion of capital. At this level, decapitalisation does nothing other than confirm the development of capital.

Expropriation now extends from the direct producers to the individual capitalists themselves. The expropriation of single individuals' means of production is the starting point of the capitalist mode of production. But it also becomes its end, now that the private means of production present themselves and can present themselves as means of production only in the hands of associated producers. Thus, capitalist expropriation presents itself as appropriation of social property on the part of a few individuals. 'The capital, which in itself rests on a social mode of production and presupposes a social concentration of means of production and labour power, is here directly endowed with the form of social capital (capital of directly associated individuals) as distinct from private capital, and its undertakings assume the form of social undertakings as distinct from private undertakings. It is the abolition of capital as private property within the framework of the capitalist mode of production itself'.[22] The 'actually functioning capitalist' is transformed 'into a mere manager, [an] administrator of other people's capital, and of the owner of capital into a mere owner, a mere money capitalist'.[23] Hence, profit presents itself directly as the appropriation of someone else's surplus-value. 'This result of the ultimate development of capitalist production is a necessary transitional phase towards the reconversion of capital into the property of producers, although no longer as the private property of the individual producers, but rather as the property of associated producers, as direct social property'.[24] This is the form assumed by the wiping out of capitalist private industry on the basis of the capitalist system: 'This is the abolition of the capitalist mode of production within

20 Ibid., 240.
21 Ibid., 245.
22 Ibid., 434.
23 Ibid.
24 Ibid.

the capitalist mode of production itself, and hence a self-dissolving contradiction … It is private production without the control of private property'.[25]

At this point, capital altogether ceases to *appear* as the property of the direct producers, gives up on many of its previous mystified forms and divests itself of some of its more obvious ideological clothes – mere remnants of the paleo-capitalist bourgeoisie. The process of the socialisation of labour is itself incarnated, indeed without mediations, in the total production of social capital, and capital presents itself as a social force of production, directly in the form of the private property of large capitalists. 'Thus grows the power of capital, the alienation of the conditions of social production personified in the capitalist from the real producers. Capital comes more and more to the fore as a social power, whose agent is the capitalist. This social power no longer stands in any possible relation to that which the labour of a single individual can create'.[26] Thus, capital rises to the level of a 'general social power', while the capitalist is reduced to the level of a simple agent, functionary, or 'delegate' of this power. So they are no longer its representative, but its direct commissar, with limited power. The fetishism of capital has practically won.

Everyone knows that the modern bourgeois political stratum is of ever more directly capitalist extraction and that this – and not the history of political thought – provides the key to grasping the real transformations that have taken place in the structure of the state. The petty-bourgeois fear of the anonymous power of technocrats now reflects only the remnants of backward sectors of capitalist development. For its part, big capital seeks only to give *political* content to technocratic power. In fact, it is unlikely that the slow and just death of representative democracy marks a simultaneous extinction of the *political power* of the ruling class. In fact, it signals only a *reform* of the state, a modernisation of its structures, an adjustment to meet its new specific functions, which will increasingly have to pay heed to the productivist schemas of some industrial machine. Clearly, power will become increasingly unified at the top, and only in this way will it be able to decentralise and articulate itself at the base. As in every self-respecting modern and rational

---

25 Ibid., 436.
26 Ibid., 263.

enterprise, decisions must be assigned to everyone, but the *power* to decide must belong to just one person. Thus, political power becomes unified and homogeneous at all levels, from the enterprise of the individual capitalist to the state of the whole people. Only at this point does the *class dictatorship* of capital become truly *democratic*: it receives the sanction of popular sovereignty and immediately puts it to work within its own industrial apparatus. The overall objective of capitalism is always *capital's own self-government*, democracy directed no longer by small proprietors, but by large capitalists, with the sovereign population reduced to the level of labour-power and capital-as-a-fetish erected as a political state within the same society. But given capitalism's intrinsic contradictions, it will not be able to achieve this objective.

If a specifically capitalist society is to be understood, it must itself be seen as a historical product of the development of capital. There is a level in the process of the socialisation of capital that materially explodes the need for a rational organisation of society. The growing rationalisation of the productive process must now be extended to the whole web of social relations. It is no longer sufficient for capitalist production as such to extend across the whole territory of bourgeois society. It is its specific characteristics, the historically attained level of the production of capital, its particular internal organisation, which must now mark the general organisation of society, to the point of repeating on the scale of capitalist society the initial relation which pitted the individual capitalist against the single worker and valorising this relation to the maximum extent. The same relation *must* now present itself anew and organise itself on the plane of *the social classes*. The recuperation of a real general terrain of the class struggle is an objective requirement of capitalist production on the level of social capital. Indeed, only through this recuperation can the class struggle be consciously regulated and organised within the plan of capital. We have seen that the working-class struggle has always objectively functioned as a dynamic moment of capitalist development. But it can also be said that only on this level can it be rationally foreseen and utilised in the total process of the production of social capital. Thus, the tension between capital and labour becomes a 'legal institution of society', and all the institutions which guarantee the orderly bourgeois development of particular working-class demands can be legally recognised in their full autonomy. The workers' own organisations acquire a decisive importance for the social interests of capital. There is a moment in which modern capital cannot do without a modern union, in the factory, in society and directly in the state. The political integration of the working-class party within the absurd antediluvian forms of the bourgeois parliament itself becomes a secondary mediating moment in arriving at the true organic integration of the workers' unions within the programmed development of capitalist society. From here, again, follows the whole restructuring which invests the general form of power, in the search for a different – difficult – equilibrium between the growing requirement for a centralisation of decision-making and the need for an effective decentralisation of the functions of collaboration and control. There is thus a tendential unity of authority and pluralism, of central direction and of local autonomy, with political dictatorship and an economic democracy, an *authoritarian state* and a *democratic society*. True, at this point there is no longer capitalist development without a plan of capital. But there cannot be a plan of capital without *social capital*. It is capitalist society which programmes its own development, by itself. And this is what *democratic planning* is.

Toward the end of *Capital* Volume 1, Marx writes: 'And since we presupposed the limits set by capitalist production, i.e. we presupposed the process of social production in a form developed by purely spontaneous growth, we disregarded any more rational combination which could be effecte directly and in a planned way with the means of production and the mass of labour power at present available.'[27] Clearly, today, we can no longer operate this same type of abstraction. Marx himself abandoned it when he went on to analyse the total process of capitalist production. Certainly, the limitations of this production must always be taken as given. The task today is not to rediscover, after decades of absolute faith in the process of capitalism's putrefaction, a similarly absolute faith in the objective rationality of this system. The modern capitalist with their science does not believe that everything is resolved. But our neoreformist ideologues, their souls wracked by crisis, do believe this: they are the pure economists, the applied sociologists, the experts of the workers' movement and those who philosophise on Marxism – all these characters are against the system but do not know how to fight it. In fact, in all of their recollections of capitalism, they regularly forget the working class.

---

27 *Capital*, Vol. 1, 758.

'The entire capitalist mode of production is only a relative one, whose barriers are not absolute. They are absolute only for this mode, i.e., on its basis'.[28] 'Capitalist production seeks continually to overcome these immanent barriers, but overcomes them only by means which again place these barriers in its way and on a more formidable scale'.[29] Everyone knows that capitalism stands historically, from the very beginning, as a system of contradictions: its internal development is the development of its contradictions. Even when the process of social production no longer takes a natural and spontaneous shape, but instead a rational and planned form, even then the articulated system of production, from the single factory to the height of the state, stands as the tendentially systematic organisation of fearsome irrationalities. The anarchy of capitalist production is not wiped away: it is simply socially organised. When the emphasis is posed always and only on the moment of development, and here even on a planned development of capital, it is an attempt to consciously react to that long religious contemplation of the general crisis of capitalism which has now fatally inverted into a profane imitation of its prodigious technical model of social development. This second attitude is the direct historical result of the first. The opportunistic empiricism that today dominates the international workers' movement is the natural daughter of Stalin's scientific opportunism. The only way to recuperate a correct discourse on the society of capital is to rediscover the concrete possibilities of the working-class revolution today. Yet these possibilities must arise materially from the necessary development of capitalist production. Doubtless, the *active* side within the economic relation, the conscious revolutionary activity of the organised proletariat, must be appreciated anew – and this is what Lenin did before 1917. This organisation of the revolution must be rooted within a historically determinate moment of capitalist development, as its external consequence and at the same time its internal contradiction – and this is what Marx did in *Capital*. Not by chance, our own sectarianism starts out, dogmatically, from these texts alone.

At the level of maximum capitalist stabilisation, the plan of capital can also come to socially organise the natural tendency of its own production. That is, the possibility can arise for a social plan of capitalist

---

28   MECW, Vol. 37, 256.
29   Ibid., 248.

production, and for it to be born directly from the now-materially objective existence of social capital. And yet throughout the historical existence of a capitalist-type socioeconomic formation, 'the cohesion of the aggregate production imposes itself as a blind law upon the agents of production, and not as a law which, being understood and hence controlled by their common mind, brings the production process under their joint control'.[30] The important thing now is to see specifically how the *internal* nexus of total production is posed at the level of social capital, and how and why it always presents itself anew, even to the eyes of the collective capitalist, as a 'blind law' – thus, the collective capitalist is unable definitively to directly control it. The internal nexus of total production is now directly given by the social class relation, which counterposes capitalist society to the working class. The national contract now engages the individual worker – or the workers of a particular sphere of production – no longer under their respective individual capitalists, but under a certain type of general development of social capital. The articulated contracting process is in this sense nothing more than a normal pluralistic structure, a guarantee of that orderly drive to efficiency both in individual enterprises and in the entire system, such as always comes from the workers' own trade-union activity. The union branch is a typical *democratic* institution of capitalist *planning*. Yet these movements of capital, camouflaged and clothed as working-class demands, themselves reveal a fundamental material fact – namely, the mounting socialisation no longer just of capital and of labour, but of the general social relation, which immediately counterposes the two within the production process; that is, a growing generalisation and socialisation of the *class struggle*, which springs from the immediate needs of the production and reproduction of social capital.

'Reproduction on an expanded scale, i.e. accumulation, reproduces the capital-relation on an expanded scale, with more capitalists, or bigger capitalists, at this pole, and more wage-labourers at the other. The reproduction of labour-power ... forms, in fact, a factor in the reproduction of capital itself. Accumulation of capital is therefore multiplication of the proletariat'.[31] It is true that the division of labour and, on this basis, its social productive power each grow at the same time; thus, the

---

30   Ibid., 256.
31   *Capital*, Vol. 1, 763–4.

possibility of engaging various forms of labour saving also grows. But accumulation, and with it the concentration of capital, also represents a material means for increasing productivity. The increased mass of means of production meant to be transformed into capital must, then, always have available a proportionately increased working population to be able to exploit it. Only the absolute increase in the mass of surplus-value renders possible an increase in the absolute mass of profit. The simultaneous relative decrease in the variable part of capital, as compared to the constant part, provokes only – and partly – a fall in the rate of profit. On the one hand, we have the growth of the absolute *mass* of profit and the relative fall of the *rate* of profit, because, on the other hand, we have an absolute increase in surplus-labour and a relative decrease in variable capital. 'The law of the progressive falling rate of profit, or the relative decline of appropriated surplus-labour compared to the mass of materialised labour set in motion by living labour, does not rule out in any way that the absolute mass of exploited labour set in motion by the social capital, and consequently the absolute mass of the surplus-labour it appropriates, may grow; nor, that the capitals controlled by individual capitalists may dispose of a growing mass of labour and, hence, of surplus-labour, the latter even though the number of labourers they employ does not increase'.[32] Marx says later on that on the basis of capitalist production, this not only *can* but *must* happen. That is, there must be a growing mass of labour and surplus-labour in the absolute sense, so that the relative decrease of living labour with respect to objectified labour does not substantially hurt the growth of the mass of profit and thus the process of capital accumulation.

If it is indeed true that the quantity of additional living labour decreases, it is also true that the unpaid part of the social working day increases relative to the paid part: surplus-value increases relative to necessary labour, and thus increases relative surplus-value and, therefore, the absolute exploitation of labour. The progress of capitalist exploitation *always* serves as the material basis for capital's development. It is, then, only the process of the socialisation of exploitation that renders capital able to organise itself on the social level. This is why the extended reproduction of social capital cannot but reproduce capitalist social relations on an extended scale. The reproduction and

32 MECW, Vol. 37, 214.

accumulation of social capital must reproduce and accumulate labour-power itself as a social class.

Individual capital – which is to say, each fragment of social capital that operates in an autonomous way and as if it had a life of its own – can give any natural form to its product. The only condition is that this natural form must have a use-value. It is indifferent to and altogether accidental whether the means of production produced will enter anew *as such* into the production process and that constant capital will thus be immediately reproduced in its natural form. The process for the product of the total social capital is different, however. Here, the part of constant capital produced reappears in the natural form of new means of production, which must again function as constant capital. 'All material elements of the reproduction must be parts of this product in their natural form'.[33] Now, if it is true that variable capital, considered according to value, is equal to the value of labour-power, it is also true that, considered according to its *material*, it becomes identical to labour-power itself, that is, with living labour put in motion. On the level of social capital, the material element of variable capital can represent itself only in its immediate *natural* form, as social *labour-power*. The individual reproduction of the single worker is no longer sufficient: a social reproduction of the collective worker becomes necessary. That is, the mere survival of labour-power as such is no longer sufficient: what is needed is a process through which labour-power is accumulated *for* social capital. Now, labour-power must reappear in that real natural form, which is its *social nature*; variable capital must directly enter back into the process of capitalist production as a *working class*. There is a long historical moment in which the production of capital finds itself gripped by this need. All of the processes of the rational decomposition of concrete labour tended to destroy the abstract possibility of its own social organisation. But they find an objective limit in the material necessity of subsequently recuperating labour-power itself as an autonomous social force within capital. The apparent 'decomposition' of capital and labour, each in its own field, is only the specific form assumed by the process of real internal unification, each on its own terrain, of the capitalist class and of the working class.

The total capital now needs the total labour to be standing visible before it, to make the necessary economic calculations for its own

---

33 *Capital*, Vol. 2, 508.

planned development. That capital, moreover, needs to see the total labour not mystified by its own exclusive class interests and not concealed in its own ruling-class ideology – hence the need to know labour through the workers and to calculate total labour through the figure of the collective worker. Social capital is forced to socialise the very knowledge of social labour. The single capitalist, with their limited perspective, realises that his profit now comes not only from their employed labour or in their branch of production and that average profit is different from immediate surplus-value. But 'to what extent this profit is due to the aggregate exploitation of labour on the part of the total capital, i.e., by all his capitalist colleagues – this interrelation is a complete mystery to the individual capitalist; all the more so, since no bourgeois theorists, the political economists, have so far revealed it'.[34]

At a certain stage of the development of capital, it is no longer only the worker but also the capitalist who must fight against the *semblances* of their own relations of production. The capitalist must eventually tear away the phenomenal veil in order to grasp the essence and the intrinsic nature of the process itself – hence the need for *science within capital*, when capital understands that it is a social force. The simple scientific reality of economic relations is no longer sufficient: the economic relations themselves need to be scientifically organised. And it is almost useless to warn that even this is a tendentious formula which seeks to grasp only one side of the problem, in order to identify a basic tendency that guides the process. We have already indicated that the capitalist system will never manage to reach a perfect objective rationality of its own development mechanism. But here we will add that it does aim at this as its ultimate programme. This is precisely the aim of the science *of* capital: its actual attempt to demystify the social process of capitalist production, rationalising the form and programming the content of capitalist development. Everything confirms as much: the pure theorist of capitalist economics today is the modern bourgeois politician: the theorist of planning is identical with the practical programmer. And, moreover, there is a politics of planning, but there is no theory of planning; the highest such theory that exists is provided by the techniques of programming. This does not mean that no bourgeois thought exists any more: rather, it means that bourgeois thought is now *wholly* integrated

---

34   MECW, Vol. 37, 169.

within capital, it functions as an internal mechanism of its development and no longer serves to justify from the outside the present forms of capitalist power. This last function is directly discharged by the traditional organisations of the workers' movement. When science is about to pass within social capital, *ideology* risks remaining in the hands of the single worker – which is to say, in the hands of the disorganised workers' movement. True: neocapitalist ideologies do not *immediately* derive from big capital's sole centre of power. They need, as a practical mediation, to pass through the trade unions' research institutes. In a capitalist society which develops on the basis of a socially organised capital, neocapitalist ideologies correspond to a capitalist organisation of the workers' movement. It is not true that at this point the working class no longer exists: there is a *working class organised by capital*.

A long series of troubling questions emerge at this level. How far can the fundamental contradiction between the social character of production and the private appropriation of the product be invested and affected by capitalist development? Does the process of the socialisation of capital not conceal a *specific form* of the social appropriation of the private product? Has the very sociality of production not become the most important objective mediation of private property? And how can such mediation *contradict* what it mediates? How can any *bourgeois* sociality of the production process pitch into crisis the capitalist appropriation of the product? In other words, how can a capitalist society enter into contradiction with the process of the production of capital? When the production relation has generalised to the level of a general social relation, when all of bourgeois society is reduced to the level of a moment of capitalist production, the social character of production *can* itself be recuperated within the mechanism of the reproduction of private capitalist property. At this point, the whole objective mechanism functions within the subjective plan of the collective capitalist. Social production becomes a direct *function* of private property. Truly, society's general representative is now *social capital*. In the social relation of production, society's mouthpiece is no longer the working class, but capital directly. The general *social* interest is left entirely in the hands of capital. Nothing is left to the workers other than their *partial* class interest. So, on one hand, we have capital's *social* self-government, and on the other, the *class* self-management of the organised workers.

The concept of the *working class* comes into being only at this histori-cally concrete level. It is specified in all its particularity, and develops in all the wealth of its determinations. Thus, the simplest social abstraction of a capitalist economic formation, which thus applies to all the succes-sive forms of its development, 'appears as effectively true in this abstrac-tion' only as a category of the most modern capitalism. The more that capitalist production attacks and dissolves its *external* contradictions, the more it is forced to bring its own *internal* contradiction into the open. The more capital succeeds in organising itself, the more it is forced to organise the working class for its own ends – to the point that the working class no longer has to become the *mirror* of all social contradic-tions: it can directly reflect itself as a social contradiction.

It is useless to pull magic words out of the archives in the hope of exorcising this vision. A cult of the workers can also be a real danger when wage-workers are a small minority among the wider working classes. But is this even possible within a process which tends to reduce every labourer to a worker? True, in the name of not chucking out the old strategy, new allies are invented for the working class: the place left empty by the once-boundless masses of poor peasants is now filled by the refined elites of the new middle classes. Thus, the workers simulta-neously free themselves both from any *sectarian* temptation and from any *socialist* perspective. The capitalists are well aware of this: the real generalisation of the working-class condition can reassert the image of its formal extinction. This is the basis on which *specifically* working-class power is immediately absorbed into the *generic* concept of popular sovereignty: the political mediation here serves to allow the explosive content of the working class's productive force to function peacefully within the fine forms of the modern capitalist relations of production. So, at this level, when the *working class* refuses politically to become *the people*, it in fact opens up the most direct path to the socialist revolution.

It is here worth resuming our discourse on the abstraction of the category 'labour'. We must return to this point, but with a separate anal-ysis. For now, the following basic considerations are sufficient. Labour 'in general' signals a developed indifference toward a kind of determi-nate labour and at the same time presupposes a very developed totality of real kinds of labour. The two processes are closely connected. The more that a particular labour becomes concrete, the greater the possibility of abstracting general labour from it. 'The most general abstractions come about only where there is the richest development of the concrete'.[35] For good reason, Marx returns to discuss labour in these terms when he addresses the levelling process that the general rate of profit undergoes through competition. Along with the almost spontaneous mobility of capital, there here intervenes a guided mobility of labour-power. Labour-power not only can but *must* be pitched as fast as possible from one sphere of production to another, from one productive site to another. There is no capitalist development without a high degree of social mobility of working-class labour-power. There is no planning of development without a programming of mobility. And this requires the 'indifference of the labourer to the nature of his labour; the greatest possible reduction of labour in all spheres of production to simple labour; the elimination of all vocational prejudices among labourers; and last but not least, a subjugation of the labourer to the capitalist mode of production'.[36] Here, too, the decisive factor is the subordination of workers to the capitalist mode of production. The worker's indifference to the nature of their labour – as the worker's labour is increasingly reduced to simple labour and the workers repudiate any *prejudices of profession or trade* – is not itself the subordination of the working class. Rather, it is a form of capitalist exploitation. This is the difference between *exploitation* and *Unterwerfung*. Everyone knows, because it is a self-evident fact, that, within the capitalist mode of production, workers certainly are *always exploited*, but they are *never subjugated*.

Workers' insubordination can advance along the same path as capitalist exploitation: that is, on each occasion, it captures the specific ways in which the two processes *combine*. For example, it is clear that today it is necessary to recognise and cultivate all the *positive* content hidden and mystified within the various so-called processes of *alienation*. If this corrupted word still has some meaning, it simply expresses a specifically determined form of capital's direct exploitation of labour. A *total* estrangement of labour with respect to the worker; useful, concrete labour which becomes objectively external, estranged and indifferent to the worker; the end of the craft, of the *profession*, of this last semblance of the worker's *individual* independence; the ultimate remnant of a

---

35 MECW, Vol. 28, 41.
36 MECW, Vol. 37, 195.

bourgeois character [*persona*] in the body of the worker. Then, the positive content of alienation is not only the positive content of capitalist exploitation, taken as the moment in which the antagonistic working-class response becomes conscious and organises. The process of the total estrangement of labour coincides with its most complete objectification within the process of the production of capital. It is only when labour is totally objectified within capitalist production that the existence of the working class comes into *specific* contradiction with the entire system of capital. Not only the product of labour, not only the instruments of production, but the conditions of labour as a whole must become *objectified* in the person of capital. They must, therefore, be torn from the subjectivity of the simple worker, if they are then to be taken back in hand as *enemies* of the collective worker. The single worker must become *indifferent* to their own labour so that the working class can come to *hate it*. Within the class, only the 'alienated' worker is truly revolutionary. In fact, there is a moment in which the capitalist is the one who directly comes to the defence of the worker's 'personality'. Only in its generically *human* figure can labour-power voluntarily submit itself to capital; only as *human needs* are workers' demands freely accepted by the capitalist. This is the point at which the worker definitively discovers that the 'cult of man' is a bourgeois sham.

There are no rights outside of capital. The workers no longer need to defend the 'rights of labour': at this point, labour's rights are the same as capital's. The trade union and its struggle cannot *alone* break out of the system; they are destined to be inevitably *part* of its development. The interests of capital are no longer corporatist; only the interests of labour outside of capital are. A trade union which, *as such* – that is, without a party and without the political organisation of the class – purports to be *autonomous* from the plan of capital succeeds in achieving nothing other than the most perfect form of integration of the working class within capitalism. Modern trade unionism, with the party as the transmission belt for the trade union, is the highest form of capitalist reformism. This is how capitalist production's objective need to regain the real political terrain of the class struggle is distorted and at the same time used within capital's subjective initiative. There are no doubts about this. If someone pretends to interpret this in economistic and objectivist terms, they have understood nothing. Marx continually uses the phrase 'in purely economic terms, that is, from the bourgeois perspective', in order to indicate that, on the terrain of economic competition with the capitalists, the workers are regularly defeated: on this terrain, they have no other choice than to improve the conditions of their own exploitation. When we ignore the system's traditional *objective* contradictions, to the point of making them all disappear within its specific development mechanism, we do so deliberately, in order to get back to the truly working-class discourse – that is, a political discourse concerning political organisation and political power. And this, too, must be done in a newly determinate sense. When science itself is objectified within capital, socialism is in turn forced to become *scientific* again. The insurrection as a work of art only now turns into a science of revolution. Social capital's programming of its own development can and must be answered by a truly working-class planning of the revolutionary process. True, it is not enough to oppose the plan of capital at the ideal level; it is necessary to know how to use it materially. And this is impossible other than by counterposing to the *economic* programme of capitalist development a *political* plan of working-class answers. Now both capital and labour, each in its own field, are very far-sighted and clash over long-term perspectives. This is a matter of strategy against strategy: the tactics can be left to the bureaucrats of the two sides.

We have already said that the working class must privilege the existence of capital, valorise the successive forms of its development and even materially anticipate them, in antagonistic form, through its own organisation. Then, within the very process of capital's socialisation, in the course of the development that leads social capital to become the representative of the general interest, the working class is forced to begin to organise its own *partial* interest and directly manage its own *particular power*. When capital reveals itself to be a social force and, upon this basis, gives rise to a capitalist society, it does not leave any alternative to the working class other than to oppose itself for the entire sociality of capital. The workers no longer have to counterpose an ideal of a *true* society to the *false* society of capital; they no longer have to dissolve and dilute themselves within the general social relation. They can now rediscover their own class as an antisocial revolutionary force. Today, the *whole* society of capital stands in front of the working class, without any possibility of mediation. The relation has finally reversed: the only thing that the general interest cannot mediate within itself is the irreducible partiality of the working-class interest. Hence, the bourgeois call to *social* reason stands against the *sectoral* demands of the workers. The bourgeois want the same relation that exists at a certain level between social capital and the single capitalists to exist between capital and labour: as the functionaries put it, a consistently 'dialectical' relationship. However, when the total labour agrees to participate reasonably in the general development, it ends up functioning as just another part of total social capital. The only thing to be attained along this path is the most balanced and rational development of *all* capital. It is at this point that the working class must instead consciously organise itself as an *irrational* element within the specific rationality of capitalist production. The growing rationalisation of modern capital must find an insurmountable limit in the growing irrationality of the organised workers – that is, in the working-class refusal of *political* integration within the system's *economic* development. Thus, the working class becomes the only *anarchy* that capitalism is unable to *organise* socially. The task of the workers' movement is to scientifically organise and politically manage *this* working-class anarchy within capitalist production. On the model of the society organised by capital, the working-class party itself can only be the *organisation of anarchy* – no longer within capital, but outside of it, meaning outside of its development.

But we need to be clear: this is not a matter of creating chaos within the productive process. It is not a matter of 'organising the systematic disorganisation of production' in the manner of the new brand of anarcho-syndicalism. And it is unnecessary to hide behind this absurd leftover the totally new perspectives which are only today opening up for the class struggle. Nor, conversely, do we want to counterpose a working-class management of the modern industrial enterprise or of the 'productive centre in itself' to the capitalist one. First of all, no 'productive centre in itself' exists – there is the capitalist industrial enterprise and nothing else. Second, the workers gladly leave the management of this enterprise up to the boss, just as they leave the general management of society to the collective capitalist, keeping for themselves only the *political* self-management of their own class power, which starts from the factory and seeks to reach the state. The simple demand of a real political working-class power, autonomous and distinct from real bourgeois political power, is now able to pitch the system's economic mechanism into crisis, thus preventing it from functioning. Here is the point where the whole discourse overturns. It is the material base upon which all that is functional to capital acquires the possibility of becoming directly functional to the revolution against capital. From the working-class point of view, the integral control of the social process becomes all the more possible as capital becomes *social capital*. The working-class articulation of the entire capitalist mechanism now unveils itself, at the very centre of the system, as the arbiter of its further development or of its definitive crisis. The internal planning of the factory and the programming of capitalist development – which is to say, the bourgeois understanding of the production process – can be utilised in a form antagonistic to the system and instrumentalised for revolutionary goals. Within capital, science can itself become the pattern of a unitary recomposition of working-class thought, thus forcibly bringing into existence a theory of revolution wholly integrated within the working class. Thus, even the company and sectoral integration of labour-power becomes an instrument of the workers' direct knowledge of the productive apparatus and the recognition of the determinate form that capitalist exploitation assumes at this level. The techniques of economic integration attempted by the boss – meeting an objective need of the production of capital – become tools of political control *over* capital, and thus means of workers' self-management.

An insubordinate use of integration then becomes possible. This is the concrete revolutionary use of capitalist development. Only at this point *can* the organised workers' movement – as, therefore, it *must* – continually *subvert* capital's tools of domination as means of labour's insubordination, violently compelling the objective needs of capitalist production to function as revolutionary workers' subjective instances.

The theoretical formulation of a total revolutionary strategy, at this level, is no longer only possible, it becomes absolutely necessary for the foundation of the revolutionary process itself. The objective anarchy of the working class within capitalism must now express itself at the highest level of consciousness. None of its elements can be left up to spontaneity any longer: everything must be tied to a scientific perspective for the revolution and to its consequent rigorous organisation. *Spontaneism* belongs always and only to 'the masses' in a generic sense and never to the workers of the big factories. The toiling people often love to explode in abrupt acts of disorderly protest. Not so with the working class. The people have only their own rights to defend, while the working class must demand power. This requires, first of all, *organising* the struggle for power. No one is more inclined than we are to wholly accept again today the Leninist thesis: 'In its struggle for power the working class has only one weapon: organisation'. Workers do not move unless they feel organised – that is, they do not know that they are *armed* in the struggle. They are serious people: they never seek their own destruction. They are a social *class* of producers and not a *mass* of the miserable and oppressed. Today, they will not move unless they have a plan for revolution which is also explicitly organised. Party programmes are useless: revolutionary strategy must not be confused with a minimum and maximum set of demands. The approach needed is not a matter of bargaining over the individual points today and then tomorrow challenging for full power. It is exactly the opposite: the demand for power must precede everything else. Only thus is *everything* organised for the conquest of power. The ruling class's political domination must be *challenged* immediately; after that, it will also be possible to *negotiate* with it over the terrain of the struggle.

The first step remains the recapturing of an irreducible working-class partiality against the entire social system of capital. Nothing will be done – neither the elaboration of theory or practical organisation – without class hatred. Only from a rigorously working-class point of view will the total movement of capitalist production be understood and utilised as a *particular* moment of the working-class revolution. Only a one-sided approach, in science as in the struggle, makes it possible both to understand everything and to destroy it. Any attempt to assume the *general interest*, every temptation to stop at the level of *social science*, will only serve to inscribe the working class within the development of capital. The workers' class-political action may also overcome the problem of sectarianism. It is the working class's thought which *must* be sectarian; that is, it must become *part* of a new organic power system organised in new revolutionary forms. No further illusions are admissible. Once the level of a developed capitalism has been reached, it is not possible to continue to follow capital's law of movement if not through the organisation of a decisive class struggle against all of capitalist society. The Marxist analysis of capitalism will not proceed unless it arrives at a working-class theory of revolution. And the latter will be useless if not incarnated in real material forces. And these forces will not exist for society unless they are politically organised in a class against this society.

Thus we find the impasse in which discourse is caught when it wants to be both sectarian and totalising. It is caught between its will to set off calmly looking for the objective reasons that guide a long historical process and the need immediately to find the subjective forces which are organising to overthrow it. It is caught between the patience of research and the urgency of the response. The theoretical void that stands between the two is a void of political organisation. There is a right to experiment – indeed, this is the only right worth insisting upon. Until that is done, everything will be expressed through abrupt clashes between immediately contradictory concepts. So, we are *forced* to jump ahead. We do so without mediation, out of hatred for opportunism.

We must now go back to look *concretely* at what wage-labour is at the highest level of capital, how the working class is composed at the ultimate degree of capitalism's development, its material internal organisation, and why and under what conditions it can come to realise a directly working-class and *thus* socialist revolutionary process. This is all nothing more than the general premise of this specific discourse, though – all the elements still need to be found. Thus, we have had only 'an attempt to break things down and the hint of a higher synthesis …'[37]

1963

---

37 Robert Musil, *Gesammelte Werke*, Vol. 7, Hamburg: Rowohlt, 1978, 942.

A New Type of Political Experiment: Lenin in England

A new era is beginning in the class struggle. The workers have imposed it on the capitalists, through the violent reality of their organised power in the factories. The power balance seems to have hardened and the relation of force is unfavourable. And yet, precisely at the points where capital's dominion appears most dominant, the deeper the working-class threat penetrates. It is easy not to see it. We need to examine the situation of the working class closely. Capitalist society has its laws of development: economists have invented them, governments have applied them, and workers have suffered under them. But who will formulate the laws of development of the working class? Capital has its history, and its historians write it. But who is going to write the history of the working class? Capitalist exploitation can impose its political dominion through many different forms. But how will we outline the future rule of the workers, organised as the ruling class? This is explosive social material; we must patiently work with it, up close and personal, from within.

We too saw capitalist development first and the workers second. This is a mistake. Now we have to turn the problem on its head, change orientation, and start again from first principles, which means focusing on the struggle of the working class. At the level of socially developed capital, capitalist development is subordinate to working-class struggles; not only does it comes after them, but it must make the political mechanism of capitalist production respond to them. This is not a rhetorical trick and does not just serve to restore our own confidence. Without a doubt, we do urgently need to shake off that sense of working-class defeat which has for decades dragged down what was born as the only revolutionary movement, and not only in our own era. But an urgent practical need is never enough to back up a scientific thesis: such a thesis must stand on its own feet, on historical scaffolding of material facts. Everyone has to recognise that, at least since June 1848 (a month cursed a thousand times over by the bourgeoisie), the workers have taken to the stage, and they have never since abandoned it. They have voluntarily taken on a series of different roles – as actors, as prompters, as technicians or stagehands – while always waiting to head down into the audience and attack the spectators. So how do they present themselves today, on the contemporary stage?

The starting point of the new discourse tells us that both nationally and internationally, the present political situation of the working class both guides and imposes a certain type of development of capital. We need to gain a new understanding of the entire worldwide web of social relations, in light of this first principle. Let's take the basic material fact of this web – namely, the recomposition of a global market, a process that has been macroscopically underway ever since the elimination of Stalinism's stranglehold over development. It would be easy to explain this in economistic terms, mathematically devoting ourselves to reconsidering the problem of markets in capitalist production. But the working-class point of view seeks a political explanation. To speak of a unified world market today is to speak of an international level of control over social labour-power. Commodity production can be organised within even a limited free-trade zone, notwithstanding some difficulty. But not so regarding the movements of the working class. Historically and from its birth, the working class's labour-power was already homogeneous at the international level, and – over a long historical period – it has forced capital to become equally homogeneous. Today, it is precisely the unity of the working class's movement at the global level which forces capital rapidly to seek out its own unitary response.

But how are we to grasp this unity in the movements of the working class? The institutional levels of the workers' movement divide everything; capitalism's own structures unify everything, but in its own exclusive interests. Nor can an act of political struggle be subjected to empirical tests. The only way to prove this unity is to work to organise it. Then we shall discover that the new form of class unity is wholly implicit in the new forms of working-class struggle and that the new field of these forms is *social capital at an international level.* At this level, the political situation of the working class has never been so clear: wherever a social mass of industrial labour-power has historically been able to concentrate, it is easily able to see the same collective attitudes, the same fundamental practices, a single type of political growth. Planned non-collaboration, organised passivity, stoppages, political refusal and a continuity of permanent struggles – these are the specific historical forms in which working-class struggle is today becoming generalised. Such are the temporary forms proper to a temporary situation, as, in social terms, the workers have already gone beyond the old organisations, but they have yet to arrive at a new one. Indeed, they are without either a reformist or revolutionary organisation. This is an interregnum in working-class history: we must examine this period deeply and understand its results, for its political consequences will be decisive.

The first consequence is, not surprisingly, a difficulty: the question of how we are to grasp the material movements of the class in the absence of corresponding institutional levels – that is, the levels at which class consciousness usually expresses itself. Hence there is a need for us to mount a higher, more abstracted theoretical effort. But this effort also has a clearer practical function, compelling us to analyse the working class independently of the workers' movement.

The second consequence is that we find contradictions and apparent uncertainties in the class's movements. It is clear that, if the working class had a revolutionary political organisation, it would everywhere seek to make use of the high point of capitalist reformism. The process for the unitary composition of capital at the international level can become the material base for a political recomposition of the working class and, in this sense, a positive strategic moment for the revolution, but only if it is accompanied by revolutionary growth not just of the class, but also in class organisation. If this element is absent, then the whole process serves the functioning of capital – it is a tactical moment of one-sided systemic stabilisation, which seemingly integrates the working class within the capitalist system. The historical operation of Italian capitalism – the organic political accord between Catholics and Socialists – could even initiate a revolutionary process on the classic model if it could also provide Italian workers with a working-class party that was committed to directly opposing the capitalist system during the democratic phase of the development of its class dictatorship. Without this, the dominion of capitalist exploitation will become more stable, for now at least, and the workers will be compelled to seek other paths toward their revolution. While it is true that the working class objectively imposes precise choices on capital, it is also true that capital then completes these choices in such a way that they work against the working class. Capital, at this moment, is better organised than the working class, and the choices that the working class imposes on capital risk strengthening it. Hence, it is in the working class's immediate interest to challenge these choices.

Today, the working class's strategic outlook is so clear that we wonder whether it is only now beginning to experience its splendid full maturity. It has discovered, or rediscovered, the true secret, which will be a violent death sentence on its class enemy: namely, its political capacity to impose reformism on capital and then to make rough-and-ready use of that reformism for the purposes of the working-class revolution. But the present tactical position of the working class, as a class without organisation, is, and must necessarily be, less clear and – we could even say – more subtly ambiguous. The working class is still forced to make use of the contradictions which pitch capitalist reformism into crisis; it has to aggravate the elements that put brakes on capitalist development, since it knows and senses that to give capital's reformist operations a free hand, in the absence of its own political organisation, would amount to closing off the entire revolutionary process over a long period – just as the existence of such an organisation would immediately instigate such a process. The two reformisms – capital's and the workers' movement's – must certainly cross paths, but only through the working class's direct initiative. When, like in the present moment, all the initiative lies in capital's hands, it is in the working class's immediate interest to keep these two reformisms separate. Also at a tactical level, it is only right that this meeting should take place once the working class is experienced not only in struggle, but specifically in revolutionary struggle, and once it has also experienced alternative models of organisation within such revolutionary struggle. Once those conditions are in place, the historic encounter of capitalist reformism with the workers' movement's reformism will really mark the beginning of the revolutionary process. But today's situation is quite different: it precedes and prepares the way for that later stage. Now is the time for the working class to both strategically support the general development of capital and tactically oppose particular modes of that development.

This means that, in the working class today, the political moment of *tactics* and the theoretical moment of *strategy* contradict one another, in a complex and highly mediated relationship between revolutionary organisation and working-class science. At the theoretical level, the working-class point of view must today be unrestricted – it must put up no barriers for itself, but must leap forward, transcending and negating all the empirical tests continually demanded by the intellectual coward-ice of the petty bourgeois. For working-class thought, the moment of discovery has returned. The time of arranging things into systems, of rote learning and of vulgarity elevated to the status of systematic discourse is definitively over. What is again needed from the outset is rigorously one-sided class logic; committed courage for ourselves and detached irony toward the rest. It would be erroneous to confuse all this with a political programme, though. We must fight the temptation to carry this theoretical outlook immediately into the arena of the political struggle – a struggle articulated on the basis of precise content, which, in some cases, may even contradict, rightly enough, our theoretical statements. The practical response to practical problems of immediate struggle, of immediate organisation, of immediate intervention in a given class situation concerning workers – all these should be judged first of all by the yardstick of what the movement objectively needs for its own development. Only secondarily should they be checked against a general line which subjectively imposes all this on the class enemy.

But the dissociation between theory and politics is only a conse-quence of the contradiction between strategy and tactics. Both have their material basis in the still slowly developing process by which the class and the historical organisations of the class – the 'working class' and the 'workers' movement' –divide and then counterpose one other. What does this discourse mean in concrete terms, and where will it take us? Right away, it is worth saying that the objective to be achieved is the solid recomposition of a politically appropriate relationship between the two moments. The separation between them ought never to be justified in theoretical terms, and they should never even temporarily be coun-terposed. If part of the workers' movement again finds the path to revo-lution as signalled by the working class, then the process of reunifying these moments will be quicker, easier, more direct and more secure.

Should that not be the case, the revolutionary process will be likewise secure, but it will also be less clear, less decisive, longer and more strewn with conflict. It is easy to see the old organisations' work in mystifying the new working-class struggles. It is harder to grasp the workers' continual, conscious instrumental use of an institution which still appears to the capitalist to be the movement of the organised workers.

More particularly, the working class has left the traditional organisations in charge of all tactical problems while reserving for itself an autonomous strategic perspective free from impediments and compromises. Again we arrive at this provisional result: namely, that we see a revolutionary strategy and reformist tactics – even if, as often happens, the opposite seems to be the case. It seems that the workers are now coming to agree with the system, and only occasionally come into friction with it. However, this is the 'bourgeois' outward appearance of the capitalist social relation. The truth is that for the workers, in political terms, even the skirmishes mounted by the unions represent a textbook exercise in their struggle for power: that is, when the workers engage the unions, make use of them and, having used them, gift them back to the bosses. The classic Marxist thesis, that the tactical moment belongs to the union and the strategic moment to the party, still holds true for the workers. Precisely for this reason, if a link still does exist between the working class and the unions, it does not exist between the working class and the party. Hence there is a freeing of the strategic perspective from immediate organisational tasks, a temporary split between class struggle and class organisation, between the permanent moment of struggle and the temporary forms of organisation. All of this is the consequence of a historical failure on the part of socialist reformism, and it is also a premise of the political development of the working-class revolution.

The attention of both theoretical research and practical work must be aggressively focused on this issue – no longer on the development of capitalism, but on the development of the revolution. We have no models. Knowing the history of past experiences serves only to free us of them. We must count on a new kind of scientific perspective. We know that the whole development process is materially embodied in the new level of working-class struggles. Our starting point thus lies in discovering certain forms of workers' struggles that spark a certain type of capitalist development which works in the direction of the revolution.

Then we will move on to articulate these experiences at the base, subjectively choosing the nerve points at which it is possible to strike at capitalist production relations. On this basis, through trial and error, we will readdress the problem of how to make a new organisation correspond to these new struggles in an ongoing way. We may perhaps discover that 'organisational miracles' have taken place already, indeed are always happening, within the miraculous struggles of the working class. No one knows about these struggles or wants to know about them. Yet they have alone made, and are making, more revolutionary history than all the revolutions of all the colonised people put together.

But if this practical work, articulated on the basis of the factory, is to function on the terrain of the social relations of production, it must be continually judged and mediated by a political level which can generalise it. We should look for or organise a new form of working-class newspaper around this political level, once distinguished. It would not have to immediately report and reflect all particular experiences, but rather concentrate them into a general political approach. In this sense, the paper would focus on monitoring, or rather self-monitoring, the strategic validity of particular instances of struggle. The formal procedure for such verification is utterly inverted. It is political discourse which must verify the correctness of the particular struggles, not vice versa. On this basis, political discourse is the total point of view of the working class and thus the true material fact is the real process itself. It is easy to see how such an approach takes us away from the Leninist conception of the working-class newspaper: namely, the collective organiser based on or anticipating a Bolshevik organisation of the class and of the party. For us, at this stage of the class struggle, such objectives are impossible: at this stage, we must discover the political organisation not of advanced vanguards but of the whole, compact social mass which the working class has become in the period of its high political maturity. Indeed, it is precisely because of these characteristics that the working class is the only revolutionary force, a threatening and fearsome force which looms over the present order of things.

We know it. And Lenin knew it before us. And before Lenin, Marx also discovered, in his own living experience, how the most difficult point is the move to organisation. The continuity of the struggle is a simple matter; the workers need only themselves, and the boss facing them. But continuity of organisation is a rare and complex thing: as soon as organisation is institutionally formalised, it is immediately used by capitalism or by the workers' movement on capitalism's behalf – hence the speed with which workers passively abandon forms of organisation that they have only just won. And in place of the bureaucratic void of a general political organisation, they substitute the ongoing struggle at the factory level – a struggle that takes ever-new forms, which only the fantastical genius of productive labour is able to discover. Unless a directly *working-class* political organisation can be generalised, the revolutionary process will not begin; the workers know it, and this is why you will not today find them in the churches of the official parties ready to sing hymns to the democratic revolution. The reality of the working class is definitively tied to the name of Karl Marx, while the working class's need for political organisation is tied equally definitively to Lenin. With his masterstroke, Lenin's strategy brought Marx to St Petersburg: only the working-class point of view could have been capable of such revolutionary audacity. Now let us try to take the opposite path, with the same scientific spirit of adventurous political discovery. 'Lenin in England' is the search for a new Marxist practice of the working-class party; it is the theme of struggle and of organisation at the highest level of the political development of the working class. It is worth convincing Marx to head back along 'the mysterious curve in Lenin's straight line'.

January 1964

An Old Tactic for a New Strategy

Our discourse has the character of political theory – and it is intended to have such a character, in this phase. But we face the problem of how to make this into something immediately practical – how to apply a new strategy tactically, in a new way. We have sought to repropose in modern terms the historic theme of the struggle against reformism. We now need to avoid reducing this to a question to be studied. We need to find a temporal articulation of this theme that shows the possibility of its concrete realisation.

One example will suffice. And this example is offered to us as a political opportunity, by the present conjunctural crisis of Italian capitalism. A merely strategic application of our discourse would mean: save the centre-left, stabilise the conjuncture and start off again with reformism on the one hand and the revolutionary use of reformism on the other. But even before we can discuss further, we should reject this purely theoretical use of a political alternative. And going further, let's say that the spontaneity of the struggle, at the highest points of the development of the working class, today moves in this direction, and that this type of spontaneity ought to be understood, criticised and defeated. In the critical passages of capitalist development, various levels of the class struggle reappear in open form. The more backward sectors of the working class today tend to assume, and indeed actively so, the traditional types of struggle – general but defensive ones. The more advanced ones instead tend to respond once again by renouncing the open struggle, wanting the organised workers' movement to have a more offensive capacity. Both choices spontaneously favour the process by which the conjuncture is stabilised. The bosses are, indeed, prompting exactly these two types of responses. They attack the advanced level of the working class because here they expect a passive response, which will allow greater capitalist power to assert itself on the factory floor and will weaken and demoralise the overly powerful working-class upsurge of recent years. They need active but backward struggles to take place elsewhere and at other points, so that they can push back the degree of development that has presently been reached by the class struggle and push forward the homogeneity of labour-power as a whole, on the social level, and thus the possibility of controlling it as a whole. These are the real conjunctural difficulties. These obstacles must likewise be overcome before a programme can be drawn up.

Let's look at how the bourgeois side presents its own conjuncture to us. It is said that the imbalances are in the market and above all in the money markets. Demand has outstripped supply, not only in terms of consumer products, but also in terms of investment goods. The consumption-investment function has been turned on its head: productive consumption is in danger. Hence, there is now a whole government economic policy directed at tightly limiting these processes, at the level of simple capital circulation. This has the following consequences: the frittering away of monetary reserves, a trade balance and a balance of payments which are both in the red, a block on liquidity, and foreign indebtedness. All this – according to Carli's line – is the only way to avoid prejudicing, and instead maintain, the recent high rate of industrial production. This is, then, nothing but a typical capitalist example of offloading difficulties in production onto the market. But what are these difficulties? The new imbalances in the capital market are the obvious consequence of new contradictions that have arisen in capital production. What, then, are these contradictions? We are told that wage rises have significantly outstripped the increase in productivity – which is to say, labour productivity has not fallen in absolute terms; the total wage bill has grown *relatively*. Labour's incomes have increased more rapidly than have capital's. This has two fundamental consequences: a 'cost-induced' inflation especially triggered by the cost of labour-power, and a relative contraction in profits with respect to wages. The science of capital has well grasped the causes of this conjunctural crisis, clearly so at the technological-economic level and, in a still opaque fashion, at the political-institutional level. It is on the basis of this science, and governed by its necessities, that some commit the error of setting the tactical cart of stabilisation before the horse of setting out strategy. In between these two moments, there today opens up a formidable opportunity for class struggle.

This separation should, in fact, be accepted and turned upside down, on the terrain of direct confrontation. It is not worth denying the facts for fear of the consequences. A process that is taking place in the structures of capitalist production ought not be denied from an economic viewpoint, but affirmed from a political one. It is true: in recent years, the increase in wages has outstripped the rise in productivity. Here, indeed, is the root of everything. The national income has, in part, been redistributed, profits have been hit, the big companies' margins of self-financing have been cut back and direct investments have remained blocked. All this even as the costs of production have gone up and labour output has fallen in the wake of workers' continued struggles, labour-power's excessive mobility and the lack of technological breakthroughs. The normal capitalist response faced with the obligation to raise the nominal wage has been to attack real wages, sparking a spiral of inflation as the only way to avoid immediate side effects at the level of production. In this sense, not even today can we speak of bottlenecks in development; what is at work here is simply a common mechanism that adjusts between the different compartments of the capitalist structure. The bottleneck, the blockage, the crisis of development are things that ought to be discovered, constructed and imposed subjectively, by force. The material conditions for this do exist. The moment is an exemplary one. The new course of working-class struggles, in these years, indicates the general tendency of movement.

It was during the 1950s, perhaps right after '53, after an open political battle that was won and lost almost at the same time, that the working class discovered a new terrain of political struggle – spontaneously so, and not for the first time. And this was the trade-union terrain, at first linked to a mass of particular demands, and then ever more connected to the occasions on which collective contracts were negotiated. In such a moment, the formal political terrain – the traditional level of struggle wholly internal to the state – is dropped, abandoned, entirely left in the hands of the 'historic' parties of the working class. The economic struggle, in a trade-union vest, was rediscovered as the only struggle able to attack the base of capitalist power and thus the only practicable political struggle in that moment. This, moreover, sprung from the objective needs of capital, which sought and prepared a developmental leap forward in Italy, pressed as it was by the need to eliminate old internal imbalances to adapt itself to the emerging new international scene. These workers' new struggles were imposed on the union and, through the union, carried directly into the sphere of production. They set a positive mechanism of capitalist development back in motion again and within this mechanism activated the demand for greater working-class power. It is not true that July 1960 opened the way to the renewed working-class upsurge.[1] This resurgence had in fact come already, and the struggle in the squares came at the end of a long chain of clashes in the factories, in production, and facing the direct bosses. July 1960 kickstarted the open, generalised struggle, as it demonstrated the workers' readiness to fight for very different objectives and indeed the existence of a force well able to achieve them. Then the institutions of capitalist power adapted to the new class situation. Both the 'modern trade union' and Italian capital's reformist movement were children of this moment. So, too, were the economic miracle and then the 'fogging up' of the miracle, when the workers continued to struggle beyond the limits allowed by the balance of development and in fact obtained more than the capitalists could give at that moment. All the economists said that the low-cost workforce had been the foundation of the boom and, likewise, that the excessive cost of labour would ultimately determine its climax. Raising the price of labour-power was a working-class act of force, which, in a certain moment, coincided with a need of capital itself and then exceeded and overwhelmed this need, turning it on its head. The imbalance between wages and productivity is a political fact, it should be understood as a political fact, and it should be used politically. Here, across this period, we find a macroscopic example of the political use of the trade-union struggle.

This strategy entailed openings and limits: struggle within the structures of production, an immediate confrontation with the bosses, the

---

1 July 1960 saw wide-scale protests owing to the creation of a Christian-Democratic government reliant on the neofascist MSI in parliament. The mobilisation took flight in anti-fascist Genoa, where the MSI provocatively attempted to hold its congress, and had an effect in reviving a wider class militancy as well as in felling Prime Minister Fernando Tambroni's short-lived cabinet.

possibility of cutting into profits right away but also trade-unionist illusions, spontaneist errors and an undervaluation of the need for organisation. This was the basis for the strengthening of the concept of the 'mass party' and, on the other hand, the opposing response that came with the minoritarian 'groups' that were organised in order to intervene in these struggles. Yet the decisive element of this process was the fact that, from the working-class point of view, the factory had resumed the lead of the effective class movement, of the two classes in struggle. It was within this struggle that the union then found itself to the left of the party, cutting and restitching the transmission belt in the opposite direction. Indeed, in these years, the working-class use of the trade union has exceeded and defeated the capitalist use of the union. Ask a trade union if it ever so happened that it had to force the workers into struggle: when the union hierarchy initiates some agitation, over a period of months the workers will always press, push and struggle on their own account. The official beginning of the agitation merely occasions the open struggle: a unique opportunity, because there was no general class organisation across the factory and society. It is true: at the highest points of the working class's political development, there has been, and continues to be, the spurning of these opportunities. For years, the Fiat workers said no to the 'class union'. It became so only at one moment, in the summer of '62, when the class confrontation suddenly became acute, general, direct and frontal. This time the opportunity did not go amiss. It is a law of development: the more the political level of the working class and the economic unification of capital grow, the more the trade union tends to separate itself from the immediately working-class interest and completely integrate itself, as an institutional mediation, within the capitalist interest. Such a history has been written before: the passage from the antistatism of the old unionism to modern unionism's integration within the state; from 'anarcho-syndicalism' to 'conflictual participation'. And it is a development now underway here in Italy. The task at hand is not to stop it, but to use it. In the factory, precisely when the instrumentalisation of the union struggle is taking place, you will find that the workers' disdain for the trade unionist has almost reached the level of their class hatred for the foremen, for the supervisors, for the technicians, for the engineers. And this will be ever more the case in the future. But how can this be organised against the social boss today?

In fact, it is precisely at the social level that capital has today understood all this. It wants first to block the working-class dynamic, which it had at a certain point needed, in order to set one of its own development mechanisms moving again. The centre-left came not too early but too late.[2] By tradition, capital is slow in its political reflexes; all the more so in Italy, where, when the workers attack it, capital must continue to converse, within itself, with all its friends: peasants, traders, priests, savers, students, intellectuals, property speculators and state employees. Thus, even as the government announces feeble counter-cyclical measures and defines the economic situation as 'alarming' – making only the left-wing parties believe this – the capitalists mount a direct attack in their own interest at the decisive point, at the level of the working class. And they do so with specific objectives: to cut back full employment, rebuild a buffer in the reserve army of labour, internally restructure the working day, upskill the workforce, better orient labour mobility and cut production costs. All of this is being done to obtain a de facto wage truce, without having to ask for one.

The attack has to be countered on the same terrain. Here an immediate programme of struggle becomes the simplest thing to put into practice. It's not up to the workers to resolve capitalism's conjunctures. May the bosses do that alone – it is their system and it's up to them to deal with it. Here, a total refusal of capitalist society must find the positive tactical forms of the most effective aggression against the capitalists' concrete power. It is not enough, then, to refuse collaboration in resolving the conjunctural difficulties; it is necessary to return these difficulties to their place of origin, in the structures of production, and avoid resolving them at the level of the market. This means obstructing from the outset the various possible anticonjunctural policies, everywhere unleashing workers' struggles as the response to the call for a truce, in this way preventing any stabilisation. Today, even the momentary shutdown of production is not tolerated: it is, therefore, necessary to shut down production at strategic points. It is in the factory that the boss attacks, in order to demolish the workers' upsurge, and it is in the

2 After the failure of the Tambroni government, in 1962 the Christian Democrats and small allies became dependent on the Socialists in parliamentary confidence votes. By late 1963, Christian Democrat Aldo Moro had formed a cabinet including Socialist ministers, the so-called organic centrosinistra bringing part of the left into government..

factory that this attack must be used to multiply this same surge. The government, acting in the name of the capitalists, proposes a pause for reflection on the workers' wages: it is necessary to put aside all their other demands and demand wage increases right away. Intervention is needed today: to push the highest levels of struggle even higher, to compel workers' spontaneity into line with these levels, to make the clash an open one, to overturn the cult of passivity through open struggle, and through this type of violence to drag the old organisations along with us. Under these conditions, no other form of workers' initiative can substitute for the traditional, fundamental form of struggle: the factory strike, the mass strike. We are asked: what will come after? And we reply: of course, it will not be the catastrophic crisis of the system. For it is clear that then there will come the stabilisation of the conjuncture, the balance of development will be recomposed, the programming will resume functioning and the state structure will, as a consequence, adapt. However, there will be a shift in relations among differently balanced forces, including a stronger working class, battle-hardened and strengthened by the struggle, organised by its experience, present on the substantial political terrain. If the programming instead comes without this type of open struggle having taken place, there will begin to be recounted also in Italy, for the first time, at various scales from the trade-union to the state level, the bourgeois legend that capitalist development can make use of the political availability of the working class. There are moments in which we find that we have to choose between two possible types of working-class defeat, and we are compelled to do so not by an objective class situation but by the frightful lack of subjective forces. Both in fact and in principle, a defeat is less unfavourable to the working class if it has come *after a struggle*. So, a concrete programme of immediate struggle is today possible. This programme and its practical application must be inserted into a strategic vision that sees a capitalism walking, in its development, along a chain of conjunctures. Every link in this chain will offer an opportunity for an open clash, a direct struggle, a test of strength; the link where the whole chain is broken will not be the one where capital is weakest, but rather the one where the working class is strongest. Hence, the working class must eliminate all the old contradictions within capitalism that mediate and blur the class struggle and make it indirect and unfocused. There is likewise a primary need for the working class to express its struggle in open forms at every opportunity, such that it can grow politically and in an organised way with and within this same struggle. Finally, there needs to be class-based political organisation to subjectively select the points and moments for a general offensive, ones which strike at the base of the system and shake its very peak. In this way, these points and moments establish a continuity of leaps connecting the entire revolutionary process. Behind the effort to discover and rediscover the most modern modes and means in which the working-class presence in capitalist society has expressed and does express itself, it is necessary to hold firm to the conviction that, at the highest level, at the decisive moment, in the frontal class conflict, the most elementary forms of the struggle and of organisation – the mass strike, the violence of the square, the permanent working-class assembly – will be recovered. A theoretical outlook that seems most abstract now appears then in a new light as the only one able practically to function, in a particular moment and given situation, as the motor of events. The most complex strategy turns out to be the one that is tactically the easiest to apply, whereas all these 'popular' routes to socialism collapse into the most ridiculous impotence when faced with an initial opportunity to attack capital's social mechanism. This is all just the latest demonstration that a new line is imposing itself at the base of the movement, in order to politically advance the working class's struggle – and we must act on this right away.

May 1964

1905 in Italy

Again, the discussion is about Italian capitalism. A web of practical problems advises that we concentrate our analytical attention on this particular point of international capital. This conjuncture is lasting too long to continue to be 'conjunctural'; either the capitalists will impose a political end to it with an open defeat of the workers, or else it risks developing into a crisis at the objective economic level, on the level of direct production. In this resides the whole dilemma that divides the ruling class in Italy. It could take the courageous initiative of mounting a general political attack that blocks and pushes back against the current working-class pressure on the capitalist accumulation process in the factory. Otherwise, the ruling class can resign itself to suffering, indeed in the foreseeable future, all the directly economic side effects that the mechanism of objective readjustment, offered precisely by the crisis itself, will inevitably cause. The first possibility terrorises the bourgeois political stratum as a whole, considering the fearsome working-class response that could result: there is good reason the governmental solution (even in the government's new clothes) seeks not to take such initiatives. The second possibility terrorises the individual capitalist, considering the brakes on his private profits, the general confusion on the market and the ever-threatening general reorganisation of the structures of production, which the crisis always entails. For good reason, private capital has for months been creating drama over the economic situation and threatening autonomous political action. It is easy to laugh at the uncertainties and the confusion that the traditional governmental and parliamentary level of politics offers upon each changing season. But it is much more useful to recognise that the capitalists' conditions in Italy today are objectively difficult. If the official workers' movement is crying, the bourgeois political institutions are not laughing. The institutional level is decidedly not the realm of happiness. Could we perhaps speak of a 'tragic' general crisis of the institutions? This is a theoretical question that we can here only mention. When capital is at a very developed level, the possibility of controlling the objective movements of economic laws is very high. The forms in which this control is expressed, from state structures to party organisations – that is, the so-called terrain of institutional politics – are, conversely, still very uncertain, unstable, uncontrolled and thus backward. It seems that all the contradictions and irrationalities typical of a capitalist society's development mechanism have been offloaded from the economic level onto the political level and concentrated there. Indeed, today the crisis always appears as a crisis of the state: what appears within the structures of production is, at most, a 'difficult conjuncture'. But if this is how things appear, we should not be deceived. The dictatorship of capital rarely enjoys political stability. And, politically speaking, the capitalists are amateurs; it is always easy to beat them on this terrain with four well-combined moves. Their practical intelligence is all in economics. But the logic of profit does not mechanically coincide with the logic of power. When, with their programming techniques, they achieve control over labour-power's movements, they notice that they cannot do anything at all without the working class's active collaboration. Then they declare themselves ready to start from scratch, but, in fact, they start making errors all over again, because they regularly confuse the workers with their so-called organisations. Then when they decide to call a 'workers' party' into government, they get the wrong party, and then it becomes *commedia dell'arte*, to which Italy's great reformist operation is reduced. Under these conditions, there is a similar need to immediately reduce the prospect of a new imminent crisis in the traditional political institutions to the real state of the relations of force between the different classes. In recent years, the initiative was directly in working-class hands, with the consequences for capital's development mechanism that everyone today knows; but this initiative has tended to pass, once more, directly into capitalist hands. The capitalists' use of class thus far in the conjuncture has been infinitely stronger than the class use that the workers could have made – and not just out of the banal consideration that sees the costs of the conjuncture overall falling on workers' shoulders. After all, it is impossible to understand how and why things should be different in a capitalist society. Rather, this disparity is visible in the outright inversion of who it is that initiates the struggle, including its possible violent conclusion. Before returning to talk about programming, from a bourgeois point of view two problems need to be resolved: the economic stabilisation of the conjuncture, and a political block on the working-class upsurge. These two issues are, in fact, one problem; unless the working class momentarily drops its struggle over wages there will be no stabilisation and, without this stabilisation, it is impossible to advance any historic proposal for workers' active collaboration in the system's own development. This is a vicious circle. Incomes policy is today nothing more than a fashionable phrase. Everyone says it is needed but no one has said how. It is difficult to admit, but the truth is that income policy, like programming, knows only one effective path: the bureaucratic, authoritarian, centralised one. Capitalist programming can also be democratic and pluralist in the sense of including the official workers' organisations, but for the workers, it will always be a varied dish of technical knowledge, authority and violence. The hardest and perhaps most far-sighted part of Italian capital has made its programme understood: to provoke the working class into a clash in the open field, with an attack in the factory that then generalises on the political terrain; we would thus move from a general working-class defeat to re-propose all long-term plans for capitalist development. The timid attempts made this spring were put off till the autumn and it may be that they are delayed again – but, however close or distant the deadlines, this is a passage the system has to go through, in Italy, in its march toward the 'mature' phase. So, one ought not make the mistake of identifying this programme with that of the stubborn traditional economic right wing. The first Moro government fell on account of its overlong indecision in adopting what is, today, big Italian capital's line. The second Moro government will again try to mediate and augment this line over time, but, ultimately, either it will assume this line in full or else be cast aside. The problem we are facing is whether a class confrontation of this kind – even one sought by the bosses for their own reasons – can prove favourable to the workers. We say that it can, and we will explain the reasons in what follows. The working class has its own internal problems and in Italy, they are still, in part, the ones present in all those counties where capital's strength seems to be based on a pedestal of fearsome weaknesses. Here, opportunities for struggle continually appear, but the momentary organisation is weak; from a working-class point of view, class confrontation is repeatedly on the advance, but the series of victories is not as continual as the opportunities for struggle. We do not make leaps forward and do not manage to introduce a lethal threat within the engine of the system. It has been said that the current relationship between the class and its traditional organisations, between the working class and the workers' movement, is 'ambiguous'. This ambiguity needs to be resolved. At the level of the class, it is high time we talked directly about the conditions of the workers' movement in Italy: now is the moment to open up a debate, to conduct an analysis, to begin specific political action on this terrain. This political labour of a new type must necessarily pass through a generalised confrontation between the classes. No grassroots pressure by organised groups among the workers and no factional activity within party structures can prompt the restructuring of the movement as a whole, on the basis of a change in its general line. Rather, this restructuring and, with it, this change become immediately possible and practicable in a moment of acute confrontation with the class enemy. With good reason, the most intelligent part of capital simultaneously both wills and fears this confrontation: as for the 'official' workers' movement, it now takes it for granted that this confrontation will happen, but it continually projects it into the future. But what is the official workers' movement, politically speaking? Perhaps we ought to begin drawing some distinctions. The Socialist Party is dead, as a class party. Any attempt to knead life back into the corpse with the moral massaging of the old red heart of the nineteenth century is pointless, harmful. In recent years, the Socialist Party has taken on the courageous historic function of helping the most modern part of Italian capitalism – since it had not managed to do this alone – impose its own line of economic development amid a situation of enduring forms of structural backwardness, political fears and institutional uncertainties. In so doing, it has contributed, or is contributing, to liberating the class movement from a series of old false dilemmas. In the present stage of the class struggle in Italy, the PSI (Italian Socialist Party) ought to be consciously used precisely in this function. And here, Nenni is much more useful than Lombardi. We ought not mistake which is which, in the manner that the bourgeois mistake what party they need: in the present moment, Lombardi's reformism remains the main enemy to be beaten. His designs for the remodernisation of capitalist society and for the gradual transformation into a socialist society presuppose that the entire workers' movement in Italy itself commit to this path. All those Communists who nod along with every word of 'comrade Lombardi's' know only too well that today even a tactical concession to Lombardi's positions means to take for granted, in strategic terms, a social-democratic or, if you will, Socialist 'evolution' of the Communist Party. At least we can say, without any doubt, that the Nennian right of the party makes no such pretence: it embraces the capitalist initiative openly, accepts the exclusion of the Communists and thus ends up handing back to the PCI (Italian Communist Party) the opposite of an integral opposition, indeed this time on the terrain of a more advanced capitalism. Given these considerations and the situation of the Socialist Party, it becomes apparent that the left's positions ought to be utterly overturned: Nenni should be used in the long term and Lombardi needs defeating in the short term. It is at this point that a direct discussion of the Communist Party opens up again, also for us, and in a new way. Up till now, it has been too easy to dismiss any new political idea that did not face being accused of abstraction. In fact, we have yet to say anything about the problem of political organisation, about the question of the party; this is because, at this level, we consider these things not as theoretical themes but as practical problems in organising the struggle and its advancement. On the terrain of practice, the objective conditions present in a given moment are always decisive. These conditions tell us: 1) that Italian capital is not subjectively ripe to extend its reformist operation so far as to include the Communist Party; and 2) that the relationship between this party and the popular masses simultaneously both expresses and mystifies a still-real relationship with the working class. These two conditions each condition the other: the subsistence of this relationship presents obstacles to the capitalist political stratum, which is widening its strategy with a little more courage; moreover, the lack of this courage continually restores this relationship and, paradoxically, consolidates it each time that it seems to be wearing away. Faced with all this stands a working class which, following one of its own laws of development, does not wholly break the link with the old political organisation so long as it cannot see and touch the new and alternative one. But in Italy at this moment, no one can see an organisational alternative at the general political level. Here, too, the circle is closed. Breaking it open requires not the abandonment of the search for this alternative, but rather planting this whole search within the heart of workers' struggles, or, rather, at the head of these struggles, as a material guide and general objective. This movement toward political unification of the various levels of the working class's struggle, which is the real basis for us being able to declare the revolutionary process officially underway, must pass by way of this moment through the reorganisation of subjective forces. This moment needs to be subjectively brought closer, as it is the only way to bring the whole perspective of revolution closer. Certainly, it is necessary to be wary. The cult of spontaneity tends always to flip into a fetish of organisation. Such is the fate of minorities. But this ought to be rejected. The Bolsheviks' whole majoritarian drive needs to be conquered anew. From the workers' point of view, an action is a mass action or is not an action at all. A vanguard that does not bring the movement along with it is no different from a rearguard. There is a dilemma not between spontaneity and organisation but between two possible ways of arriving at the new organisation. We say that today it is possible to choose a path that proceeds by way of a positive crisis of at least a part of the old organisations. This clears the immediate terrain of the risk that we will end up starting all over again only to erect a new bureaucratic structure. But this choice can be made only on one condition, the fundamental stipulation that distinguishes and discriminates this movement from all the other now-traditional positions under the petty-bourgeois and semi-proletarian misery in both the old entryism and the new one. This condition is the fact that this political labour, which must function as a material force, must be conducted not within the party but outside it, in the factory, in production, among the workers – all workers, the few who are organised like the mass of unorganised. Again today, as always, all this labour ought to be tactically determined within a specific moment of the working class's struggle. We said that the initiative in the class struggle is again passing into capitalist hands. We need to prevent this. Still highly relevant today is a programme for genuinely tackling this conjuncture. To the most difficult point in the evolution of the conjuncture, there ought to respond the most acute moment of workers' struggles. They've already said that the critical limit for the increase in wage levels has been surpassed for this year: so, in every government statement, they are forced to register a victory for the workers. It is necessary to start from here, from this result, to generalise trade-union struggles, so that they take to the political terrain. We should not be waiting for the bosses, *en bloc*, to take the initiative in the confrontation, since, for now, they may well not do so. And if they do so because they are forced by the economic situation alone and not by workers' political drive, the clash will take place on bases too backward and positions too defensive for it to be possible to reap fruits at the organisational level. It is necessary to exacerbate the wage dynamic, and by articulating it, before they manage to establish an effective block on wages. Before they attack employment levels, it is necessary to strike against labour productivity, with a clear threat of reprisal. Before they manage to freeze the contracts that have already been signed, it is necessary to take to the offensive against some of them, including through shop-floor actions at strategic points. Before they again begin to look at state force as a panacea, we must remind them that there is a much greater force in the factories. A few initiatives would thus suffice to seize up the whole arduous mechanism of economic recovery and to blow up all the programmes for stabilising the conjuncture – that is, to provoke a real political crisis, which is not just a crisis in the government but a crisis of power and thus a substantial shift in the relations of force between the two classes in struggle. Here is the starting point for taking the initiative in the general confrontation back into working-class hands. We already know that the official leadership – well, since we've learned to name names, let's also say the current Communist leadership of this movement – will tend to deflect this confrontation onto a position of generic popular protest. It will be necessary, then, to find the strength to nail the whole thing down to the political content of a working-class revolt. It is through foreseeing and searching out this moment of working-class revolt that the revolutionary imaginary of an Italian 1905 takes form. Yes, we know the enormous differences. Here, we are not interested in historical philology. But what is decisive are the few things that are similar. In 1905, the Bolsheviks went through their test of fire; in 1905, the soviets were born; without 1905, there would have been no October 1917. At this point, a general test is necessary for each and every one of us. And from this, we should draw rich insight into forming new organisations and laying down a fixed point beyond which there can now be nothing other than the process of working-class revolution true and proper. The subjective conditions for this minimum programme today all seem to be there. The Putilov Works – which at this time have 100,000 workers – are ready to give the sign for the attack. A battleship Potemkin can easily be found in any Piazza Statuto. And Father Gapon is no more. We have buried the sacred icons along with him.

September 1964

Class and Party

On the agenda today is the search for a new strategy for the class struggle in advanced capitalism. The urgent need to recompose a general perspective on this terrain is a pressing one for the movement and pushes with the force of great historic necessities. This immense work will be collective or it will not be; it will either immediately cross paths with the daily movement of the social mass of workers or it will remain blocked, it will stagnate and regress. There is no autonomous development of theoretical discoveries that is separate from organisational practice. It is impossible to foresee the struggle when one is not in it. No slogan truly exists in the absence of the weapons with which to impose it. Such are the laws that govern the history of working-class experiences. Of course, there have already been moments where the relation between the class and its political organisation assumed the violent aspect of a problem that needed resolving before all others. But perhaps never like today has this violence imposed itself with the pressure, the imminence, the clarity of a historic node that must be politically solved in a short period, given the current state of things – that is, the current state of social relations, including the subjective forces present therein. Today's discourse on the party must first of all plunge into that melting pot of still-open problems and then fuse into the new form that working-class thought is able to give to the new class realities. It must be shaped and remoulded around those harsh realities, all the while keeping a critical eye on all the past models and a sharp tactical eye toward certain organisational solutions offered by the current situation. Each of these moments must appear explicitly in our analysis, if we want to be able to confront the theme of the class-party on the political field. To do this, we immediately need to introduce a new concept of working-class political struggle in place of the old one.

There is a well-known Leninist distinction between economic struggle (the fight against the individual capitalists or groups of individual capitalists in order to improve the workers' situation) and political struggle (the fight against the government to extend the people's rights, or, in other words, for democracy). Lenin's Marxism united these two moments of the working-class struggle into an indissoluble whole. Without Marxism and without Lenin, these two moments have separated again. Once divided, they entered into a dual crisis which is, indeed, the current crisis of the class struggle, understood in the Leninist sense of the term – that is, in the sense of the organisation and direction of this struggle. Understood literally, this distinction leads to a class union and a people's party: an 'Italian' reality plain for all to see, an opportunism that has not even had to cut ties with Leninism. From this follow two consequences: a union that finds itself managing the concrete forms of the class struggle without being able even to speak of their political outcomes and a party whose function is limited to talking about this political outcome without the least reference and with only the most distant link to concrete forms of the class struggle. And extreme confusion demands an extreme remedy. To get rid of the consequences, it is necessary first to destroy the premises. The old distinction between economic struggle and political struggle must be exploded; this will blow up one of the cardinal points of reformism in its most modern – post-Leninist, Communist – form.

This should not be a difficult task. If we look at advanced capitalism, we see that this distinction has already disappeared. At the stage of social capital, when we see the implementation of integration processes on the grandest scale between the state and society, between the bourgeois political stratum and the social class of capitalists, between the workings of institutional power and the mechanism of production for profit – at this stage, all working-class struggle that limits itself voluntarily to the economic terrain ends up coinciding with the most reformist politics. When the historical democracy/capitalism nexus definitively stabilises for the first time in the only possible form – that is,

authoritarian planning that requires the 'active' consensus of the productive social forces through the increasingly direct exercise of popular
sovereignty – at this point, all working-class struggle that limits itself
voluntarily to the 'political' field (no longer for democracy, but for
democratic planning!) and ends up blending into the most opportunist
economism. To avoid being trapped and divided between these two
fields, which are artificially proposed to the workers' movement by capital in its own efforts to put a cage around the class struggle, we again
need to assert at every opportunity the struggle's character as a single,
global clash, probably the only one that is historically feasible and possible today. From the workers' point of view, from within modern capitalism, the political struggle is the one that aims consciously to pitch into
crisis the economic mechanisms of capitalist development. The elements
of this definition are all equally important. The new strategic approach,
which seeks an active inversion of the relation between the working-
class political movement and the economic crisis of capitalism, has been
the object of only a minimum of theoretical analyses; we will soon go
back to this, in order to deepen these analyses and to elaborate them
over a longer period. The possible tactical application of this strategic
reconstruction can be informed by interpreting the present conjuncture
of Italian capital that has already been expounded in these columns.
This analysis, notwithstanding its simple exposition, is rich in practical
findings that now only need experimentation. But what interests us
today is to foreground an element that we have thus far scarcely taken
into account: namely, the subjective consciousness, which is internal
and essential to the very concept of political struggle, and constitutive of
all active intervention by the revolutionary will, insofar as it is the fruit
of organisation. In fact, it is within this definition of the political content
of the class struggle that we will discover, reaffirm and impose anew the
irreplaceable function of the working-class party.

If the different moments of working-class struggle precede and
impose the various moments of the capitalist cycle, we should add that,
to give a revolutionary content to these struggles, it is necessary to
precede and impose capital's moves in a conscious way at the social,
mass level – meaning in an organised manner at the level of political
intervention. If this is done, then the working class will dominate the
capitalist production process, and this should constitute the immediate
premise of capitalist overthrow. But the necessary mediums for this are

the organisation of this domination, the political expression of this organisation and the mediation of the party. Only through a subjective, conscious intervention from above, through material force that returns to the workers ownership of the functional mechanism of the system that is to be destroyed … only through the social use of this power will it be possible not only to foresee and anticipate the turning points in capital's development cycle, but also to measure, to control, to manage and thus to organise the political growth of the working class. This will itself be done by forcing the working class to pass through a chain of clashes at different levels and on various occasions, until the one where it is necessary to decide to break the chain, to invert the relations between the classes and to break the state machinery.

In these conditions, it is necessary to establish a new relation between spontaneity and organisation, for the old one no longer functions. It relied on the illusion that it is enough to know capital in order to under-stand the working class. From this stems the fact that at the top of the present-day party, one may have only a rather loose knowledge of either phenomenon. This has also led to the current attempts to adapt the organisational instrument of the party to the needs of the development of capitalist society rather than to the needs of the revolutionary work-ers' revolt. It is necessary to repeat, once again, that the establishment of a correct relationship between class and party first supposes that the party has a scientific knowledge of the material, objective, spontaneous movements of the working class. On this condition alone is it possible to have scientific knowledge of the movements of the capitalist class and its social organisation. It is in this sense that the party presents itself as the theoretical organ of the class, as the collective brain which captures the material reality of the class, of its movements, its development and its objectives. The party leader must necessarily have that quality of politi-cal judgement, capable of synthesis, which can derive only from great experience, in a long-term experiment that makes use of refined, modern, complex and piercing instruments. The leadership group as a whole must be able to express the synthetic unity of working-class science. It cannot ask for this from someone else; it must be able to embody it. The function of the party intellectual has definitively come to an end: the savant has no place in the working-class party. A science of social relations is no longer possible if separated from the practical capacity to overthrow them, if such science ever was. Consequently, a correct relationship between class and party supposes in the second place precisely this practical capacity to foresee and orient the class's movements in historically determinate situations: not only to know the laws of action, but to be able to act concretely, on the basis of an intimate understanding of what might be called the theory and practice of the law of tactics. In this sense, the party is not only the scientific bearer of strategy, it is equally the practical organ of its tactical application. The working class spontaneously possesses the strategy of its own move- ments and its development; the party has but to identify it, express it and organise it. But the class does not possess the properly tactical moment at any point, either at the level of spontaneity or at the level of organisa- tion. All the missed historical opportunities, all the failed offensives against the class enemy, all the employers' attacks that were not punished with the working-class response that they deserved, owe to this and this alone: that only the party could have, and can, isolate and grasp the determinate point at which the class confrontation turns and can be pitched into social revolution. The great Leninist moment of the party marks the historic working-class conquest of the world of tactics; not by chance, it is bound up with the first concrete revolutionary experiment in history.

But there is no need to delude ourselves: in none of these historic moments will the relationship between class and party, between the working class and workers' movement, find perfect expression. If this was the case, we should declare the history of the class already concluded, as indeed it has seemed finished every time it was claimed that it had achieved its perfect form. No party will ever manage to express, in its entirety, the incomparable wealth of experiences of struggle that are lived at the level of the class itself. The party must continually aim to capture within itself the global reality of the working class as it antici- pates and guides its movements. It must do so even though it knows that there will always be a gap between its own margins of subjective action and the overall pressure that is exercised on it by its base, which constrains its ability to act. The party must approach this tension toward the working class as its very *raison d'être*. And the party leader, the professional revolutionary, must be the living mirror of this revolution- ary tension at once toward his own class and against the opposing class. The working-class leaders' whole activity finds itself trapped between these two contradictory extremes. From constraint stem all true theoretical discoveries, all the unforeseen intuitions, the inspired syntheses of social reality, of which the working-class point of view alone is capable. Thus is born simultaneously the tactical capacity to move within realities, to shift them at one's own will, to destroy and rebuild them, with all the subjective violence of self-organised forces. The revolutionary leader is this living contradiction, which has no solution. But when we depart from this and find ourselves facing a party bureaucrat, we are pressed by the urgent need to mine the deepest shafts of the history of the workers' movement to find out what has happened in recent decades.

Nevertheless, it would be an error of abstract moralism to stop here. It would be easy, at this point, for our discourse to wander away from the heart of the matter, but we are deliberately overlooking questions concerning the party's internal institutional problems and those regarding its organisational structures; however, these are the easiest problems to resolve and they will settle themselves, in time. The new course imposes a new organisation and not the opposite, and we have learned to attach little importance to moments of internal democracy that do not question the general course. It is evident that the political relationship between class and party must be born in the factory, that it is the site from which it must then head off to take hold of the whole society, including its state. Likewise, the political mechanisms of the revolutionary process must return to the factory, to this decisive terrain, if they are to be able to progress. That is the right path to take, so long as we hold to the scientific concept of the factory. This will prevent us from falling short of taking the relations of production and remaining tangled up in the empirical web of relations with the individual employer. At the same time, it stops us from immediately going all the way to tackling the generic relation with the social bosses and the formal political level. If the party's maxim is to obtain in the factory, the factory must already be inside the party. If the party's organisation is to materially survive and grow in every factory, the relations of production must first become politically alive within the party line. And when we take a closer look, we discover that none of these two moments truly precedes the other; they exist in combination, and can only live in combination in an organic whole, in a historical relationship of movement and organisation, of spontaneity and leadership, of strategic line and tactical shifts. This is the decisive problem around which the solution of all the other problems must be oriented: the point at which party and class converge, the terrain of struggle that the social class and political party have in common, on which basis alone a class party can possibly exist, from the working-class point of view.

Of course, the road to be travelled is still a long one. Beyond all the democratic chatter on the concept of autonomy, one cannot deny that, on certain occasions, some of which are very much relevant, it still seems that the most practicable method of class struggle is the linking of the union to the party with a transmission belt. But it is clear that, beyond these occasions, the belt tends to break and the relationship reverses. We can foresee that in the long run there will inevitably come to be an association between the party and the union, on the class terrain. And the reduction of the union to a party, or rather of the class union to a class party, will constitute perhaps the first scientific formulation of the workers' party in advanced capitalism. At this stage, the union will increasingly be reduced to defending the conservation and development of the material and economic value of social labour-power, while the party will increasingly have to grow as an offensive weapon of working-class political interest against the system of capital. In the presence of a working-class party – and on this condition alone – the union will be able to fully resume its natural role as defender of the rights of the working people. Ultimately, the new definition of the political struggle requires a class party and a people's union. There will necessarily be a moment in which the union will be home to nothing more than the working-class mediation of the capitalist interest, while the directly working-class interest will live only in the party. This will occur to such an extent that, outside of the party, the working class will seem to have politically disappeared, only to reappear in the phases of acute social tension in the presence of a general confrontation. When revolutionary organisation finds its first successful application in developed capitalism, it will work wholly in function of the revolutionary process – a foreseen, prepared, practised process, only momentarily reaching its conclusion and constantly reopened anew. This will be nothing other than the organisation of an ever-stronger continuity and an accelerating succession from the class's underground phases of growth to the party's abrupt revolutionary offensives. At a certain stage of the struggle, it will be necessary, in reality, to make capital dance to this music for a long time, before we knock it down with the decisive blow.

Our task for today is to discover and clear the road that will bring us to this stage. The task remains that of laying the foundations of a revolutionary process by advancing the objective conditions for it and by beginning to organise the subjective forces. We will not achieve this without the immediate combination of a great strategic insight and a strong dose of political realism. In his mature phase, Marx had already understood that the weapons to fight the present society must be drawn from within this same society. We need to set out from this same starting point today if we want to avoid just rerunning the workers' movement's more infantile experiences. It is obvious, for example, that the working class possesses very different levels of political development (as will always occur) and that the most advanced sectors will always be posed with the problem of how to lead the most backward sectors, just as the whole of the class will be posed the problem of a real political unity that cannot be achieved except through and in the party. It is just as clear that there is a problem of working-class hegemony; a hegemony not over the other classes, but over the other parts of what are loosely and generically termed the working masses. At the theoretical level, this constitutes a difference that demands much further investigation – namely, the difference between the direct and indirect forms of productive labour, expressed on the directly political level precisely through the hegemony of the working class over the entire people. How to make 'the people' operate within the working class remains a real problem of the revolution in Italy, specifically in the interest not of winning a democratic majority in the bourgeois parliament, but of constructing a political bloc of social forces and using it as a material lever that will blow up each of the connections internal to the enemy's political power and then all of them at once. This demands a fearsome popular power, deployed, controlled and directed by the working class through its tool, the party. This excludes from the party's tasks something that had hitherto instead seemed to characterise it: namely, the task of mediating the relations that exist between related classes – that is, between the different stratums and all their ideologies, in a system of alliances. The reduction of the party to the wax holding together the historic bloc was one of the most determinant factors, if not the most, in blocking off any revolutionary perspective in Italy. The Gramscian concept of the historic bloc did nothing but reveal a particular stage, a national moment of capitalist development. Its immediate generalisation, in Gramsci's carceral writings, was a first error. The second error, and a much more serious one, was the Togliattian vulgarisation of Gramsci in the form of the 'new party'. This party's intention was to identify itself more and more with this historic bloc, going as far as to dissolve itself into it, as the history of the nation became identical with the national policy of the party of the whole people. It is easy to say today: the plan failed. The truth is that it could not have succeeded – capitalism does not allow those who speak against it (however formally) to do these kinds of things. Capitalism keeps this programme for itself, adapts it to its level and uses it for its own development. Everyone said that Togliatti was a realist. He was perhaps the man most removed from the social reality of his country that the Italian workers' movement has ever known. One wonders if his realism was really calculating opportunism, or a fine and little-thought-through utopia.

For good reason, at this point, the discussion resumes on the current phase of this social reality. Our accounts with Italian capitalism are still all to be settled. Italy currently finds itself in the phase that immediately precedes the stabilisation of capitalism at full maturity. Both the domestic conjuncture and international ties are pressing this process forward with irresistible force. It is just as clear that the Italian workers' movement finds itself in the phase that immediately precedes a social-democratic compromise at the traditional political level. And there again, both the domestic conjuncture and the international situation are pushing toward a strong acceleration of this development. We would hypothesise that these two processes do not present the same mechanical and irresistible objectivity; on the contrary, the present moment of class struggle in Italy must more so divide these two processes, to set them in contradiction in such a way as to make them progress in opposite directions. This would achieve – for the first time and thus on the basis of an original revolutionary experience – an economic maturity of capital in the presence of a politically strong working class. To accomplish this, it is necessary, first of all, to block the realisation in Italy of the historic path that all the advanced capitalist societies have followed; this is only feasible by stopping the stabilisation of the system at new levels from conquering for itself all the available margins of political manoeuvre on the new terrain. This is also the only way to maintain in working-class hands a threat which, everyone knows, risks disappearing over the horizon for decades if it does not find, in the decisive moments and crucial points, explicit forms of functioning and organisation. Maturity without stabilisation, economic development without political stability: capital must be made to walk this tightrope, so that, in the meantime, we can build the working-class forces that will ultimately knock it off. Without the general defeat of the working class, there will be no political stabilisation – this defeat is what the capitalist initiative wants to bring about. Working-class defeats on the general level are also the ones (maybe the only ones) that mow down the base and decapitate any prospect of forming immediate organisation, dispelling any concrete possibility of offensive struggles, by pushing the mass of workers back toward now traditional behaviours of political passivity and of purely economic refusal. When the entire official workers' movement in a capitalist country stands on openly social-democratic positions, it is necessary to have an alternative organisation already prepared to take over from it and able right away to pull behind it the majority political support of the working class. The experience of international capitalism shows that if this condition is not met, all prospects of revolution will be closed for a long period. Consequently, this is the condition that needs preparing. The preparation of this alternative organisation demands work that starts right now, combining our utmost forces with clear-sighted perspectives and practical skill to attain the greatest possible control over the situation.

Today, as indeed in other moments of history, the struggle inside the working-class movement is an essential part and a basic moment of the class struggle in general. If we ignore it, we lose the complexity, the knowledge, the control of the class struggle against capital and, thus, the possibility to act. The task today is not to use the PCI (Italian Communist Party) in a revolutionary way; the situation is far more backward than that. Rather, the task is to prevent the explicit social-democratisation of the Communist Party, in order to block the political stabilisation of capitalism in Italy. This means not allowing the whole of the Italian workers' movement to sign up to the new expressions of capital's own reformism at a moment where, outside of the official workers' movement, on the class level, no truly organised power and consequently no seriously feasible offer of an alternative political organisation exists. Taking this action will ultimately avoid a terrible defeat for the working class that would set the struggle back for years, put an end to the prospect of a rupture of the system in the short run and that would therefore push the Italian class situation back into line with Western capitalism. Thus far, the Italian working class has not been pushed back into line – indeed, this must be prevented whatever the cost in personal sacrifices, theoretical backward steps or even practical compromises. The first political objective of organisational practice is to avoid abandoning the PCI to capital's reform-ist operation, even if this operation did push forward to that extent. Only within and through the struggle for this objective will it be possible, any time soon, to recompose the political relation between class and party on the basis of revolutionary action. Revolutionary prospects in Italy 'in the short run' are bound up with this perspective. This is a tough perspective, which cannot be realised without certain courage in taking positions, patience in continuous political initiatives and violence in open struggle. Everyone can see that the last act of the comedy, which should result in the class party's complete liquidation, has already practically begun. The liquidators of the party will have to be liquidated in turn and right away. As Lenin explained, 'The liquidators are not only opportunists. The opportunists push the party in a bourgeois and erroneous direction on the path of a liberal policy for the working class, but they do not renounce the party itself, they do not liquidate it. The liquidators represent the form of opportunism that goes as far as to renounce the party.' This extreme form of opportunism, which renounces all, is the target in our next battle. And we must not stop there but go beyond, toward the work-ing-class party.

But if all of these are temporal processes, what might their spatial limits be? What historical horizon can they assume? Is there not again, here, the danger of overestimating a national moment, a specific stage of capitalist development? Does this analysis not leap across the huge complexity of working-class revolutionary problems, today present at the international level? This issue is vastly complex, it is true. We could not escape it even if we wanted to. All that has been said so far repre-sents only a tenth of what needs to be said. We do not even know if this is what is most important. But, certainly, this is what is most urgent, the precondition, the premise from which to begin. Today, there is a curious form of opportunistic 'internationalism' (one that has become strangely relevant today) which also needs defeating – namely, the idea that everything can only be resolved on a worldwide and generic scale, in the overall battle between revolution or integration. This is one of the many ways of detaching oneself intellectually from the concrete moments of the true class struggle. But we do not think that any key idea today is more important than the Leninist thesis that envisages the chain of capitalism breaking at a certain point, and which demands that we identify and resolve the various problems of organisation and direction with a view to this essential objective. This thesis has grown and is growing in importance alongside the supranational integration of contemporary capitalism. The channels of communication which capital has established to serve its own interests today constitute an objective fact, including for the working class. It is only today that a revolutionary rupture at the national level really begins to have the possibility of generalising along the chain internationally. Indeed, this increasingly proves to be the only possibility. For it now appears clear that only a real revolutionary experience will be able to set the overall mechanism of the international revolution back in motion. No theoretical discourse, no political alternative that remains at the stage of a programme will be able to have this impact, this value as a model, this role as a sharp practical proposition. And in the most advanced capitalism today, the latter constitutes the minimum for breaking the de facto truce between the workers' revolution and the development of capital. Of course, it is necessary to correct the Leninist thesis on one point. We put less emphasis today on the inequalities of capitalist economic development than on the inequalities of the political development of the working class; this is in order to accept the neo-Leninist principle that the chain will not break where capital is weakest but where the working class is strongest. And we need to get it into our heads – and this is not easy to do – that there is no mechanical coincidence between the level of capitalist development and the level of the development of the working class. Again, the practice of the struggle reveals itself richer than all the wealth that working-class thought has accumulated thus far. This means choosing the link in the chain where we find ourselves in the presence of both sufficient capitalist economic development and a very high degree of the political development of the working class. Is Italy therefore on the way to becoming the epicentre of the revolution in the West? It is too early to say. All depends on how much time we take to get the line across and to open the way.

December 1964

Initial Theses

Marx, Labour-Power, Working Class

Let's start from the fundamental discovery which – according to Marx – is at the basis of *Capital*, namely the *Doppelcharakter* of labour represented in commodities. Even in Marx's time it was obvious that the commodity was something double, at once use-value and exchange-value. But what had remained unknown to the thought of the time was that the labour expressed in value has different characteristics to those of the labour that produces use-values. Near the beginning of *Capital*, Marx says: 'I was the first to point out and to examine critically this twofold nature of the labour contained in commodities' (*zwieschlächtige Natur*: a nature at once double, divided, and riven by contradiction). Indeed, in the 1859 *Contribution to the Critique of Political Economy* Marx had attempted an analysis of the commodity 'as labour presenting a double form'. This was an analysis of use-value as real labour or productive activity in accordance with the scope and analysis of exchange-value as labour-time or equivalent social labour. Here Marx discovered the final, critical result of a hundred and fifty years of classical economy, in England running from William Petty to Ricardo, and in France, from Boisguilbert to Sismondi. Marx's discovery, on this terrain, is 'the transition from concrete labour to labour which produces exchange-value, i.e. the basic form of bourgeois labour'.[1]

Already in 1859, Marx's concept of value-producing labour presented three well-defined facets: simple labour, social labour, and general

---

1 Marx and Engels Collected Works (MECW), Vol. 29, 299.

abstract labour. Each of these facets is in itself a *process*, which immediately presents itself as intimately linked to the processes of the other two: it is precisely the combination of these processes which permits the transition from precapitalist forms of labour to capitalist ones. And each process is an objective fact governed by the force of a nascent capitalism's laws of development. Simple labour means the *reduction* of all labours to a simple, undifferentiated, uniform labour, which is always qualitatively the same and only differs in quantitative terms. Complex labour is nothing other than simple labour elevated to the nth power; labour of greater intensity, of greater specific weight, is always reducible, which is to say *must* always be reduced to unskilled labour, stripped of quality. But labour without quality and 'general human labour' are the same thing: not the labour of different subjects, but different individuals 'as mere organs *of* labour'. 'This abstraction, human labour in general, *exists* in the form of average labour which, in a given society, the average person can perform, productive expenditure of a certain amount of human muscles, nerves, brain, etc.'[2] The specific form in which labour acquires its *simple* character is therefore that of human labour in general. The reduction to simple labour is a reduction to *abstract human labour*. The same goes for the *social* character of value-producing labour. As the analysis of value demonstrates, the conditions of this labour are social determinations of labour, or determinations of social labour. In either case, they are not social *tout court*; they become so through a particular process. And what is the particularity of this social character? Two things: (1) the undifferentiated simplicity of labour, which is to say the equivalence among the labours of different individuals, the social character of the equivalence of the labours of each; (2) the general character of individual labour, which presents itself as its social character – for it is, indeed, the labour of the individual, but also the labour of an individual undifferentiated from any other. In the logical passage between these two things – which is also the historic passage from the social determinations of labour to the determinations of social labour – the *different* exchange-values find *one* general equivalent: which is only a *social* magnitude insofar as it is a *general* magnitude. But for a product to assume the form of a general equivalent, it is necessary for the labour of the individual itself to assume a general abstract character.

---

2 Ibid., 272.

The specific form in which labour acquires its *social* character is therefore the form of abstract generalisation. The particular trait of this social labour is that it is also *abstract human labour*. When they produce value, simple labour and social labour are reduced to abstract labour, to labour in general. It is thus mistaken to see in labour the *only* source of material wealth; for here again, as always, this would mean the concrete labour that creates use-values. We must instead speak of abstract labour as the source of exchange-values. Concrete labour is realised in the infinite variety of its use-values; abstract labour is realised in the equivalence among commodities as general equivalents. That labour which creates use-values is the natural condition of human life, the condition of the organic exchange between man and nature; conversely, that labour which creates exchange-values is a specifically social form of labour. The first is particular labour that splits up into infinite types of labour; the second is always general, abstract and equivalent labour. 'Labour as a source of material wealth was well known both to Moses, the law-giver, and to Adam Smith, the customs official.'[3] Value-creating labour is the first fundamental discovery of the working-class point of view's application to capitalist society.

With the publication of the first volume of *Capital*, Marx wrote to Engels: 'The best points in my book are: 1. (this is fundamental to all understanding of the facts) the *two-fold character of labour* according to whether it is expressed in use-value or exchange-value, which is brought out in the very first chapter; 2. the treatment of *surplus-value regardless of its particular forms* as profit, interest, ground rent, etc.'[4] A few months later – in another letter – he criticized Dühring's review of *Capital* for having failed to grasp the 'fundamentally new elements' of the book, namely: '(1) That in contrast to all former political economy, which *from the very outset* treats the different fragments of surplus value with their fixed forms of rent, profit, and interest as already given, I first deal with the general form of surplus value, in which all these fragments are still undifferentiated – in solution, as it were. (2) That the economists, without exception, have missed the simple point that if the commodity has a double character – use value and exchange value – then the labour represented by the commodity must also have a two-fold character,

---

3 Ibid., 278.
4 MECW, Vol. 42, 407.

while the mere analysis of labour as such, as in Smith, Ricardo, etc, is bound to come up everywhere against inexplicable problems.'[5] We will later return to the organic connection that intimately links the content of these two discoveries: the concept of labour-power, and the concept of surplus value. For the moment, we will push on in tracking down the origin of this first concept, in the works of Marx and in his sources.

'If then we disregard the use-value of commodities, only one property remains, that of being products of labour.' But even the product of labour can have a use-value. We can look beyond this and erase all the commodity's tangible qualities: this latter will, then, no longer even be the product of a determinate productive labour. 'The useful character of the kinds of labour embodied in them also disappears; this in turn entails the disappearance of the different concrete forms of labour. They can no longer be distinguished, but are altogether reduced to the same kind of labour, human labour in the abstract.' What then remains of the products of labour, at this point? Nothing if not 'the same phantom-like objectivity; they are merely congealed quantities of homogeneous human labour'. There is only 'human labour-power expended without regard to the form of its expenditure'. Only as crystals of this common social substance – human labour-power – are things 'values, commodity-values'. A common social substance (*gemeinschaftliche gesellschaftliche Substanz*) of things, common among commodities, which is to say common among the products of labour and not 'the common social substance of exchange value' (see the beginning of the 'Critical Notes on Adolph Wagner's *Treatise on Political Economy*'), but *wertblindende Substanz* (valorising substance). This is the first definition of the concept of labour-power that we find in *Capital*. Here Marx says *Arbeitskraft*, whereas in *Theories of Surplus Value* he instead used the term *Arbeitsvermögen*, and in the *Grundrisse* he had mostly used *Arbeitsfähigkeit*. The concept is the same. Here we are not interested in the philological shift from one term to another. In Marx, the distinction between labour and labour-power is found in already-complete form in all the works preparing his *Contribution to the Critique of Political Economy* (see the *Grundrisse*, for the years 1857–8); if we consider that these works span a decade (from 1849 to 1859), we would properly locate just after 1848 Marx's definitive discovery of the concept

---

5 Ibid., 514.

of labour-power, in all its significance. And naturally enough, we can also find seeds of this discovery in all the works before this date. Through these works we can document a development internal to the concept of labour-power itself – that is to say, its gradual internal specification, giving it ever-greater scientific qualifications, up till the decisive encounter, and its definitive identification, with the concept of the working class, amidst the revolutionary experience of 1848.

Already in some of Marx's notebooks of excerpts from the works of the greatest economists, which he compiled in Paris in 1844 – and which thus prepared or were contemporary to the *1844 Manuscripts* – we can find the concept (the term) *Erwerbsarbeit*. We think this can be translated directly as 'industrial labour'. Marx tells us that in industrial labour we have: '1) estrangement and fortuitous connection between labour and the subject who labours; 2) estrangement and fortuitous connection between labour and the object of labour; 3) that the worker's role is determined by social needs which, however, are alien to him and a compulsion to which he submits out of egoistic need and necessity, and which have for him only the significance of a means of satisfying his dire need, just as for them he exists only as a slave of their needs; 4) that to the worker the maintenance of his individual existence appears to be the *purpose* of his activity and what he actually does is regarded by him only as a means; that he carries on his life's activity in order to earn means of *subsistence*.'[6] Given these foundations, the unity of human labour is considered only in terms of the *division of labour*. Once we have presupposed the division of labour, then for the individual the product – the material of private property – increasingly assumes the significance of an equivalent. And the equivalent acquires its existence as an equivalent *through money*. The total domination of the estranged object *over man* manifests itself already in money: 'The separation of work from it*self* [*Trennung der Arbeit von sich selbst*] – separation of the worker from the capitalist – separation of labour and capital.' The economists distinguish between production, consumption, and as the intermediary between the two, exchange or distribution. But 'the separation of production and consumption, of action and spirit, in different individuals and in the same individual, is the *separation of labour* from

---

6 MECW, Vol. 3, 220.

its *object* and from itself as something spiritual.'[7] It is the separation of 'labour from labour' (*Trennung der Arbeit von Arbeit*). In the first of the *1844 Manuscripts*, in the section on the wage, Marx writes: 'It goes without saying that the *proletarian* [*Proletarier*], i.e., the man who, being without capital and rent, lives purely by labour, and by a one-sided, abstract labour [*rein von der Arbeit und einer einseitigen, abstrakten Arbeit lebt*], is considered by political economy only as a *worker* [*Arbeiter*] ... In political economy labour occurs only in the form of *activity as a source of livelihood* [*unter der Gestalt der Erwerbstätigkeit*].' But if we 'rise above the level of political economy', two decisive questions arise, which for good reason occur to Marx precisely at this point '(1) What in the evolution of mankind is the meaning of this reduction of the greater part of mankind to abstract labour [*auf die abstrakte Arbeit*]? (2) What are the mistakes committed by the piecemeal reformers, who either want to raise wages and in this way to improve the situation of the working class, or regard equality of wages (as Proudhon does) as the goal of social revolution?'[8] Only much later, in *Capital*, would Marx give a likewise decisive and wholly accurate response to this question. Given their strongly 'ideological' form, in the *Manuscripts* it is difficult to find practically anything more than the indication of direction for future research, which is doubtless already present. 'True, it is as a result of the *movement of private property* that we have obtained the concept of *alienated labour* (*of alienated life*) in political economy. But on analysis of this concept it becomes clear that though private property appears to be the reason, the cause of alienated labour, it is rather its consequence, just as the gods are *originally* not the cause but the effect of man's intellectual confusion. Later this relationship becomes reciprocal. Only at the culmination of the development of private property does this, its secret, appear again, namely, that on the one hand it is the *product* of alienated labour, and that on the other it is the *means* by which labour alienates itself, *the realization of this alienation*.'[9] The reversal of the relation between labour and capital is all already here, in the form of a seed; already here we can grasp all the possibilities that it offers of a revolutionary methodological approach,

---

7 Ibid., 221.
8 Ibid., 241.
9 Ibid., 279.

which throws open the door to immediately subversive solutions, simultaneously both at the level of theoretical research and the level of practical struggle. We will show that this is the red thread running through all of Marx's work. Yet already at this point we can observe that in this present work this discovery has not gone further than a brilliant intuition, still subject to the uncertainties of an objective path through the history of capital. And the path it is taking is slower and more complex, more indirect and unsure than the one that Marx's working-class point of view was able to consider. This strategic reversal of the relationship between labour and capital today needs to be wholly rediscovered; it needs to be expounded anew, and in full, as a method of analysis and as a guide to action. Even a minimal tactical grasp on the present situation makes the truth of this principle visible to the naked eye. The culmination point of capital's development in fact again reveals its secret, and emphatically so.

'The *subjective essence* of private property – *private property* as activity for itself, as *subject,* as *person* – is *labour.*' It was political economy that first acknowledged labour as its principle: 'it thus revealed itself to be a product of private property and modern industry. Those who fetishised the mercantilist monetary system only knew of an objective essence of wealth. The Physiocratic doctrine represented a decisive phase in the discovery of a subjective existence of wealth in labour, but this was more a question of a concrete, particular labour, linked to a determinate natural element serving as its material. Starting with Adam Smith, political economy recognised the general essence of wealth, and was then led to 'the raising up of *labour* in its total absoluteness (i.e., its abstraction) as the *principle.*' 'It is argued against physiocracy that *agriculture,* from the economic point of view – that is to say, from the only valid point of view – does not differ from any other industry; and that the *essence* of wealth, therefore, is not a specific form of labour bound to a particular element – a particular expression of labour – but *labour in general* [*Arbeit uberhaupt*].'[10] In the process of scientific understanding of the subjective essence of private property, labour initially appeared only as agricultural labour, and then made itself recognised as a general labour. At this point, 'All wealth has become industrial wealth, the wealth of labour; and industry is accomplished labour, just as the factory

---

10   Ibid., 292–3.

system is the perfected essence of industry, that is of labour, and just as industrial capital is the accomplished objective form of private property.'[11]

In the *Arbeiterslohn* manuscript, dated Brussels, December 1847, we read right at the beginning: '*die menschliche Tätigkeit = Ware*' ('Human activity = commodity'). Further on we read: 'The worker [*der arbeiter*: the labourer, not labour] becomes an increasingly one-sided productive force [*Produktivkraft*] which produces as much as possible in as little time as possible. Skilled labour increasingly transformed into simple labour.'[12] So here already we have the general human activity of the worker reduced to a commodity, the most complex labour reduced to the simplest. At the end of the manuscript we moreover find a paragraph put in parentheses by Marx, indicating that he wants to consider the problem 'in general form' 'since labour has become a commodity and as such subject to free competition, one seeks to produce it as cheaply as possible, i.e., at the lowest possible production cost. All physical labour has thereby become infinitely easy and simple for the future organisation of society.'[13] Thus already here we have the theme of social labour, even if its particular content remains in doubt, not yet having been well-defined.

This manuscript, *Wages*, provides a trace of the lectures that Marx gave to the German Workers' Association in Brussels in 1847. It develops some points which he would not take up any further even in the famous *Neue Rheinische Zeitung* articles on 'Wage Labour and Capital' from April 1849. If we treat the 1847 manuscript in the same way that Engels did these 1849 articles – that is, substituting the word *Arbeitskraft* for *Arbeit* every time that we are dealing with abstract labour, which is to say everywhere – this has a notable practical result. That is to say, the concept of labour-power (and the word itself) appears in the works of Marx not only before *Capital*, but also before the *Manifesto*, and as a specific discovery of his, dating back – as we see it – to that first and still-insufficient critique of political economy that appeared in the *1844 Manuscripts*. The worker 'does not sell labour ... but puts his labour power at the disposal of the capitalist for a definite time ... in

---

11 Ibid., 292.
12 MECW, Vol. 6, 415, 422.
13 Ibid., 436.

return for a definite payment: he hires out, or sells, his labour power. But this labour power is intergrown with his person and is inseparable from it. Its cost of production, therefore, coincides with his cost of production; what the economists called the cost of production of labour is really the cost of production of the worker and therewith of his labour power,'[14] says Engels in the 1891 introduction to 'Wage Labour and Capital'. Here lies the whole difference between labour and labour-power. In the concept of *labour-power* there is the figure of the worker, whereas this is not true of the concept of *labour*. And the figure of the worker, who, in selling her own 'labour sells herself as 'labour-power', appears (in her entirety) in the works of Marx, right from his youthful analyses of alienated labour. This is, indeed, the precondition for his whole discourse: in the conditions imposed by capital, the alienation of labour and the alienation of the worker are one and the same thing. Otherwise, we would have to conclude that this analysis does not concern capitalist society, but society in general; not the worker, but in general. Such is the error of those who try to find in the young Marx nothing more than old philosophy of totality. But the limit of Marx's pre-1848 works instead lies elsewhere. It lies in the still-insufficient definition of labour-power as a commodity – or rather, in the absence of an analysis of the *particular* characteristics of this commodity and of the consideration of labour-power as an 'entirely special' commodity. Already in the Marx of before 1848 we find abstract labour as labour-power, and then labour-power as commodity. But it was only the revolutionary turning-point of 1848 that exposed, within Marx's own head, the theoretical process that would lead him to discover the *particular* content of the commodity labour-power. This commodity was linked no longer only – through the alienation of labour – to the historical figure of the worker, but to the birth of capital itself – through the production of surplus value. Near the beginning of 'Wage Labour and Capital', we find this enlightening statement: 'Now, after our readers have seen the class struggle develop in colossal political forms in 1848, the time has come to deal more closely with the economic relations themselves on which the existence of the bourgeoisie and its class rule, as well as the slavery of the workers, are founded.' We can say that only in 1848 – or rather after June 1848 – did the concept of labour-power

14   MECW, Vol 27, 199.

first encounter the movements of the working class in Marx's thought, thus giving rise to the truly Marxian history of the commodity labour-power. This latter reappeared better-defined in the *Contribution to the Critique of Political Economy* and later in *Capital*, now endowed with all its 'special characteristics' – that is, with all its specifically working-class content. In this sense, even though it had beaten the workers on the battlefield, the bourgeoisie of the time was right to lament 'Woe to June!'

Labour as abstract labour, and thus as *labour-power*, is present already in Hegel. Labour-power – and not only labour – as a *commodity*, is present already in Ricardo. As for the commodity labour-power as *working class*: this is Marx's discovery. The double character of labour is only the premise to this: it does not constitute the discovery, but only the means of reaching it. We arrive at the working class not from labour but from labour-power. To speak no longer of labour, but of labour-power, is to speak of the worker and no longer of labour. The terms *labour-power*, *living labour*, and *living worker*, are synonymous. The critique of the expression 'the value of labour' and the definition of the 'value of labour-power' allows an avenue to the concept of surplus-value. Pre-Marxist (and indeed, post-Marxian) socialist ideology never completed this path and thus never brought out the historical existence of the working class. And what, indeed, is this latter, at this level, if not the social labour-power that produces surplus-value? From surplus-value to profit, and from profit to capital – that is the path that it follows. The living commodity which is the socially organized worker thus proves to be not only the theoretical origin, but also the historical-practical precondition, that we can call the *fundamental articulation* of capitalist society (*Glied* and *Grund* at the same time).

But these are the conclusions of our discourse: we still need to demonstrate the premises. The search for the main sources of the concept of labour in Marx does not arise out of any scholastic need to philologically specify the terms of the problem. Rather, it stems from the practical need to identify Marx's *true* discoveries, to be able to recognise and develop them, as well as the tendentious choice to separate out, from the outset, everything that painfully comes to life on the terrain of working-class thought, precisely in order to use – for our own ends – parts of the adversary's thought. What Schumpeter called 'the impressive synthesis that is Marx's work' almost always has the following characteristic: it is not his own individual discovery that counts, but rather his integrated use of discoveries by others, and their collective reorganisation by reference to a single direction of thought, with the specific and unilateral orientation provided by this single point of view. The sectarianism of working-class science is all here. Marx provided a model, which he himself was not always capable of following in his analyses and conclusions. No Marxist after him did. The only decisive exception was Lenin and *his* revolution. In this case, the method of unilateral synthesis – the approach to comprehensively grasping a given social reality, starting from the deliberate choice of a tendency – had a practical result in concrete forms of political organization. This was the most important phase in the history of working-class thought since Marx. From that point, the bourgeois mystification of an *immediate* identification between the particular interests of a class and the general interest of society proved no longer tenable at either a theoretical or practical level. Control over society in general *is to be attained* by struggle, imposing the explicit domination of a specific class. On this terrain, two viewpoints of near-equal force and power collide. The universal reign of *ideology* crumbles. There is now only room for two antithetical class positions, each looking to impose, through dexterity and violence, its exclusive domination *over* society. Lenin imposed this on the capitalists of his time, in practice, by organising the revolution *prematurely*. Marx's own analysis of capitalist society was also 'premature' with respect to its era. That is why *Capital* and the *October Revolution* had the same historical destiny. It is easy to list the enormous historical and logical contradictions that made both of them 'impossible': but ultimately, the conclusion to be drawn is that all this does not even slightly put into doubt their validity. The truth is that each involved one same method applied at two different levels: that is, the theoretical and practical use of a web of material conditions (a series of concepts and circumstances) from a rigorously working-class point of view, in a process aimed at the subversion of capitalist society. Marx's treatment of the categories of political economy and the concepts of classical philosophy is the same treatment that Lenin reserved for the intermediate layers of the old society and the historic parties of the old Russian state. Marx powerfully discovered a *tactical moment* of research: the practical capacity to use certain results obtained by the science of the time, inverting them in the opposed dimension of a strategic alternative. Lenin – the only Marxist to have understood Marx on this point – directly translated this theoretical approach into *laws for action*. The Leninist discovery of tactics is only the extension, in the practical domain, of a theoretical discovery of Marx's: namely, the, conscious, realistic, and never ideological unilateralism of the working-class point of view on capitalist society. Our ambition is to demonstrate that 'all the value in labour' and 'all power to the soviets' are one and the same thing. They are two *watchwords* that encompass a tactical moment of struggle yet do not contradict any of its possible strategic developments. They are *two laws of movement* – not those of capitalist society (this may have been an error of Marx's, since here we risk losing the tactical moment), but those of the working class within capitalist society (and this is the Leninist correction of Marx).

For clarity's sake, a reference to Marx's sources, regarding the specific and decisive question of the definition of the concept of labour, is here essential. The Marx-Hegel relationship has long been studied, but almost nothing has been done on Marx's relationship to Ricardo. Most interesting would be to study the *Hegel/Ricardo* relation. If we had the time and the political calm to do so, we might consider mounting a detailed comparative analysis of Hegel's *Phenomenology* and Ricardo's *Principles*: we would find that the material dealt with is identical, as is the way of treating it (their method); the difference lies only in the 'form' with which it is treated, which oriented Hegel and Ricardo towards different disciplines, unable to communicate with one other. Here we shall limit ourselves to bringing out the Hegel/Ricardo relation, in its objective terms, by means of a separate although parallel analysis. As Marx put it: 'if the Englishman transforms men into hats, the German transforms hats into ideas. The Englishman is Ricardo, a rich banker and distinguished economist; the German is Hegel, an ordinary professor of philosophy at the University of Berlin.'[15]

---

15 MECW, Vol. 6, 161.

1

Hegel and Ricardo

Let's take the chapter from Hegel's *Phenomenology* on the independence and dependency of self-consciousness, on master and slave. Self-consciousness has escaped itself; for this reason, it turns into another self-consciousness. But it is not immediately seen as a different essence: in the other, we first of all see ourselves. The duplication of self-consciousness, in its unity, presents us with 'the movement of recognition': a double movement of both self-consciousnesses. 'Each sees the other do the same as he does; each himself does what he demands of the other and for that reason also does what he does only insofar as the other does the same. A one-sided doing [*einseitige Tun*] would be useless because what is supposed to happen can only be brought about through both of them bringing it about.'[1] So, only through the way in which the process of mutual recognition appears to the self-consciousness will the aspect of inequality and thus of opposition present itself. The exhibition of itself as the pure abstraction of self-consciousness consists in showing itself to be the pure negation of its objective mode. 'This display is the doubled act [*gedoppelte Tun*] namely, both what the other does and what is done through oneself.'[2] The relationship of both self-consciousnesses is thus constituted in such a way that they offer proof of one another, by

---

1 G. W. F. Hegel, *The Phenomenology of Spirit*, Cambridge: Cambridge University Press, 2018, 109.
2 Ibid., 111.

way of the struggle for life and death. 'And it is solely by staking one's life that freedom is proven to be the essence.'[3] But this test, by way of death, risks concluding in a natural negation of consciousness itself, a negation without any independence of its own; 'negation without self-sufficiency, which thus endures without the significance of the recognition which was demanded'.[4] The two moments recognise each other anew as essential; precisely because they are unequal and opposed, they are like two opposed figures of consciousness. 'One is self-sufficient; for it, its essence is being-for-itself. The other is non-self-sufficient; for it, life, or being for an other, is the essence. The former is the *master*, the latter is the *servant*.'[5] The master enters into relation with two moments: to the thing, to the object, to the appetite, and also to consciousness, whose thinghood is essential. But not only that: the master 'relates himself to the servant mediately through self-sufficient being'.[6] This is precisely how he is attached to the servant: 'it is his chain, the one he could not ignore in the struggle, and for that reason he proved himself to be non-self-sufficient and to have his self-sufficiency in the shape of thinghood'.[7] And 'the master likewise relates himself to the thing mediately through the servant'.[8] For the servant to negate the individual thing does not amount to destroying it: 'the servant only *processes* [*bearbeitet*] it'.[9] The lord, conversely, does not go beyond a pure negation: he tends to be satisfied by his enjoyment of the thing, until he has exhausted it. For this reason, the master is forced to introduce the servant in between the thing and himself; he thus obtains the dependency of the thing and pure enjoyment of it. But 'he leaves the aspect of its self-sufficiency in the care of the servant, who works [again, *bearbeitet*] on the thing'. For the master, 'it is in these two moments that his recognition comes about through another consciousness'. Conversely, in his own recognition, the master cannot do toward himself what he does toward the other; whereas what the servant does with regard to himself, he also is supposed to do with regard to the other. 'As a result, a form of recognition has arisen that is

---

3 Ibid.
4 Ibid., 112.
5 Ibid., 112–13.
6 Ibid., 113.
7 Ibid.
8 Ibid.
9 Ibid.

one-sided and unequal'.[10] Where the master has found completeness, this has become to him the dependency of his own consciousness. 'The truth of the self-sufficient consciousness is thus the servile consciousness.' And 'in its consummation' servitude will 'become … the opposite of what it immediately is. As a consciousness forced back into itself, it will take the inward turn and convert itself into true self-sufficiency'.[11] The conditions are all in place for what the servant does to become 'mastery' proper. But if servitude is a self-consciousness that arrives at self-sufficiency, it is thus possible and necessary to consider what it is in itself and for itself. First of all, for servitude, the essence is the master: for servitude, the truth is the self-sufficient consciousness, which is for itself and thus no longer in servitude. And yet already in this phase, servitude 'has this truth of pure negativity and of being-for-itself in fact in servitude in its own self, for servitude has experienced this essence in servitude'.[12] This absolute negativity is not, therefore, only a pure and universal movement in general: in his service he effectively accomplishes it: 'In his service, he sublates all of the singular moments of his attachment to natural existence, and he works off his natural existence [*und arbeitet dasselbe hinweg*]'.[13] It is thus through labour that the servile consciousness arrives at itself. In the consciousness of the lord, the pure negation of the object seemed reserved to the appetite. But this satisfaction merely disguises matters: both the objective aspect and the essence are missing. 'In contrast, work is desire held in check, it is vanishing staved off, or: work cultivates and educates [*bildet*]. The negative relation to the object becomes the form of the object; it becomes something that endures because it is just for the laborer himself [*eben dem Arbeitenden*] that the object has self-sufficiency. This negative mediating middle, this formative doing, is at the same time singularity, or the pure being-for-itself of consciousness, which in the work external to it now enters into the element of lasting. Thus, by those means, the working consciousness [*arbeitende Bewusstsein*] comes to an intuition of self-sufficient being as its own self'.[14] Nonetheless, the formation of this consciousness has not only this positive meaning, but also a negative

---

10 Ibid., 114.
11 Ibid.
12 Ibid.
13 Ibid., 115.
14 Ibid.

one faced with its first moment, the fear of the master, which is always 'the beginning of knowledge' for the servant. This objective negative, this alien essence before which the servant's consciousness trembled, is now destroyed. The consciousness of the servant 'posits himself as such a negative within the element of continuance. He thereby becomes for himself an existing- being-for-itself'.[15] Given the fact that it is externalised, the form does not become another consciousness apart from a servile consciousness: precisely the form is its pure being-for-itself that here becomes truth. 'Therefore, through this retrieval, he comes to acquire through himself a mind of his own [*eigner Sinn*], and he does this precisely in the work [*in der Arbeit*] in which there had seemed to be only some outsider's mind [*fremder Sinn*].'[16] And when we are reading this famous text of Hegel's properly, and also keep an eye on the purposes of our research, we must also keep in mind one of Marx's observations, albeit also adapting it, when he said that 'Hegel should not be criticised for describing the essence of the modern state as is, but because he passes off what is as the essence of the state'. Let's open up Ricardo's *Principles* at Chapter Twenty:[17] 'an examination of the difference between use-value and exchange-value, i.e. a supplement to the first chapter "on value"' as Marx defined it. It begins "A man is rich or poor"', says Adam Smith, 'according to the degree in which he can afford to enjoy the necessaries, conveniences, and amusements of human life.'[18] Ricardo comments: 'Value, then, essentially differs from riches, for value depends not on abundance, but on the difficulty or facility of production. The labour of a million men in manufacturing will always produce the same value, but will not always produce the same riches'. The invention of machines, progress in individuals' abilities, the better division of labour, and the discovery of new markets can lead to the doubling or tripling of the existing wealth, without thereby increasing its value. The value of each thing in fact increases or decreases on the basis of the greater ease or difficulty of production, in other words on the basis of the quantity of labour employed to produce it. 'Many of the errors in political economy have arisen from errors on this subject, from

---

15 Ibid., 116.

16 Ibid.

17 David Ricardo, 'Value and Riches, Their Distinctive Properties', in *On The Principles of Political Economy and Taxation*, available at marxists.org.

18 Ibid.

considering an increase in riches, and an increase in value, as meaning the same thing'. A long discussion has developed on what constitutes a typical measure of value, without this discussion ever arriving at sure conclusions. It would be necessary to find some invariable community, whose production at any given time requires the provision of the same sacrifice in toil and labour. 'Of such a commodity we have no knowledge, but we may hypothetically argue and speak about it as if we had'. One thing is for sure: 'But supposing either of these to be a correct standard of value, still it would not be a standard of riches, for riches do not depend on value'. The confusion of the idea of value with the idea of wealth has led to the assertion that wealth can be increased even where the quantity of commodities falls. This would indeed be correct if value were a measure of wealth, given that scarcity increases the value of commodities. But if Adam Smith is right and wealth consists of necessary or pleasurable things, then it cannot increase on account of a fall in quantity. From this, we can conclude that the wealth of a nation can be increased in two ways: 'it may be increased by employing a greater portion of revenue in the maintenance of productive labour ... [or] without employing any additional quantity of labour, by making the same quantity more productive'.[19] In the first case, the nation becomes wealthier and, at the same time, the value of its wealth increases; in the second case, given that more is produced with the same quantity of labour, wealth increases but value does not. Mr Say, for example, is considered synonymous with not only the terms *value* and *wealth* but also riches and *utility*. Thus a quantity of wealth, utility or use-value is easily exchanged for what is, instead, a quantity of value. Following this path, he comes to evaluate the value of a commodity on the basis of the quantity of other commodities that can be obtained in exchange for it. Yet, before then, a 'very distinguished writer', Mr Destutt de Tracy, had said 'To measure any one thing is to compare it with a determinate quantity of that same thing which we take for a standard of comparison, for unity'. The measure of the value of a thing is precisely the thing that needs measuring: they need to be able to be referred to some other measure commensurate with both. 'This, I think, they can be, for they are both the result of labour and, therefore, labour is a common measure, by which their real as well as their relative value may be estimated.

---

19 Ibid.

This also, I am happy to say, appears to be M. Destutt de Tracy's opinion.' He adds: 'He says, "as it is certain that our physical and moral faculties are alone our original riches, the employment of those faculties, labour of some kind, is our only original treasure, and that it is always from this employment, that all those things are created which we call riches, those which are the most necessary, as well as those which are the most purely agreeable. It is certain too, that all those things only represent the labour which has created them, and if they have a value, or even two distinct values, they can only derive them from that of the labour from which they emanate."' Ricardo did not cite what comes next in Destutt de Tracy's exposition: 'Wealth consists of possessing means for satisfying one's desires ... We call these means goods, because they do us good. They are all the product and representation of a certain quantity of labour.'[20] Say ascribes to Smith the error of having attributed the power to produce value to man's labour alone and of thus forgetting the value attributed to commodities by natural agents, which sometimes substitute for human labour and sometimes combine with it in the production process. In reality, it was Say himself who had forgotten that while these natural agents do increase the use-value of a commodity they do not, of course, increase its exchange-value. 'M. Say constantly overlooks the essential difference that there is between value in use, and value in exchange.'[21] 'M. Say accuses Dr Smith of having overlooked the value which is given to commodities by natural agents, and by machinery, because he considered that the value of all things was derived from the labour of man; but it does not appear to me that this charge is made out; for Adam Smith nowhere undervalues the services which these natural agents and machinery perform for us, but he very justly distinguishes the nature of the value which they add to commodities – they are serviceable to us, by increasing the abundance of productions, by making men richer, by adding to value in use; but as they perform their work gratuitously, as nothing is paid for the use of air, of heat, and of water, the assistance which they afford us adds nothing to value in exchange.'[22] David Ricardo, Marx tells us, 'unlike Adam Smith, neatly

20 Destutt de Tracy, *Élements d'idéologie; tome quatrieme, Traité de la volonté et de ses effets*, Paris, 1815, 103.
21 Ricardo, 'Value and Riches, Their Distinctive Properties'.
22 Ibid.

sets forth the determination of the value of commodities by labour time, and demonstrates that this law governs even those bourgeois relations of production which apparently contradict it most decisively.'[23] So value and wealth are not the same thing. But are the two things opposed? If wealth can be reduced to use-value and value to exchange-value, between value and wealth there is the same opposition combined with constant co-presence that exists between exchange-value and use-values. It is true, Marx observed in one of his interpretations of this chapter of the Principles, that 'With the pure and simple conceptual distinction between value and wealth, Ricardo does not remove the difficulty. Bourgeois wealth and the scope of all bourgeois production is not enjoyment but exchange-value. To increase this exchange-value … there is no means other than to multiply the products, to produce more. To achieve this greater production it is necessary to multiply the productive forces. But in the same proportion as the productive force is increased by a given quantity of labour – a given sum of capital and labour – the exchange value of products reduces, and the doubled production has the same value as half did before … The scope of bourgeois production is not to produce more commodities, but more value.'[24] And thus the aim of bourgeois production is not wealth, but value. But, Marx adds: without wealth there is no value; without use-value, no exchange-value arises. The aim of bourgeois production is not the mass of necessary object-commodities that are useful and pleasurable in life, but the mass of values that are realised within them; it is not the quantity-quality of products, but the quantity of their qualitative content. And yet without the mass of commodities, there is no mass of values: without the quantitative vest, the product, the quality that it contains would have no form. Capitalist production does not eliminate wealth, but makes it serve value: it casts it aside as an end while maintaining it as a means. Wealth – as use-value – becomes the phenomenal form of what is opposed to it – that is, value. The reduction of wealth to a crude instrument of value production is, indeed, the condition of capital. When in the same section cited above Ricardo said that 'capital is the part of the nation's wealth employed in view of future production', Marx

---

23   Marx and Engels Collected Works (MECW), Vol. 29, 300.

24   Karl Marx, *Notizen und Auszüge über Ricardos System*, March–April 1851, Appendix to the Grundrisse, Berlin 1953, 804.

rightly continued 'Here Ricardo confuse capital with the material of capital. Wealth is only the material of capital. Capital is always a sum of values.'[25] The equation, therefore, is not between wealth and capital but between capital and value. The distinction between value and wealth is the distinction between capital and wealth. When wealth – which is to say, everything necessary, useful or pleasurable to human life – becomes the matter of a social production relation, there then springs into action the mechanism of capitalist production proper – and from here stems the construction process of a society of capital. Can we say that at this point (all) the other fundamental conditions have been realised? If capital is a sum of values, is it not also a sum of labour? From labour to value and from value to capital we pass by way of the use of wealth as the material of production. On the other hand, wealth is already in this phase a freeing-up of labour, the creation of a disposable reserve of labour. And here, naturally, we are always speaking of labour-power, like more or less everyone speaks about it. Have we not seen even Destutt de Tracy speak of '[the employment of] our physical and moral faculties ... labour of some kind'? And what is *travail quelconque* if not *Arbeit über-haupt*? Too often, 'so-called primary accumulation' is confused with the general process of capitalist accumulation, as if they were one and the same. But the process through which value is separated from wealth is no different from the process by which the worker is separated from property over the conditions of labour, the producer from the means of production, and labour – as labour-power and thus as the worker – from capital. Except that these latter separation processes do not have to be taken as 'processes of capital'. Marx himself called them the 'prehistory of capital'. But even this definition is a perilous one: in Marx's work (and beyond), too many prehistorical characters remain attached to the true and proper history of capital. It is necessary to free it of them with the coolest critical courage, by combining a historical labour that reconstructs the processes and a theoretical labour that systematises the concepts anew. 'In themselves, money and commodities are no more capital than the means of production and of subsistence are. They need to be transformed into capital.'[26] For this transformation into capital to be possible it is necessary: 1) that labour has already emancipated itself

25 Ibid., 805.
26 *Capital*, Vol. 1, 874.

from servitude; 2) that value has already subjected wealth to itself. Necessary, then, is the free worker, and also wealth – which, through accumulation, becomes money, means of production and means of subsistence – subjected to the valorisation process, which is to say, compelled to purchase labour-power (or better, compelled to pay for labour-power). The whole movement thus returns to the side of labour – or, rather, to the moment that labour achieves freedom, emancipation and independence, as labour-power and thus as the worker; a moment which can be isolated in the true and proper historical passage from labour to labour-power, from labour as servitude and service to labour-power as the only commodity able to subject wealth to value, able to valorise wealth and thus to produce capital. Here is the key that opens up the mechanism of capitalist production. Had Hegel said anything differently, in his own language, when he said that: 'the master is forced to introduce the servant in between the thing and himself'? He thus leaves the whole question of the thing's independence up to the slave who expresses it. It was Marx who said that 'Hegel's standpoint is that of modern political economy'.[27] He grasped the essence of labour and conceived of labour as the essence of man; he thus only saw the positive side of labour and not the negative one: 'The only labour which Hegel knows and recognises is abstractly mental labour'.[28] Löwith is wrong when he says, in this regard: 'for Marx, labour is "abstract" no longer in the Hegelian sense of a positive universality of the spirit, but in the negative sense of an abstraction from the totality of concrete man, which he wishes to actuate with labour in its integrity'. This is not right, if – Löwith himself says lower down in a note – 'this unilateral transformation of the dialectical negation into a simple annihilation characterised the radical attitude of all Left-Hegelians'. What Marx criticises in Hegel is not abstract labour, but the spiritual, logical, speculative character of this abstraction of labour. Here, too, the movement of history describes humanity's real history, but in the form of a dialectic of abstract thought. At no point in Hegel does the concept of abstract labour go beyond this empirical abstractness: from the Jena *Realphilosophie* to the *Phenomenology* and the *Philosophy of Right*, we are always and only dealing with the real development of the abstract form. 'The I's being for

27 MECW, Vol. 3, 333.
28 Ibid.

itself is something abstract; rather, it labours, but its labour is something
likewise abstract [*ein ebenso Abstraktes*]: Universal labour and the division of labour are the same thing. Our working activity becomes ever
more mechanical and tends to belong to a single determination. But 'the
more [labour] becomes abstract, the more [man] becomes pure abstract
activity'. 'Since this labour is this abstract labour, he thus behaves
abstractly, according to the mode of thinghood, not as the comprehensive, perspicuous spirit rich in content that dominates a large domain
and is master of it. Here, there is not concrete labour, but rather his force
[*Kraft*] consists of analysing, abstracting, breaking down [*Zerlegung*] the
concrete into many abstract parts.'[29] In the preface to the *Phenomenology*
he would say that 'in modern times, the individual finds the abstract
form ready-made.'[30] But already earlier he had spoken of the multiple
works of needs, and of things that must themselves, too, realise their
concept, their abstraction. 'Need and labour are thus elevated into
universality and construct themselves an immense system of commonality and mutual dependence. A life of the dead that moves itself within
itself [*ein sich in sich bewegendes Leben des Toten*]', which in its motion
blindly ebbs and flows like the elements [*blind und elementarisch*], and
like a fierce beast needs to be constantly harnessed and tamed.[31] This
need, which is found in the universal interpenetration of the dependence of all, is now, for each person, the general and permanent wealth.
'The possibility of sharing in the general wealth [*Vermögen*] … presupposes skill, health, capital, and so forth as its conditions.'[32] Elsewhere he
had said: the first essence is the power of the state, the other is wealth:
'Whether wealth is the passive or the null, it is in any case a universal
spiritual essence; it is the result which is continuously coming to be,
just as it is the work and the doings of all, as it again dissolves within
everyone's consumption of it.'[33] Again, labour and wealth, positive and
negative, appear in that mechanism of commonality and reciprocal

---

29 *Jenenser Realphilosophie, II, Die Vorlesungen von 1805–1806*, Sämtliche Werke,
XX, Leipzig 1931, 214–15.

30 Hegel, *Phenomenology of Spirit*, 21.

31 *Jenenser Realphilosophie, I, Die Vorlesungen von 1803–1804*, Sämtliche Werke,
XIX, Leipzig 1932, 239.

32 G. W. F. Hegel, *Outlines of the Philosophy of Right*, translated by T. M. Knox, New
York: Oxford University Press, 2008, para 237.

33 Hegel, *Phenomenology of Spirit*, 288.

dependence that is the 'system of needs'. What is missing is value, the mediation of value, and its link with labour emancipated from wealth. In Hegel, the passage from labour to value to capital stops at a correct concept of labour. He aptly starts out from labour as labour-power but does not arrive at value. If abstract labour does not meet concretely with the worker, nor does it meet with the relative abstraction of value. Capital is thus reduced, in banal fashion, to a particular wealth and labour itself to the mechanical ability of those who work. Indeed, the subject of the first chapter of the *Principles* is precisely 'On Value'. Hegel without Ricardo would not have allowed Marx to pass from labour to capital by way of the valorisation of value. 'But at last Ricardo steps in and calls to science: Halt! The basis, the starting-point for the physiology of the bourgeois system – for the understanding of its internal organic coherence and life process – is the determination of value by labour time'.[34] 'If men employed no machinery in production but labour only, and were all the same length of time before they brought their commodities to market, the exchangeable value of their goods would be precisely in proportion to the quantity of labour employed'.[35] Again: given fixed capitals of the same value and duration, the value of the commodities produced would vary only with the variation of the quantity of labour employed to produce them. Any progress in machinery, tools, manufactured goods and the extraction of raw materials allows for labour-saving; it allows for the easier production of the commodity to which the improvement is applied. 'In estimating, then, the causes of the variations in the value of commodities, although it would be wrong wholly to omit the consideration of the effect produced by a rise or fall of labour, it would be equally incorrect to attach much importance to it; and consequently, in the subsequent part of this work, though I shall occasionally refer to this cause of variation, I shall consider all the great variations which take place in the relative value of commodities to be produced by the greater or less quantity of labour which may be required from time to time to produce them'.[36] On this point, we have taken the most cautious of Ricardo's definitions in this regard, namely the one from the third edition of the *Principles* and not from the first, in the

---

34 MECW, Vol. 31, 392.
35 Ricardo, *Principles*, 32.
36 Ibid, 36–7.

context of the fourth section of the first chapter, which sees the employment of fixed capital intervene to modify the labour principle of value
'considerably'. Marx got to the bottom of this discussion in Volume 2 of
Capital. 'Ricardo', Marx tells us, 'constantly confuses the ratio between
variable and constant capital with the ratio between circulating and
fixed capital. We shall see later on how this vitiates his investigation of
the rate of profit.'[37] The real material of the capital paid out in wages is
labour itself, the labour-power entering into action that creates values,
and the living labour that the capitalist has exchanged against objectified dead labour and which he has incorporated in his capital; for this
reason, only the value found in his hands has transformed into a self-
valorising value. But 'the capitalist does not sell this power of self-valor-
ization. It forms throughout simply a component of his productive capital, just like his means of labour, and is never a component of his
commodity capital, like the finished product that he sells, for instance.'[38]
Within the production process, the means of labour *qua* constitutive
parts of productive capital do not stand in relation to labour-power as
does fixed capital; just as the material of labour, *qua* circulating capital,
does not coincide with labour-power. From the viewpoint of the labouring process, labour-power stands counterposed to the means of labour
and the material of labour, as a personal factor [*persönlicher Faktor*] to
objective factors [*sachlichen Faktoren*]. From the viewpoint of the valorisation process, these same objective factors stand counterposed, as
constant capital, to the subject labour-power, as does variable capital.
'Alternatively, if we are to speak of a material difference that affects the
circulation process, this is simply that it follows from the nature of value,
which is nothing other than objectified labour, and from the nature of
self-acting labour-power, which is nothing other than self-objectifying
labour, that labour-power continually creates value and surplus-value so
long as it continues to function; that what presents itself on its side as
movement, as the creation of value, presents itself on the side of its
product in a motionless form, as created value.'[39] Myrdal asked himself
why Ricardo and the other classics after him decided to see the real
value of a commodity in the labour embodied in it – the metre of value

---

37 *Capital*, Vol. 2, 304.
38 Ibid., 299.
39 Ibid., 299–300.

thus being a commodity that always contains the same quantity of labour. For Myrdal Ricardo gave no satisfactory response to this question. He ought to have looked in Marx for the answer he did not find in Ricardo. The response to this question – why labour? – would have resolved in the simplest of ways a curious problem of his, namely: 'for the historian of thought the real puzzle is why the classics did not draw' the same "radical conclusions" that the socialists did.'[40] These were not the last of Ricardo's uncertainties on this problem. On 13 June 1820, he wrote to McCulloch: 'I sometimes think that if I were to write the chapter on value again which is in my book, I should acknowledge that the relative value of commodities was regulated by two causes instead of by one, namely, by the relative quantity of labour necessary to produce the commodities in question, and by the rate of profit for the time that the capital remained dormant, and until the commodities were brought to market.'[41] But Ricardo, Marx tells us, never distinguished between surplus-value and profit, just as he never distinguished between variable and constant capital. Thus, he did not arrive at a correct conception of capital; instead, he reduced it to accumulated labour, to something simply objective, to a simple element of the labouring process, from which the relationship between labour and capital, between wages and profit, could not be further developed. The same letter continued, 'Perhaps I should find the difficulties nearly as great in this view of the subject as in that which I have adopted. After all, the great questions of Rent, Wages, and Profits must be explained by the proportions in which the whole produce is divided between landlords, capitalists, and labourers, and which are not essentially connected with the doctrine of value.'[42] Ricardo makes a bold attempt to try to separate the theory of value from the theory of distribution, which makes him move decisively toward conceptualising value as a cost of production. His starting point, value, was right. In the passage from labour to value to capital, though, Ricardo starts out from value but does not arrive at either labour or capital. For Marx, 'instead of labour, Ricardo should have discussed labour capacity. But had he done so, capital would also have been revealed as the

---

40 Gunnar Myrdal, *The Political Element in the Development of Economic Theory*, London: Routledge, 2017.

41 David Ricardo, *Works and Correspondence*, Vol. 8, Letters 1819–June 1821, Cambridge: Cambridge University Press, 1952, 194.

42 Ibid.

material conditions of labour, confronting the labourer as power that had acquired an independent existence. And capital would at once have been revealed as a definite social relationship.'[43] So he lacks a correct conception of labour, as labour-power, as abstract labour. Ricardo without Hegel would not have allowed Marx himself to pass from value to capital by way of production and the reproduction of labour-power.

---

43   MECW, Vol. 32, 36–7.

2

The Exchange of Money for Labour

Let's call labour-power L, money M and the means of production MP. The sum of commodities C becomes L + MP and, more succinctly, C^L_{MP}. Considered according to its content, M – C thus appears as M – C^L_{MP}. That is, M – C subdivides into M – L and M – MP. 'The sum of money M is separated into two parts, one of which buys labour-power, the other the means of production. These two series of purchases belong to entirely different markets, the one to the commodity-market proper, the other to the labour-market'.[1] When M – CMP is completed, the buyer not only disposes of the means of production plus labour-power; he also possesses a greater availability of labour-power – that is to say, a quantity of labour bigger than that necessary to substitute for the value of the labour-power; and, simultaneously, he disposes of the means of production required for the realisation and objectification of this sum of labour. The value antici-pated in the form of money is thus now found in a natural form, in which it can be realised as a value that produces surplus-value. Money capital (M) has transformed into productive capital (P). The value of P = the value of L + MP = M converted into L and MP. Thus 'M – L is the charac-teristic moment in the transformation of money-capital into productive capital, because it is the essential condition for the real transformation of value advanced in the form of money into capital, into a value that produces surplus-value. M – MP is necessary only for the purpose of

---

1 Karl Marx, *Capital*, Vol. 2, translated by David Fernbach, London: Penguin, 1978, 1.

realising the quantity of labour bought in the process M – L.' From the capitalist's point of view, labour-power appears on the market just like any other commodity, possessed by no matter whom; its sale and purchase ('the sale and purchase of human activity' [*Kauf und Verkauf von menschlicher Tätigkeit*]) represents nothing more out of the ordinary than the sale and purchase of any other commodity. From the worker's point of view, the productive application of their labour-power becomes possible only after it is sold, when it is set in mutual connection with the means of production. For each of them, 'before its sale, labour-power exists therefore separately from the means of production, from the material conditions of its application'. Before its sale – which is to say, before the formal act of exchange and outside of circulation – the elements of production are themselves divided and counterposed, with the objective factors concentrated on one site and working activity – in isolation from these factors – on the other. 'True, in the act M – L the owner of money and the owner of labour-power enter only into the relation of buyer and seller, confront one another only as money-owner and commodity-owner … Yet at the same time the buyer appears also from the outset in the capacity of an owner of means of production, which are the material conditions for the productive expenditure of labour-power by its owner. In other words, these means of production are in opposition to the owner of the labour-power, being property of another. On the other hand, the seller of labour faces its buyer as labour-power of another, which must be made to do his bidding and must be integrated into his capital, in order that it may really become productive capital. The class relation between capitalist and wage-labourer therefore exists, is presupposed from the moment the two face each other in the act M – L (L – M on the part of the labourer)'.[2] It is only when this class relation already exists that circulation is necessarily interrupted. Capital value, in the form of productive capital, cannot continue to circulate; it must pass into consumption, and more specifically into productive consumption: 'The use of labour-power, labour, can be materialised only in the labour-process'. The capitalist cannot resell the worker as a commodity, for the latter is not his slave: he has only purchased the use of her labour-power for a determinate time. On the other hand, he can use labour-power only by making the worker use the means of production to create commodities. Thus, 'Whereas labour-power is a commodity

---

2 *Capital*, Vol. 2, 22–30.

only in the hands of its seller, the wage-labourer, it becomes capital only in the hands of its buyer, the capitalist, who acquires the temporary use of it. The means of production do not become the material forms of productive capital, or productive capital, until labour-power, the personal form of existence [*persönliche Daseinsform desselben*] of productive capital, is capable of being embodied in them. Human labour-power is by nature no more capital than by means of production. They acquire this specific social character only under definite, historically developed conditions, just as only under such conditions the character of money is stamped upon precious metals, or that of money-capital upon money'. It is for this reason that capitalist production concerns itself not only with producing commodities and surplus-value, but so too with reproducing the class of waged workers in ever-greater numbers, transforming the huge majority of direct producers into wage-labourers. M – C ... P ... C' – M', the total circuit of the first stage of capital, has as the first presupposition of its development the 'existence of a class of wage-labourers on a social scale'. Money capital (*Geldkapital*) – productive capital (*produktives Kapital*) – commodity capital (*Warenkapital*) are the three forms of the circuit: two stages of circulation on either end, and between them the intermediate stage of production: 'The form pertaining to the stage of production is that of productive capital. The capital which assumes these forms in the course of its total circuit and then discards them and in each of them performs the function corresponding to the particular form, is industrial capital [*industrielles Kapital*], industrial here in the sense it comprises every branch of industry run on a capitalist basis'. The other forms are not autonomous kinds of capital, but only successive, particular forms of the functions of industrial capital. This, in fact, is capital's only mode of existence in which the function of the appropriation of surplus-value accompanies the process of its creation. It is true, therefore, that only with industrial capital is 'the capitalist character of production ... a necessity'. But as we have seen, 'Its existence implies the class antagonism [*Klassengegensatz*] between capitalists and wage-labourers'. Indeed, if we return to the process of capital production, particularly its earliest historical forms – the process of the production of relative surplus-value – we immediately find the basic fact that 'capitalist production only then really begins, as we have already seen, when each individual capital employs simultaneously a comparatively large number of labourers ... A greater number of labourers working together, at the same time, in one place (or, if you will, in the same field of labour), in order to produce the same sort of commodity under the mastership of one capitalist constitutes, both historically and logically [*historisch und begrifflich*], the starting-point of capitalist production.[3] And 'this point coincides with the birth of capital itself'. Labour objectified in value is always labour at an average social quality, and thus always the explication of average labour-power. And yet the concept of average social labour implies the historical realisation of a total working day: 'Thus the laws of the production of value are only fully realised for the individual producer, when he produces as a capitalist, and employs a number of workmen together, whose labour, by its collective nature, is at once stamped as average social labour'. The specific productive power [*forza*] of the collective working day is greater than that of an equal number of single, individual working days: this is the 'social productive power of labour, or the productive power of social labour'. 'When the labourer co-operates systematically with others, he strips off the fetters of his individuality, and develops the capabilities of his species [*sein Gattungsvermögen*]'. At the outset, the command of capital over labour presents itself only as a formal consequence of the fact that instead of working for herself, the worker works for the capitalist, and thus under the capitalist. With the cooperation of many wage-labourers, the command of capital evolves in accordance with the requirements of the execution of the labour process itself, which is to say, the real conditions of production. On the one hand, the functions of direction, oversight [*sorveglianza*] and coordination become functions of capital. On the other, the directive function *qua* specific function of capital takes on special characteristic notes: 'As the number of the co-operating labourers increases, so too does their resistance to the domination of capital, and with it, the necessity for capital to overcome this resistance by counter-pressure. The control exercised by the capitalist is not only a special function, due to the nature of the social labour-process, and peculiar to that process, but it is, at the same time, a function of the exploitation of a social labour-process, and is consequently rooted in the unavoidable antagonism between the exploiter [*Ausbeuter*] and the living and labouring raw material [*Rohmaterial*] he exploits'. So long as she negotiates with the capitalist, the worker does so as the proprietor of her own labour-power. She sells what she possesses: her own individual, singular power to work. The capitalist concludes the

---

3 *Capital*, Vol. 1, Chapter 13.

same contract with other isolated workers: he thus pays the value of each autonomous labour-power but does not pay for the workers' combined labour-power. Thus, 'being independent of each other, the labourers are isolated persons [*Vereinzelte*], who enter into relations with the capitalist, but not with one another. This co-operation begins only with the labour-process, but they have then ceased to belong to themselves. On entering that process, they become incorporated with capital. As co-operators, as members of a working organism, they are but special modes of existence of capital. Hence, the productive power developed by the labourer when working in co-operation [*Arbeiter als gesellschaftlicher Arbeiter; come operaio sociale*] is the productive power of capital'. Thus a considerable number of workers – which is to say, the workers socially combined within one same production process under the same capitalist – become productive power for capital. The social productive power of labour does not exist outside of capital; this power is not elaborated by the worker before the worker's own labour belongs to the capitalist. It is an unpaid productive power. Marx says that it thus 'presents itself' (usually: *erscheint*) as a productive power that capital naturally possesses, as its immanent productive power. And this is not just how things seem. As a producer, the worker does not have autonomy from the conditions of capitalist production. She would never have begun to produce if she had not first of all produced capital. In the passage from individual labour-power to social labour-power, from the worker to the social worker, labour transfers into capital, becomes a social productive power for capital. When labour-power presents itself socialised in its productive functions, there has already been a production of capital. The production of capital alone renders possible the process of the productive socialisation of labour-power, the birth of the social worker as a historical figure, as a social productive power of labour – a power incorporated in capital. This is another – perhaps the greatest – of the examples of historical progress brought by capital. And yet, precisely within this 'progress', labour-power, which at first presented itself as a presupposition of capital, independent of and counterposed to capital, is subordinated to capital, becomes 'part' of it, and is made an object of social exploitation. What does Marx mean, then, when he speaks of a 'class relation' (*Klassenverhältnis*) already present in the moment in which capitalist and worker stand counterposed in the act of M – L, in the formal act of exchange between money and labour-power; when he speaks of the [constant] 'existence of the class of wage-labourers

[*Lohnarbeiterklasse*]' as the first presupposition for the unfolding of the circuit of money capital; and when he says that the existence of industrial capital implies the existence of the 'class antagonism [*Klassengegensatz*] between capitalists and wage-labourers'? He means precisely this: the historical figure in which the wage-labour appears for the first time before the capitalist is the figure of the seller of labour-power. Here, at the same time, is the first elementary form of antagonism between two classes, which already sees as counterposed the contracting parties in a necessary relationship between the possessors of opposed commodities. This is M – L, but, Marx tells us, L – M from the labourer's side. The wage-labourer's decisive characteristics, as far as the market is concerned, are already present at this stage: that is, labour-power purchased with money in the form of the wage. It is thanks to and through this form that this market transaction between money and labour-power is recognised as character- istic of the capitalist mode of production. Yet the truth – the content of this form – is that within the contract for the purchase of labour-power, what is in fact agreed is the provision of a quantity of labour greater than that necessary to compensate for the price of the labour-power, and thus to cover the total wage: therefore, a provision of surplus-value is already presupposed and arranged by contract. This provision of surplus-value is the fundamental condition for the capitalisation of the value anticipated for the production of surplus-value and thus of capital. It is true that when the worker takes on the auspices of an antagonistic figure, she first does so as the seller of labour-power; but it is also true that the figure of the producer of surplus-value is already presupposed within this antagonist. Is it this presupposition that makes the worker an antagonist, at the class level, on the labour market? Or is the class antagonism already there in the worker being forced to become a wage-labourer – that is, being forced to sell the only commodity that she possesses, her labour-power? Marx says 'The capital-relation during the process of production arises only [*kommt nur heraus*] because it is inherent in the act of circulation, in the different fundamental economic conditions in which buyer and seller confront each other, in their class relation. It is not money which by its nature creates this relation; it is rather the existence of this relation which permits of the transformation of a mere money-function into a capital-function'. Thus, for Marx, there is no doubt that the class relation already exists in itself (indeed, *an sich*) in the act of circulation. It is precisely this aspect that reveals the capitalist relation, makes it come out, during the production process. The class relation (*Klassenverhältnis*), therefore, precedes, brings into being and produces the capitalist relation (*Kapitalverhältnis*). Or, better: it is the existence of the class relation that makes the transformation of money into capital possible. This is rather an important point. For, in general, Marx is made to say exactly the opposite, and it is today commonly 'Marxist' to say the opposite: namely, that the counterposition, the antagonism comes only *from* the capitalist production relation, and this antagonism is, then, only a new type, compared to the old one, which has existed ever since human society was no longer a primitive community. Hence, it would be capital that made classes – or better, that transformed the old classes – into new counterposed agglomerates that are still equivalent to what they were before. So how can we instead say that the class relation precedes the capitalist relation? In the act of the sale – we repeat, an obligatory sale – of labour-power, can we see (and in what sense can we see) the already-complete class relation of a social relation that allows the production of capital? Do wage-labourers therefore first constitute themselves as a class precisely *as* sellers of labour-power? We think yes, on one condition: namely, that the concept of the working class is not fixed in a single and definitive form without development or history. With great strain, slowly and, in truth, without much success, the Marxist camp has acquired the idea of an internal history of capital such as would involve a specific analysis of the various determinations that capital assumes in the course of its development: this will, appropriately enough, lead to the goal of historical materialism, with its overstretched *Weltgeschichte*. But what is still far from being assumed as a programme of work – or, indeed, as a principle of our research method – is the idea of an internal history of the working class, such as would reconstruct the moments of its formation, the changes in its composition, the growth of its organisation, according to the various successive determinations that labour-power assumes *qua* power producing capital, according to the diverse, recurrent and ever-new experiences of struggle that the working-class mass chooses *qua* the only antagonist of capitalist society.

The sale of labour-power thus offers the first, elementary stage of a composition of wage-labourers into a class; a social mass obliged to sell labour-power is also the general form of the working class. This is the case in Marx's sense, when he says that there is capital in money as soon as – at some point, at least – money has already been transformed into capital; when he says that the circuit of money capital, the first stage in the total circulation of capital, is also the general form of the circuit of industrial capital, in which the capitalist mode of production is, however, presupposed; when he says that cooperation, the first elementary method of the production of relative surplus-value, is also the fundamental form of capitalist production, even if its simple figure presents itself as a particular form alongside other, more evolved forms, which are, besides, already presupposed in this more simple figure. The sale of labour-power presupposes the existence of labour-power, its existence as a commodity, and as a particular condition: three conditions which alone found the capitalist mode of production. And there's more. An act of sale of this nature is simultaneously both free and necessary. Free, because she who possesses the commodity is not juridically forced to sell it; necessary, because in effect she cannot *not* sell it, on pain of the extinction of her kind. We have seen that the sale of labour-power already means the unpaid provision of surplus-value and thus the production of surplus-value, and thus the reproduction of the capital relation. So, the principal secret of capitalist production does not lie in the generic human capacity to work, but, rather, in the specific labour-power of the wage-labourer, as in its reduction to a wholly particular community; not, therefore, in labour-power in itself, but in the exchange of labour-power for money – which is to say, in the passage of the ownership of the only power that produces capital in the hands of those who already possess money. But, then, the power that produces capital exists prior to and independently of the conditions of production that make it function as such, prior to and independently of money *qua* possessor of means of labour and the material of labour. It is the encounter with money, its being put on an equal footing with the means and material of labour – in a word, the reduction of labour-power itself to a condition of production – that incorporates it into capital and makes it part of it, as a living appendage of capital. On the working-class side of things, the historic passage sees first a seller of labour-power, then the individual productive power, and then the social productive power. In the individual labour-power, in its character as a particular commodity, the capacity to produce capital is already there. But only in capital, in its need to be a social production relation, is there the capacity to socialise labour-power. Labour-power has no possibility of autonomous socialisation independent of capital's needs. For this reason, once again, labour's social productive power presents itself as capital's productive power. It is precisely in the moment in which social labour-power enters into production and transforms the collective labouring process into a social process of valorisation, the very moment in which it essentially comes to coincide with a social mass of producers and thus touches on the natural confines of the 'working class', that it appears as nothing more than an internal part of capital, even in the antediluvian form of individual capital. The process through which labour-power is socialised within capitalist production does not begin or conclude the process of the working class's historical formation; rather, it is an essential intermediate moment of development in the organisation of class antagonism, which can be used in practice – depending on the relation of forces – by either the capitalists or the workers.

When the unpaid productive power of the social worker is added to the unpaid labour of the single worker, it advances a true and proper socialisation of capitalist exploitation. This is now the exploitation not of the worker, but of the working class; this in turn is the true and proper birth certificate of a capitalist society: a leap in the history of capital, which will, in the long term, lead it to overthrow the relations in its society and begin an inverse process of the socialisation of capital, up to its highest forms of social capital. And to speak of the exploitation not of the worker but of the working class means that the working class already exists. The transition, in the history of capital, to the capitalist society, implies the necessary existence of a class of capitalists. The process through which exploitation is socialised by way of capitalist production, which seems to mark the birth of the working class, in reality marks the birth of the opposed class, or the self-constitution of the opposed interest – that of the individual capitalists – as a class. Only by incorporating the social productive power of labour into each individual capital was it possible to make each individual capitalist into a conscious member of a social class of capitalists. But the social productive power of labour, of the particular commodity labour-power, was already, in its elementary and general form, the working class. Only by incorporating the working class into capital, only by making the working class part of capital (its living, mobile, variable part), was it possible to make the whole of capital (and not just the other dead, immobile, constant part) into a class counterposed to that of the workers. The process of the historical formation of a class of capitalists follows, copies, repeats the analogous process of the formation of the working class. Even to recognise this still raises scandal, and yet it is already banal. All the same, this is not everything, and it is not the fundamental thing. It is a methodological principle that ought to overturn the search for further perspective and instead guide the new strategy both from above and from afar. The fundamental thing is something else, for it comes even to imbue the everyday tactics of the class struggle: namely, that from the outset, from the early forms of this struggle, the workers as a class find themselves within capital and must fight it from within, whereas the class of capitalists is only counterposed to the workers and can strike it *en bloc* from without. This, which has been the working class's greatest point of weakness, should instead become the greatest sign of its power. The workers enter the capitalist's factory already as a class: only thus can their social productive power be exploited. Constrained – not by juridical laws but economic ones – to sell labour-power, which is to say, to sell themselves on the market as a commodity, they find themselves already individually united against the capitalist even before they begin to produce capital. On the other hand, the worker can function as an instrument of production only in association with other workers; the productive worker is a social labour-power; workers, like commodities, always appear in the plural; the single worker does not exist. We need only recall the historical concept from which capitalist production originated: a considerable number of workers, at the same time, in the same place, there for the production of the same kind of commodities, under the command of the same capitalist. Social labour-power, the particular commodity labour-power, begins to produce capital already *as* a working class. Labour's social productive power becomes a social productive power of capital, *as* a working class. Workers enter into capital, are reduced to a part of capital, *as* a working class. Capital now has its enemy within. This is how we prefer to interpret the meaning of Marx's opaque phrase that 'the true limit to capitalist production is capital itself'. A need of production becomes a threat to the system. Capitalists respond by attempting, with great strain, to compose their single, disparate interests into the single social interest of an antagonist class.

3
Critique of Ideology

But we are getting ahead of ourselves here. These are problems in Marx, in the advanced mature phase of his thought. We have to take the proper path to arrive at these conclusions. This path is itself important, because it wipes the slate of the old problems and poses the new ones. Let's turn, for example, to look at Marx coming to grips with the critique of ideology. And, we will say, a little arbitrarily, coming to grips with the critique of communism and socialism. Here, naturally, we are referring to his critique of pre-Marxist communism and socialism. But anyone can see that, after Marx, these "ideologies" did not much change. His 1844 manuscript on private property and communism does contain a critique of private property from the perspective of communism, but also, and together with this, contains a critique of communism from the perspective of private property. This last point has not been properly brought into relief. On the one hand, Marx tells us, there is labour, the subjective essence of private property, *qua* exclusion from property; on the other hand, there is capital, objective labour, *qua* exclusion from labour: together they make up 'private property as its developed state of contradiction – hence a dynamic relationship driving towards resolution'.[1] First, private property was considered only in terms of its objective aspect, but still also with labour as its subjective essence; it thus exists in the form of capital which, as such (*als solches*)

---

1 Marx and Engels Collected Works (MECW), Vol. 3, 294.

is to be suppressed; this is what Proudhon says. Or else a particular mode of labour – for instance, an agricultural labour, levelled-down, parcellised and unfree – is considered the cause of the harmful character of private property and its alienated existence from humanity; this is what Fourier says. Or industrial labour is considered the decisive thing, and this should lead to the exclusive predominance of industrialists and the improvement of the labourers' conditions; this is what Saint Simon says. And, finally, comes communism, which is 'the positive expression of annulled private property – at first as universal private property [*das allgemeine Privateigentum*]'.[2] Insofar as it embraces the relation of private property as a whole, it is 'in its first form only a generalisation [*Verallgemeinerung*] and consummation [*Vollendung*] of it [of this relation]'.[3] The domination of the property of things presents itself, at this point, as so vast as to be bent on cancelling out everything that cannot be possessed by all as private property: 'The category of the worker is not done away with, but extended to all men'; the relationship of private property remains the community's relationship to the world of things. 'The community is only a community of labour, and equality of wages paid out by communal capital – by the community as the universal capitalist. Both sides of the relationship are raised to an imagined universality – labour as the category in which every person is placed, and capital as the acknowledged universality and power of the community'.[4] This first positive suppression of private property, this 'crude communism ... is thus merely a manifestation of the vileness of private property, which wants to set itself up as the positive community system'.[5] Assuming historical forms counterposed to private property, communism seeks historical proof for itself, a proof in the existent, picking out single moments from the overall movement and pinning them down as proof of its own historical reality: 'By so doing it simply makes clear that by far the greater part of this process contradicts its own claim, and that, if it has ever existed, precisely its being in the past refutes its pretension to reality'. There were indeed good reasons why communism immediately coincided with atheism – just look at Owen.

---

2 Ibid.
3 Ibid.
4 Ibid., 295.
5 Ibid., 296.

It is true that atheist philanthropy is from the outset only an abstract philosophical philanthropy, while communism's philanthropy is from the outset real and immediately tends toward action. But there remained a substantial affinity between atheism and communism, in both method and content. In its attempt to affirm the essentiality of nature and of humanity, atheism is the negation of God; and it presents humanity's existence by way of this same negation. Socialism, as such, no longer needs this mediation: it 'proceeds from the theoretically and practically sensuous consciousness of man and of nature as the essence'.[6] It is humanity's positive consciousness of itself, no longer mediated by the suppression of religion; 'man's positive self-consciousness, no longer mediated through the abolition of religion, just as real life is man's positive reality, no longer mediated through the abolition of private property, through communism'.[7] For its part, 'Communism is the position as the negation of the negation, and is hence the actual phase necessary for the next stage of historical development in the process of human emancipation and rehabilitation. Communism is the necessary form and the dynamic principle of the immediate future, but communism as such is not the goal of human development, the form of human society'. Here, Marx seems to place communism in a subordinate position relative to socialism. He practically sets communism on the same footing as atheism: it is posed as a negation of the negation, rather than as an immediate positive affirmation. Communism is reduced to being a means, an instrument, a real and necessary moment for arriving at socialism: this is communism, then, as a negation of the present, as an instrument of struggle against the present, and not yet as an affirmation of a future state of affairs; communism as a transitional phase within capitalism. This is no paradox, if we think that just a few years later Marx himself would reduce communism to the Communist Party, '[meeting the] nursery tale of the Spectre of Communism with a Manifesto of the party itself'.[8] Moreover, even in the *German Ideology*, he had said: 'Communism is for us not a state of affairs which is to be established, an ideal to which reality [will] have to adjust itself. We call communism the real movement which abolishes the present state of

---

6 Ibid., 306.
7 Ibid.
8 MECW, Vol. 6, 481.

things'.[9] But nor is it a paradox, even if we think of the development of the objective structures of capitalist society, which sees in community capital, in the community as general capitalist and as generalisation of wage-labour, a highly developed form of capital's socialised existence. In critical-utopian communism, the infant working class expressed the principles it had drawn from 1789 – and according to Marx, in a rather hapless fashion. The first formless masses of proletarians felt that they needed real equality in order to establish their own power, to build their own society. It is this that revealed, to the first capitalist's thought, capitalist production's unavoidable need for formal equality. It is not true that communist social egalitarianism is an illegitimate extension of bourgeois political egalitarianism. The opposite is true: the latter is the first concrete historical realisation of eternal ideas on levelling linked to the eternally misery-stricken layers of the toiling population. In the *Manifesto*, Marx said of the utopian socialists and communists that 'only from the point of view of being the most suffering class does the proletariat exist for them'.[10] This left them unable to find the material conditions for the proletariat's emancipation. Instead of the gradual self-organisation of the proletariat as a class, they proposed a form of social organisation that would spring from a blueprint. 'They want to improve the condition of every member of society. Hence, they habitually appeal to society at large, without distinction of class; nay, by preference, to the ruling class ... Hence, they reject all political, and especially all revolutionary, action; they wish to attain their ends by peaceful means, and endeavour, by small experiments, necessarily doomed to failure, and by the force of example, to pave the way for the new social Gospel'.[11] Everyone knows that this critical-utopian form of the first communism – knocked down by Marx – did not then disappear; rather, it grew and developed to the point of becoming dominant precisely in the so-called Marxist current of the workers' movement. And since it is this current that has set itself the goal of socialism in the most practical terms, the result has been the following curious yet logically consistent conclusion: critical-utopian communism has become the ideology of practical socialism. Thus, the scientific working-class perspective and

---

9   MECW, Vol. 5, 49.
10   MECW, Vol. 6, 515.
11   Ibid.

Marx's analysis on capitalist society have everywhere been replaced by a resounding 'return to ideology'. Likewise, the whole organised workers' movement lives a pre-Marxist existence. The clash – a historically recent one – between Marxism and communism, between science and ideology, between theory and propaganda, which, from the working-class point of view, found its greatest representative in Lenin, concluded – for well-determined, material reasons – with the opportunistic synthesis of an 'ideological' science, a 'propagandistic' theory. Even to the point that the working class, which had together with Marx criticised the ideologies of capital, is today obliged to criticise its own ideology – and again, to do so together with Marx. We do not know yet whether this critique will only partly, or wholly, concern Marx's own work. But what we do already know is that, as a scientific self-critique from the working-class point of view, it will coincide with the historical experience of a concrete revolutionary process. Nonetheless, the real starting point again seems to be to reduce communism to a party; practice again seems to impose the temporary solution of seeing it as a simple instrument of struggle within capital; never must it instead be seen as an end point in the evolution of the organisation, as a 'form' of the workers' party. It seems that the only page left to us of Marx's draft for the *Manifesto* was written more for yesterday's capitalists than for today's reformists. It concludes: 'The Communists do not put forward any new theory of property. They state a fact. You deny the most striking facts. You have to deny them. You are backward looking utopians'.[12] The rejection of the concept *labour-value* is the starting point of the Marxian critique of 'socialism'. For Marx, this critique was already finished business in his 1847 *Poverty of Philosophy*. Proudhon's fundamental error was that he confused the quantity and value of labour as if they were one identical measure for the value of commodities. If that were so, then the relative value of any commodity could be measured without regard for the quantity of labour contained within that commodity, the quantity of labour that it could purchase, or the quantity of labour that could purchase it. But that is not how things are: the value of labour cannot serve as a measure of value, any more than the value of any other commodity can. A relative value cannot be determined by a relative value which, in turn, needs to be determined. Again,

---

12   Ibid., 578.

this error is rooted in the logical conflict between Adam Smith's two
concepts of value: embodied labour and commanded labour, though
they are no longer counterposed, but identified outright. Ricardo, who
had already unveiled this error, was reinterpreted by Smith: the 'egalitarian' consequences of Ricardo's theory of value were similarly
re-explained. Marx speaks of how 'it is in order to find the proper
proportion in which workers should share in the products, or, in other
words, to determine the relative value of labour, that M. Proudhon
seeks a measure for the relative value of commodities'.[13] In order to
achieve this, he found nothing better than giving, as the equivalent of a
certain quantity of labour, the sum of products that it created. The wage
thus becomes the true value of labour, 'which is as good as supposing
that the whole of society consists merely of immediate workers who
receive their own produce as wages'.[14] Taken as an already entirely
determined fact, the equality of wages amounts to seeking 'the measure
of the relative value of commodities in order to arrive at equal payment
for the workers'.[15] This is the egalitarian application of the Ricardian
theory, which almost all British socialists had proposed in various eras
even prior to Proudhon. For example, Marx cites communist J. F. Bray's
1839 *Labour's Wrongs and Labour's Remedy*: 'Men have only two things
which they can exchange with each other, namely, labour, and the
produce of labour ... If a just system of exchanges were acted upon, the
value of all articles would be determined by the entire cost of production; and equal values should always exchange for equal values'.[16] We
would thus arrive at a giant joint-stock company, made up of an infinite
number of smaller joint-stock companies, all of which work, produce
and exchange their products on the basis of the most perfect equality.
'The joint-stock modification (which is nothing but a concession to
present-day society in order to obtain communism), by being so constituted as to admit of individual property in productions in connection
with a common property in productive powers – making every individual dependent on his own exertions, and at the same time allowing
him an equal participation in every advantage afforded by nature and

13   Ibid., 129.
14   Ibid.
15   Ibid.
16   Ibid., 139

art'.[17] So, Marx comments, at root there is not the exchange of products but the exchange of the workers who combine in production. An hour of labour is exchanged for an hour of labour: the fundamental axiom from which everything starts. But what remains to be established is the peculiarity, insignificant for the communist J. F. Bray's socialism, of the mode of this exchange. From the moment in which social labour begins to be exchanged on an individual basis, the mode of exchange of the productive forces determines the mode of exchange of products. Individual exchange thus already corresponds to a determinate system of associated production. And this, we have seen, is nothing other than the product of the antagonism between two classes. On this basis, therefore, there cannot be individual exchange without class struggle. All the honest bourgeois consciences refuse to accept this self-evident fact. 'Mr Bray turns the illusion of the respectable bourgeois into an ideal he would like to attain. In a purified individual exchange, freed from all the elements of antagonism he finds in it, he sees an "equalitarian" relation which he would like society to adopt. Mr Bray does not see that this equalitarian relation, this corrective ideal that he would like to apply to the world, is itself nothing but the reflection of the actual world; and that therefore it is totally impossible to reconstitute society on the basis of what is merely an embellished shadow of it. In proportion as this shadow takes on substance again, we perceive that this substance, far from being the transfiguration dreamt of, is the actual body of existing society'.[18] The concept of *labour-value*, putting value and labour on an equal footing – that is to say, labour-value as the measure of value – would remain common in every socialist critique of capitalism that sought to do without a treatment of class relations. The maximum programme of struggle that can be extracted from such premises is that of a 'fair price' for the wage-labourer's work, and thus a reform of society that transforms all people into immediate labourers who exchange equal quantities of labour. This is why Lassalle's formula of the payment of the 'full fruits of one's labour' made such headway in the workers' movement, notwithstanding the *Critique of the Gotha Programme*. Yet even before 1848, Marx had already expounded the great opposing thesis: labour does not have a price, for the simple

---

17 Ibid., 140.
18 Ibid., 144.

reason that it does not have value; nothing like the value of labour, in the common sense of the term, exists; there cannot, therefore, exist a price for something that has no value. If the value of a commodity is given by the quantity of necessary labour contained within it, then what is the value of a working day? The quantity of a day's work. But to say that the value of a working day is given by the quantity of labour contained in a working day is a mere tautology. 'Value of labour' does not mean measuring value with the time laboured, with the quantity of labour, but rather measuring value with value and labour with labour. It is here that the relationship between antagonistic classes goes awry, for here the individual exchange is reduced to an exchange of labour for labour and thus to an exchange of equal values. There remains, then, no fundamental social demand other than equal wages, demanding equal (or even simply fair) pay on the basis of the wage system. This, Marx tells us, is like demanding freedom on the basis of the system of slavery. The honest capitalist's dream has always been that of seeing socialism precisely as the realisation of capital's ideas. Socialists, before and after Marx, have always tried to make this chimera into a practical, living reality. The consequence has been the realisation of socialism as the ultimate phase of capitalism: a capitalist society made of workers alone; a society under the real power of capital, but without a formal class of capitalists, with capitalism in the relationship of production and socialism in the mode of exchange and distribution; labour exchanged against labour, but for the production of capital; and, through capital, the extended reproduction of class dominion over the workers. When, within capital, the single capitalist no longer exists, the capitalist class has truly reached perfection. When the capitalist is no longer distinct from capital, the class dictatorship over the workers is complete; it no longer bears internal contradictions (on this point). The working class can no longer locate its adversaries. The workers, as a class, remain alone and without the possibility of struggle. But one class cannot exist all by itself. There is no class without the struggle against the other class. The working-class mediation of capitalist power, a genuine workers' power of capital, thus remains the only way for the only socialism that has yet come about – namely, the socialism of capital: a system of exploitation made of the exploited alone without exploiters – the dream of the bourgeois socialist's honest conscience, now realised. Indeed, Marx noted back in his day that this dream achieves its most perfect expression when it can blend into some rhetorical figure: 'Free trade: for the benefit of the working class. Protective duties: for the benefit of the working class. Prison reform: for the benefit of the working class.'[19] Since the days of the *Manifesto* the slogans of 'bourgeois socialism' have changed in form but the method remains the same. And it will remain the same so long as the organisation of the struggle on the workers' side sets out not from what is most necessary but from what seems most just. Indeed, speaking to the worker representatives in the General Council of the International, Marx advised that 'What you think just or equitable is out of the question. The question is: What is necessary and unavoidable with a given system of production?'[20]

19   Ibid., 514.
20   MECW, Vol. 20, 129.

4

Woe to June!

But then came the lightning bolt of 1848. Even for Marx, this was a hoped for but feared moment, one that had been predicted but not prepared for. Europe was suddenly awoken from its bourgeois slumber. 'By dictating the republic to the Provisional Government and through the Provisional Government to the whole of France, the proletariat stepped into the foreground forthwith as an independent party'.[1] Of course, the proletarians did not thereby conquer revolutionary emancipation itself, but they did conquer the terrain of the struggle for that same emancipation. They had made the February revolution together with the bourgeoisie; they now sought to bring their interests to bear alongside the bourgeoisie and not against it. 'As soon as it has risen up, a class in which the revolutionary interests of society are concentrated finds the content and the material for its revolutionary activity directly in its own situation: foes to be laid low, measures to be taken, dictated by the needs of the struggle; the consequences of its own deeds drive it on. It makes no theoretical inquiries into its own task. The French working class had not attained this level; it was still incapable of accomplishing its own revolution'.[2] The struggle against capital in its modern form, at an already-advanced level of development, the struggle of the industrial salariat against the industrial capitalist, was in France still a very partial

---

1 Marx and Engels Collected Works (MECW), Vol. 10, 54.
2 Ibid., 56.

phenomenon: 'the struggle against capital's secondary modes of exploitation'[3] blended into the general uprising against the financial aristocracy. In this sense, the February republic was truly the bourgeois republic and nothing more, albeit one conquered by the proletarians with the passive aid of the bourgeoisie. And the proletarians 'rightly regarded themselves as the victors of February, and they made the arrogant claims of victors'.[4] However, not only did their demands not coincide with the bourgeoisie's, but they contradicted them. This contradiction in demands opposed two camps with contrasting objectives, not only on the political level but also in the social realm. On the one side, alone, was the Paris proletariat, and on the other all the factions of the bourgeoisie and all layers of French society, now all welcomed into the circle of the republican authorities. A contest of this kind could only be resolved with arms. These proletarians had to be defeated in the streets: 'they had to be shown that they were worsted as soon as they did not fight with the bourgeoisie, but against the bourgeoisie'. 'They answered on June 22 with the tremendous insurrection in which the first great battle was fought between the two classes that split modern society'.[5] Long trains of men and women criss-crossed the city, repeating: 'Bread or lead! Lead or bread!' On the morning of June 23, barricades were erected. What Marx a few days later called *Der proletarische Löwe* – the proletarian lion – was now on its feet. The menace of the proletariat in arms had taken to the stage of history. It had been compelled to mount its insurrection. And its doom was already contained within this fact. On the workers' side in the class struggle, only an attacking strategy can secure victory. And the defeat now convinced Marx of a definitive truth: 'the slightest improvement in its position remains a utopia within the bourgeois republic, a utopia that becomes a crime as soon as it wants to become a reality'.[6] After the defeat of June, there would no longer be a place in the proletariat's political class struggle for 'demands' to be wrested from the adversary as concessions: rather, in future it would be replaced by the fiery slogan of revolutionary struggle: 'Tear down the bourgeoisie! For the dictatorship of the working class.' Advancing in its

---

3 Ibid., 57.
4 Ibid., 66.
5 Ibid., 67.
6 Ibid., 69.

development, the bourgeoisie would respond with its own program: the dominion of capital and the enslavement of labour. But it would henceforth find itself faced with the irreconcilable, invincible proletarian enemy, 'invincible because its very existence is a condition of the bourgeoisie's existence'. The proletarian defeat in June thus created, for the first time, the conditions within which the initiative for a workers' revolution could take shape. Its full historical significance lay in this very fact. 'February 25, 1848, had granted the republic to France, June 25 thrust the revolution upon her. And revolution, after June, meant: overthrow of bourgeois society, whereas before February it had meant: overthrow of the form of government'.[7] It was 1848 that revealed to Marx a classic revolutionary movement of the working class. Or – and this is not the same thing – based on the earlier development of his point of view, Marx found himself ready to see a movement of this kind within the events of 1848 in Paris. Engels says in his reminiscences on Marx's activity with the *Neue Rheinische Zeitung* that 'the insurrection of the Paris workers in June 1848 found us at our post. From the first shot we were unconditionally on the side of the insurgents. After their defeat, Marx paid tribute to the vanquished in one of his most powerful articles'.[8] By chance (or foresight?) at that moment he found himself in possession of an instrument through which he could publicly issue his political judgements. On 1 June 1848, the first issue of the *Neue Rheinische Zeitung* was published. And the practical, immediately political origin of what would be called Marx's 'historical' works – the *Class Struggles in France*, the *Eighteenth Brumaire* and so on, later published elsewhere – should be sought out within the pages of this same paper. Any historian reading these works as a historian will all too easily find basic grammatical errors. But there is no revolutionary workers' leader who does not have to turn back to this political source periodically, each time to decide, in practice, a mode of conduct in the class struggle. The experience of editing this paper at the turn of 1848 and 1849 was a fundamentally important turning point in Marx's discourse on labour and capital: we realise as much immediately afterward, indeed precisely from the form of his 'historical' works. These politically crude, violent, sectarian, one-sided writings are not justified by the facts. But they have

---

7 Ibid., 71.
8 MECW, Vol. 26, 126.

a clear-sightedness in foreseeing future developments such as only class hatred could provide. And, in these writings, we see, for the first time, the overlapping and conjugation of the abstract concept of labour and the concrete reality of the worker. The synthesis is that of an already-wholly defined idea of the proletariat, and not only solely intuited through the power of Marx's genius as it had been in his previous works. But this concept of the proletariat did not yet contain all the characteristics of what would become the working class. For us, it is satisfying to see the same historical succession, the same logical difference between the proletarian and the worker that we already found between the seller of labour-power and the producer of surplus-value. The proletarian is the simple, elementary political figure and, for this reason, the more general class form of the industrial worker, of the wage-labourer in industry. After June 1848, the particular character of the commodity labour-power presented itself on the political terrain, as the proletariat: not simply the proletariat against the bourgeoisie, but against all of bourgeois society, and not only in the form of a democratic opposition, but in the organisation of a violent alternative to the established power; a class in arms against the whole of society, as if it, too, were another single class. From this point, the discourse on labour and labour-power, on labour and capital, became definitively intertwined with the political analysis of workers' movements in their permanent struggle against capital, searching for the laws that alone can decide the practical solution to any theoretical problem. From this point, no one who identifies with Marx's working-class perspective can continue to divide these levels among themselves. If we need further persuasion on this, we need only follow – again, in Marx – the process through which labour-power is ever more wrapped up with the working class, as the development of capital advances.

5

The Particularity of the Commodity Labour-Power

In his effort to grasp the process by which money is transformed into capital, Marx stops at one point and says, 'we have to consider more closely that peculiar commodity that is labour-power'. In the decisive section on the 'purchase and sale of labour-power', which concludes the second section of Volume 1 of *Capital*, we find a note which refers – not by chance – to both Ricardo and Hegel. Marx says that the change in the value of money, and thus its transformation into capital, cannot take place within money itself; rather, it has to take place within the commodity; and not in value, but in use-value, and thus in the consumption of a commodity which is exchanged for money. Ricardo had said already, on this point, that 'in the form of money ... capital does not produce profit'. Marx says that the sale of the commodity labour-power cannot take place *en bloc* and once and for all; rather, it must always and only take place for a determinate time; she who possesses this commodity concedes the temporary consumption of her labour-power but not ownership over it; otherwise, she would no longer be free, but a slave. Hegel had already said that 'Single products of my particular physical and mental skill and of my power to act I can alienate to someone else and I can give him the use of my abilities for a restricted period, because, on the strength of this restriction, my abilities acquire an external relation to the totality and universality of my being. By alienating the whole of my time, as crystallised in my work, and everything I produced, I would be making into another's property the substance of my being, my universal activity and actuality, my personality.'[1] Money is not capital and does not become capital but must *transform* into capital. If this transformation takes place in the commodity, the use-value of this commodity must possess a particular quality: namely, that it is itself a source of value. Its real consumption must itself be an objectification of labour and thus a creation of value. And there is already a specific commodity of this type on the market: the capacity to labour, labour-power. 'We mean by labour-power, or labour-capacity, the aggregate of those mental and physical capabilities existing in the physical form, the living personality, of a human being, capacities which he sets in motion whenever he produces a use-value of any kind.'[2] The presence of labour-power on the market presupposes the existence of the seller of labour-power. The seller presupposes the proprietor. And the proprietor's sale of labour-power presupposes the free ownership of the commodity. And this, too, is a wholly particular freedom: the freedom to sell a single commodity, which is also the impossibility of not selling it – a freely accepted constraint, which is indeed the freedom at the foundation of capital. In this sense, we would more rightly say that the first condition, from which stem all the other conditions that make the transformation of money into capital possible, is the existence of the historically determinate figure of the *free worker*, who is 'free in the double sense that as a free individual he can dispose of his labour-power as his own commodity, and that, on the other hand, he has no other commodity for sale, i.e. is free of all the objects needed for the realization [*Verwirklichung*] of his labour power.'[3]

If labour-power is a commodity, then it has a value like all other commodities. For the same reason that we could not speak of 'the value of labour', we can instead speak of the 'value of labour-power'. Labour is not a commodity; it is only the use-value of a commodity, in particular the commodity labour-power. And a use-value has no value as such, only as an exchange-value. Labour-power, as a commodity, has an exchange-value and a use-value. There is nothing peculiar about its exchange-value: like that of any other commodity, it is determined by the labour-time necessary for its production, which then breaks down

1 Hegel, *Philosophy of Right*, par. 67

2 Karl Marx, *Capital*, Vol. 1, translated by Ben Fowkes, London: Penguin, 1990, 270.

3 Ibid., 272.

into the production of the means of subsistence necessary for the
conservation and thus for the reproduction of the possessor of labour-
power. The formal particularity of labour-power, as a commodity, is
concealed within its use-value. In the meantime – remaining within the
sphere of circulation – we see the peculiar nature of this specific
commodity in the fact that when the contract is concluded between
buyer and seller, its use-value has not yet really passed into the hands of
the buyer. The value of this commodity, like the value of any other, is
already determined at the point at which it enters into circulation – but
unlike in the case of other commodities' use-values, its use-value is not
already objectively contained in its very existence. Rather, the use-value
comes only afterward, as the subjective unfolding of a possibility, a
capacity, a potentiality. The sale of labour-power and thus its existence
as an exchange-value, and the consumption of labour-power and thus
its existence as a use-value, are staggered over time. In this case, as in
other, similar cases, money functions as a means of payment. And the
commodity is paid for not at the moment of sale, but after it has been
consumed. 'In every country where the capitalist mode of production
prevails, it is the custom not to pay for labour-power until it has been
exercised for the period fixed by the contract, for example, at the end of
each week. In all cases, therefore, the worker advances the use-value of
his labour-power to the capitalist. He lets the buyer consume it before he
receives payment of the price. Everywhere the worker allows credit to
the capitalist.'[4] But this is, so to speak, a reflected particularity of
labour-power's use-value. To understand this, we need to connect back
to this commodity's original particularity, which comes to light only
within the inner workings of the production process, specifically in one
part of it – the valorisation process proper, the process of the production
of surplus-value and thus of capital. Marx's conception of surplus-value
has always been connected back to the classical theory of value, but it
would instead rightly be connected back to Marx's own conception of
labour-power, in the moment in which it meets the concept of productive labour. Only this makes possible an independent treatment of
surplus-value, in its general form, before and above any treatment of its
particular forms such as profit, interest, annuities, and so on. And this
is, indeed, the other fundamental discovery in *Capital*. The use of

---

4 Ibid., 278.

labour-power, Marx tells us, is labour itself. To consume labour-power, whoever has bought it must make whoever has sold it work. This consumption process is, at the same time, a production process, producing commodities and surplus-value. And it is within this process that the seller of labour-power becomes, *in actu*, what she previously was only in potential: she becomes labour-power in action, transforming into a worker. The value of labour-power is then equitably paid in the form of a wage: the worker becomes a wage-worker. But what had already been contracted *before* is only paid in wages *after*. The form of the wage does not specify the figure of the worker in any way that was not already contained within the figure of the seller of labour-power. In the consumption of labour-power – in labour – what is added is the concrete act of production, within determinate conditions, in the valorisation process. It is at this point that the specific use-value of the commodity labour-power comes out – its wholly special nature, its historical particularity: not that it is a source of value, as in the particularity of the exchange-value of labour-power; rather, it is the particularity of being the source of a greater value than it itself has. In the commodity labour-power, value does not coincide with valorisation. Not only that, but labour-power is the sole commodity that through the process of its consumption, produces a valorisation greater than its own value – it produces surplus-value, produces capital. Labour-power is not, therefore, just potential labour but also potential capital. The use of labour-power is not only labour, but also surplus-labour; not only the production of value, but also the production of surplus-value. The use of labour-power, therefore, is not only labour, but also capital. Yet the use of labour-power is inseparable from the complete figure of the worker-turned-producer. Just as the relation between two antagonistic classes is already contained within the act of the sale and purchase of labour-power – the relation that founds the entire successive history of capital proper – so too is the entire terrain of the direct struggle between the two classes already prepared within the process of the consumption of labour-power, at the moment of production. And it is this struggle that will determine the birth, development and collapse of capitalist society, one after the other. Indeed, this is the manner in which the process of capital production first ought to be considered from the working-class perspective; that is, as the natural home of the expression of its own antagonism, as a specific terrain of class struggle. Labour-power, we have seen, is introduced and must be introduced into the production process as a class and as an antagonistic class. However, as a social productive force, it cannot only produce capital, but also belongs to capital, becoming an internal part of it. The process of capitalist production thus presents itself as the process of the capitalist appropriation of workers' labour-power. It is no longer simply the purchase of that commodity, but the reduction of this commodity's particular nature under its own dominion; no longer the individual act of exchange, but a process of social violence; not only exploitation, but control over exploitation. The consumption, in production, of the commodity labour-power, the productive use of the worker by the capitalist, thus becomes – must become – the capitalist use of the working class. We must look within this process to unearth the historical birth of a class of capitalists. The capitalist use of the workers as a class is not possible without the capitalists constituting themselves into a class – and their model cannot but be that of the only class hitherto constituted, the class of workers.

From this, then, begins the whole history of the movements of the class of workers. But the – both logical and historical – passage from the proletariat, which sells its labour-power, to the working class, which produces surplus-value, marks the beginning of the working-class history of capital, which is then the history of capitalist society proper as well as the only materialist conception of 'history' thus far acceptable from a Marxist point of view. We will return to this. For now, what concerns us is to conclude the point that we had left hanging: namely, that the character – the particularity – of the commodity labour-power is that it is, potentially, the working class. This particular use-value is workers in general, what Marx calls 'this peculiar breed of commodity owners'. The realised value of labour-power, in the form of the wage, is once again capital, part of it, as variable capital. This point however, cannot be the site of the working-class specificity of this commodity, since this is not where capital is born. The whole particularity of the commodity labour-power lies not in its value, but in its use-value, for it is the latter that produces surplus-value. It is the use of labour-power, labour, that contains (presupposes) surplus-value – and not surplus-labour in general, but the worker's surplus-value; like labour, the use of labour-power and the worker's labour, the concrete explication, the concretisation of abstract labour – abstract labour which, in turn, already reduced to a commodity, realises its value in the wage. Thus, the point at which abstract labour flips into the concrete figure of the worker is the process of the consumption of labour-power, the moment in which labour-power becomes in actuality what it had earlier been in potential. It is the point of the realisation of the labour-power's use-value. What had been a simple, elementary and general class relation within the act of purchase and sale now definitively acquires its specific character, its total and complex nature. The particularity of labour-power as compared to all the other commodities thus coincides with the specifically working-class character that the process of capital production assumes. Within this, it also coincides with the concretisation of a working-class initiative in class relations, which leads to a leap in the development of the working class and to the subsequent birth of a class of capitalists. All this is definitively expounded in the first exposition Marx provides of the transformation of money into capital – the 1858 urtext to his *Contribution to the Critique of Political Economy*. *Qua* the result of simple circulation, capital exists first in the simple form of money. Its existence in money is, rather, only its existence as an adequate exchange-value, which can convert into all kinds of commodities indifferently: it is exchange-value made autonomous. And this autonomisation consists of precisely this: the fact that the exchange-value remains limited to itself as an exchange-value, be it in the form of money or in the form of a commodity; it transforms into a commodity only in order to valorise itself. Money is simply a form of capital, insofar as it is now objectified labour. None of labour's objective modes of existence are counterposed to this capital, but all of them present themselves as its possible mode of existence. 'The only opposite of reified labour is unreified labour, and the opposite of objectified labour, subjective labour. Or, the opposite of past labour, which exists in space, is living labour, which exists in time. As the presently existing unreified (and so also not yet objectified) labour, it can be present only as the power, potentiality, ability, as the labour capacity of the living subject. The opposite of capital as the independent, firmly self-sufficient objectified labour is living labour capacity itself, and so the only exchange by means of which money can become capital is the exchange between the possessor of capital and the possessor of the living labour capacity, i.e. the worker.'[5] In money, exchange-value had to maintain its independence; that is, in abstraction

---

5   Marx and Engels Collected Works (MECW), Vol. 29, 502.

from use-value. Yet now exchange-value – precisely in its real and not formal existence as a use-value – has to maintain itself as an exchange-value; and not only maintain itself as an exchange-value within use-value, but produce itself on this basis. 'The real being of use values is their real negation, their absorption, their annihilation in consumption.'[6] The true reality of exchange-value is no longer in the *abstraction from* use-value, but precisely in the *consumption of* use-value. 'The real negation of the use value which exists not in an abstraction from it (not in a stoppage tensely opposed to it) but in its consumption, this real negation of it, which is at the same time its actualisation as use value, must for that reason become an act of self-assertion, self-actualisation of the exchange value.'[7] Yet this is possible only insofar as the commodity is consumed by labour and its very consumption presents itself as an objectification of labour, and thus as a creation of value. 'For money, use value is now no longer an article of consumption in which it loses itself, but only a use value through which it preserves and increases itself. No other use value exists for money as capital. That is precisely the relation of capital as exchange value to use value. Labour is the only use value which can present an opposite and a complement [*Gegensatz und Ergänzung*] to money as capital, and it exists in labour capacity, which exists as a subject. Money exists as capital only in connection with non-capital, the negation of capital [*Nicht-Kapital*] the negation of capital, in relation to which alone it is capital. Labour itself is the real non-capital.'[8] Standing counterposed to exchange-value in the form of money is exchange-value in the form of a particular use-value. That is, exchange-value can be realised as such only because it is counterposed not to this or that use-value, but to the particular use-value that concerns it. The particular use-value which concerns exchange-value, even while being its negation, is labour. In simple circulation, the content of the use-value was a matter of indifference, and fell outside of the economic relation: here, conversely, it is its essential moment. But the specific use-value of at least one of the commodities being exchanged itself leads outside of the confines of simple circulation. It is not the particular form of exchange that provokes this shift: for insofar as there is an exchange of

---

6 Ibid., 503.
7 Ibid.
8 Ibid.

equivalents, here all the sacred rights of freedom and equality are respected. Rather, what provokes it is the particular content of the use-value of the commodity labour-power, again meaning labour. But 'the exchange between capital and labour, once it itself exists as the simple relationship of circulation, is not the exchange between money and labour, but the exchange between money and living labour capacity'.[9] As a use-value, labour-power is realised in working activity itself. But this working activity falls outside of the circulation process. It is true that 'the buying of the labour capacity [is] the appropriation of the ability to dispose over the labour'.[10] But this available labour can be consumed only within production. The consumption of labour-power is the production of capital. Indeed, within the commodity labour-power the great, vital contradiction of capitalism – the contradiction between production and consumption – is resolved, for the consumption of this commodity is nothing other than the productive consumption of its use-value. Thus, the secret of capital lies not in the value, but in the use-value of labour-power. 'It is only the specific nature of the use value bought with the money – namely, that its consumption, the consumption of the labour capacity, is production, labour time which objectifies, consumption which posits exchange value; that its real being as use value is creation of exchange value – that makes the exchange between money and labour the specific exchange M–C–M in which the exchange value itself is posited as the aim of the exchange, and the bought use value is immediate use value for the exchange value, i.e. is value-positing use value.'[11] The use-value that produces value is the labour that produces surplus-value. Indeed, on the following page, where the manuscript is interrupted by Marx's first exposition of the passage to capital, we find the title: 'Productive and unproductive labour'.

---

9   Ibid., 506.
10   Ibid.
11   Ibid., 506.

6

Productive Labour

Productive labour, in the sense of capitalist production, is that waged labour which in the exchange with the variable part of capital not only reproduces this part of capital but also produces surplus-value for the capitalist. 'Only labour which produces capital is productive labour. Commodities or money become capital, however, through being exchanged directly for labour capacity, and exchanged only in order to be replaced by more labour than they themselves contain.'[1] And here Marx adds a further observation, indeed one of fundamental importance: 'The mere existence of a class of capitalists, and therefore of capital, depends on [beruht] the productivity of labour.'[2] With the relative productivity of her work, the worker not only reproduces the old value, but creates a new one: that is, she objectivates in her product a greater labour-time than that objectified in the product that maintains her life as a worker. 'It is this kind of productive wage-labour that is the basis for the existence of capital [seine Existenz].'[3] One of Smith's greatest scientific merits is that he defined productive labour as that labour which is directly exchanged for capital: it is in this exchange that the conditions for the production of labour and value in general, money and the commodity, transform into capital, and labour transforms into

---

1 Marx and Engels Collected Works (MECW), Vol. 31, 12.
2 Ibid., 8.
3 Ibid., 9.

wage-labour 'in the scientific sense'. With this, we also get an absolute definition of the meaning of unproductive labour: 'It is labour which is not exchanged with capital, but directly with revenue.'[4] Smith's distinction between productive and improductive labour is correct, but 'from the standpoint of the capitalist', not the worker.[5] The material determinacy of labour, and thus of its product, does not in any way enter into this distinction as a determining factor: the particularity of labour and the particular use-value in which it is realised are here wholly inessential. For the capitalist, indeed, the use-value of labour-power consists not of its effective use-value, in the utility of this particular concrete labour, and still less in the use-value of the product of this labour. What interests him in the commodity is that it possesses an exchange-value greater than what he paid for it. What interests him in labour is that in its use-value he recuperates a quantity of labour-time greater than what he paid out in the form of wages. But the productive worker's labour-power is a commodity for the worker herself; so too is that of the unproductive labourer. The difference is that the productive worker produces a commodity for the buyer of her labour-power, while the unproductive labourer produces a mere use-value for this buyer. 'It is characteristic of the unproductive labourer that he produces no commodities for his buyer, but indeed receives commodities from him.'[6] In this case, labour does not transform into capital, for it does not create a profit for the capitalist: labour is a simple expense (*Ausgabe*), one of the articles through which income is consumed. There is labour-power here, and this labour-power is a commodity, but the labour that emanates from this labour-power is not productive labour. It is possible, on this basis, to establish a more modern distinction (than was possible in Marx's times) between the productive worker and the unproductive labourer. From this point of view, we can say that the seller of labour-power is the simplest form of the worker, only in the sense that the commodity is the most elementary form of bourgeois wealth and the productive labour producing commodities the most elementary form of the productive labour producing capital. Indeed, Marx tells us that the whole world of commodities can be broken down into two categories: first,

4 Ibid., 13.
5 Ibid.
6 Ibid., 16.

labour-power and second, the commodities distinct from labour-power. But the concept "commodity" implies that the labour concerned is incorporated, materialised, realised in its product. Labour, as such, in its immediate existence, cannot be directly conceived as a commodity; only labour-power can be. Moreover, only the use-value of this commodity labour-power is capable of creating new value. The commodity, differently from labour-power, is something that stands materially counterposed to humanity. Yet even the commodity labour-power, as capital, stands counterposed to the worker: all the more so when labour-power's use-value becomes productive labour. The productivity of labour always belongs to capital. When Marx writes that it is a sad fate to be a productive worker, he is not issuing a moral protest but recognising this fact. To be a productive worker means to produce capital, and thus also to continually reproduce the dominion of capital over the worker. Not only the existence, but likewise the development of capital, and thus of a class of capitalists, is founded on productive labour. For Marx, 'labour is productive only when it produces its own opposite'.[7] The history of the different ways in which productive labour is extorted from the worker – which is to say, the history of the various forms of the production of surplus-labour – is the history of capitalist society from the working-class point of view. It is one of the two 'histories of capital' that we think can appropriately be written from the two opposed points of view, by virtue of which capital exists. For example, from the capitalist point of view, productive labour appears as labour exchanged for capital; from the working-class view, as labour which produces capital. Both definitions are correct. It is just that one is seen from the circulation side and the other from the production side – the two 'natural' points of view for the two classes. Indeed, there is no need to think that bourgeois science is always ideology, that the capitalist point of view is always the prisoner of appearances and mystificatory by nature. It sometimes is, indeed consciously so, to serve its brutal class interests: these are the cases in which it is necessary to expose and defeat it with arms of struggle more than with arms of critique. And it is true that in capitalist society, what appears to be the case is, too often, the opposite of what it is, and each of these appearances is functional to the totality of the real phenomena that express it. But this comparison of appearances with reality cannot

7   MECW, Vol. 28, 231.

– as often happens – entirely explain the theoretical clash between the two points of view. The dazzling games so much in fashion today, which take the name of a critique demystifying bourgeois ideologies, now serve only to mask the tough demands of a direct engagement with the science of capital. On this point, the situation within which Marx found himself working has now been completely turned on its head. He had to confront the great bourgeois systems, in which science and ideology fused and contradicted one another; we need only think, once more, of Hegel and Ricardo, and of the incalculably rich material that found a classic synthesis in the works of each of these figures. Marx's method was to immediately clear the field of all the ideological functionalities that connected these systems together internally, in his own bid to grasp the isolated scientific data that they were nonetheless forced to register. Only at this level did the use of these data intervene in Marx, now seen from the opposite point of view. And yet it is clear that this latter point of view preexisted all the rest or, better, founded it. Just as the class relation comes historically prior to the capitalist relation proper, thus the antagonism between the two classes' opposing points of view logically comes before the attempt at a general social science of capital. Today's situation returns us continually to this attempt, in an ever-harsher way. For now we face not the great abstract syntheses of bourgeois thought, but the cult of the most vulgar empirical trivia that has become capital's praxis. No longer the logical system of knowledge, the principles of science, but an orderless mass of historical facts, of fragmented experiences, of great *faits accomplis* that no one has ever thought about. Science and ideology again merge with and contradict one another, but no longer in a systematisation of ideas meant for eternity, but rather in the day-to-day happenings of the class struggle. And this struggle is now dominated by a new reality that would have been inconceivable in Marx's time. Capital has placed the whole functional apparatus of bourgeois ideology into the hands of the officially recognised workers' movement. Capital no longer manages its own ideology but has the workers' movement manage it in its stead. This 'workers' movement' thus functions as an ideological mediation internal to capital; through the historical exercises of this function, the entire mystified world of appearances that contradict reality is attached to the working class. That is why we say that today the critique of ideology is a task internal to the working-class point of view, and has only in the second instance to do with capital. The political task of a working-class auto-critique must question the entire past historical course of the workers' class struggle and do so starting from the current state of organisation. In the present, the working class does not have to criticise anyone outside of itself, its own history, its own experiences and that corpus of ideas that has been gathered together by others around it. At this point, we can reply, in part, on the question as to whether this critique ought to implicate Marx's own work: we think that there is a single critique of Marx that can be not only accepted, but even proposed from the working-class point of view, and that is a Leninist critique of Marx. Already in Lenin, and in other words through Leninist praxis, Marx was criticising himself. In the organisation of neo-Leninist praxis, we today need to resume the critique of workers' movement ideologies. Does that mean that all science has been left in the hands of capital? No, it means that the real scientific data that also exist in bourgeois thought have today been materially incorporated into capital. Thus, such data no longer exist as a scientific reality of capitalist relations but as a direct awareness – even if a short-term one – of capital's own needs and objective movements, and as a forecast, if an approximate one, of its class antagonist's possible subjective deviations. In these conditions, it is better from the working-class point of view to recognise that the capitalist point of view also has the possibility of scientific understanding; to deny this today would amount to maintaining that the working class alone, in the persons of its official representatives, is the sole depository of true science (and the true history, etc.), including the science of all, the general social science, which fully applies to capital, too. But it is better to recognise that, in the reorganisation of the productive process in a big factory, there is at least as much scientific understanding as there is in Smith's discovery of the productive labour that is exchanged for capital. Indeed, in each of these cases, the capitalist interest is expressly without ideological mediations, and is at the same time a fact of capitalist production and a form of dominion over the working class. For the working class, nothing is left but to counterpose its own exclusive and alternative interest, on the terrain of science as on the terrain of struggle. These two terrains are now just one. Just as the one science is wholly incorporated into capital, the other, opposed science must be fully incorporated into the working class and its struggles. Again, differently to Marx's case and to our great regret, there is no British Museum open to us. Classical political economy, Marx says, always made the production of surplus-labour the decisive characteristic of productive labour – hence, definitions of the productive worker varied with the changing conceptions surrounding the nature of surplus-value. The 'Theories on Surplus-Value' – in the text not manipulated by Kautsky – begins with these words: 'Before the Physiocrats, surplus value – that is, profit, in the form of profit – was explained purely from exchange, the sale of the commodity above its value'.[8] First 'the Physiocrats transferred the inquiry into the origin of surplus value from the sphere of circulation into the sphere of direct production, and thereby laid the foundation for the analysis of capitalist production'.[9] Here we again find what Marx called 'my own particular way of dealing with the Physiocrats – i.e., as the first methodical (not, like Petty, etc., merely casual) exponents of capital and of the capitalist mode of production' (in his 7 March 1877 letter to Engels).[10] For Marx, precisely because the analysis of capital essentially belonged to the Physiocrats, within a bourgeois horizon, they were the genuine 'fathers of modern economics'. But this analysis of capital belongs to them because they gave a correct definition of productive labour. Productive labour is that labour which creates a net product and thus a surplus-value, and whose product thus contains a value superior to the sum of values consumed during its production. The Physiocrats had not yet reduced value to labour-time, for they had not yet reduced labour to abstract labour. For them, value consisted of matter, land, nature. They thus looked for surplus-labour in concrete agricultural labour. In agriculture, the difference between value and valorisation directly manifests itself in the excess of use-values produced relative to the use-values consumed by the workers; it can thus be understood without any analysis of value in general and without any clear insight into the nature of value. For them, it suffices to reduce value to use-value, and use-value to natural material. Land rent thus becomes not only the sole form, but indeed the general form of surplus-value; agricultural labour is likewise the natural source of surplus-value not only in agriculture but in all other branches of labour. In the Physiocratic reading, there is productive labour without labour-power; there is the concept of surplus-value without the concept

---

8   MECW, Vol. 30, 348.
9   Ibid., 354.
10   MECW, Vol 45, 208.

of value, which means that there is surplus-value without surplus-labour; there is the production of capital without the exchange between capital and labour. In the first bourgeois analysis of capitalist production, industrial workers are part of the 'sterile class'. The Physiocrats conjectured an ideal capitalist system without a working class; this is the classic form of the transition between two systems of property and power, between two historical types of social organisation. This is the sense in which they ought to be studied anew. The Physiocrats did not discover the concept of labour-power-as-commodity but did discover the difference between value and valorisation, which is precisely the specific trait of the commodity labour-power. How did they discover this? It was because they recognised surplus-value as an excess of use-values produced over the use-values consumed; this presents itself first of all and in the most manifest fashion in agriculture, in the original form of production. Moreover, this is the branch of production that can be imagined as being autonomous and independent from circulation and exchange. Precisely because the discovery of the surplus-value produced by productive labour takes place on the land, in agricultural production – and this productive labour is still, concrete, determinate labour, not labour-power – surplus-value presents itself as a gift of nature, as a productive force that belongs to nature itself. Agriculture thus becomes the only branch of production in which capitalist production, as the production of surplus-value, directly manifests itself. Hence Marx says that the Physiocratic system 'has rather the character of a bourgeois reproduction of the feudal system, of the dominion of landed property ... Feudalism is thus portrayed and explained sub specie of bourgeois production ... While feudalism is thus made bourgeois, bourgeois society is given a feudal semblance.'[11] It was no accident that the homeland of the Physiocrats was France, an agricultural country, and not England, a country of trade and industry: there, conversely, all attention was devoted to circulation, and surplus-value still appeared as profit upon alienation. If, in order to uncover the origin of surplus-value in production, it was necessary to go back to the branch of labour in which surplus-value appeared independently of circulation, then such an initiative could be taken only in an agricultural country. The Physiocratic system thus started out from the feudal landowner, though he appears

---

11   MECW, Vol. 30, 358.

not as such but rather as the simple possessor of commodities. He values the commodities he exchanges for labour and draws not only their equivalent, but an excess on top of this equivalent, for even if he does not yet know it, he pays for labour-power as a commodity. This land-owner is thus essentially a capitalist: he stands as a possessor of commodities, counterposed to the free worker, and exchanges the objective conditions of labour for labour-power. For Marx, 'in this respect too the Physiocratic system hits the mark, inasmuch as the separation of the labourer from the soil and from the ownership of land is a fundamental condition for capitalist production and the production of capital'.[12] Thus, even in the consequences that the Physiocrats themselves drew, the apparent glorification of land ownership flips into its most complete negation. These are all contradictions of capitalist production, as it opened up the path out of feudal society, and the Physiocrats limited themselves to interpreting this in the most bourgeois sense, without having yet found 'its specific form'. In the Physiocratic system, we thus find not only the theoretical source that comes prior to the concept of productive labour, but also the starting point for the analysis of its historical origin. Productive labour is borne on the land; it is no chance thing, then, that it was unearthed by the Physiocrats. Likewise, this labour was then organised by industry and, not by chance, it was grasped in systemic terms by Smith, who rightly relates the general form of surplus-value to industrial profit. Can we say that the first capitalist rela-tion, with its respective and preceding class relation, takes place within agriculture? And that industry is a successive form of social organisa-tion as well as a reduction of these two processes into one? If we can indeed say this, then of the two classic routes to capitalism, the very one that Marx called the effectively revolutionary path is exploded, for it did not exist historically. And the only route that remains standing is the other one, which passes through a long stage of transition and which, as such, does not in itself lead to revolution in the old mode of production. Rather, it conserves this old mode and safeguards it as its own condition until *qua* an obstacle to the capitalist mode of production it disappears through the development of the latter. In the passage to capitalism there is not, then, a revolutionary road that begins from within production and a reformist (gradualist) road that besieges production from the

---

12 Ibid., 359.

outside, to use our own more modern terms. Rather, there is just a single road that sets out from a determinate form of production, from a particular production, to arrive at the production of capital in general. The concrete labour that produces surplus-value is not an invention dreamt up by the Physiocrats or a simple bourgeois appearance: it is the objective way in which the use-value that produces value, and thus the working-class labour-power that produces capital, first appears historically. The uneliminable, or at least not-eliminated, historical passage seems to be that of a first appropriation of the new type of surplus-labour on the basis of the old mode of production. Marx says: it remains true that 'taking a single country (excluding foreign trade), surplus labour must first be applied to agriculture before it becomes possible in the industries which get their *matière brute* from agriculture'.[13] Here, he is already talking about the modern form of surplus-labour: the simple increase in the amount of labour (with an unchanged number of workers) persists but added to this are productivity gains. Originally, too, this did not presuppose the accumulation of capital, but its concentration: two discrete processes, these, which only subsequently integrate together. This integration takes place in the passage from agricultural to industrial labour, from concrete to abstractly general labour, from that labour which produces more use-values to the labour that produces more value; that is, having started out from the agricultural production of absolute surplus-value, we arrive at the industrial production of relative surplus-value. The latter can arise only on the basis of industry and *from there* be extended, *as a reflection*, into agriculture; indeed, the production of relative surplus-value presupposes not the simple concentration of capital, but its accumulation, as well as the finished integration of these two processes, which then lays the foundations of capitalist production proper. Now, the need for a bourgeois reproduction of the feudal system becomes a museum piece, like so many historical leftovers. There is a fundamentally important point of method here, though. In the whole epoch that has been under the dominion of capital, we see the repetition of what is now almost a natural progression in the analysis of social phenomena: the real process, in all its complexity, which we can say emerges only at the most historically advanced point, is instead discovered *at a logical level* at a more backward point, insofar

---

13 MECW, Vol. 31, 25.

as it emerges still free from the mediations of development; this discovery is then instrumentalised precisely on the most advanced terrain and serves to liberate development from its mediations. The working-class point of view has, on many occasions, made use of this operation, in the moments in which the objectives of organising the struggle against the immediate enemy turned out to be the most urgent tasks for the entire movement; from this have sprung impressive indications that are likewise purposive for analysing phenomena theoretically. Again, Lenin has much to teach us here. The Marxian methodological formula on the most advanced point that explains the most backward point is a theoretically accurate one, but it conceals within itself – in its vulgar interpretation – the possibility of political opportunism, as when it leads us to conclude that, in the unequal development of capitalism around the world, all that has been at one point must also be so in the others. The practical needs of the class struggle have never known the comfort of this imperative. Within the bounds of capitalist structures that are, in themselves, already complete, it is not true that the class situation of the more advanced countries explains and prefigures the class situation of the more backward ones. Or, it explains and prefigures it from the capitalist point of view – that is, from the point of view of understanding a possible path of development. But from the working-class point of view, the important thing is precisely to impede this development in practice, to break it at some point – to impose a non-normal class situation, unnatural with respect to theoretical-analytical models. To begin from a midpoint of development, and thus from its innermost point, is perhaps the only way still open to bring down the whole thing at its very highest point. The ineliminable condition for this is that the subjective forces called on to carry forth this process of rupture and overthrow have a degree of organisation that already has a lead on the objective level of development. So, a passive correspondence between the organisation of revolutionary working-class forces and the level of capitalist development is insufficient to win in the long term. Rather, it is necessary for these forces to have actively gone beyond this level by some margin and to have deliberately organised themselves at the highest point conceivable in that moment of the history of capital, even if this point is still materially absent in the given situation. If this condition is not fulfilled, or only appears to be fulfilled – that is, existing only as an ideological illusion – then the vast material power in capital's coffers will take the lead once more, overturning the class situation in its own favour and crudely instrumentalising the very subjective forces that wanted to destroy it, now within its own very rapid new growth cycle. Hence, as a result of the revolutionary passage, we have nothing more than a reproduction of the old mode of production in new forms. What did the first historic attempt to build socialism result in, along this route, if not a working-class reproduction of the capitalist system? Through their resolve, the Bolsheviks demonstrated, for the first time, that it was possible to defeat capitalism in the open field. They transported the revolution from the world of books into the world of things, from theory to practice. But they did not have a clear concept of the working class and its higher organisational needs. They are our own 'Physiocrats'. 'Building socialism in one country' is their *Tableau économique*.

The question is posed: in what way, or why, does labour faced with capital present itself as productive labour, now that labour's productive forces have transferred into capital? Can the same productive force be counted twice – once as a productive force for labour and once as a productive force for capital? Marx's reply immediately poses another question: what is productive labour, from capital's point of view? As a producer of value, labour always remains the labour of the *individual*, which is only expressed in a *general form*. Productive labour – as labour that produces surplus-value – is thus always, with respect to capital, the labour of individual labour-power, of the *isolated worker*, regardless of the social combinations into which these workers enter within the production process. Thus, while faced with the worker, capital represents labour's social productive force; facing capital, the worker's productive labour always and only represents the labour of the isolated worker. As we have seen, money transforms into capital when part of it is converted into commodities that serve labour as means of production, while the other part is employed in the purchase of labour-power. Nonetheless, this original exchange between money and labour-power is only the condition that renders possible the transformation of money into capital, and not the transformative act itself. Indeed, this transformation can take place only within the real productive process, where living labour reproduces the wage – the value of the variable capital – and also a surplus-value, which is to say that it leaves part of the living labour in the hands of the money-holder. 'It is only through this immediate transformation of labour into labour power, belonging not to the worker but to the capitalist, that money transforms into capital ... Before money is only capital in itself (*an sich*)'. It is capital because it presents itself in an independent form faced with labour-power, and vice versa; thus, it is capital on account of the class relation that founds it. Money – either as a commodity (as a provision of means of production for labour) or as money (as the provision of means of subsistence for the worker) – at this stage represents all of the objective conditions of production. And these 'already possess at the outset the social determinacy vis-á-vis the workers, which makes them into capital and gives them command [*das Kommando*] over labour'. Thus, from the outset, the objective conditions for production are the social conditions and the conditions of social command over the workers. Even before the transformation of money into capital and even before the birth of the specific form of the capitalist relation of production, the class relation sees the workers on one side and, on the opposite side, the social conditions of labour as a power over them. In other words, on the one side is a mass of isolated individuals who are necessarily united by their common situation as sellers of labour-power, and on the other side the pure and simple consistency of the objective conditions that deserve the title 'dead labour'. On the one side, a first, simple, embryonic, proletarian form of working class, and facing it, against it, not the class of capitalists or even an already self-developed capitalist relation of production, but only capital in itself, capital in potential and nothing else. 'Productive labour can therefore be characterised as labour which exchanges directly with money as capital, or, and this is merely an abbreviated expression of the same thing, labour which exchanges directly with capital, i.e., with money which is in itself capital, has the determination of functioning as capital, or confronts labour capacity as capital'.[14] But, in the exchange between capital and labour, two essentially different moments again need to remain distinct, even though they also condition each other. The first of these is a formal process in which capital figures as money and labour-power as a commodity: it is, in fact, an exchange of labour for labour, or labour objectified in money for the living labour that exists within the worker; yet it is in this transaction with itself that labour becomes the property of wealth. The second moment of exchange

---

14 MECW, Vol. 34, 132.

between capital and labour is the total opposite: the money-holder now functions as a capitalist and the workers' labour-power is only a function in use by capital; the exchange here is thus effectively between capital and itself, the exchange between two of its parts. 'Labour therefore directly objectifies itself in this process, converts itself directly into capital, after it has already been incorporated formally into capital through the first transaction'.[15] And yet it is precisely in this process that capital divides internally into two counterposed parts, each the enemy of the other. The class relation is now introduced into the very relation of social production. Only at this cost can 'capital in itself' become a capitalist relation of production. At this point, wage-labour meets with productive labour: the sale of labour-power for a wage becomes the use of labour-power for profit. The process that the worker had first set in motion is now moved by the capitalist through the use of the worker. There has been a decisive shift in the relation of force: all power has passed into the hands of capital – that is, the power of command over labour and of exploitation of the workers. From this moment onward, the movements of capital always seem to precede and condition the movements of the working class, seem continually to impose on it the reflections of its own figure. This, too, is no mere outward appearance. This is how things are *in fact* to those who look at them from the capitalist point of view: this is, indeed, the day-to-day political effort that fills the days of a functionary of capital. But can this also be the case from the working-class point of view? It can be, albeit only on condition that workers' labour is seen as part of capital but not a part counterposed to it; only on condition that the working-class point of view is assumed on capital's behalf, on the now sadly 'historical' condition that it settles into the seat of reformism. But if it is discovered that the class relation comes before the capital relation, if it is discovered that within this preliminary class relation the only class already embryonically constituted is that of the proletarians who sell their labour-power, who, once inserted into production and socially organised, develop into a working class, even before capital passes from potential to actuality – are not all the bases then laid for continuing to construct the entire history of capital starting from the historical development of the working class? The working-class point of view on productive labour is an essential point in the

---

15 Ibid., 133.

conquest of this 'strategic overturn'. Did Marx not say that 'productive labour' is only an abbreviation, which in fact means to indicate the entire relation, the whole way in which labour-power figures in the process of capitalist production? So, faced with the question 'what is productive labour from capital's point of view?', the response ought to be: productive labour, as a concrete production of use-values, 'reproduces for the worker only the previously posited value of his labour capacity' as an activity that creates value, 'valorises capital, and counterposes the values created by labour to the worker himself as capital'.[16] It is true: labour's productive forces are indeed transferred into capital. And yet, even after this transfer, labour presents itself in the face of capital precisely as labour that produces capital. The real process is one and the same: in the first case, it is seen from the capitalist side and in the second case from the working-class one. These two points of view are no less real than the process that underpins them. So, yes, when we are talking about the working class within the system of capital, the same productive force really can be counted twice: one time as a force that produces capital and another time as a force that refuses to produce it; one time within capital, another time against capital. When the two times are subjectively unified on the working-class side, the route is opened to dissolve the capitalist system and the practical process of the revolution begins.

The necessary next step in this research is to see 'how capital produces'. But, at this point, it is all too interesting to go back and see 'how it is itself produced'. These are two eras in the history of the working class that we will keep distinct in order to make our exposition easier. But, in fact, they make up a single whole – and, in their continuity, they recount the entire life of the working-class articulation of capitalist development. What jumps to the foreground, again, is the original relation between labour and capital as a relation between labour and the objective conditions of labour, which present themselves as capital. Behind this is that long historical process which, in Marx's words, dissolves the various forms in which the worker is a property owner – which is to say, the different forms in which the property owner works: the dissolution of the property relation with the land; the dissolution of the property relation with the tool; the dissolution of the property relation with the

---

16   Ibid., 447.

means of subsistence; and, finally, the dissolution of all the relations in which the labourers themselves, the living bearers of the capacity to labour themselves, still directly belong to the objective conditions of production. One same historical process, on the one hand, liberates a mass of individuals from the positive relations that they entertained with the conditions of labour, and it thus makes wage-labourers *dunamei* free individuals compelled to work and to sell their labour, precisely because they have been liberated from property; on the other hand, it liberates the very conditions of labour – land, raw materials, means of subsistence, the tools of labour, money and so on – from their previous tie to the individuals who are now unbound from them. The whole process thus consists of the separation of elements that were hitherto united. As Marx would elsewhere put it, in this society separation appears as a normal relationship. Capital's historic power owes precisely to its ability to unite under its own command two separate material entities – the subjective and objective conditions of production: 'The only characteristic of capital is that it brings together the masses of hands and the instruments which are already there. It agglomerates them under its sway. This is its real accumulation; the accumulation of workers along with their instruments at particular points.'[17] It is important to note the previous (*ursprüngliche*) accumulation of capital, the prehistory of the capitalist economy – the formation of a monetary base that is in itself and as such unproductive, but also able to exchange the objective conditions of labour for labour-power, which is to be able to purchase living labour by paying with dead labour. Quite another thing is the true and proper accumulation of capital, which generalises and, at the same time, makes specific the exchange between objectified labour and the capacity to labour, thus establishing the appropriation of social living labour without exchange – which transforms labour's social productive forces into productive forces that directly belong to capital, to the point that the latter presents itself as productive capital. This accumulation of capital is thus also a production of capitalists. Marx tells us that the capitalist is contained within the concept of capital. And Engels was grossly mistaken in his *Wage-Labour and Capital* when he substituted 'capitalist' for 'capital'. If he did so in order to make himself understood among the workers, this was still unjustified. '*Im Begriff des Kapitals ist der*

---

17 MECW, Vol. 28, 431.

Kapitalist enthalten'. Accumulation is itself – in a wholly different sense – the reproduction of waged workers. 'In as much as this process posits objectified labour as simultaneously the non-objectification of the worker, as the objectification of a subjectivity confronting the worker, as the property of someone else's will, capital is necessarily also a capitalist. The idea of some socialists that we need capital but not capitalists is therefore completely false. It is inherent in the concept of capital that the objective conditions of labour – and these are its own product – acquire a personality confronting labour, or, and this amounts to the same thing, that they are posited as the property of a personality alien to the worker.'[18] Thus, at the surface-level, capitalist production always presents a free and equal exchange between equivalents, but fundamentally it is nothing other than the exchange of objectified labour *qua* exchange-value for living labour *qua* use-value 'or, as it may also be expressed, labour relating to its objective conditions – and hence to the objectivity created by labour itself – as to alien property: the alienation of labour'.[19] That is, as the exchange of labour for labour, within capital and by work of capital. Living labour and objectified labour, labour-power and the conditions of labour, the subjective and objective presuppositions of production are subsumed economically under capital and politically subordinated to it. Along this route, the logical difference, the historical separation between these two moments is negated, and in accumulation, in the true and proper production of capital, it is reduced to a single unity. When Marx says that separation is the normal relation in this society, he means that this is the normal class social relation. The political history of capital is the history of its various attempts to free itself of the destructive practical consequences of this relation, or to control it in its irrational twists and turns, and thus to use it in the continual unitary recomposition – one with a rationalising tendency – of its own development. Capital's most mature vocation, as a historical force of governance, decisively proceeds from division toward unity. This refers to the unity – and not identity – of every antagonism and unity in every struggle, the unity between subjective and objective, between its own objectivity and the counterposed subjectivity wholly left in the hands of the worker – a unity, therefore, within itself, between the capitalist mode of

18 Ibid., 436.
19 Ibid., 438.

production and its functionaries, who express and manage it. The concept of capital contains not only the capitalist, but also the class of capitalists. The history of this class is a short one: its birth comes after that of capital, and it dies sooner. It emerges outside of the indistinct objectivity of the production relation when the workers threaten this relation, subjectively as a class. And in this objectivity is wholly recuperated as soon as this class threat, now being overturned, becomes the bearer of the general interests of capitalist society. When the working class disappears politically, what purpose does it serve capitalists to politically organise themselves as a class? The conditions of the struggle thus have to be followed back to their origins, but elaborated from the working-class point of view alone. In the passage from capital to the class of capitalists, and from the latter to capitalist society, the terrain of the class struggle develops positively – but on just one condition, that the freedom of property, in which the figure of the first proletarian emerged in rough form, transforms into a conscious and organised freedom of society, in the evolved stage that the modern working class has now reached. Of course, along this path, the conditions of the struggle will become harsher to the point of the most violent rupture, and even go beyond that. The outcome will long remain uncertain. The clash will take place between two likewise powerful forces on a completely new terrain: on the one side, a class; on the opposite side, society. Marx tells us that 'in bourgeois society, e.g., the worker stands there purely subjectively, without object [*objektvlos*]; but the thing which confronts him has now become the true community, which he tries to make a meal of [*verspeisen*]and which makes a meal of him.'[20] Even if we consider only the formal side of the capitalist relation – the general form that the least-developed capitalist mode of production has in common with the most-developed – it is easy to see how the conditions of labour never appear as subsumed under the worker, but, rather, the worker always appears subsumed under them. This is precisely the reason that the conditions of labour are capital. Marx tells us that capital employs labour. So even if we consider the simple formal subsumption of labour under capitalist conditions of production, the productivity of capital consists first and foremost in the compulsion to provide surplus-labour (*Zwang zur Surplusarbeit*), a compulsion thus now exercised in a manner

---

20 Ibid., 420.

much more favourable to production. And this privilege, now handed to production, derives precisely from the fact that 'The capitalist himself only holds power [*ist Gewalthaber*] as the personification of capital … the capitalist does not rule the worker in any kind of personal capacity, but only in so far as he is "capital"; his rule is only that of objectified labour over living labour; the rule of the worker's product over the worker himself.'[21] If Marx himself expresses his thinking using the terms 'personification of the thing' and 'thingification of the person' thus analysing these processes in terms of fetishism, this should not offer the opportunity – as too often happens – to head off down one of the neutral pathways of contemporary philosophy. The product that dominates the worker here is not simply a generic object, perhaps an object of consumption, but something very socially determinate, from the point of view of production. As a use-value, it is identified with the objective conditions of labour; as an exchange-value, it is identified with general objectified labour-time – which is to say, with money. So, it is identified with things that are immediately material, but which stand counterposed to the worker, dominate the worker, as capital. And this is the simplest capitalist relation, offering the fewest obstacles to under-standing; it is the formal and general aspect which, indeed, even a philosopher is able to grasp. Capital becomes highly mysterious in the immediately subsequent historical process, 'the forms of socially devel-oped labour, cooperation, manufacture (as a form of the division of labour), the factory (as a form of social labour organised on the material basis of machinery) appear as forms of the development of capital, and therefore the productive powers of labour, developed out of these forms of social labour, hence also science and the forces of nature, appear as productive forces of capital'.[22] Thus, this unity in cooperation, the combination in the division of labour, the employment of natural forces and science, the organisation of machines for production – all these now-fully social conditions of labour stand counterposed to the workers themselves, dominate them, in an extraneous and objective way, as functions of capital and thus of the capitalist. 'The social forms of their own labour, or the form of their own social labour, are relations consti-tuted quite independently of the individual workers; the workers as

21   MECW, Vol. 34, 123.
22   Ibid.

subsumed under capital become elements of these social constructions, but these social constructions do not belong to them. They therefore confront the workers as shapes of capital itself, as combinations which, unlike their isolated labour capacities, belong to capital, originate from it and are incorporated within it.'[23] In the development of this historical process internal to capitalism, no longer only the simple objective conditions of labour but the more complex 'social characteristics of labour' themselves rise up *in front* of the workers, *against* them, 'so to speak, capitalised [*kapitalisiert*]': means of exploiting social labour, social means for the appropriation of surplus-labour. 'And thus the development of the social productive powers of labour and the conditions for this development appear [*erscheinen*] as the work of capital [*Tat des Kapitals*], and not only does the individual worker relate passively [*passiv verhält*] to this work, it also takes place in antagonism to him.'[24] On the one side, then, at this point are the social productive forces of labour as the action of capital; on the other side, and counterposed to this, the passive attitude of the single worker – a condition of the class struggle that should not be unknown even to neutral worshippers of the social sciences. A problem of considerable importance is posed here. Is the productive force of labour – as a social force introduced into the production process – not to be identified with the working class at a rather advanced level of its development? And, if that is so, what does it mean to say that this power belongs to capital? Perhaps it means that the workers, as a class, are not only introduced into the production process *of capital*, but are even incorporated into capital itself, as a relation of production? Does the working class, then, as soon as it has begun to be a class, become a function of capital? Following Marx's research up to this point, it seems that all the conditions of production – and, foremost, the social productive forces of labour, which is to say, the social force of productive labour – have passed into capital's ownership and what has remained outside of it is only labour-power 'taken in isolation', as the ineliminable property of the single worker. The workers *as a class* now contract the value and price of individual labour-power with the capitalists *as a class*. The primordial relation of the purchase and sale of this particular commodity now reappears in a form managed by social

---

23 Ibid.
24 Ibid., 124.

classes or, better, by the institutions that represent each of them. The
radical order of institutionalised conflict replaces the irrational disorder
of the class struggle. The moment of the contract negotiations becomes
the only opportunity for struggle and the trade union the highest stage
of organisation. This is what we can conclude here. It would be all too
easy to reply that while this is how things appear, the reality is opposite
to this appearance. But we have decided that we will no longer entertain
ourselves with this game of appearances. Of course, the 'intellectual'
functionaries of capital, professional 'social researchers', charge all these
processes with so much ideology as they explain them. And we ought
not believe that they pluck these ideological trappings from their own
empty heads: rather, they simply see them as attached to the single real
phenomena, because they see the whole process from the standpoint of
capital; not only that, but they view it as a necessarily ideological 'defence'
of capital's point of view. From such a stance, in the totality of this
process there is no difference between what is and what appears to be,
but only between different parts, different moments of one same social
reality. Thus, the ideological appearance is not only functional to the
social relation; it is the social relation itself, as it appears to the capitalist.
And it then presents itself before the worker as it appears to the capitalist. From the worker's point of view, the process is turned on its head.
This self-presentation, this way of going forward, this counterposition
of the relation with the worker is often a wholly real fact and hardly ever
a merely apparent phenomenon. It is necessary, therefore, to start out
from how the relation really presents itself, if we want to not only know
it but destroy it. Hence the slight ambiguity in Marx's use of the verb
erscheinen: on very few occasions – and only in some of the cases in
which he is referring to the capitalist point of view – can it be translated
as 'appear'. But most of the time, including in every case where we are
referring to the working-class point of view in Marx, it should be translated as 'presents itself', a meaning very close to the verb 'to be'. As we
well know, 'ideology' also means the bourgeois will to make the capitalist relation appear to the workers in a certain way. But we consciously
tend to underestimate this aspect, in order to avoid making even a small
opening for behavioural psychology, or, to be more precise, not to dip
even a toe into the muddy terrain of 'class consciousness'. If we speak of
the worker as a single labour-power outside of capital and the workers
as a social class within capital, this does not owe to some false

appearance, and our task is not to exercise a critique at this level; rather, it is a harsh reality, and the important thing is to measure the needs of organisation against this reality. The antagonism, indeed, is not within the figure of the free worker taken in isolation, but in the massive presence of the working class within capital, compelled to combat its entire enemy while itself being part of it. But to convince ourselves of this, and to see more closely in practice what it entails, we need to respond to the aforementioned questions. Thus, first of all: at what point of its own development is the working class identical to labour's social productive power, as in the social power of productive labour? And, from that point onward, does this identification account for the entire factual reality of the working class, or does something of this reality remain outside of this concept? We need, therefore, to quickly pick up on a thread in Marx's research that we had deliberately allowed to fall to one side: namely, the one that from the outset regards the workers' directly political movements – which is to say, the definition of the working class as a rebellious force in the capitalist system, as a revolutionary potentiality. And we think it right to uphold the thesis that, in Marx, this definition preceded and anticipated all of his subsequent research into labour, labour-power, value and thus capital. Insofar as, in Marx, the proletarian is identical to the seller of labour-power, the concept of the 'proletariat as a class' is an original discovery of his. Here, we are not interested in the philological origin of the term, which is, of course, very ambiguous ideologically and as such extraneous to Marx's own scientific point of view. What interests us is a political fact: that even the roughest Marxian definitions of the proletariat, its political content, its practical needs, its destructive function within bourgeois society, come far before his refined analyses of the corresponding abstract categories which the classical sources would deposit on his desk. Marx did not start out from the 'critique of political economy', even if this is understood to mean a critique of capitalism. Rather, he arrived at this and passed through it, having earlier started out from an attempt at a theory of revolution. At the outset, there was nothing other than a choice – elementary in its violence and violent in its elementary character – to oppose the entire world of bourgeois society, as well as deadly class hatred against it. This, the simplest form of Marx's working-class science, would remain – as it had to and must remain – as a general form in all the further developments of this science. Here, we find for the motives behind something that later put Marxist thought into difficulty and created dangerous delays in the development of Marxist analysis, but in recompense for this also kept Marx distant from the petty-bourgeois plague of philistines, as indeed it continues to do. And it is a fact that, amid the most developed analyses in *Capital*, in the mature phase of Marx's thought, we find the most elementary definitions of the working class as a proletariat, and thus a wholly practical judgement on its historical formation and its political function. Undoubtedly, when it comes to the analysis of the working class, Marx's point of view did not manage to develop from the simple form to the general form of working-class science, which bears within it all past journeys and judges them from the height and the needs of the present struggle – a present which, in turn, is wholly projected into the future. This does not mean to say that the historical level of the working class's development could not offer any more to Marx. That is not right; after all, the same thing could be said of the level of development that capital had reached, and yet, in the latter case, his masterly strokes anticipate decades of future history. In this, so to speak, 'proletarian' definition of the working class, which Marx constantly supplies at the political level, we see how much he is missing a proper mediation between the correct theoretical starting point – class hatred against the entire society – and the successive articulation of practical action tending toward the concrete objective of revolution. Here, in Marx's lack of direct political activity – and he could never approach the level of his research subject itself – we think we can see the practical origin of some of the errors he made in his analysis. We need only think of the chapter on primitive accumulation, which discussed the formation of the proletariat, or of the laws of immiseration, which were meant to regard the development of the working class. The error here lies not in any lack of serious scientific objectivity on the part of the researcher, but in a lack of practical long-term foresight on the part of the politician. Again, the exchange is between tactics and strategy, between theory and politics. Marx is rarely clear about the distinction between these two moments. He wanted to demonstrate that, even with the most formidable development of capital, the division into classes, as the class counterposition between two classes, remained politically the same as at the outset, and even that it was this counterposition that had founded the capitalist production relation. Faced with the processes that socialise capital, which he intuited with such genius, he found nothing better than the exasperation of an aggressive proletarianisation of working-class labour-power as the only antithesis that could not be absorbed by the system. Instead of politically developing the concept of the working class, he continually tried to draw this concept back to its historical origins. If the workers – as productive labour – were incorporated into capital, and the proletarians – as sellers of labour-power – continued to be counterposed to capital, then there was no other political route to revolution other than to precipitate the working class into the proletariat once more. It was thus necessary to twist the historical analysis, the scientific foresight, in this direction. But the whole origin of this error of substance lies in an overly impassioned participation in the most immediate happenings of the class struggle. Not that we would want to condemn this. When, in spring 1848, the Paris proletariat applauded the city's lumpenproletarians, dressed as *gardes mobiles*, through the streets, (mis)taking them for their own vanguard fighters, Marx commented that its error was pardonable.

To who then asks us: 'why still Marx', we reply with two reasons. First, and in general, because Marx and the point of view of working-class science make up a single whole. Second, and more particularly, because, on the theme of labour, labour-power, and the working class, the path internal to Marx's work is the historical path of the development of the problem itself. First the proletariat, then labour-power; first the workers as a class politically, then the economic category as an articulation of production; first the antagonistic class, then the function of capital. The working class had a political birth, in that it presented itself from the outset as an alternative power to the system of capital; it grows up economically, in that it is, by necessity, introduced into this system's mechanism of production and reproduction; on this basis, it must organise its own development in a revolutionary way, in order to blow up the whole of the very system of which it is itself part. Cassirer had to come along to explain that the criterion of truth in Marxism is posed within the historical outcome – that is, in the revolution not as idea, but as a real fact. Lenin tells us that, after Marx, none of the Marxists understood this. Marx's path, completed by Lenin, leads from the theory of the revolution to the critique of capitalism, and from here to the practical revolution – and this path thus ought to be reproduced also in terms of the specific theme that we are dealing with here. If, in our analysis, we started out from the second moment, readers will have understood that the first moment was already presupposed: not as an ideological programme but as a political forecast. For us, too, the theory of revolution is wholly contained within the political definition of the working class. Today's Marxists have still not understood such a simple idea. And yet it is perhaps the first fundamental discovery of 'their' young Marx.

7

What the Proletariat Is

Already back in his day, Lukács had set these imposing words of Marx's as the epigraph for one of his own later-disavowed youthful essays: 'It is not a question of what this or that proletarian, or even the whole proletariat, at the moment regards as its aim. It is a question of what the proletariat is, and what, in accordance with this being, it will historically be compelled to do.' In the *Holy Family*, faced with the critical critique, the worker is presented as he who 'creates everything' to the point that even in his spiritual creations he puts all critique to shame; something of which the British and French workers had provided a great deal of evidence. 'The worker creates even man' for it is true that 'man has lost himself in the proletariat' but at the same time 'has not only gained theoretical consciousness of that loss, but through urgent, no longer removable, no longer disguisable, absolutely imperative *need* – the practical expression of *necessity* – is driven directly to revolt against this inhumanity'. The form of this rebellion, first of all, comes out in the most evident, strident and immediately revolting way, on account of poverty and misery, as part of the contradictory essence of private property. The proletariat and wealth are, indeed, antithetical terms, within a whole that comprises both. 'Private property as private property, as wealth, is compelled to maintain itself, and thereby its opposite, the proletariat, in existence. That is the positive side of the antithesis, self-satisfied private property. The proletariat, on the contrary, is compelled as proletariat to abolish itself and thereby its opposite, private property, which determines its existence, and which makes it proletariat. It is the negative side of the antithesis, its restlessness within its very self, dissolved and self-dissolving private property.' The proletariat-class thus feels itself continually being destroyed in this condition and it, in turn, continually rebels in order to destroy this condition. 'It is, to use an expression of Hegel, in its abasement the indignation at that abasement.' Out of the two antithetical terms, the first thus works to conserve the antithesis and the second works to destroy it. 'Within this antithesis the private property-owner is therefore the conservative side, the proletarian the destructive side. From the former arises the action of preserving the antithesis, from the latter the action of annihilating it.' It is true that through its economic movement, private property itself heads toward its own dissolution, but only by means of a development that is independent of it, of which it is unconscious, and which takes place against its will. 'Private property drives itself … towards its own dissolution … only inasmuch as it produces the proletariat as proletariat … The proletariat executes the sentence that private property pronounces on itself by producing the proletariat.'[1] This is the sense in which 'Its aim and historical action is visibly and irrevocably foreshadowed in its own life situation as well as in the whole organisation of bourgeois society today.'[2] All this was clearly expressed already in the *Deutsch-Französische Jahrbücher*: 'If constructing the future and settling everything for all times are not our affair, it is all the more clear what we have to accomplish at present: I am referring to ruthless criticism of all that exists.'[3] Of course, this is not a matter of raising the banner of dogma. Quite the contrary. Communism, above all, is a dogmatic abstraction, insofar as it is 'itself only a special expression [*Erscheinung*] of the humanistic principle, an expression which is still infected by its antithesis – the private system.'[4] Not without good reason, communism has seen other socialist doctrines rising up before it, and today it is itself but a particular, unilateral realisation of the socialist principle. And the whole socialist principle, in turn, is nothing but one aspect of the problem, that which concerns the reality of the true human essence. But we likewise ought to concern ourselves with the other object: the judgement

---

1 Marx and Engels Collected Works (MECW), Vol. 4, 36.
2 Ibid., 36–7.
3 MECW, Vol. 3, 142.
4 Ibid., 143.

on things such as they really are, as they exist. 'There is nothing to stop us 'making criticism of politics, participation in politics, and therefore real struggles, the starting point of our criticism, and from identifying our criticism with them.'[5] The positive possibility of emancipation in fact resides only 'in the formation of a class with radical chains [mit radikalen Ketten],'[6] a class that does not demand 'any particular right' for itself and which, through its universal existence, heralds the dissolution of society as a particular state. 'By proclaiming the dissolution of the hitherto exist- ing world order the proletariat merely states the secret of its own exist- ence, for it is in fact the dissolution [faktische Auflösung] of that world order. By demanding the negation of private property, the proletariat merely raises to the rank of a principle of society what society has made the principle of the proletariat, what, without its own co-operation, is already incorporated in it as the negative result [negatives Resultat] of society.'[7] Hence, the more that the working-class revolt makes headway on this material-practical terrain, the more it acquires a theoretical and conscious character. 'Recall the song of the weavers, that bold call to struggle, in which there is not even a mention of hearth and home, factory or district, but in which the proletariat at once, in a striking, sharp, unrestrained and powerful manner, proclaims its opposition to the society of private property. The Silesian uprising begins precisely with what the French and English workers' uprisings end, with conscious- ness of the nature of the proletariat [mit dem Bewusstsein über das Wesen des Proletariats] (Vorwärts, 10 August 1844).'[8] In the German Ideology, Marx would start out from the principle that 'The separate individuals form a class only insofar as they have to carry on a common battle against another class; in other respects they are on hostile terms with each other as competitors.'[9] And this general law has its ultimate and highest particu- lar application in modern society. 'Thus, on the one hand, we have a totality of productive forces, which have, as it were, taken on a material form and are for the individuals themselves no longer the forces of the individuals but of private property, and hence of the individuals only insofar as they are owners of private property ... On the other hand,

---

5 Ibid., 144.
6 Ibid., 186.
7 Ibid., 187.
8 Ibid., 201.
9 MECW, Vol. 5, 77.

standing against these productive forces, we have the majority of the individuals from whom these forces have been wrested away, and who, robbed thus of all real life-content, have become abstract individuals, who are, however, by this very fact put into a position to enter into relation with one another as individuals [*miteinander in Verbindung*].[10] The only connection that still binds them to the productive forces and their very existence – labour – has lost in these latter any semblance of personal expression. Their enemy is not, therefore, only the capitalist, but also labour itself. Hence, from the outset, their struggle is directed against the entire social relation. These are the 'proletarians of the present time' a class which, insofar as it has to bear all the burdens of society' is 'forced into the sharpest contradiction to all other classes'; it is 'a class which forms the majority of all members of society, and from which emanates the consciousness of the necessity of a fundamental revolution [*einer gründlichen Revolution*]'.[11] In all the revolutions that have thus far taken place, indeed, the 'mode (Art) of activity' has remained unchanged. They have always and only had to do with a different distribution of these activities, a new distribution of labour to other people, whereas 'the communist revolution is directed against the hitherto existing mode [*Art*] of activity, does away with labour [*die Arbeit beseitigt*] and abolishes the rule of all classes with the classes themselves'.[12] A line in the manuscript after 'does away with labour' that was later crossed out continues, with an interrupted definition of labour as 'the modern form of activity under which the dominion of.'[13] Marcuse seeks to emphasise the gravity of these claims, noting that here there appears the trusty old *Aufhebung*, which, even as it suppresses also restores and so on. He then notes that this explanation is too banal and thinks about how he can get rid of the category of the future that is non-labour and restore the antiquated, philistine, reactionary idea of happiness. But separate from all this, the previous discourse ends as follows: what is needed, for both the mass production of this communist consciousness and for the success of the thing itself, is a transformation of the mass of humanity, which can take place only in a practical revolutionary movement. 'The revolution is

---

10 Ibid., 86–7.
11 Ibid., 52.
12 Ibid.
13 Karl Marx, *Werke*, Vol. 3, 70.

necessary, therefore, not only because the ruling class cannot be over-
thrown in any other way, but also because the class overthrowing [*die
stürzende Klasse*] it can only in a revolution succeed in ridding itself of all
the muck of ages …'[14] The theoretical struggle against Proudhon achieved
a notable leap forward in Marx's analysis of these problems. Not by
chance, the *Poverty of Philosophy* contains Marx's first and important – if
not yet satisfactory – definitions of the concept of class. The relations of
production that the bourgeoisie moves within present themselves not
with a simple single character, but rather with a dual character. Within
these same relations, there is the production of wealth, but also of
poverty; there is development of the productive forces, but also of a force
that produces repression; that is, 'these relations produce bourgeois
wealth, i. e., the wealth of the bourgeois class, only by continually annihilating the wealth of the individual members of this class and by producing an ever-growing proletariat.'[15] And this is the basis upon which a
struggle develops between the proletarian class and the bourgeois class;
this struggle has a whole history of its own, its own development and a
series of phases that it passes through. 'There develops a struggle between
the proletarian class and the bourgeois class, a struggle which, before
being felt, perceived, appreciated, understood, avowed and proclaimed
aloud by both sides, expresses itself, to start with, merely in partial and
momentary conflicts, in subversive acts.'[16] Yet the development of modern
industry necessarily also leads to coalitions among workers. Workers'
first attempts to associate themselves always took this form. Economists
and socialists then agreed to tell the workers: do not build coalitions
among yourselves. 'Large-scale industry concentrates in one place a
crowd of people unknown to one another. Competition divides their
interests. But the maintenance of wages, this common interest which
they have against their boss, unites them in a common thought of resistance – combination. Thus combination always has a double aim, that of
stopping competition among the workers, so that they can carry on
general competition with the capitalist. If the first aim of resistance was
merely the maintenance of wages, combinations, at first isolated, constitute themselves into groups as the capitalists in their turn unite for the

14 MECW, Vol. 5, 53.
15 MECW, Vol. 6, 176.
16 Ibid., 175.

purpose of repression, and in face of always united capital, the maintenance of the association becomes more necessary to them than that of
wages.'[17] In this struggle, 'a real civil war', all the elements that will be
necessary for the future battle come together and develop. Once the association has reached this point, it takes on a political character. 'Economic
conditions had first transformed the mass of the people of the country
into workers. The domination of capital has created for this mass a
common situation, common interests. This mass is thus already a class as
against capital, but not yet for itself. In the struggle, of which we have
pointed out only a few phases, this mass becomes united, and constitutes
itself as a class for itself. The interests it defends become class interests.
But the struggle of class against class is a political struggle.'[18] Taken to its
highest expression, this political struggle of class against class, between
proletariat and bourgeoisie, 'is a total revolution'. And 'indeed, is it at all
surprising that a society founded on the opposition of classes should
culminate in brutal contradiction, the shock of body against body, as its
final denouement?'[19] Combat or death, the bloody struggle or the void –
this is 'the last word of social science'.[20] So, when the Second Conference
of the Communist League mandated Marx and Engels to write the
Manifesto, its content was in fact all already in Marx's head. The
programme of the proletarian revolution responded like a fusillade to the
bourgeois revolution of February 1848. 'The old motto of the League of
the Just, "All men are brothers", was replaced by a new, Marxist one:
"Working Men of All Countries, Unite!"'.[21] Too many intellectuals,
so-called serious scholars, even ready to admire the scientific Marx of
Capital, shut their eyes in dismay at the raw, wholly political pages of the
Manifesto. But for us, this text remains a model for a practical intervention of the working-class point of view in the class struggle. The battlecry
of which Engels spoke lay not only in the final slogan but in the very
construction of the entire text: 'But not only has the bourgeoisie forged
the weapons that bring death to itself; it has also called into existence the
men who are to wield those weapons – the modern working class – the

---

17 Ibid., 210–11.
18 Ibid., 211.
19 Ibid., 212.
20 Ibid.
21 Ibid., 671.

proletarians'.[22] For this is the class of those who are compelled to sell themselves by the minute, who live so long as they can work and find work so long as their labour augments capital. Thus, the proletariat passes through different degrees of development. But its 'struggle against the bourgeoisie begins with its existence'. First off, individual workers struggle one by one, and then the workers of a factory struggle – that is, the workers of a given category in a certain place struggle against the individual bourgeois, who directly exploits them. At this stage, the workers form a mass dispersed across the country and divided by competition. As a mass, they are already united; not, however, through their own initiative but through the initiative of the bourgeoisie, which must set the whole proletariat in movement in order to achieve its own political goals. This is the long historical stage in which proletarians do not fight their enemies but their enemies' enemies. At this point, the whole movement of history is concentrated in the hands of the bourgeoisie. Every victory is a victory for the bourgeoisie. But, with the development of industry, the proletariat multiplies, concentrates, is internally levelled-out, unifies; its power grows enormously and together with this, its awareness of its power. The conflict between individual workers and individual bourgeois disappears; what arrives in its place is the open clash between the two classes. The workers form coalitions, unite in associations, and with the latter drive the first forms of struggle, up to and including the pure and simple violence of the riot. Now and then, they win, but only ever temporarily. 'The real fruit of their battles lies, not in the immediate result, but in the ever-expanding union of the workers'.[23] Local struggles link together and concentrate in a single class struggle against a nation's whole bourgeoisie. 'But every class struggle is a political struggle'. There thus emerges the problem of the 'organisation of the proletarians into a class, and consequently into a political party'.[24] Only at this point does the theoretical programme of the revolution become practically realisable. The most important condition for the existence and the dominion of the bourgeois class is the accumulation of wealth in private hands, the formation and the multiplication of capital. But 'the condition of capital is wage-labour'. The progress of industry – of which the bourgeoisie is the

---

22 Ibid., 490.
23 Ibid., 493.
24 Ibid.

involuntary and passive vehicle – necessarily leads to the association of the workers among themselves, to their 'revolutionary union'. With the development of big industry, the very terrain on which the bourgeoisie produces and appropriates products is thus pulled from under its feet. Rather, it produces its own gravediggers (*Sie produziert vor allem ihre eigenen Totengräber*). Both Marx and Engels repeatedly referred to the 'decisive event' that had taken place in Paris on 13 June 1849. About a month earlier, the two men's time at the *Neue Rheinische Zeitung* had come to an end with a 'glorious defeat' – the experience of the political periodical had reached its conclusion. Marx was in Paris. From there, on 7 June, he wrote to Engels, who was volunteering in Kaiserslautern among Willich's troops: 'never has a colossal eruption of the revolutionary volcano been more imminent than it is in Paris today'.[25] On 11 June, Ledru Rollin, leader of the Montagnards, asked the Chamber to put Bonaparte and his ministry under investigation for having violated the constitution. This was another case of an attempt, such as had become traditional since the time of the Convention, at a parliamentary insurrection, 'an insurrection within the limits of pure reason'.[26] The aim was the same one the democratic petty-bourgeoisie had always had: 'breaking the power of the bourgeoisie without unleashing the proletariat or letting it appear otherwise than in perspective; the proletariat would have been used without becoming dangerous'.[27] In these conditions, it was natural that the cry 'long live the constitution' took on no other meaning than 'down with the revolution'. Having been consulted, the delegates of the workers' secret associations did the only thing that would have been reasonable to do in that moment: they forced the Montagnards to commit themselves and to break out of the limits of the parliamentary struggle if the bid to charge Bonaparte were thwarted. And indeed it was. But when, on the morning of 13 June, they read the 'proclamation to the people' in the socialist papers *La démocratie pacifique* and *La réforme* – namely, the appeal from the petty bourgeois for the proletarians to rise up – they refused to give their backing and watched passively as the democrats went down to a ridiculous defeat. 'During the whole of June 13, the proletariat maintained this same sceptically watchful attitude, and awaited a

---

25 MECW, Vol. 38, 199.
26 MECW, Vol. 10, 103.
27 Ibid., 103–4.

seriously engaged irrevocable mêlée between the democratic National
Guard and the army, in order then to plunge into the fight and push the
revolution forward beyond the petty-bourgeois aim set for it. In the event
of victory a proletarian commune was already formed which would take
its place beside the official government. The Parisian workers had learned
in the bloody school of June 1848'.[28] The battle did not take place. Regular
troops mounted a bayonet charge against the peaceful procession by the
disarmed national guards. Only from Lyons did there come the sign –
one that was not heeded elsewhere – of a bloody working-class insurrection; but here 'where the industrial bourgeoisie and the industrial proletariat stand directly opposed to one another, where the workers'
movement is not, as in Paris, included in and determined by the general
movement'.[29] In all the other provinces where the lightning struck, it did
not catch fire. On 29 June, Marx wrote in the *Volksfreund*: 'Taken as a
whole, June 13, 1849, is only the retaliation for June 1848. On that occasion the proletariat was deserted by the "Mountain", this time the
"Mountain" was deserted by the proletariat'.[30] 'If June 23, 1848, was the
insurrection of the revolutionary proletariat, June 13, 1849, was the
insurrection of the democratic petty bourgeois, each of these two insurrections being the classically pure expression of the class which had been
its vehicle'.[31] But the starting point was still there, in June 1848: 'the most
colossal event in the history of European civil wars' (as Marx put it in his
Eighteenth Brumaire). 'On its side stood the finance aristocracy, the
industrial bourgeoisie, the middle class, the petty bourgeois, the army,
the lumpenproletariat organised as the Mobile Guard, the intellectuals,
the clergy and the rural population. On the side of the Paris proletariat
stood none but itself'. The bourgeois republic emerged triumphant. 'With
this defeat the proletariat recedes into the background of the revolutionary stage'.[32]

The proletariat sought to push itself forward once more, each time
that the movement seemed to produce a new upsurge but did so with
ever less energy and with increasingly meagre results. As soon as one of
the social layers above it entered into revolutionary ferment the

---

28   Ibid., 104.
29   Ibid., 106.
30   MECW, Vol. 9, 479.
31   MECW, Vol. 10, 106.
32   MECW, Vol. 11, 110.

proletariat established ties with it, and the former thus itself shared in all the defeats that the various parties suffered, one after the other. The most outstanding representatives of the proletariat gradually fell victims to the courts and increasingly dubious figures took their place. The official workers' movement abandoned itself to doctrinaire experiments, public exchange banks and secret workers' associations; it thus '[renounced] the revolutionising of the old world by means of the latter's own great, combined resources, and [sought], rather, to achieve its salvation behind society's back, in private fashion, within its limited conditions of existence, and hence necessarily [suffered] shipwreck'.[33] Faced with the bourgeois republic, now discovered to mean nothing more than 'the absolute despotism of a class', there arose the urgent need for a coalition between the workers and the petty bourgeois. 'The revolutionary point was broken off from the social demands of the proletariat and a democratic turn given to them; the purely political form was stripped from the democratic claims of the petty bourgeoisie and their socialist point turned outward. Thus arose Social-Democracy'.[34] The revolutionary goal henceforth became 'the reformation of society in a democratic way'.[35] All this was a prelude to the events of June 1849 and explains how 'the blaring overture that announced the contest dies away in a faint grumble as soon as the struggle has to begin, the actors cease to take themselves au sérieux, and the action collapses completely, like a pricked balloon'.[36] The deep and real aversion toward the democratic petty bourgeoisie cultivated by the proletariat of June 1848 was stronger than all the much-invoked 'great common interests'. It was the first time an autonomous movement, a class movement of proletarians, of workers, escaped the control and plans of the formal democratic logic. 'The democrats concede that a privileged class confronts them, but they, along with all the rest of the nation, form the people. What they represent is the people's rights; what interests them is the people's interests. Accordingly, when a struggle is impending, they do not need to examine the interests and positions of the different classes. They do not need to weigh their own resources too critically. They have merely to give the

---

33 Ibid.
34 Ibid., 130.
35 Ibid.
36 Ibid., 133.

signal and the people, with all its inexhaustible resources, will fall upon the oppressors'.[37] But in practice, 'their interests prove to be uninteresting and their potency impotence'[38]; the 'indivisible' people had divided into enemy camps: '*Das unteilbare Volk in verschiedene feindliche Lager spalten*'. From this point, each and every popular uprising would be conditioned by the movements of the working class. The popular masses no longer stood independent from the workers.

Popular struggles would no longer even exist without the working-class struggle. The people's tribunes were impotent without the power of the workers. Social democracy had lost its political autonomy forever: henceforth it would be either a function of capital or a crude, conscious, instrument of workers' power. What Marx called the collapse of democratic institutions was not an objective fact that followed from the defeat in 1848, but a subjective initiative that the very workers who had then been defeated took with regard to their former false allies. This would give 13 June 1849 its true meaning, when, for the first time, in the refusal of democratic struggle, the workers' passive response to the petty-bourgeois call on them to limit their demands within the confines of democracy itself emerged as a specific form of working-class struggle. So it was not, therefore, an error, as Maenchen-Helfen and Nikolaevsky have commented, but rather another clear-sighted product of Marx's 'analytical intelligence', when, in the wake of the decisive event in Paris in 1849, he adjudged that 'awkward though the present state of affairs may be for our personal circumstances, I am nevertheless among the *satisfaits. Les choses marchent très bien* and the Waterloo suffered by official democracy may be regarded as a victory'.[39] Lenin could not fail to grasp the significance of this passage, in his own way and in terms of the needs of his own struggle. In the preface to the Russian edition of Marx's letters to Kugelmann, he did not only highlight Marx's enthusiastic approval of the fresh uprising by the Parisian workers in his 12 April 1871 writing – a text which, in Lenin's view, ought to be displayed in the bedroom of every revolutionary, 'of every Russian worker who can read'. Rather, together with this, he also highlighted another consideration. 'Kugelmann apparently replied to Marx expressing certain doubts,

---

37 Ibid.
38 Ibid.
39 MECW, Vol. 38, 209.

referring to the hopelessness of the struggle and to realism as opposed
to romanticism – at any rate, he compared the Commune, an insurrection, to the peaceful demonstration in Paris on June 13, 1849. Marx
immediately (April 17, 1871) severely lectured Kugelmann.' Lenin wrote
this before continuing: 'In September 1870, Marx called the insurrection an act of desperate folly. But, when the masses rose, Marx wanted to
march with them, to learn with them in the process of the struggle, and
not to give them bureaucratic admonitions. He realised that to attempt
in advance to calculate the chances with complete accuracy would be
quackery or hopeless pedantry. What he valued above everything else
was that the working class heroically and self-sacrificingly took the initiative in making world history. Marx regarded world history from the
standpoint of those who make it without being in a position to calculate
the chances infallibly beforehand, and not from the standpoint of an
intellectual philistine who moralises: "It was easy to foresee ... they
should not have taken up ..." Marx was also able to appreciate that there
are moments in history when a desperate struggle of the masses, even
for a hopeless cause, is essential for the further schooling of these masses
and their training for the next struggle.'[40] Marx sharply reproached
Kugelmann in his 17 April 1871 letter: 'How you can compare petty-
bourgeois demonstrations à la 13 June 1849 etc., with the present struggle in Paris is quite incomprehensible to me. World history would indeed
be very easy to make if the struggle were taken up only on condition of
infallibly favourable chances'. Without a doubt, the conditions of the
struggle – above all due to the presence in France of the Prussians –
were unfavourable to the workers. The 'bourgeois *canaille* of Versailles'
knew as much. 'Precisely for that reason they presented the Parisians
with the alternative of taking up the fight or succumbing without a
struggle. In the latter case, the demoralisation of the working class
would have been a far greater misfortune than the fall of any number of
"leaders". The struggle of the working class against the capitalist class
and its state has entered upon a new phase with the struggle in Paris.
Whatever the immediate results may be, a new point of departure of
world-historic importance has been gained'. All of Marx's political
advice to the Communards pointed in the direction of a more decisive,

---

40   Lenin, 'Preface to the Russian Translation of Karl Marx's Letters to Dr.
Kugelmann', 1907, text from marxists.org.

more violent resolve, more daring in taking on the open struggle. As he put it in his 12 April 1871 letter to Kugelmann, 'They did not want to start the civil war ... If they are defeated only their "decency" will be to blame. They should have marched at once on Versailles'.[41] This would henceforth return in every decisive struggle, in every direct clash, as the watchword for the workers' revolutionary viewpoint, in the face of the leaders' eternal opportunist call for moderation. Indeed, there is no need to think that the passive refusal to fight for democratic demands is the only specific form of working-class struggle. Rather, it is just one of these forms. The one that always and immediately accompanies it is the class's active refusal to allow itself to be defeated without engaging in battle. And this always brings with it the search, at whatever cost, for an open clash on the terrain of mass struggle. In the first case, the various factions of the class of capitalists are allowed to resolve their unsettled accounts among themselves; the working-class's force is spared and kept intact, so that it might instead be deployed at a new and more advanced level of struggle. At this point, there are no demands coming from the working class. In the second case, it is the workers and big capital directly who are settling accounts – and this is the opportunity for all the poten- tial for struggle hitherto accumulated to enter into play. And the degree of violence will now depend only on the greatness of this potential and how well organised it is. A single demand comes forth, one that negates all the others and thus negates itself together with them; indeed, this is no longer a subjective demand from the workers themselves, but a simple and necessary historical consequence of their existence, their presence as a class. In the Inaugural Address to the First International (1864), Marx establishes that 'the great task of the working class is the conquest of political power'. The experience of the Commune took on such importance more as a first general realisation of this task than in terms of the particular ways in which power was organised therein; the Commune was 'our party's most glorious action since the June insurrec- tion' and the 'first revolution in which the working class was openly acknowledged as the only class capable of social initiative'.[42] Marx's writings on the Commune are themselves often considered part of his 'historical' works. It is often forgotten that they were addresses by the

---

41 MECW, Vol. 44, 131–2.
42 MECW, Vol. 22, 336.

General Council of the International Workingmen's Association regarding the civil war in France. When he defined the Commune as an 'essentially working-class government', 'the political form at last discovered under which to work out the economical emancipation of Labour',[43] he was not making an empirical observation or still less a historical judgement, but drawing a simple political watchword. The proletariat of Marx's first works – a force for dissolving the old world – had here become a working class – a social power that decisively snatches the offensive weapon of power from the hands of the capitalists. The political form has changed, the social composition has transformed, the structural economic power has shifted and grown, the level of struggles has repeatedly leapt forward: all this took place within the permanently erupting revolutionary volcano that is the class of workers. But the objective, the purpose, the programme with which to assail and bring down the rotten old world – which is not different to, but rather forms a single whole together with capital's most modern social forms and its modern power apparatus – all this remains identical throughout the passage from proletarians to workers. And this demonstrates another thing: that on the political terrain, there is also, and must continually be, the inverse passage, from the modern working-class forms to the crude proletarian forms of the class struggle, if we do not want to remain within the – this time, truly apparent – game of a concerted 'conflictual' evolution in the relations between the two enemy classes. The point that unifies the forms of struggle is always precisely in the objective, the purpose, the programme. Amid so much transformation, this is the thing that does not and cannot change. On this, in 1871, Marx repeated almost to the letter what he had said in 1843: 'The working class did not expect miracles from the Commune. They have no ready-made utopias to introduce *par décret du peuple*. They know that in order to work out their own emancipation, and along with it that higher form to which present society is irresistibly tending by its own economical agencies, they will have to pass through long struggles, through a series of historic processes, transforming circumstances and men. They have no ideals to realise, but to set free elements of the new society with which old collapsing bourgeois society itself is pregnant'.[44] Thus, the afternoon of 13 June

---

43 Ibid., 334.
44 Ibid., 335.

1849, when the most active members of the proletariat watched the democrats' procession from the pavement, and the morning of 19 March 1871, when the obscure figures of the central committee governed Paris alone, provide two opposed and specific forms of the working-class struggle. They are two limit-models, between which are located an infinite, extraordinarily varied series always rich in new 'technical' inventions regarding the practical applications of those elementary reforms which – as such – remain the complete expression, at the political level, of working-class antagonism. Analysing the forms of struggle is an important passage in reconstructing the working-class point of view we seek, and it will be necessary to insist on this analysis in future with particular studies. Once we resolve the problem of what workers set forward as their purpose, it is necessary to understand what the working class is; this is not possible without seeing how it struggles.

8

The Forms of Struggle

The fight for the legally limited working day, for example, sets us in front of the working class as a positive articulation of capitalist development, as a propulsive force behind development, as its dynamic foundation: the working class as a motor that drives capital. 'If then the unnatural extension of the working day, that capital necessarily strives after in its unmeasured passion for self-expansion, shortens the length of life of the individual labourer, and therefore the duration of his labour-power, the forces used up have to be replaced at a more rapid rate and the sum of the expenses for the reproduction of labour power will be greater; just as in a machine the part of its value to be reproduced every day is greater the more rapidly the machine is worn out. It would seem therefore that the interest of capital itself points in the direction of a normal working day'.[1] Yet everyone knows that this interest of capital's was imposed upon it by a succession of very hard-fought working-class struggles. At the outset, the capitalist does not worry himself with the possible length of the lives of the individual labour-powers. The single and only thing that interests him is the maximum amount of labour-power that can, in general, be released within a working day. '*Aprés moi le déluge!*' is the watchword of every capitalist and of every capitalist nation. Capital therefore takes no account of the health or length of life of the worker,

---

1 Karl Marx, *Capital*, Vol. 1, translated by Ben Fowkes, London: Penguin, 1990, 377.

unless society forces it to do so.'[2] When, at its origins, capital was left to its own devices, it lengthened the working day to its normal maximum limits and then beyond them, to the limits of the natural day, excepting the few hours of rest without which labour-power would absolutely recuse from providing its services once more. Capital thus obtained more absolute surplus-value, but, at the same time, it made the costs of the reproduction of labour-power more expensive, having shortened its lifetime. This, moreover, violently hit the workers' living conditions, and they, indeed, were the first to react: 'As soon as the working class, stunned at first by the noise and turmoil of the new system of production, had recovered its senses to some extent, it began to offer resistance, first of all in England, the native land of large-scale industry.'[3] The first consequence was the Factory Act of 1833, which dates the existence, for modern industry, of a normal, ordinary working day prescribed by law; from there began the successive series of coercive laws on the limitation of labour-time. In the working-class attempt to shorten this labour-time and in the capitalist resistance to conceding this shortening, the level of the workers' class struggle grew. The internal history of the Chartist movement itself ought to be seen in terms of the needs of this struggle. For Engels, in his *Condition of the Working Class in England*, 'The movements against the New Poor Law and for the Ten Hours Bill were already in the closest relation to Chartism'.[4] When the working-class populations of the industrial districts of the northwest entered into play, when the proletariat of Lancashire and Yorkshire took to the streets, 'moral-force Chartism' collapsed, and the violent appeal to physical force took its place. It was at this moment that Feargus O'Connor counterposed the "guance non rase, dalle mani callose e dalle giacche di fustagno" to the skilled artisans of the London Working Men's Association. Not least, given the movements in Manchester in 1842, Engels could say 'in general, all the workers employed in manufacture are won for one form or the other of resistance to capital and bourgeoisie; and all are united upon this point, that they, as working-men, a title of which they are proud, and which is the usual form of address in Chartist meetings, form a separate class, with separate interests and

---

2 Ibid., 381.

3 Ibid., 390.

4 Marx and Engels Collected Works (MECW), Vol. 4, 519.

principles, with a separate way of looking at things in contrast with that of all property-owners.[5] The result: the Ten Hours Law, which came into effect on 1 May 1848. But the defeat in Paris in June again intervened to overturn the relation of forces. All the factions of the ruling classes – in England, too – were once again united. The factory lords no longer needed to be circumspect. There broke out an open capitalists' rebellion against the law, and against all the legislation from 1833 onward that had sought to put brakes on the 'free' bloodletting of labour-power: 'It was a pro-slavery rebellion in miniature, carried on for over two years with a cynical recklessness and a terroristic energy which were so much the easier to achieve in that the rebel capitalist [*der rebellische Kapitalist*] risked nothing but the skin of his workers.'[6] For two years, these workers put up a ' resistance which was passive, although inflexible and unceasing' in opposition.[7] Then they began to protest full-throatedly in 'threatening meetings', which again took place in Lancashire and Yorkshire. The factory owners divided once more. Between 1850 and 1853, the 'legal' principle passed into all major branches of industry. And then, between 1853 and 1860, a marvellous industrial development went 'hand in hand with the physical and moral regeneration of the factory'. Then, 'the very manufacturers from whom the legal limitation and regulation of the working day had been wrung step by step in the course of a civil war lasting half a century now pointed boastfully to the contrast with the areas of exploitation still "free"'.[8] It is, nonetheless, easy to understand 'that after the factory magnates had resigned themselves and submitted to the inevitable, capital's power of resistance gradually weakened, while at the same time the working class's power of attack [*Angriffskraft*] grew'.[9] Marx thus drew two political-practical lessons from his analysis of the working-class struggle for the regulated working day: First, the changes in the material mode of production and in the corresponding social relations among producers 'gave rise to outrages without measure, and then called forth, in opposition to this, social control, which legally limits, regulates, and makes uniform the working

---

5 Ibid., 529.
6 *Capital*, Vol. 1, 397–8.
7 Ibid., 405.
8 Ibid., 408–9.
9 Ibid., 409.

day and its pauses'.[10] Second, 'the history of the regulation of the working day' shows 'that the isolated worker, the worker as "free" vendor of his labour-power succumbs without resistance [widerstandslos], when capitalist production has reached a certain stage of maturity. The establishment of a normal working day is therefore the product of a protracted and more or less concealed civil war [Bürgerkrieg] between the capitalist class and the working class. Since the contest takes place in the arena of modern industry, it is fought first of all in the homeland of that industry – England. The English factory workers were the champions, not only of the English working class, but of the modern working class in general'.[11] These workers had the historic merit of having shown for the first time, in practice – that is, in struggle – that 'the worker comes out of the production process different from how he went in'. This difference is a true and proper political leap forward. It is the leap that the passage via production provokes, in what we can call the composition of the working class or composition of the class of workers. Yet this production is the production of capital. And the production of capital presupposes a capitalist relation. This, we have seen, presupposes a class relation. A class relation is a struggle between antagonistic classes. This is why the production process – as a process that produces capital – is inseparable from the moments of class struggle, which is to say, it is not independent of the movements of the working-class struggle. It is made, composed, organised by the successive series of all such moments. The development of the capitalist production process makes up a single whole, together with the history of the workers' class movements. For the worker, to pass through the production process means to pass through the specific terrain of the class struggle against the capitalist. It is thus the terrain of struggle which the worker leaves 'different from how she went in'. This, in order to immediately clear the field of any inverted cult of technology, any attempt to reduce the production process to a labour process – which is to say, to a relation between worker and the tool of her labour, as if it were the eternal relation between humanity and some malign gift of nature. This is important in order to avoid falling into the trap of reification processes, which are always preceded by an ideological lament for the living life of the machine operative

10   Ibid., 411–12.
11   Ibid., 412–13.

reduced to a dead object, and always followed by the mystical cure for this worker's class consciousness, as if in the search for modern humanity's lost soul. It is the viewpoint of the individual capitalist which sees the working-class struggle as a moment – however impossible to eliminate – of the production process. Conversely, from the working-class point of view – and in production, this can no longer be the viewpoint of an individual worker – the opposite is true, once more: the production process is revealed to be a moment – again, an ineliminable one – of the working-class struggle. That is, it is revealed to be the tactical terrain most favourable to the development of this same struggle.

There is class struggle even before the act of production itself begins: there is class struggle on the labour market, where the buyer and seller of labour-power confront one another with opposed interests. In negotiating a contract, they each demonstrate the same weapons that they will be able to use in the future. But at that point, the terrain is more favourable to the boss: the money, the means of labour, the conditions of production, all the capital in itself are on his side, and on the other side is the simple compelled freedom to sell a commodity, which alone can guarantee the worker's survival. Of course, the commodity that the worker possesses is the end of the exchange and also the principle that moves this exchange. It is the condition of all the other conditions of production and, as such, is also at the beginning of the whole process. It is true that labour-power is the foundation of the whole mechanism of capitalist production, but it is also true that in the act of the sale and purchase of labour-power the worker does not have the power to impose this same priority on the capitalist: the relation of forces is unfavourable to her, and the weapons she can count on right away are weaker. The will to struggle and the consciousness of the need to wage this fight may not be lacking; rather, what are lacking are the material tools adequate to wage it victoriously. There are good reasons why the heroic history of proletarian revolts is a history of bloody defeats for the working class. But this is the school of the class struggle, and it is necessary to learn from this. Among her various predecessors, the advanced worker in massive modern industries ought to choose the figure of those whom Marx called the 'fathers of the present-day working class', the *vogelfreie Proletarier*, the labouring poor. For they were at the same time both poor and free. Yet there is also a class struggle after the act of production has finished: in the distribution of income, when it comes to sharing the fruits of workers' labour among the classes recognised by society. Everyone knows that the extravagant laws of distribution are compiled in the dark laboratory of production and that the question of who among all the state's citizens will have more and who will have less depends on the relations of force established therein by the two classes. And everyone also knows that the realm of distribution was the first real homeland of socialism, and it was first the dreamers with their utopias and then the reformists with their realism – ultimately, all the 'beloved leaders' who have, through such misadventure, afflicted the workers' movement – who have long seen this as the terrain for realising social harmony, the end of struggles among the classes and eternal peace between all people. This, of course, after a fair profit has been secured for the capitalists, a fair wage for the workers, a state that is fair to its citizens and a fair salary for its functionaries. Here, too, the relation of forces for the working-class side is unfavourable. When it comes to distributing what has been produced, the whole jurisdiction over distribution is already in the hands of those who have exercised command over production. And we have seen that this command over production does not exist outside of capital. The general dictatorship of capital and its political power concentrated within the state machine are nothing other than an extension into society of the capitalist command over the production of capital. The more the specific relation of capitalist production takes charge of the general social relation at every point, the more complete becomes capital's power over the whole society. To challenge this power at the level of distribution is the usual ridiculous error of reformist utopias: that is, they want capital without capitalism. The hard reality is that, after production, a vast amount of dictatorial command has already accumulated in the hands of the bosses: not only money, means of labour, conditions of production, but so too the condition at the root of all the other conditions of production – the commodity labour-power, at first autonomous and for itself, has now become an internal part, a merely variable moment of capital. And this is no longer a matter of capital in itself, but a wholly unfolded capital, which exclusively commands the process from the exchange with labour-power to the production of surplus-value, to the distribution of income and even, if you will, the consumption of the product. And the exclusive forms of its command are, in turn, summed up not in the mediating jurisdictions of the single modes of public governance, but in the singular continuity of that always one-sidedly oppressive machine that is state political power. Compare capital's victorious power to the whole succession of defeats for the working class – regularly abandoned to itself by all the parties in history that were born in its name – and you will have grasped today's situation. From these parties' point of view, the conclusion drawn is that the working class does not even exist anymore; the working class, however, has concluded that its parties no longer exist. In the parties' estimation, the working-class point of view has failed, and the workers think the same of the party. Yet no revolutionary process is possible without the class and party aligning. Today, this is our 'hic Rhodus, hic salta!' So, let's ask ourselves: where, at what point, in what moment, are the workers by themselves stronger than the capitalist? Can we establish, as a general law, that here and now the working class is always stronger than capital? We can do this only if we find, concretely, the point, the moment, in which the relation of forces between the two classes is always in the workers' favour. But can this really exist in a capitalist society that lies under the exclusive command of capital, which subordinates everything to itself?

Yes – not only can it, but it must in fact exist.

Its existence is linked to the existence of capital. The production of capital begins with the working class on the one side and the capitalist on the other. If the individual labour-powers are not first forcibly associated under a single power, they cannot assert the particular power of the commodity labour-power in general at the scale of society; that is, they cannot make abstract labour concrete at this level, and thus they cannot realise the use-value of labour-power, in whose effective consumption lies the secret of the process of valorising value, as in the process of the production of surplus-value and thus of capital. The workers are bought on the market as individual labour-powers, but they must function in the production process as a social labour-power. It is true that the relation of sale and purchase is already a social relation, but it is a social relation that presents itself in the figure of two single commodity-holders, without any other specific characteristics. It is not this generic social relation that characterises the act of the sale and purchase of labour-power; rather, its very particular trait is that it is already a class relation, which is such a determinate characteristic that it appears for the first time here within a social relation. The passage to production – to capitalist production, obviously – marks a forced process of the socialisation of the class relation. After this passage, in all moments of the overall cycle of capital's development – from initial circulation to final distribution – there will be now only a place for a class social relation. After this passage, the very exchange – the purchase and sale – of labour-power will no longer have as its protagonists the individual figures of two isolated commodity-holders on the market, but two great social aggregates, each with its own respective institutionalised organisation for collective bargaining. It is on this basis that capital – as a production relation, and thus as a class relation – undergoes an indefinite process of socialisation, in its spiralling development. At each passage through an acute moment of confrontation between the two classes, which is to say, each time the class relation emerges as the force driving the whole process, there takes place as a consequence a leap forward in socialisation. And this, in turn, reproduces, in an enormously expanded form, the class relation itself. The historical characteristic that marks out the commodity labour-power is a capacity for valorisation greater than the value that it itself has. This constitutes its power [*potenza*] and, at the same time, its misfortune, for the value of labour-power, and thus the worker's life itself, is in the hands of capital. Thus, we find the burning contradiction that while the workers as a class present themselves as the vastest aggressive political force ever to have appeared in human societies, as single individuals, they instead present the extreme image first of misery, then of subordination, and always of exploitation. That is why those who consider the class as a sum of individuals have never understood anything of the working class. But what is the particular historical characteristic of capital, whether corresponding to all of this or in opposition to it? We respond that it is a capacity for socialisation that is greater than its own social relation. If capital in itself, divided by labour-power, is a social relation, insofar as it stands before labour-power, then the act that introduces labour-power into the production process and the production process that incorporates labour-power into capital place in the hands of capital itself a dynamic force for socialisation that is magnified far beyond the static level of the general social relation. On this basis, the degree reached by the socialisation process within the capitalist production relation will always be higher than the degree reached by this same process within the general social relation. Even if there is a tendency toward the coincidence of these two relations, there is good reason to believe that they will never fully coincide. There will always remain a gap between capital as a production relation and capital as capitalist society. The socialisation of production will always run ahead of the organisation of society itself. The historical margin between these two moments is an imposing form of political domination, which capital has well experienced to its own advantage. But this is not the point of the positive contradiction. Rather, we must make the point here of seeing social labour-power as a mediation on the socialisation of capital. Which is to say that capital does not and cannot directly bear its own capacity for socialisation; it makes labour-power do so, as it must. It is true that labour-power cannot carry forth this burdensome endeavour alone, and its true that only insofar as it is socialised by capital can labour-power then drive all the processes of capitalist socialisation. But this suffices not to subordinate it to this process, but rather to place it at its heart, as a vital, pulsating motor, through which all and any social action must pass. So what appeared to be capital's eternal power now presents itself gripped by the everyday need to head via this passage. Again, what presents itself to the workers' point of view is far different from what appears to the capitalist. Given that, within the terms of capitalist society's laws of motion, labour-power must produce more than it itself costs, it cannot but continually go beyond the limits that society itself imposes on its socialisation processes. But if it is to transgress these limits, to break the forms of passive resistance – which is to say, go effectively beyond these limits – capital no longer just needs this living mediation, this dynamic articulation that only labour-power can supply and indeed exercise within the production process. For it now needs something new, different and higher; it needs the offensive weapon of the working-class struggle to be pointed in threat against it. Not only in Marx's *Capital* but in the very history of capitalist development, the struggle for the regulated working day preceded, imposed and caused a change in the form of surplus-value, 'a revolution in the means of production'. Since the law set a normal duration for the working day, the expansion of surplus-labour must derive from the shortening of the necessary labour-time – that is, the shortening of necessary working time could not derive from the prolongation of surplus-labour. Not only was it necessary for the value of labour-power to be reduced and the productive power of labour increased, but the value of labour-power also had to be reduced through an increase in the productive power of labour. There began a continuous series of upheavals in the labour process itself; through these upheavals developed the 'specifically capitalist' history of the production of relative surplus-value. The working-class struggle had thus imposed capital's own interest upon it; that is, capital had imposed its own interest on itself via the mediation of the working-class struggle. And this fact is no exception within the history of capitalist development. This time, it is a model not so much of struggle as of the conclusion of the struggle, which would repeat itself in different forms at various levels of that development. Indeed, we should avoid confusing the *forms* of struggle with the use that the stronger of the two sides in that moment makes of the struggle as such. When workers struggle, they do so to defeat the boss, not in order to develop capital. If they then win, and the present defeat of the capitalist becomes the future victory of capital, then, in the model that we are examining, this depends neither on errors in the workers' subjective movements for their demands or on the diabolical nature that their enemy's initiative seems to assume within this framework. Rather, it has to do with a wholly objective mechanism that effectively puts the active factor in the whole process within the variable part of capital, in capital as living labour, which is to say, in labour-power as capital. And this active factor is that 'negative side of the antithesis', that 'internal agitation', which – for good reason – we now see no longer expressing itself in the concept of the proletariat, but coinciding, merging, becoming identical with the act of the working-class struggle. In this sense, we can say that, in the modern class struggle, there are never decisive victories and defeats. When the workers win a partial battle, they later realise that they have won it to capital's benefit. When the capitalists call the working class into an open confrontation, in order to defeat its political movement on the battlefield, the workers then pay for their momentary success with the long periods of passivity that living labour introduces, in response, into the economic mechanism. Capitalist society's laws of motion do not allow one class to eliminate the other. So long as capital exists, both classes must exist within it, and they must struggle. The working-class point of view begins from the principle that, when there has been a struggle, it has never been futile. A terrible defeat that momentarily forces the movement to fold but then brings it to its feet even stronger has more value than all the opportunist surrenders that keep the relation of forces unaltered for decades in immobilism – that is, in reformism. And yet, we should not forget that from the working-class side, rejection of the struggle can, in certain cases, itself be a form of struggle. Such is the case when the working-class mediation of the capitalist interest has been fully unveiled and is visible to the naked eye while, at the same time, presenting itself as too urgent and necessary for capital's immediate needs and, moreover, cannot, in that moment, be managed by the workers directly and must by necessity be placed in the hands of their false representatives. This is the point at which, faced with the capitalist need for the working class to take the initative, the workers spontaneously respond en masse with a passive attitude toward the struggle, with the passive rejection of the working-class struggle itself. It is possible to get a general sense, within such a response, of the presence of a new type of contradiction, a new way in which the continual historical separation between labour-power and capital presents itself. For it now turns up mediated by the separation between workers and 'their' organisations, between the working class and the workers' movement. Certainly, this line of argument is not easy to grasp: if a mass of concrete historical experiences shows all this, the whole tradition of vulgar Marxist thought – which is the only tradition of thought that the working-class vision finds behind it – fiercely denies it. We cannot, moreover, start out by refutating the various moments or passages in this tradition; we would draw nothing from this and the demands of the polemic would suffocate the impact of the new hypotheses. And yet these hypotheses are precisely the thing that we need to work on before anything else, articulating in principle the theoretical premises at their foundation and ultimately pulling together the practical consequences that derive from them. These consequences are decisive for the choice of these premises. The form of struggle on the working-class side is chosen on the basis of which form can impose the greatest possible damage on the boss in that moment. The form of science is chosen from the working-class point of view on the basis of which weapons this form can provide for fighting capital. Neither the forms of science or those of struggle are given once and for all. For Marx, historical materialism – the attempt to reconstruct the whole history of human societies in terms of the principle of class struggle – was probably a means of practically overturning, on the terrain of science, the bourgeois ideological thesis that capital has an eternal history, as well as an alternative way of counterposing to this a subaltern history of the exploited classes, for the purposes of the struggle. Without doubt, to consider historical materialism still now to be the modern form of working-class science means to begin writing this science of the future with a medieval scribe's quill. We think that, with every upheaval that starts a new era in the history of working-class struggles, the working-class point of view is posed the question of changing the form of its science. The fact that this change has not taken place, even after the greatest practical overhaul that the workers have provoked in the contemporary world, is at the root of all of the difficulties of Marxism today. We will need to return to this.

9

Labour as Non-Capital

It was Marx who spoke of the *Angriffskraft* (attacking power) of the working class and of the *Widerstandskraft* (power of resilience) of capital. We need to put these terms back into circulation in today's struggle. For within them is contained that strategic overturn that has only been attempted once in practice after Marx, and which, after Lenin, was stashed away in both theory and practice. If we want to demonstrate how this overturn can function once more – that is, in forms of struggle – we need to carry further the process of reconstructing the objective movements of the forces that find themselves in struggle. In the meantime, we have conquered one point that some people are even ready to admit in principle, but which no one is ready to consider for all its weight of consequences – namely, that first there exists the poor, free labourer and thus the proletariat as the 'party of destruction', then there develops the commodity labour-power and thus the single worker as a producer-in-potential, and finally comes the social force of productive labour *in actu* and thus the working class in the process of production. These are, in turn, conceptually and historically speaking (*begrifflich und geschichtlich*), the true and proper dynamic elements of capital, the primary cause of capitalist development. In this sense, *Arbeitskraft* is not only a commodity-object that passes from the workers' hands into the hands of capital; rather, it is an active force that all the more passes from the working class to the class of capitalists the more that it precedes development. Marx's eulogy to the powerful and incessant activity of the bourgeoisie would correctly be redirected toward the proletarian threat that was snapping at its heels; the charge of ever-agitated dynamism that seems to push capital forth in each moment of its history is in reality the aggressive thrust of class movements pushing within it. Schumpeter portrays the figure of the entrepreneur with his innovating initiative; it is pleasing for us to see this figure turned inside out, as the permanent initiative-in-struggle of the great masses of the working class. Through this passage, *Arbeitskraft* can and must become *Angriffskraft*. This is the passage – this time, a political one – from labour-power to the working class. Marx shows his greatest awareness of this problem in the *Grundrisse*. And perhaps this is simply due to form: here obliged neither to arrange his arguments in an ironclad logical order nor to take any particular care for language in expounding them, in a phase of research that was wholly his own – that is, in a work that stood far from publication – Marx here made a more expeditious advance in his fundamental discoveries and thus discovered more and more new things that did not appear in his finished works starting with *Contribution to the Critique of Political Economy* and Volume 1 of *Capital*. It follows from this that politically the *Grundrisse* – the internal monologue that Marx built up with himself, in his own time – turns out to be a more advanced book than the other two, for it is a text that leads more directly, through thrown-together, practical pages, to a new type of political conclusion. Look, for example, how, before arriving at the concept of living labour and thus before he gets stuck in the original exchange relation between capital and labour, Marx poses the problem '*was ist unter "Gesellschaft" zu verstehen*': 'nothing is more erroneous than the way in which both the economists and the socialists consider society in relation to economic conditions.'[1] Proudhon saw no difference for society between capital and the product. But does the difference between capital and the product not lie precisely in the fact that as capital, the product expresses a determinate relation relative to a historical form of society? 'This so-called consideration from the point of view of society means nothing more than to overlook precisely the differences which express the social relation (relation of civil society). Society does not consist of individuals, but expresses the sum of the relationships and

---

1   Marx and Engels Collected Works (MECW), Vol. 28, 195.

conditions in which these individuals stand to one another'.[2] This definition of society is important precisely for the purposes of defining the
social substance common to all commodities as if they were single
individuals. This common substance can no longer be their singular
material content, their individual physical determinations; it must be
the fact that their form – indeed, a social form – is the product of a
social relation. But it is possible to speak of this form – insofar as it is
value, insofar as it is a determinate quantity of labour – only by looking for an antithesis to capital.[3] And what constitutes the common
substance of all commodities is the fact that, socially, they are all
objectified labour. But 'the only thing distinct from objectified labour
is non-objectified labour, labour still objectifying itself, labour as
subjectivity. Or objectified labour, i.e., labour present in space, can
also be opposed as past labour to labour still present in time. If it is to
be present in time, present alive, it can only be present as a living
subject, in which it exists as capacity, as potentiality; therefore as
worker'.[4] We have already seen that, in the urtext to the *Contribution to
the Critique of Political Economy*, from the same period as the
Grundrisse, Marx would draw the even more concise synthesis that
'The only opposite of reified labour is unreified labour, and the opposite of objectified labour, subjective labour'.[5] Subjective labour counterposed to objectified labour, living labour counterposed to dead
labour, is labour counterposed to capital: labour as non-capital (*die
Arbeit als das Nicht-Kapital*). It has two fundamental characteristics,
both of which mark labour as a non-something, a *Nicht* planted in the
heart of a network of positive social relations and which entails the
possibility of both their development and their destruction. As the
Grundrisse puts it: 'Labour as non-capital, posited as such, is: 1) Not
objectified labour, negatively conceived (itself still objective; the not-
objective itself in objective [*objectiver*] form). As such it is non-raw
material, non-instrument of labour, non-raw product: labour separated from all means of labour and all objects of labour, from its whole
objectivity [*Objectivität*]. Living labour existing as abstraction from

---

2 Ibid., 195.
3 Ibid., 202.
4 Ibid.
5 MECW, Vol. 29, 502.

these moments of its actual reality (likewise, non-value); this complete denudation, the purely subjective existence of labour lacking all objectivity [*Objectivität*]. Labour as absolute poverty: poverty, not as shortage, but as a complete exclusion of objective wealth. Or also as the existing non-value and hence purely objective use value, existing without mediation, this objectivity can only be one not separated from the person; only one coincident with his immediate corporality. Since the objectivity is purely immediate, it is also immediately non-objectivity. In other words: not an objectivity falling outside the immediate existence of the individual himself. 2) Not-objectified labour, non-value, positively conceived; or negativity relating itself to itself. As such it is not-objectified, therefore non-objective, i.e., subjective existence of labour itself. Labour not as object but as activity; not as itself value, but as the living source of value. General wealth, in contrast to capital, in which wealth exists objectively, as reality – general wealth as its general possibility, which [possibility] proves itself as such in activity'.[6]

There is, therefore, absolutely no contradiction, Marx continues, in labour being 'on the one hand absolute poverty as object, and on the other the general possibility of wealth as subject and activity'. Better, it is wholly contradictory, but precisely due to the fact that labour itself is a contradiction of capital – and, even before that, a contradiction for itself. Abstract labour that has a use-value, or, rather, labour pure and simple (*schlechthin*) is the pure and simple use-value that stands counterposed to capital: it is labour as worker, 'absolutely indifferently of its particular determination' and yet 'capable of any determination'. The interest of the worker is always for labour in general and never for its determinate character. Such character is, in fact, only use-value for capital. For this very reason, since labour is as such only in opposition to capital, the worker is thus only in opposition to the capitalist. 'This economic relation – the character which capitalist and worker bear as the extremes of a relation of production – is therefore developed the more purely and adequately, the more labour loses all craft-like character, the more its particular skill becomes something abstract, irrelevant, and the more it becomes purely abstract, purely mechanical activity, hence irrelevant, indifferent to its particular form; the more it becomes merely formal

---

6 Ibid.

activity or, what is the same, merely physical [*stoffliche*] activity, activity pure and simple, indifferent to its form'.[7]

Arbeitsprozess in das Kapital aufgenommen: 'By the exchange with the worker, capital has appropriated labour itself, which has become one of the moments of capital, and which now acts as a fructifying vitality upon its merely present and hence dead objectivity'.[8] Capital, at this point, cannot continue passively to identify itself with objectified labour (that is, as money); rather, it must establish an active relationship, as capital, with living labour, with 'labour existing as process and action'. This, indeed, is the qualitative difference between the substance and the form in which it also exists as labour. It is the process of this distinction [*Unterscheidung*] and of its overcoming [*Aufhebung*]: the path through which 'capital itself becomes process'.

'Labour is the yeast thrown into capital, bringing it now into fermentation [*zur Gärung*]. On the one hand, the objectivity in which capital exists must be processed, i.e., consumed by labour. On the other hand, the mere subjectivity of labour as pure form must be transcended [*aufgehoben*], and it must be objectified in the material of capital. The relation of capital in accordance with its content to labour, of objectified labour to living labour – in this relation where capital appears as passive towards labour, it is its passive being, as a particular substance, that enters into relation with labour as creative activity – can in general only be the relation of labour to its objectivity, its physical matter [*Stoff*] – (which must be dealt with already in the first chapter which must precede that on exchange value and must treat of production in general) – and with regard to labour as activity the physical matter, the objectified labour, has only two relations: that of the raw material, i.e., of the formless physical matter, of mere material for the form-giving, purposive activity of labour; and that of the instrument of labour, of the means, itself objective, by which the subjective activity inserts an object as its conductor [*Leiter*] between itself and the object'.[9]

Produktionsprozess als Inhalt des Kapitals: 'In the first act, in the exchange between capital and labour, labour as such, existing for itself, necessarily appeared as the worker. Similarly, here in the second process:

---

7   MECW, Vol. 28, 223.
8   Ibid., 224.
9   Ibid., 224–5.

capital in general is posited as value existing for itself, as egotistic value, so to speak (something which was only aspired to in money). But capital existing for itself is the capitalist. Of course, socialists say: we need capital, but not the capitalist. Capital then appears as a pure thing, not as relationship of production, which, reflected in itself, is precisely the capitalist. I can indeed separate capital from this individual capitalist and it can pass on to another one. But, when the former loses his capital, he loses the quality of being a capitalist. Capital is therefore quite separable from an individual capitalist, but not from the capitalist who as such confronts the worker. In the same way, the individual worker can cease to be the being-for-itself of labour; he can inherit money, steal, etc. But then he ceases to be a worker'.[10] 'By the incorporation of labour into capital, capital becomes process of production; but initially material process of production; process of production in general, so that the process of production of capital is not distinct from the material process of production in general. Its determinateness of form is completely extinguished. Since capital has exchanged a part of its objective being [*Sein*] for labour, that objective being [*Dasein*] itself is internally divided [*dirimiert in sich*] into object and labour; the relation of the two constitutes the process of production, or more precisely the labour process. Thus the labour process, posited as point of departure before value – a process which because of its abstractness, its pure materiality, is equally common to all forms of production – here reappears again within capital, as a process which proceeds within its physical matter, forms its content'.

Surplusarbeitszeit: 'If a whole working day were required in order to keep a worker alive for a working day, capital would not exist, because one working day would exchange for its own product. As a result, capital could not valorise itself as capital and thus could not preserve itself. The self-preservation of capital is its self-valorisation. If capital had to work in order to live, it would not preserve itself as capital but as labour'.[11] But 'if the worker requires only half a working day to live for a whole day, he needs to work only half a day to eke out his existence as a worker. The second half of the working day is forced labour; surplus labour. What appears on the side of capital as surplus value, appears on the

---

10 Ibid., 229.
11 Ibid., 249.

worker's side precisely as surplus labour over and above his requirements as worker, hence over and above his immediate requirements to
sustain his vitality'.[12] In this sense, a complete historical determination
of capital presupposes: 1) needs so developed that surplus-labour
beyond the necessary level itself becomes a general need; 2) a general
industriousness which, through the rigorous discipline of capital, develops into a general possession; 3) such a mature development of the
productive forces of labour that the possession and conservation of the
general wealth 'requires from the whole of society only comparatively
little labour time on the one hand',[13] 'and on the other labouring society
takes a scientific attitude towards the process of its continuing reproduction, its reproduction in ever greater abundance; so that labour in
which man does what he can make things do for him has ceased'.[14]

'As the ceaseless striving [*rastlose Streben*] for the general form of
wealth, however, capital forces labour beyond the limits of natural need
and thus creates the material elements for the development of the rich
individuality, which is as varied and comprehensive [*allseitig*] in its
production as it is in its consumption, and whose labour therefore no
longer appears as labour but as the full development of activity itself, in
which natural necessity has disappeared in its immediate form; because
natural need has been replaced by historically produced [*geschichtlich
erzeugte*] need. This is why capital is productive, i.e., an essential relationship for the development of the productive forces of society. It ceases
to be such only where the development of these productive forces themselves encounters a barrier in capital itself'.[15]

This is the new path that Marx himself here proposes. The starting
point: labour as non-capital, and thus labour as the living subject of the
worker as against the dead objectivity of all the other conditions of
production; labour as the vital ferment of capital – another active determination added to the activity of productive labour. The point of arrival:
capital, which itself becomes productive, an essential relation to the
development of labour as a social productive power and thus an essential relation to the *development* of the working class – a new function of

---

12 Ibid., 250
13 Ibid., 250.
14 Ibid., 250.
15 Ibid., 251.

capital that now makes it serve the worker. Along this path, between these two points, is labour as non-value, and, for this very reason, a living source of value; absolute misery and, for this very reason, the general possibility of wealth; again, surplus-labour and, for this very reason, surplus-value – the modern figure of the collective worker that now comes to produce capital precisely as an antagonistic class that combats it. This is the decisive point that now needs bringing into focus. The production process, the act of producing capital, is contemporaneously the moment of the working-class struggle against capital: the specific moment to which all the other generic levels of the struggle are compelled to refer in order themselves to become productive. In the act of production, the relation of force between the two classes is favourable to the working-class side. Let's ask why that is. Well, we have seen already: for labour-power to pass into the capitalist relation of production is a need of capital's. Indeed, capital needs it to do so no longer only as a social productive power objectified in capital, but as the living active subject of the worker, thus associated and thus objectified. Upon the act of purchase and sale on the market, labour-power distinguishes itself with two fundamental characteristics: 1) that of being already in substance counterposed to capital; and 2) that of being still formally autonomous of it. Its autonomy, the charter of its rights on which the word 'freedom' is written in gothic letters, consists of the fact that it is still outside of the capitalist relation of production. The moment of exchange is not only the realm of freedom because the buyer and seller deal as free individuals, but because capital and labour here present themselves – at least formally – as free of each other. It is this freedom that they must lose if they want to live. This is the sense in which Marx sees, in the passage to production, the dissolution of capital as a 'formal relation'. What in fact falls away here is precisely the form of the reciprocal autonomy between the moments of the relation, and what remains is the relation itself in its substance, in its raw and immediate reality, without the mediation of a formal expression – we would say, without ideology. But the substance of the relation is given from the outset by the antithetical counterposition between labour-in-potential and capital-in-itself – the simple figures of labour and capital, of worker and capitalist. The content of the capitalist relation is, in each moment, the class relation. And the class relation sees the initiative in struggle on the working-class side as the initial point in the process, the permanent motor of this process, the absolute negation of capital as such and at the same time the dynamic articulation of the capitalist interest. In the passage to production, this class content of capital as a 'substantial relation' is not only conserved in substance, not only liberated from the form, but is and must be specifically socialised and objectified. It must be socialised in the sense that the single individual labour-powers must become a social productive power, or a social power of productive labour. It must be objectified in the sense that this social power of productive labour must become a social productive power for capital. These two processes – the socialisation of labour-power and its objectification in capital – are gripped within a single necessity: namely, the need to break the autonomy of labour-power without destroying its antagonistic character. Capital's existence, its birth, its development, are all linked to the presence of this antagonism. Not only can capital not exist without labour-power, but it cannot exist without the socialisation of labour-power; not only can it not do without the working class, but it cannot do without introducing the working class, itself within capital, as its own living part. The process of capitalist socialisation can proceed very far; it has possibilities for development that seem unlimited; it leaps backward from the production relation to the exchange relation and forward toward the relations of distribution; it takes hold of the general social relation and continually pushes it up a degree, a level, a moment. And yet there is a marked limit to this which it is unable to surpass: the process of general socialisation cannot go so far as to liquidate the workers as a specific class; it cannot, it must not, dilute, dissolve, dismember the working class amid the whole of society; it can and must increasingly socialise the class relation, such as it is, and ever renew the workers as an antagonistic class within it. On the capitalist side, this is the road to social control over the movements of the working class; on the working-class side, this is the perspective of unlimited political growth of its own, counter to the unsurpassable limit that capital places on itself. Thus, the process of the objectification of each social relation within capital carries with it a historic charge that accumulates as it advances. This builds up an irresistible force: from commodity fetishism to capital fetishism, by way of a whole era of positive violence, the reduction of everything that is socially alive to something dead seems practically complete. Yet here, too, an insurmountable barrier impedes the completion of this operation: the process of total objectification cannot go so far as to liquidate the individual life of labour as active subject, cannot and must not reduce to passive, dead objectivity the same vital ferment that sets everything into activity through production: the more that there grows and advances the objectification-in-capital of all that is social, the more the activity, the initiative, the 'entrepreneurial' interest of the working class must advance and grow within capital. On the capitalist side, this conditions the system's rational economic development, whereas on the working-class side it is the opportunity to politically subordinate capital's movements to itself. The initial class content is thus revealed to be ever more present and ever more determinant in the capitalist relation of production, its substance life-giving precisely because it is its immanent contradiction, precisely because it is a continual striving on the working-class side to make political, subjective use of an objective economic mechanism. The socialisation and objectification processes augment these possibilities of its alternative use, which are, moreover, implicit in every capitalist production process. From capital's practical point of view, there is no choice other than to guide these processes by making the working class carry them forward. The working-class practical point of view can choose to carry them forward while also refusing capital's direction. It thus enjoys a position of potential advantage. It needs only that this working-class choice not be left up to spontaneity, that it finds the way to express itself in a powerful subjective organisation and that the relation of forces is effectively overturned, with the workers' attacking power pushing the capitalists' resistance into a defensive position. In the factory, in production, when the workers serve the capitalist as the machines do capital, but moreover have the possibility of choosing not to serve him, and when labour is within capital and at the same time against it, then the collective boss is enormously weak, for he has left – for a moment – the arms with which he was fighting, the productive forces of labour socialised and objectified in the working class, in the hands of his enemies. If labour's activity should cease, then capital's life also ceases. A closed factory is already dead labour, capital-at-rest that does not produce and does not reproduce itself. The strike is, not by chance, a permanent form of working-class struggle and thus its primitive form, which develops but without ever negating itself. And the recognition of this basic fact has the vast power that simple things sometimes do: since the strike is a cessation of activity by living labour – which is to say, its reduction to dead labour, its refusal to be work – the strike is thus the collapse of the distinction, the separation, the counterposition between labour and capital. And this is the most terrible threat that can be wielded against the very life of capitalist society. Living labour's refusal of activity is the recovery of its autonomy, which is to say, precisely the autonomy that the production process has to break. And this is the other thing that capital cannot withstand. It must keep labour distinct from itself and counterposed to itself as an economic potential, yet, at the same time, subordinate it to its own command as political potential. Capital must, that is, counterpose itself to labour-power without leaving the working class autonomous; it must conceive labour-power itself as a working class, but within the capitalist relation of production; it must, therefore, conserve, reproduce and extend the class relation while also controlling it. And this is the thread that links together capital's modern history. Today the strategy of the working-class revolution is to break the thread of this control at some point. To this day, the starting point in the struggle is a separate political autonomy of the two sides' class movements: hence, once more, all the problems of organisation are on the working-class side. Capital strives to shut off the moment of antagonism within the economic relation, incorporating the class relation into the capitalist relation as its social object. Opposite to this, the effort on the working-class side must be to continually try to smash open this economic form of the antagonism; it must have as its day-to-day objective the restoration of political content to each elementary moment of confrontation; it must thus make the capitalist relation work subjectively within the class relation, conceiving capital as a production relation always and only as a moment of the working class's struggle. This is the route through which labour's living activity, socialised by capital and objectified in it, can be made roughly to serve the work of positive destruction that the working-class viewpoint materially entails. This fermenting vitality of working-class labour is, in fact, still nothing more than an antagonism. And the antagonism is nothing other than its antithetical character, its position of permanent negation, this continually repeated no, this rejection of everything which, when left up to spontaneity, whips the capitalist and makes him run and forces him to repeat to himself – as Marx said – onward, onward; this, which, when channelled between the iron limits of revolutionary organisation, first sets up the economic barrier of capital before itself like a dam and then politically besieges, overwhelms and destroys it. We start out from this presupposition: that capital has now arrived at retracing the natural law of its own social development. In these conditions, the ultimate end of working-class thought is no longer to reveal capitalist society's economic law of motion. At this point, every phase of capitalism's unfolding ought to be at once reduced to a practical means of its possible dissolution. It ought to be shown how capital's laws of development are laws of the capitalist development of the working class, as the organisation of the workers by the capitalist. There is a fetishism of labour-power that attaches itself to the producers of capital as soon as they begin to produce social capital. What first of all needs doing is to violently suppress this modern bourgeois semblance, which subordinates labour to capital, and to do so in struggle: it is within such action that we will find the decisive political terrain for defeating the capitalists. And what then needs doing, on this basis, is to set off in discovery of the working class's political laws of movement, which materially subordinate the development of capital to the working class itself. Thus will be found the definitive theoretical task, from the working-class point of view. From this point onward, capitalism must begin to interest us only as a historical system of the reproduction of the working class.

10

The Labour Theory of Value as Watchword

This is the decisive point of the strategic overturn. For now, it will not proceed to activate itself in research 'in the field'. It does not have the immediate possibility of sowing any seeds in the present desert of contemporary Marxism. This is not the thing that we need to aim for. Only an imposing political experience tactically guided by this new strategic criterion will be able to explode once and for all the crust of opportunism, of surrender, of passive obedience to the tradition that accepts only the innovations proposed by the opposite camp, and under which the working-class point of view has remained buried for decades. Only the new forces that produce this practical experience, and which are reproduced by it, will then be able to carry forth the work of theoretical reconstruction, the labour of scientific modelling, to the very end. We ought not believe that the opposite would be possible. To reveal only the new possibilities for the course of struggle does not change the real conditions in which the struggle unfolds. But, when we really do change these conditions, according to the new point of view, this imposes a decisive victory also with regard to the future. Again, here, we find that we have to proceed through a narrow gate. Each and every time that the working-class point of view advances, it finds itself having to demonstrate through practical example what it has proposed in theory; by its very nature, it finds that it has to put politics ahead of science. This is the reason that working-class science will never offer itself up to the 'scholar' in an internally complete form. The working-class point of view *qua* science is already a contradiction. For it not to be so, it must be more than science, or, in other words, a conscious grasping of phenomena or means of predicting them. It has to be revolution, an actual process of taking realities and overturning them. It is hardly strange that, a century on, the economist will continue to find economic errors in Marx, the historian historical errors, the politician political errors, and so on – all of this is normal. The reason all of this is normal is that from the economist's, the historian's, the traditional politician's point of view, these are outright errors. But none of these ask themselves whether they can, indeed, judge Marx from their point of view, from the point of view of their disciplines. If Marx's *oeuvre* is reduced to a phenomenon in the history of doctrines, then one may indeed be a Marxist or not, in a more or less refined way – to each their own doctrine. But, if this *oeuvre* itself is seen as a practical moment in the class struggle, from the working-class point of view, then the important thing is to be Marxists in a single, rough sense, namely as revolutionary militants on the working-class side. If this is the case, then we should understand that this has hefty consequences on the objectively scientific terrain. We should accept, then, that we are working clandestinely, on the underground, at a wholly different level to recognised science. So, it will often not be possible to compare like with like. We demand the right to be despised as scholars, and by the scholars. In capitalist society, research, study, science, from the working-class point of view, must consciously choose to take on the honour of isolation. That is the only way to provide the class's movements with an untroubled understanding of that aggressive antagonistic force which they so need. This restores to the workers what Marx aptly indicated to them as an unavoidable choice: 'the honour of being a conquering force [*die Ehre eine erobernde Macht zu sein*]'.[1]

What if we today propose an overturning of the historical priority between capital and labour, beginning to see capital as a function of the working class or, more precisely, the capitalist economic system as a moment in the working class's political development, thus breaking and inverting through research the subaltern history of the working-class movements in order to recuperate in practice the possibility of forcibly imposing on capital its own movements? All this would methodologically be no different from what Marx himself did when he took on the

---

1 Marx, *Werke*, Vol. 8, 157.

labour law of value and interpreted it, brought it to completion and made it serve his purposes, which was not exclusively the goal of his analysis, but it was one of the overall goals of the struggle of his class. It was not Marx who discovered the labour law of value. He found it already fundamentally complete, in the existing thought of his time. But while it is true that this was the contemporary bourgeois thought, it was precisely the thought of that advanced part of the industrial bourgeoisie which, in its life-and-death struggle against the passive survivals of the past, had an interest in realistically presenting its own theories as a 'scientific subsistence' of economic relations. Simply to face the facts was already, in that case, a break with the old equilibrium. Besides, it was precisely this truth that made a relation with this bourgeois science productive. And the truth that this science sought to impose, in the crudest way, on political attention was – for good reason – the new, simultaneously both economic and political knot of the labour-value, labour-capital reality. So, heading along this path is not a matter of giving credit to the historic illusion that, when the bourgeoisie is revolu-tionary, it has no fear of telling the truth, but becomes more dishonest the more reactionary it is, and that while before it takes power it is good and after it has taken power it becomes wicked. These are but fables for children at the nursery of historical materialism. The realism of classical bourgeois thought is not an isolated fruit of the golden age of capital – it repeats itself every time that the most advanced capitalist element decides to attack and defeat the most backward capitalist element on the working-class terrain. That is, every time that the working-class articu-lation of capitalist development is brought into play, it must be enacted in a direct and now-open fashion. Now it again becomes possible for the alternative, working-class use of some of the scientific findings obtained by the opposing point of view. This is why Ricardo's bourgeois cynicism on the conditions of labour for profit was more useful to Marx than all the laments in communist literature about the misery of the toiling classes. When Marx rejected the idea that labour is the source of all wealth and assumes a concept of labour as a measure of value, the social-ist ideology was defeated once and for all and working-class science was born. And for good reason, as this is a choice that goes for all time. Labour does not create anything, it does not create value, just as it does not create capital, and thus labour has no need to ask anyone to compen-sate it for the full fruits of what it has created. How many times did Marx tell us that labour is a presupposition of capital and, at the same time, in turn presupposes capital? And what else can this mean if not the very simple fact that for capital to become capital, to become a production relation, it presupposes a workforce and labour-power to work – that is, for capital to be able to produce, it presupposes the conditions of labour? And these are not simple reciprocal presuppositions, what we may call static conditions. Rather, they have to do with a dynamic, very mobile, even agitated counterposition between two classes. And this counterposition sees – and this is the point of discrimination – one class, one active force of living labour, a social mass of proletarians, already long in advance standing counterposed to the dead conditions of labour as capital in itself; that is, as the single capitalist. This situation has unfolded to the point of forcing the latter to live and to constitute himself on this same model, as an antagonistic class. The passage via a concept of labour as a moment that homogenises social realities, as a yardstick that measures values, as the reduction to living units of what in capitalist society is simultaneously both multiple and dead – this passage via labour now acquires its fundamental and ineliminable importance. Labour can make realities more homogenous among themselves insofar as the proletarian mass from which it originates is the only homogeneous force society provides. Labour can measure value because its working-class articulation is, from the outset, present in all the decisive structures that make the machine of capital move; it is an objective measure of value insofar as it is a potential check on capital. Labour can reduce everything to itself and thus render everything alive, because the class movement that expresses it has a univocal antagonistic direction, a single enemy to defeat and a single available force of attack. In this sense, it is true that the substitution of labour with labour-power changes the nature of the law of value, from how Marx found it to how he left it. But that is true only on the condition that economic analysis does not reduce labour-power to a normal commodity, and only on the condition that it is politically exalted as a particular commodity. And we can say that the particularity of the commodity labour-power – the possibility of it valorising more than its own real value – coincides with the fact that it is living labour associated by capital and objectified in it, and the fact that it is not only the working class, but the working class within the capitalist relation of production – not labour that creates wealth and thus lays claim to this wealth for itself, but workers who, as a class, produce capital and can thus refuse, as a class, to produce it. At this point, the particular character of labour-power as a commodity is now discovered to be not an economic fact passively incorporated into the workers' existence, but an active political possibility that the working class holds in its power with its sole presence as a living part within capital. Thus, the valorisation of labour-power beyond its own value, the modern compulsion to surplus-labour, the extortion of surplus-value by industry – all these economic laws of movement in capitalist society ought to be discovered anew as the political laws of movement of the working class, forced by the subjective power of organisation crudely to serve the objective revolutionary needs of class antagonism and the struggle. And we should understand that in the case of overturning the content of the laws of development, it will not arrive through its immediate spontaneous power. Certainly, spontaneity also comes into play here, just as it has thus far. Yet it does so in the opposite sense, in the sense of the gradual disintegration of all subjective political will under the iron mechanism of the economy. Nor will a simple strategic call, the wholly theoretical appeal to a new strategy, suffice to turn this tendency around. So, we are instead forced to take direct interest in tactically preparing the terrain on which the most subversive praxis thus far conceived can properly be planted, in such a way that it will seek deep roots. And this praxis is subversive twice over – once against the power of capital and once against the tradition of the workers' movement. Of course, the Marxian labour law of value does not already implicitly include all this. And yet, if we consider this law – as is our intention – to be working-class science's first model hypothesis to be put into the field, then there is also the possibility of finding therein something more than Marx himself wanted to see. At this point, the economists' fuss about the non-functioning of this law within real economic relations is overwhelmed by the realities themselves, as they present themselves from a working-class political point of view. And what are these realities if not the simplest, most elementary, facts from the everyday common sense of the class struggle? For at the very moment that the labour law of value entered Marx's head, it became something different than what it had been up to that point. Having been a law of movement of capitalist society – a discovery of the most advanced bourgeois science – it became a law of movement of the working class and thus a practical moment of attack, of material aggression against capitalist society itself – no longer only from the theoretical point of view of a counterposed working-class science, but from the political camp of a possible organised revolutionary movement. Now bourgeois science itself intervened to uncover the contradictions of this law. It's true: when Marx took on the law of value as his own, he set it into crisis, in practical terms. Indeed, from the point of view of objective economic science, after Marx the law of value no longer works. And we can no longer implicate Marx in the crisis, in the economic collapse of this law. We cannot criticise Marx for what would instead rightly be blamed on Ricardo. That is why every defence of the Marxian theory of value, or any attempt to justify it – even more serious examples like Sweezy or Pietranera – on the objective economic terrain turns out to be politically unproductive, which is to say neutral in practical terms. For Marx, the labour law of value is a political thesis, a revolutionary rallying cry; it is not a law of economics, or a means of scientific interpretation of social phenomena. Or, better, it *is* these two last things but on the basis of the first two and in consequence of them. In this sense, again, the law of value is truly an economic error from the point of view of capital's science. And the modern instruments of this science have well identified the internal difficulties of this law. But the correct relationship is between the law and its object. And the object in Marx is not the economic world of commodities but the political relation of capitalist production. The economist comes along and closes *Capital* after the first section of Chapter One because Marx's theory of value does not explain prices. Yes, this is the eternal bourgeois pretence: to put science before science, of wanting to explain *a priori* all the phenomena that apparently contrast with this law. But it is also the organic historic vice of the intellectual who mistakes *Capital* for a 'treatise of political economy', while, in fact, it is nothing other than a 'critique of political economy', a critique of its scientific tools and ends, the preparation of new tools for new ends, both of which go beyond the limits of science. Labour-value, then, means first labour-value and then capital; it means capital conditioned by labour-power, moved by labour-power, value measured by labour. Labour is the measure of value because the working class is the condition of capital. This political condition is the true, presupposed starting point of Marx's economic analysis itself. The reconstruction of Marx's discourse on the concept of labour, and the gap in quality that divides him from his own theoretical sources on this problem – see Hegel and Ricardo – and, at the same time, his reference back to the concrete experiences of working-class struggle as the true practical source of a possible solution – all this tended to privilege the class relation over all other social relations and make it the one that conditions the others. And at the centre of these others is capital's relation with the working-class part of itself. The moment of mediation that now, indeed, enriches the problem is the possibility of tying together in a single bundle, within capitalist society, labour as measure of value – the first homogenising element, indispensable to the bourgeois understanding of social phenomena – and the working class as an articulation of capital – the primary factor in the organisation of the capitalist system of production. We say that this working-class articulation of capitalist production still today expresses the bourgeois contradictions of the labour law of value, without resolving them but also without using them. This demands that a new form be given to this same law, or – and this is the same thing – that its content is made fully explicit. The working-class point of view no longer needs an economic solution to the theoretical problem of labour-value; there is only the search for a political outlet for the practical relation between working class and capital. So, according to Marx's own indications, the task of working-class science is still precisely to 'show how the law of value asserts itself'.[2] However, there is one condition: that this elaboration is not trapped in the phoney contradictions of economic science. The way in which the law imposes itself is a problem of the political organisation of the class relation. And everywhere in the production process where there exists a class relation, it is necessary to uncover the objective functioning of the content of this law and, at the same time, fix the political forms with which to impose this law subjectively. The labour law of value, in Marx's interpretation, cannot in fact be extrapolated from the capitalist relation of production and from the class relation at the former's foundation. Where the laws of the market pretend that it no longer exists, it must still and always be maintained that the law of value is indeed functioning. What does this mean, if not that the class struggle lives, still now as always, within the production relation? This is the historical paradox of realised 'socialism': an orthodox loyalty to Marxist tools of analysis is to be discovered precisely in the living presence of each of the classical laws of capital's development. When asked whether it was possible to see the law of value

---

2 Marx and Engels Collected Works (MECW), Vol. 43, 68.

functioning in an economy planned in a socialist sense and the answer was affirmative, this was therefore a fundamentally important turning point. If we want to proceed further, here – even if also with the preoccupation, on this terrain and at the current stage of research, to break through an intellectual *omertà* that blocks the working-class point of view behind a now useless barrier of political opportunism – then we have to pose this scandalising theme as a real problem. Namely, that if we can speak of the *objective economic functioning* of the labour law of value, we can speak of this precisely – and only – with reference to the very society that claims to have realised socialism. If, indeed, we dovetail – as is quite legitimate – placing value and capital on one side and labour and the working class on the other, and say that the modern, wholly developed form of the labour law of value now presents itself as the working-class articulation of capitalist development, then we must conclude that it is possible to elaborate this law wherever capital exists as a production relation, but that the way in which this law effectively imposes itself today has, as its historical condition, a management of the capitalist relation of production that is working class in form. That is: wherever all the laws of capital's development function openly under the subjective command of a class of capitalists, the working-class conditioning of development can be imposed only in the various – but all-open and all-subjective – forms of the working-class struggle. Here, the capitalist has no need to refer to the law of value for his own economic calculations, for he has no interest in making the working class function as the active political motor of the whole process; it is enough for him to use the working class economically as such in the production process. But where, on account of a determinate context of historical circumstances, a concentrated nucleus of the working class is the only homogenous social force able to carry forth the development of capital, then there the conditions are prepared for labour to objectively impose itself as a homogenous yardstick of all value and for the working class to objectively impose itself as such a material articulation of capital that it no longer has to express itself in the openly subjective forms of the struggle. We have to find the courage of our convictions and recognise as a real historical fact the absurdity that the political power of capital can take the form of a workers' state. When working-class conditioning goes beyond the terms of the production relation alone and takes hold of the general social relation, it brings into being, imposes on itself, perhaps through a revolutionary rupture, a class dictatorship in its own name. Mind you, the working-class articulation of capital does still exist. But, in today's capitalism, it operates as a struggle, while, in today's socialism, it functions as a law. Hence, once more, a chain of paradoxes. Capital presents itself as the definitive political terrain in which the class relation effectively develops, and socialism presents itself as the possible form of its static economic regulation. Faced with capitalism, socialism will no longer succeed in losing its character as a temporary experiment in managing capital. Capitalism has chosen directly to pay for living labour's activity even at the price of an open class confrontation, which is subsequently also opportunely institutionalised. Socialism has anticipated these institutional political forms with a kind of working-class self-control, but it has done so at the price of the mass passivity of the workers with regard to 'their' system. Thus, the capitalist economy turns out to be infinitely rich in possibilities on account of the working class's political laws of movement, whereas the socialist state presents itself as a closed juridical organisation of collective passivity. But it is important not to make a mistake here. The class struggle doubtless assumes more direct and acute forms in today's capitalism, but the content of this struggle perhaps has a higher level precisely within the structures of today's socialism. Once passivity is extended to a mass social scale, it can be a very high form of working-class struggle. We should never confuse the lack of open forms of struggle with a lack of struggle itself. The more the economic mechanism of development becomes wholly objective, the more the working-class rejection of exploitation – if restricted to mere spontaneity – will tend to follow and not precede capital's laws of movement. Thus, where the capitalist relation of production has reached a high degree of socialisation, now not only the working class as a social productive power, but the class struggle itself and, moreover, the very organisation of the working-class antagonism, present themselves materially incorporated in capital, as its internal part, as its moment of elaboration. But the level of social capital is not exclusive to the socialist solution to capital's problems; it likewise captures what we might call classic capitalism at its highest point. Rather, everything suggests that, at its most extreme, social capital will constitute the level at which the two systems converge and reunite. In this sense, it is possible to foresee that, in the long run, capital will use the experiences of building socialism for its own ends, within its own logic. Unless, that is, an autonomous

resumption of the working-class struggle – a working-class revolutionary experience at a strategically chosen and tactically prepared point –
should intervene to block and overturn this process. The theory of a
rupture at the middle point of development must consciously find its
application at the centre of this context of historical conditions. And it is
only in order to prepare ourselves for engagement, for this concrete
experience, that it becomes important to know what the process's objective tendency in the absence of this experience is. The fatal error that the
revolutionary movement is making today is that it passively obeys this
objectivity, allowing capital to choose the terrain of the struggle on the
field of its iron economic laws, and it refuses to organise to aggravate
irrationality from the capitalist point of view of the political rejection of
the workers as a class. This means giving up on making the working-
class articulation of capital operate in a subversive way through a heightened external subjective intervention. The more we reflect on this, the
more we discover that in the 'purgatory of revolution', the working-class
point of view hives off all its sins of economism, objectivism, and opportunistic political subordination to the movements of capital.

11

The Class

Behind and before the class of capitalists, there is capital. Capital does not alone constitute itself into a social class. Rather, it first needs to see the working class before it, already formed. But even after capital has achieved a subjective, class expression, what guides the process still remains an object, a thing, a material relation in the form of a social relation, a development mechanism. The bourgeois ideologue is still scandalised by this, but fetishism, reification and alienation are permanent realities in the history of capital. Only that the object, the thing, alienated labour itself, are all historically determinate, which is to say, more precisely, socially specific. If behind labour-power as a commodity, we find the workers as a class – the proletariat in its political definition – the reverse happens on the opposite side. Behind the class of capitalists there is capital as an economic category, there is the capitalist production relation as an economic relation. 'Economic determinism' is synchronous with the capitalist point of view. Amid so many transformations in the practice – the history – of capital, the classic figure of the bourgeois theorist always remains that of the economist. Economics is the bourgeois science *par excellence*. Sociology itself is nothing other than an ideology of economics. Indeed, no question is more 'ideological' than the one that asks, at this point, 'what is a social class'? The sociologist starts reading *Capital* from the end of Volume 3 and stops reading when the chapter on classes breaks off. Then, every now and then someone, from Renner to Dahrendorf, has a grand old time of completing what had remained incomplete, and what results from all this is libel against Marx, which should, at a minimum, be punished with physical violence. But there was a reason the chapter on classes remained incomplete. The essential things regarding the concept of class had already been said throughout *Capital*'s entire analysis. And this interruption of the manuscript on *spaltet* says more than any continuation of the text ever could. After the discourse had again started out from the real separation, the one governed by the law of movement of the capitalist mode of production, between means of production and labour, with the transformation of labour into wage-labour and of means of production into capital, an internal dissection of the *drei grossen Klassen*, governed by the division of labour, was so ines-sential and even perilous that it could not be continued. When Marx stopped there, it had every air of a sudden decision to stop pursuing a line of reasoning that had taken a wrong course. Moreover, it is hard to understand why the chapter on classes should have been part of the section on incomes, if Marx himself ruled out any idea that identical sources of income would be enough to indicate belonging to one same class. The existing ambiguity at the outset perhaps lies precisely in the 'trinity formula' – we cannot say, as Marx does, that this holds all the secrets of the social process of production. If the social process of produc-tion is capital at the level of its full development, then it cannot be defined by any formula that contains more than two protagonists – that is, capital itself and then the working class facing capital, within capital and against capital. This applies to any definition of this process that counts as 'science'.

On the terrain of political practice, a further reduction needs to be made. By its very nature, the trinity ought to be reduced to a singular. When we ask ourselves why the secret of capitalism can be grasped only from the working-class point of view, the only possible response is that the working class is the secret of capitalism. What Marx said in 1857 is still true: capitalist society is the most complex and developed organisa-tion of production in history. But we ought not set off from here and reconstruct the past history of all human societies from the heights of capital; it is hard to understand whom or what purpose this would serve. It may even be true that the bourgeois economy provides the key to the ancient economy, but, without doubt, this is of no use for our purposes. What does interest us is to focus on capital as the highest point of organ-isation not only of production, but also of society as a whole, and then locate within this point the successive level of development which explains, judges and conditions it. And this higher level of development internal to capital is, indeed, the working class: which, moreover, we have already called the key to the mechanism of capitalist production. Can we say that the working class explains capital as capital explains land rent? Certainly not. For if we reduced everything to a history of 'categories', we would have to conclude that capital cannot be understood without the working class, but the working class can very well be understood without capital. Yet capital and the working class can only be understood in combination, the one always against the other. The working class is not for capitalism what capital was for premodern social categories; that is, a point of arrival for historical development and thus a starting point for its logical succession. Otherwise we would have to dig up a neo-objectivism of perhaps political rather than economic content, and that leads to a new type of reformism, which will indeed perhaps emerge in the coming years and which we need to prepare to crush in the egg. The development of our discourse is a wholly different one. Here, the working class is the historical starting point for the birth and growth of capitalism. And we can also start out from capital in order to arrive at a logical understanding of the working class. Is this not, perhaps, the path Marx himself took? To conceive capitalism as a historical system of the reproduction of the working class means to take this path to its conclusion. But in what sense, then, can we say that it is possible to grasp the secret of capitalism from only the working-class point of view, if it is, instead, capital that brings to light the historical nature of the working class? It is possible, so long as we bear in mind this very simple fact: the working class is not the secret of capitalism in terms of explaining it, but in the sense that it is the secret to its dissolution. Capital can explain everything about the working class theoretically but cannot eliminate it practically. The working class, with its science, may not be able to explain everything about capital, but can succeed in destroying it in the revolution. For this very reason, it will always be a pious illusion, from the working-class point of view, to want to know more about capitalist society than do the capitalists themselves; every form of working-class management of capital will necessarily fall short compared to a directly capitalist one, and it will be discovered, perhaps before not too long, that the realistically most practicable path, the 'easiest' one for the working-class side, is precisely the path of destruction through revolution. Thus, from the capitalists' point of view it is only right to study the working class; only they can study it well, but even with the ideological smoke and mirrors of industrial sociology they will not manage to cancel out the death sentence that this class represents for them. If 'capital is the economic power in bourgeois society that dominates everything', the working class is the only political power that can dominate capital. If anything, this is also the way to explaining capital – but then it is an explanation that has to be imposed by force. We should account for the fact that in its objectivity, which is to say, in its spontaneity, the working-class articulation of the capitalist mode of production functions as an economic law of movement of capital. To make this articulation function as a political law of movement of the working class, the vast task of organising that attacking force of workers, which alone can force the capitalists onto the defensive, is a necessary passage that is impossible to leap over. The working-class secret to capitalism, from a revolutionary point of view, is not a theoretical law but a practical possibility. It does not function objectively, but rather has to be imposed subjectively. It must be torn from the society of capital and handed to the party of the working class. Thus, for the first time in the history of any social formation, capital's laws of development will be made to serve the process of its overthrow. And this is what needs finally to be understood. For good reason, thus far we have always spoken of the working class and never of the concept of class in general; we have spoken of working-class struggles and never of class struggle in general. Marx himself refused to be credited with having discovered the existence of classes and the struggle between them, instead attributing these discoveries to bourgeois economists and historians. Indeed, Lenin could even comment that 'the theory of the class struggle was created not by Marx, but by the bourgeoisie before Marx, and, generally speaking, it is acceptable to the bourgeoisie ... Only he is a Marxist who extends the recognition of the class struggle to the recognition of the dictatorship of the proletariat'.[1] If this is indeed true, and if what is decisive is the point that the process arrives at – the overthrow of capital, the dictatorship of the proletariat, then from a Marxist point of view, from the

---

1   Vladimir Ilyich Lenin, *The State and Revolution*, text from marxists.org. Here Lenin comments on Marx's 5 March 1852 letter to Weydemeyer published by Mehring in the *Neue Zeit*, XXV, 2, 1907, 164.

working-class point of view, classes and the class struggle can be conceived only through and within capitalist society. Or would you have it that the class struggle between the serfs and feudal lords, or perhaps between Spartacus and Licinius Crassus, ought to have ended with the dictatorship of the proletariat? It is not that 'Marxist' historians have not tried their hand at this: out of the usual determination to compete with the bourgeoisie, which finds capital in the ancient world, these historians call the pyramid builders 'workers'. We can separate out who is a Marxist and who is not by pulling everyone back from these appeals to history and instead identifying a possible conclusion for political practice, today; that is, by pulling everyone back from the class struggle in general to look at the particular needs of the revolution against capital. For Lenin, this is 'the touchstone on which the real understanding and recognition of Marxism should be tested'.[2] And this holds today. We need, then, to proceed in this direction and go further still. It is hard to understand how Schumpeter can call the Marxist theory of social classes the 'crippled sister' of his 'economic interpretation of history' and five pages later describe it as 'a bold stroke of analytical strategy ... which linked the fate of the class phenomenon with the fate of capitalism'.[3] It is true that here he means the end of capitalism, in traditional fashion, as the end of classes. But the real strategic audacity – indeed, valid not only on the field of analysis – is today quite different: namely, that which turns the problem on its head and sees the birth of classes as the birth of capitalism. It is in this sense that the fate of the phenomenon of class and the destiny of capitalism ought to be bound together in a single political perspective of the dissolution of capital's class society – that is, the only social formation historically founded on the class struggle. Perhaps Parsons saw part of this problem when he linked, in Marx, 'the fact of an organised productive unit' and 'the inherent class conflict' 'given that the immediate interests of the two classes were completely opposed'.[4] It is true, he restores this to the history of social thought, because he found a precedent in the Hobbesian factor of power differences: this does not, however, stop him from recognising the reinsertion of this same factor

---

2 *The State and Revolution*, Chapter 2, text from marxists.org.

3 Joseph Schumpeter, *Capitalism, Socialism and Democracy*, London: Routledge, 2013.

4 Talcott Parsons, *Structure of Social Action*, New York: Free Press, 1967, 108.

as the specific determinant of a grave instability in the economic system and this instability, in turn, as 'the result of a power relation within a determinate institutional framework, implying a definite social organisation: the capitalist enterprise'.[5] Here, naturally, we will not manage to place the class relation before the capitalist relation of production: it would moreover be to ask too much, and the important thing is not to ask these people about these things. Capital's scientific point of view can also go so far as to close off the course of the class struggle within the history of capitalism. The direct capitalist at the social, collective level is compelled to do this daily, to meet his own practical needs. And this is why, on this terrain, the modern science of capital does not only seem but *is* more advanced than the currently dominant archaeological Marxism. What absolutely cannot be seen, standing outside the working-class point of view – which is to say, outside of the organisation of the working-class struggle – is the fact that the class relation historically preceded the capital relation – and thus classes historically preceded capital, and thus the working class historically preceded the class of capitalists. Indeed, this historical precedence is nothing other than the workers' permanent and aggressive political pressure against the bosses.

Does not the very birth of the working-class point of view, the possibility of a non-objective social science without pretensions to objectivity, the practicability of a unilateral synthesis which grasps all the phenomena of all present society from one side – not to know them but to overthrow them – the 'imposing synthesis' of Marx's *oeuvre* – does not all this find its material *raison d'être* precisely in the birth of the first social class to have historically existed, the working class? The historical starting point in capitalist society saw the workers on one side and the capitalist on the other. This is another of those facts that imposes itself with the violence of simplicity. We can, historically, speak of the single capitalist: that is, the socially determinate figure who presided over the constitution of the capitalist relation of production. As such, at least in the classic development of the system, this historical figure does not disappear and is not extinguished or suppressed. Rather, he is collectively organised, being socialised – so to speak – in capital, precisely as a class relation. But at no historical moment can we speak of the single worker: the materially, socially determinate material figure of the worker

---

5   Ibid., 110.

arises already collectively organised. From the outset, the workers, like the capitalist's exchange-values, proceed in the plural: the worker in the singular does not exist. Dahrendorf reproaches Marx for his error of 'sometimes' recognising only the proletariat as a class. But for us, this error is very easy to understand. Such are the conditions of the class struggle that almost every day each of us is led to see, on the one side, a social class that moves as such, and on the other side something that is always either less or more than a social class. Something less, because the capitalist side's directly economic interest has continued to present itself in divided fashion and perhaps will never cease to do so. Something more, because capital's political power now increases its apparatus of control, its dominion of repression, beyond the traditional forms of the state such as to take hold of all the structures of the new society. So, on each occasion, we need to strive to reduce to the class level, the level of the two classes, all the phenomena that apparently seem to contradict this level or not concern it. And this is, not least, the burdensome task of theory and the reason why it is necessary. But for theory, all this is insufficient. The next step – or better, the premise at its foundation and which must make itself explicit in the conclusion – is the qualitative difference between the two classes, the effective historical priority of the one over the other, the possible political subordination, which is never decided once and for all within capitalist society, of the one over the other. If the class relation precedes the capital relation, the class relation at the origins presents, on the one hand, living labour-power and, on the other, the dead conditions of production; on the one hand, the proletariat, already partly elaborated as a class, and, on the other, capital still wholly in itself, still wholly in potential; that is, on the one hand, the social mass of sellers of the commodity labour-power, gripped within a single collective condition that makes them all together antagonists of a single enemy, and, on the other, the single capitalist, the true and only sovereign individual, the prince-entrepreneur who conquers command over living labour with the power of all that is dead – money, land, work tools – and thus seizes power over everything. Power over everything and dominion over labour are, then, a single thing. But here, labour is the living activity of labour-power, working-class labour. In capitalist society, the class that becomes the ruling class is that class which holds working-class labour, reduced to a dead object, beneath itself. With an act of violence, capital takes labour's life and incorporates it within itself; thus

capital itself becomes a living subject, makes itself a formally autonomous activity, proceeds as a class of capitalists. Just as, from a rigorously
working-class point of view, it is easy to make the mistake of recognising
the compact social mass of factory workers as a single class, so too, from
a rigorously capitalist point of view, it is easy to make the mistake of
recognising the absolute dominion of capital at the social level as the
only power. The consequences: in the first case, ineliminable 'revolutionary illusions' on the working-class side; in the second case, the web
of 'practical errors' that link together the political history of capitalist
initiatives. Each of these errors has provided – provides – a 'historic
opportunity' for the revolution, and it is possible to profit from this, or
not, depending on the degree to which the subjective forces are prepared.
If they are well prepared, then even these illusions – overturned into a
rational plan of battle – can indeed function. What will never function
is the cold logic of reason when it is not moved by class hatred. We
should concede nothing – other than a healthy dose of disdain – to the
philistine who reproaches Marx for having constantly seen the revolution behind the corner and Lenin for having wanted it in the improper
time and moment. An elementary rule of practical conduct ought to be
immediately – intuitively – applied in these cases. When, on the one
hand, we find those who say that tomorrow everything will blow up and
the old world will crumble, and, on the other hand, we find those who
say that nothing is going to budge for fifty years, and the former are
denied by the facts and the second proven correct, we are with the
former – here, we must be with those who are mistaken.

12

The Strategy of Refusal

Adam Smith says – and Marx notes the accuracy of his observation – that the effective great development of labour's productive power begins when labour is transformed into wage-labour; that is, when the conditions of labour confront it in the form of capital. One could go further and say that the effective development of labour's political power really begins from the moment that labourers are transformed into workers; that is, when the whole of the conditions of society confront them as capital. We can see, then, that working-class political power is intimately connected to the productive power of wage-labour. The power of capital, conversely, is primarily a social power. Working-class power is a potential power over production – that is, over a particular aspect of society. Capitalist power is a real dominion over society in general. But such is the nature of capital that it requires a *society centred on production*. Production, a particular aspect of society, thus becomes the aim of society in general. Whoever controls and dominates it controls and dominates everything. Even if factory and society were to become perfectly integrated at the economic level, at a political level they would, nonetheless, forever continue to be in contradiction. One of the highest and most mature points of the class struggle will be precisely the frontal clash between the *factory as working class* and society *as capital*. To deny capital's interests a way forward in the factory is to block the functioning of society itself – and the way is then open to overthrow and destroy the power of capital. To instead seek to take over the running of the 'general interests of society' would, however, mean simplistically reducing the factory itself to capital, indeed by reducing the working class – a part of society – to society as a whole. But, if the productive power of labour makes a leap forward when it is put to use by the individual capitalist, it is also true that it makes a political leap forward when it is organised by social capital. This political leap forward may not express itself in organisational terms, and hence, from the outside, one might conclude that it has not happened at all. Yet it still exists as a material reality, and the fact of its spontaneous existence is sufficient for the workers to refuse to fight for old ideals – though it may not yet be sufficient for the working class to take on the initiative in elaborating a new plan of struggle, based on new objectives. So, are we still living through the long historical period in which Marx saw the workers as a 'class against capital', but not yet as a 'class for itself'? Or should we not perhaps say the opposite, even if it means muddying the waters of Hegel's triad a little? That is, that initially, faced with the direct boss, the workers *immediately* become 'a class for itself' and indeed are recognised as such by the first capitalists. And only afterwards, through a historical travail which is perhaps not yet over, passing through terrible practical experiences which are still ongoing, do the workers arrive at the point of being actively, subjectively, 'a class against capital'. For this transition to take place there needs to be political organisation, the party, which demands all power. In the period in between there is the workers' collective, mass refusal, expressed in passive forms – to reveal themselves as a 'class against capital' before they have this organisation of their own, before they have this total demand for power. The working class *makes* its own existence. But it is, at the same time, an *articulation* and *dissolution* of capital. Capitalist power seeks to use the workers' antagonistic will-to-struggle as a motor for its own development. The working-class party must take this real working-class mediation of capital's interests and organise it in an antagonistic form, as the tactical terrain of struggle and as a strategic destructive potential. Here, there is only one point of reference, only one set of bearings, for the opposed viewpoints of the two classes – and it is the class of workers. Whether one's aim is to stabilise the development of the system or to destroy it forever, it is the working class that decides. The society *of capital* and the *working-class party* find themselves to be two opposite forms with one and the same content. And in the struggle over that same content, the one form excludes the other. They can only both coexist during the brief period of the revolutionary crisis. The working class cannot constitute itself as a *party* within capitalist society without preventing this society from continuing to function. As long as it continues to function, this party is *not* the working-class party.

Remember: 'the existence of a class of capitalists is based on the productive power of labour'. Productive labour, then, stands in relation not only to capital, but also to the capitalists as a class; in this latter relationship, it exists as the working class. This is probably a historical transition: it is productive labour which produces capital; it is capitalist production that 'organises' the working class, through industry; it is the organisation of industrial workers into a class that prompts the capitalists in general to constitute themselves as a class. At an average level of development, workers thus already present themselves as a social class of *producers*: industrial producers of capital. At this same level of development, the capitalists present themselves as a social class not so much of *entrepreneurs* as of *organisers*: that is, the organisers of workers by means of industry. A history of industry cannot be conceived other than as a history of the capitalist organisation of productive labour, and thus as a working-class history of capital. There is no forgetting the 'industrial revolution' here. Our research must start out from this point, if it is ever to get to grips with the contemporary forms of capital's dominion over workers –which is, indeed, increasingly exercised through the objective mechanisms of industry – and then investigate the possible working-class uses of them. This is the point at which the development of the relationship between living labour and the constant part of capital is violently subordinated to the emergence of the class relationship between the collective worker and the whole of capital, as social conditions of production. Every technological change in the mechanisms of industry thus turns out to be determined by the specific moments of the class struggle. Proceeding along this path would achieve two things: first, we would escape the trap of the apparent neutrality of the relationship between humanity and machinery; and, second, we would locate this same relationship in the combined history of working-class struggles and capitalist initiative. It is wrong to define modern society as 'industrial civilisation'. The 'industry' mentioned therein is just a means to be used. In truth, modern society is the civilisation of labour. And a capitalist society can never be anything but this. Precisely for this reason, in the course of its historical development, it can even take on the *form* of 'socialism'. So, we have not an industrial society – the society of capital – but the society of industrial labour, and thus the society of working-class labour. We must find the courage to fight capitalist society on these terms. Are the workers doing anything else when they struggle against the boss? Are they not above all fighting against labour? Are they not first and foremost saying 'no' to the transformation of labour-power into labour? Are they not, more than anything, refusing to *receive* work from the capitalist? Stopping work does not in fact mark a refusal to *give* capital the use of one's labour-power, since it has already been given to capital through the legal contract stipulating the sale and purchase of this particular commodity. Nor is it a refusal to hand capital the products of labour, since this is legally already capital's property, and the worker does not in any case know what to do with this property. Rather, stopping work – the strike, as the classic form of working-class struggle – is a refusal of capital's command, its role as organiser of production. It is a way of saying 'no' to the offer of concrete labour at a particular point in the process, a *momentary* blockage of the labour process as a recurrent threat which cuts into the process of value creation. The anarcho-syndicalist 'general strike', which was meant to provoke the collapse of capitalist society, is doubtless a romantic naivety owing to a primitive phase. It in fact already implies a demand, which it appears to oppose – that is, the Lassallean demand for a 'fair share of the fruits of one's labour' – in other words, a fairer 'stake' in capital's profits. In fact, these two perspectives converge in that incorrect correction which was imposed on Marx, and which has subsequently enjoyed such success within the practice of the official workers' movement – namely, the idea that those who really 'create work'[1] are 'working people' and that it is their concern to defend the dignity of this thing which they provide, against all those who would seek to debase it. No, the commonplace terminology is correct, and it really is the capitalist who creates work. The worker is the *creator of capital*. She in fact possesses a unique, particular commodity that is the condition of all the other conditions of production. For, as we have seen, at first all these other conditions of production are but capital in itself – a dead capital which, in order to come to life and develop into a social relation of production, needs to subsume labour-power as an

---

1 *Datori del lavoro*, work-givers, a term for employers today more common than *padrone* with its implications of 'mastery' and private ownership.

activity under itself, as a subject of capital. But as we have also seen, it cannot become a social relation of production unless the class relation is introduced into it, as its content. And the class relation is imposed from the proletariat's very *first* self-constitution as a class confronting the capitalist. Thus, the worker *creates* capital, not only insofar as she sells labour-power, but also insofar as she *bears* the class relation. Just like the sociality implicit within labour-power, this is another thing the capitalist does not pay for, or rather pays the cost (never subject to contract) of the working-class struggles which periodically shake the production process. Not by chance, the workers choose this as the terrain on which to attack the employers, out of their own tactical interest, and this is thus the terrain on which the employer is forced to respond with continual and disruptive technical developments in the organisation of work. In this whole process, the only thing that does not come from the worker's side is, precisely, work. From the outset, the *conditions of labour* are in the hands of the capitalist. And the only things in the worker's hands from the outset are the *conditions of capital*.

This is the historical paradox which marks the birth of capitalist society, and, indeed, an 'eternal rebirth' that will continue throughout its development. The worker cannot be *labour* other than in relation to the capitalist that stands against her. The capitalist cannot be *capital* other than in relation to the worker that stands against him. It is often asked what a social class really is. The answer is: these *two* classes. The fact that one is dominant does not imply that the other becomes subaltern. Rather, it implies a struggle, on equal terms, to break that domination and to reverse it into new forms, into a domination over those who have thus far dominated. We urgently need to resume circulating an image of the working-class proletariat that represents it as it really is – 'proud and menacing'. It is high time for a fresh comparison, in a new historical experience that directly sets the working class against capital, of what Marx called 'the gigantic infant shoes of the proletariat with the dwarfish, worn-out political shoes of the German bourgeoisie.'[2]

We have said that the conditions of capital are in working-class hands; that there is no active life in capital without the living activity of labour-power; that capital is already, at its birth, a consequence of productive labour; and that there is no capitalist society without the working-class

---

2   Marx and Engels Collected Works (MECW), Vol. 3, 201.

articulation of capital – in other words, no social relation without a class relation and no class relation without the working class. If all of this is the case, then we can conclude that the capitalist class, from its birth, is in fact subordinate to the working class. Hence the need for exploitation. Working-class struggles against the iron laws of capitalist exploitation cannot be reduced to the eternal revolt of the oppressed against their oppressors. For the very same reason, the concept of exploitation cannot be reduced to the individual employer's desire to enrich himself by extracting the maximum possible amount of surplus-labour from the bodies of his workers. As always, the economistic explanation has no weapons to deploy against capitalism other than a moral condemnation of the system. We are not here out of some intention to turn the problem on its head. In fact, the problem was already the other way around, right from the start. Exploitation is born, historically, from capital's need to escape from its de facto subordination to the class of worker-producers. It is in this very specific sense that capitalist exploitation in turn provokes working-class insubordination. The growing organisation of exploitation, its continual reorganisation at the very highest levels of industry and society are again capitalist responses to the working-class refusal to bow to this process. Now it is the working class's directly political thrust that imposes economic development on capital – a development which, starting from the site of production, extends to the general social relation. But this political vitality on the part of its antagonist – which it can also not do without – is, at the same time, the most fearsome threat to capital's power. We have already envisaged the political history of capital as a succession of attempts by capital to free itself from the class relation as a normal moment of 'separation'. Now we can envisage it at a higher level as the *history of the capitalist class's successive attempts to emancipate itself from the working class*, through the medium of the various forms of capital's political domination over the working class. This is the reason capitalist exploitation, a permanent form of the extraction of surplus-value within the production process, has throughout the history of capital been accompanied by the development of ever more *organic* forms of political dictatorship at the level of the state. In the society of capital, there is a truly economic need for political power: namely, the need forcibly to make the working class renounce its own social role as the dominant class. From this point of view, the present forms of economic planning are nothing more than an attempt to impose this *organic* form of dictatorship within democracy as the modern political form of a class dictatorship. Myrdal has spoken of the intellectual consensus on the future state of well-being – the society of which J.S. Mill, Marx and Thomas Jefferson alike would each approve. Such a state may even be realisable. We would then have a synthesis of liberalism, socialism and democracy. The potential accord between liberalism and democracy would finally find its ideal *mediation* in the shape of the social state – a system commonly known as 'socialism', indeed. But here, too, we run into the need for a working-class mediation, even at the level of political erudition. But, for their part, the workers would find in this 'socialism' the ultimate form of automatic – in other words, objective – control over their movement of insubordination – a political control now in economic form. The transcendence of state capitalism by a capitalist state is not something that belongs to the future: it is already a matter of the past. We no longer have a bourgeois state *over* a capitalist society, but directly, capitalist society's own state.

When does the political state start to direct at least part of the economic mechanism? When this economic mechanism can begin to use the political state itself as an *instrument of production*; in other words, in the sense that we have used it thus far, as a moment of the *political reproduction* of the working class. The 'end of laissez-faire' means, in substance, that working-class articulation of capitalist development can no longer function on the basis of spontaneous objective mechanisms; rather, it must be subjectively imposed by way of the political initiative of the capitalists themselves, as a class. Leaving aside all the post- and neo-Keynesian ideologies, it was Keynes alone who took the capitalist point of view on a formidable *subjective* leap, perhaps comparable in historical importance with the leap that Lenin imposed on the working-class point of view. However, this is not to concede that this was a 'revolution' in capital's way of thinking. When we look more closely, we can see that this was all already embodied in its prior development. The capitalists have still not invented – and in fact, will obviously never be able to invent – a non-institutionalised political power. That type of political power is specific to the working class. The difference between the two classes at the level of political power is precisely this: the class of capitalists does not exist independently of the formal political institutions through which, in different but permanent ways, it exercises its domination. For this very reason, the smashing of the bourgeois state marks the true destruction of the capitalists' power, and, indeed, it is only possible to destroy that power by smashing the state machine. The opposite is true of the working class: it exists independently of the institutionalised levels of its organisations. The destruction of the working-class has never amounted to the dissolution, dismemberment or destruction of the workers' class organism as a whole. The very possibility of the withering-away of the state in a society in which workers are in the saddle is to be found within the specific nature of this problem. For the class of capitalists to exist, it needs the mediation of a formal political level. Precisely because capital is a social power which, as such, purports to dominate over everything, it needs to articulate this domination in political 'forms' which can bring to life its dead essence as an objective mechanism and provide it with subjective force. By its very nature, capital is immediately and only an *economic* interest, and, at the beginning of its history, it was nothing more than the egotistical point of view of the individual capitalist. But, faced with the threat posed by the working class, it is forced to organise itself into a *political force* and to subsume under itself the whole of society in its own self-defence. It becomes the class of capitalists or, equivalently, it organises itself into a repressive state apparatus. If it is true that the concept of class is a political reality, then no capitalist class exists without the state of capital. And the so-called bourgeois 'revolution' – the conquest of political power by the 'bourgeoisie' – amounts to nothing more than the long historical transition through which capital constitutes itself as a class of capitalists in antagonistic relation to the workers. Once again, the development of the working class is totally the opposite: when the working class begins to exist formally at the level of political organisation, it directly initiates the revolutionary process and poses a single demand – its claim to power. But it has long since existed as a class and, as such, posed a threat to the bourgeois order. The collective worker is that wholly particular commodity which stands counterposed to all the conditions of society, including the social conditions of her own labour. And precisely for this reason, she presents the direct political subjectivity, that partiality, which constitutes her class antagonism, as something which she has already incorporated. At the outset, the proletariat is nothing more than an immediate *political interest* in the destruction of all that exists. In its internal development, it has no need for 'institutions' to bring its essence to life, since this essence is nothing other than the *living force* of that immediate destruction. Yet the proletariat does need *organisation* in order to objectify the political power of its antagonism against capital; in order to articulate this power within the material reality of the class relationship in any given moment; and in order to fruitfully shape this power into an aggressive force, in the short term, through the *weapons of tactics*. It needs organisation to do all this, even before it needs it in order to seize power from those who have it now. Marx discovered the existence of the working class long before any forms existed to express it politically: thus, for Marx, there is *a class even in the absence of the party*. On the other hand, the very existence of the Leninist party created the real illusion that a specific process of working-class revolution was already underway; for Lenin, in fact, *when the class organises itself into a party, it becomes revolution in action*. Here are two mutually complementary theses, just as the figures of Marx and Lenin are complementary. What do these two figures fundamentally represent for us today if not admirable anticipations of the class's future?

If the class is not identical to the party and yet we can speak of class only at a political level; if there is class struggle in the absence of the party, and yet every class struggle is nonetheless a political struggle; if the class makes the revolution through the party – or, in other words, puts into action what it is – by dissolving *in practice* everything that it must dissolve in theory, *taking the leap* from strategy to tactics, and only by these means *seizes* power from those in whose hands it previously lay, before organising that power in its own hands, in new forms … if all of this is true, then we must draw the conclusion that the class-party-revolution relationship is far tighter, more determinate and much more historically specific than is currently presented, even by Marxists. We cannot split the concept of revolution from the class relation. But a class relation is posed for the first time by the working class. *The concept of revolution and the reality of the working class thus become the same thing.* Just as there can be no *classes* before the workers begin to exist as a class, so there can be no *revolution* prior to the embodiment of that destructive will which the working class bears through its very existence. The working-class point of view has no interest in defining the upheavals of the past using the concept of 'revolutions'. To hark back to some 'historical precedent', which supposedly anticipates and prefigures the workers' movements in the present, is always simply reactionary, a conservatism that blocks the movement and recuperates it within the limited horizons of those who control the course of history today, of those who thus dominate society's development. Nothing is more alien to the working-class point of view than the opportunistic cult of historical continuity, and nothing more repugnant to it than the concept of 'tradition'. Workers recognise only one continuity – that of their own, direct political experiences; and only one tradition – that of their struggles. So why should we concede that the bourgeoisie was ever capable of organising a revolution? Why passively take as fact the intrinsically contradictory concept of the 'bourgeois revolution'? Has there ever even been a *bourgeois* class? For if, following historical materialism's own error, we choose to confuse the bourgeois class with the subsequent class of capitalists, then we have to explain how the organic relation between class and revolution functions – and do so in light of an historical experience which sees not the so-called bourgeois class making its revolution, but, if anything, the so-called bourgeois revolution laying the necessary foundations for the emergence of a class of capitalists, only after a long process of struggle. At this point, we need extensive concrete research in order to invert an interpretation that the Marxist 'tradition' has too long suffocated within schemas that are as theoretically false as they are politically damaging. We think that this is possible today even at the level of a basic historical investigation. We also think that the time has come to begin the work of reconstructing the facts, the moments, the transitions, which the inner reality of capitalism reveals – and can only reveal – precisely to the working-class viewpoint. It is now time to start building that *working-class history of capitalist society*, which alone can provide rich, fearsome, decisive weapons of theory to this moment of practical overthrow. Theoretical reconstruction and practical destruction can henceforth run only together, as the two legs of that single body which is the working class. Proletarian revolutions, Marx told us, 'criticise themselves constantly, interrupt themselves continually in their own course, come back to the apparently accomplished in order to begin it afresh, deride with unmerciful thoroughness the inadequacies, weaknesses of their first attempts, seem to throw down their adversary only so that he may draw new strength from the earth and rise again, more gigantic, before them, recoil ever and anon from the indefinite prodigiousness of their own aims, until a situation has been created which makes all turning back impossible, and the conditions themselves cry out: Hic Rhodus, hic salta!'³ (from *The Eighteenth Brumaire of Louis Bonaparte*). But we would say that this is not the process of proletarian revolutions. This is the process of revolution *tout court*. This is the *revolution as a process*. Because the working class is what it is, because of the point where it acts, because of the mode in which it is forced to fight – only the working class can be a *revolutionary process*. Bourgeois revolutions, says Marx, 'storm swiftly from success to success; their dramatic effects outdo each other; men and things seem set in sparkling brilliant; ecstasy is the everyday spirit; but they are short-lived; soon they have reached their highest point and a long crapulent depression lays held of society before it learns soberly to assimilate the results or its storm-and-stress period'.⁴ We must go further and say that these are not revolutions, but something different on each occasion: they may be coups d'état; crises in the regime; upheavals in the form of power; the exchange of power from one faction of a class to another faction of the same class; or sudden restructurings of that class's domination over the other class. The classic model of bourgeois 'revolution' – invented by historical materialism – sees a sudden seizure of political power only after the completion of a long, gradual assumption of economic power. Hence the class that has already come to dominate society as a whole now lays claim to the direction of the state. If these infantile schemas served to illustrate a history book or two, fair enough; it's the least one might expect in a 'history book'. But in the Marxist camp, errors of theory are paid for in very practical terms; this is a law whose harsh consequences the workers have all too often felt on their own hides. When it was attempted to apply the model of the bourgeois revolution to the course of working-class revolution, this led to the strategic collapse of the movement. And we must always bear this in mind. Copying this model, the workers would supposedly demonstrate in practice their ability to manage society economically – naturally having far more ability than the capitalists, in this regard – and on this basis lay claim to direct the state. This was to see the working-class management of capital as the highest, most 'classic' road to socialism. From the viewpoint of historical materialism, social democracy is theoretically the most orthodox workers' movement. The communist movement has fundamentally done nothing

---

3 MECW, Vol. 11, 106.
4 Ibid.

other to break and overturn in certain aspects of its practice, as necessity demanded, the logic of this essentially social-democratic theory.

And yet, at the beginning the dividing line between social democracy and the communist movement was clearly established. And if an internal history of the working class is to be reconstructed – alongside the history of capital – it will certainly include both of these organisational experiences, although they cannot be conceived at the same level or attributed the same significance. There is in fact a qualitative difference between different moments of the working-class struggle. When 10,000 workers marched on Manchester on 9 August 1842, with the Chartist Richard Pilling at their head, to negotiate with the manufacturers at the Manchester Exchange, and to see how the market was going, it was *not* the same as Sunday 28 May 1871 in Paris, when Gallifet picked out all the grey-haired prisoners and ordered that they be shot immediately, because they had been there not only in March '71 but also June '48. And we should not reduce the first case to an offensive action by the workers and the second to an act of repression by the capitalists, because perhaps things are, in fact, the other way around. It is true that here emerges the working-class articulation of capitalist development. The first time, however, was a positive initiative for the system's functioning, an initiative that only needs to be institutionally organised; the second time, as a 'no', as a refusal to manage the mechanism of the society as it stands, merely to improve it – a 'no' which must be repressed by pure violence. Such is the qualitative difference that may exist, even within one same working-class context, between *trade-union demands* and *political refusal*. Social democracy, even when it has conquered state political power, has never gone beyond the limited demands of a trade union faced with a boss. The communist movement has, in individual, short-lived experiences, blocked the peaceful development of the capitalist initiative by using the weapon of the party-of-non-collaboration. If workers simply had to choose between these two *historical* bearings, the choice would be fairly simple. But this is not the problem faced. The problem is the price we might pay at the level of theory if we adopt the communist movement's tradition of struggles as our own, and any answer to this problem is circumscribed by the question of what immediate practical results are to be achieved by taking this path. At this point, we must guard against the subjective illusion that conceives the strategic overthrow here proposed as the birth *first* of working-class science and *subsequently* as the first real possible organisation of the class movement. Instead, we must set our minds on a specific type of internal development of the working class, a political growth of its struggles, and use this as a lever for a further *leap forward*. And we must do without objectivism, without harking back to our origins and without having to start from scratch. Once again, we must grasp the crude proletarian origins of the modern worker and work them in service of the present needs of struggle and organisation. Nothing should be resisted more strongly than the modish image of a 'new working class' which is somehow continually being reborn and renewed by capital's various technological breakthroughs, as if in some scientific production laboratory. At the same time, what needs disowning is not the working class's rebellious past – that violent series of insurrections known as its 'desperate follies'. We should not make the mistake of those detached historians who dismiss as a 'popular revolt' every occasion on which the masses have put up barricades and then find the 'real' working-class struggles only in more recent forms of bargaining with the collective capitalist. Were 1848, 1871 and 1917 *working-class struggles*? Empirically, historically, we could demonstrate that they fell below the threshold of development that would have justified the objectives actually put forward in those events. But just try to reconstruct the concept and the political reality of the working class without the June insurgents, without the Communards and without the Bolsheviks. You will have a lifeless model on paper, an empty form in your hands. Of course, the working class is not 'the people'. But the working class comes from the people. And this is the basic reason why all – like ourselves – who adopt the working-class viewpoint no longer need to 'go out among the people'. We ourselves *come from the people*. And, just as the working class politically frees itself from the people when it no longer takes the stance of a subaltern class, so too does working-class science break with the heritage of bourgeois culture at the moment that it no longer takes the viewpoint of society as a whole, but of that part which wishes to overthrow it. Culture, in fact, like the concept of Right, of which Marx speaks, is always bourgeois. In other words, it is always a relation between intellectuals and society, between intellectuals and the people, between intellectuals and class; it is thus always a mediation of conflicts and their resolution through something else. If culture is the reconstruction of the totality of man, the search for his humanity in the world, a vocation to keep united that which is divided – then it is by nature reactionary and should be treated as such. The concept of working-class culture as *revolutionary culture* is as contradictory as the concept of bourgeois revolution. And this idea also contains that wretched counterrevolutionary thesis whereby the working class supposedly has to relive the whole experience of the history of the bourgeoisie. The myth that the bourgeoisie had a 'progressive' culture, which the working-class movement is now supposed to pick up from the dust where capital dropped it along with the usual old banners, has taken Marxist theoretical research into the realm of fantasy. But it has also imposed as a 'realistic' everyday practice the *preservation of a tradition* that is to be accepted and safeguarded as the heritage of the whole of humanity advancing along its path. Unblocking this kind of situation, as in other cases, will take the violent force of a destructive blow. Here, the critique of ideology must consciously assume the working-class perspective as a *critique of culture* and work towards a dissolution of all that already exists, refusing to continue to build on the old foundations. Man, Reason, History … these monstrous divinities must be fought and destroyed just like the boss's own power. It is not true that capital has abandoned these ancient gods. It has simply turned them into the religion of the official workers' movement: that is how they actively continue to govern the world. Meanwhile, the negation of these gods, which, in itself, presents a mortal danger for capital, is in fact managed directly by capital. Thus, antihumanism, irrationalism, antihistoricism become not practical weapons in the hands of the working-class struggle but cultural products in capitalist ideologies. In this way, culture – not because of the particular guise that it momentarily assumes in the contemporary period, but precisely through its ongoing form, *qua* culture – becomes a mediation of the social relation of capitalism, a function of its continued conservation. 'Oppositional' culture does not escape this fate, either; it merely presents the body of the workers' movement ideologies in the common clothing of bourgeois culture. Here, we are not interested in whether or not the historical figure of the intellectual-on-the-side-of-the-working-class could have existed at some point. Because what is decidedly impossible is for such a political figure to exist *today*. The organic intellectuals of the working class have, in reality, become the only thing that they could be: organic intellectuals of the workers' movement. The old party, the old form of organisation outside of the class, needs them. For decades, they have assured the relationship between the party and society without passing through the medium of the factory. And now that the factory is imposing itself, now that capital itself is calling them back into production, they become the objective mediators between science and industry. Such is the new form that is being assumed by the traditional relationship between intellectuals and the party. The most 'organic' intellectual today is one who *studies* the working class, putting into practice the most reprehensible bourgeois science that has yet existed – namely, industrial sociology; in other words, the study of the workers' movements, performed on behalf of the capitalist. Here, too, the whole problem needs rejecting *en bloc*. The solution here is not culture that is 'on the side of the working class', or a working-class intellectual figure. There is no culture, no intellectuals, apart from those who serve capital. This is the counterpart of our solution to the other problem: there can be no working-class re-enactment of the bourgeois revolution, no retracing of its path by the working class. For there is no revolution, ever, outside of the working class, outside of what the class is, and thus outside of what the class is forced to do. A critique of culture means a *refusal to become intellectuals*. A theory of revolution means the direct practice of class struggle. This is the same relation as the one between working-class science and the critique of ideology. And between these two things is the moment of subversive praxis. We said earlier that the working-class point of view cannot be separated from capitalist society. We should add: it cannot be separated from the practical necessities of the class struggle within capitalist society.

What, then, are these necessities? And, most importantly, is a *new strategy* needed? If it is indeed necessary, then one of the most urgent tasks in the struggle is to discover it, to put it together and to elaborate it. At the level of science, there is no other task beyond this. Formidable and new powers of the intellect must be organised around this work. Powerful brains must begin to function collectively within this single, exclusive perspective. A new form of antagonism must take to the level of working-class science, bending this science toward new ends and then transcending it in the wholly political act of practice. The form of this struggle is the refusal, the organisation of the working class 'No': the refusal to collaborate actively in capitalist development, the refusal to put forward a positive programme of demands. We can identify the germ of these forms of struggle and organisation right from the very start of the

working-class history of capital, right from the time that the first proletarians were constituted as a class. But the full development, the real
significance of these forms, comes much later, and they still exist as a
strategy for the future. Their possibilities of material functioning increase
as the working class grows quantitatively, as it becomes more concentrated and unified, as it gradually develops in quality and becomes internally homogeneous, and as it increasingly succeeds in organising itself
around the movements of its own total power. These forms thus presuppose a process of accumulation of labour-power, which – unlike the
accumulation of capital – has a directly political meaning. It implies the
concentration and growth not of an economic category, but of the class
relation which underlies it; an accumulation, therefore, of a political
power which is immediately alternative, even before it comes to be
organised through its own particular 'great collective means'. The refusal
is thus a form of struggle which grows simultaneously with the working
class. And the working class is, at the same time, both a political refusal
of capital and the production of capital as an economic power. This
explains why the working class's political struggle and the terrain of capitalist production always form a single whole. Insofar as they could not be
absorbed by the capitalist, the very first proletarian demands objectively
functioned as forms of refusal which put the system in jeopardy.
Whenever the workers' positive demands go beyond the capitalist-
granted margins, they repeat this function – the objective, *negative* function of a pure and simple political blockage in the mechanism of economic
laws. Every conjunctural transition, every structural advance in the
economic mechanism, must therefore be studied in terms of its specific
moments – but only so as to ask from the working-class point of view
what capital cannot now give. In such circumstances, the *demand-as-
refusal* sets off a chain of crises in capitalist production, each of which
demands the tactical ability to drive forward the level of working-class
organisation.

As workers and capital together grow, there is a process of *simplifica-
tion* of the class struggle, whose full, fundamental strategic importance
needs to be grasped. It is not true that the 'elementary' nature of the first
clashes between proletarians and individual capitalists later became
enormously more complicated as the working-class masses found themselves faced with the modern initiative of big capital. In fact, precisely
the opposite is true. In the beginning, the content of the class struggle

had two faces – that of the working class and that of the capitalists – which were not yet separated by any radical division. The struggle for the limiting of the working day is instructive in this respect. Moreover, the platforms of demands which workers have for decades presented to the capitalists have had – and could only have had – one result: the improvement of exploitation. Better living conditions for the workers were inseparable from a greater economic development of capitalism. As far as the official workers' movement is concerned, both the trade-union strand and later the reformist strand have functioned within the terms of this development, in their attempts at the economic organisation of the workers. For good reason, in our exposition, we have preferred to emphasise those moments of working-class struggle that challenge the political power of capital, even at a less advanced social level. The fact remains that this historical terrain of the class struggle, which has not disappeared from the world, should be reduced to a simple and direct clash between antagonistic forces only on the condition that we work to analyse the high points of successive developments and criticise the results at which they arrived. This presents a landscape in which the class struggle has always been complicated and mediated in its outward relations by situations, even political situations, which were not themselves class struggle. These situations increasingly lose importance as the residues of the precapitalist past burn up, and all the utopian futures built on top of the working class fall away. This finally offers the subjective possibility of wrapping the class struggle within the chain of the present, precisely in order to smash it. In this process, we have to grasp from the working-class point of view not only the quantitative growth and massification of the antagonism, not only its ever more homogeneous internal unification, but also, through this, the gradual reacquisition of its primitive, direct, elementary nature; in other words, as a counter position between the two classes, each of which gives life to the other but only one of which holds in its grasp the possible death of the other. Leaving aside earlier periods of history and moving forward to the highest point of development, we can see how self-evident is that simplest of revolutionary truths: capital *cannot* destroy the working class, but the working class *can* destroy capital. The cook who ought to be able to govern the workers' state, as Lenin put it, must henceforth be enabled to function, on the basis of these fundamental categories, as a theorist of working-class science.

The masses of working-class demands thus become ever more simple and united. There must come a point where all of them will disappear, except one – the demand for power, all power, to the workers. This demand is the highest form of refusal. It already presupposes a de facto inversion of the relation of domination between the two classes. In other words, it presupposes that henceforth it will be the capitalist class that makes demands, issues positive requests and presents its bill of rights – in the name, naturally, of the general interests of society. And it will be the workers who are rejecting what is asked of them. There must also be a point, here, where all the requests and demands will come explicitly from the capitalists and only the 'no' will be openly working class. These are not stories from some far-off future – the tendency is already under way and we must grasp it as it emerges in order to be able to control it.

When capital reaches a high level of development, it no longer limits itself to guaranteeing workers' collaboration – in other words, it only ensures the active extraction of living labour within the dead mechanism of its stabilisation, which it needs above all else. At significant points, it now makes a transition, to the point of expressing its objective needs through the subjective demands of the workers. It is true, as we have seen, that this has already happened, historically. The needs of capitalist production have imposed themselves throughout the history of capital as working-class demands, and the only thing that can explain this is the permanent working-class articulation of capitalist society. But, whereas in the past this happened as an objective part of the system's functioning, making it almost self-regulating, today it instead owes to the conscious initiative of the capitalist class, via the modern instruments of its power apparatus. In between the two moments came that decisive experience of working-class struggle, which no longer limited itself to demanding power but actually conquered it. It was with 1917 and the Russian Revolution that the working-class articulation of capital was subjectively imposed on the capitalists. What had previously functioned all by itself, controlled by nobody, as a blind economic law, from that moment had to be operated from above, politically promoted by those who held power. This was the only way to control the objective process, the only way to defeat the subversive threat of its possible consequences. This is the origin of that major development in capital's subjective consciousness, which led it to elaborate and put into practice a plan of social control over all moments of its cycle, all seen within a directly capitalist use of this working-class articulation. Thus, once more, an experience of working-class struggle spurred a major advance in the capitalist point of view – an advance which it would never otherwise have made out of its own impulse. The workers' subjective demands are now recognised by the capitalists themselves as objective needs of the production of capital; as such, they are not only subsumed, but solicited; no longer simply rejected, but collectively negotiated. The mediation that takes place at the institutional level of the workers' movement, and particularly at the trade-union level, here acquires a decisive and irreplaceable importance. The platform of demands that the trade union puts forward is reviewed and checked by the very people on whom it is supposed to be imposed – the same bosses who are supposed to take it or leave it. Through the trade-union struggle, working-class demands can do nothing more than reflect capital's own needs. And yet capital cannot pose this necessity directly, all by itself – not even if it wanted to, not even when it reaches its highest point of class consciousness. Rather, at this point, it acquires precisely the opposite consciousness: it *must* find ways to have its own needs put forward by its enemies, it *must* articulate its own movement via the organised movements of the workers. We might ask: what happens when the form of working-class organisation takes on a wholly alternative content? When it refuses to function as an articulation of capitalist society? When it refuses to *shoulder* capital's needs through meeting working-class demands? The answer is that, at that moment and starting from that moment, the system's whole development mechanism is blocked. This is the new concept of the *crisis of capitalism* that we must start to circulate: there will no longer be an economic crisis, a catastrophic collapse, a *Zusammenbruch*, however momentary, that owes to the impossibility of the system's continued functioning. Rather, it will become a political crisis imposed by the subjective movements of the organised workers, through a chain of critical conjunctures provoked by the working-class strategy of refusing to resolve the contradictions of capitalism and by the tactic of organisation within the structures of capitalist production, but outside of and free from its political initiative. Of course, it remains necessary to block the economic mechanism and, at the decisive moment, to incapacitate it. But the only way to achieve this is via the working class's political refusal to be an active part of the whole social process and, furthermore, its refusal to even *passively* collaborate in capitalist development – in other words, the renunciation of precisely that form of mass struggle which today unites the movements led by the workers in advanced capitalist countries. We must say clearly that this form of struggle – for that is what it is – is no longer enough. For decades, the working-class struggle has been reduced to non-collaboration, passivity (even on a mass scale) and refusal, but it has not been political, nor subjectively organised, nor inserted into a strategy, nor practised in tactical terms; but all this marks the highest form of spontaneism. Not only is this no longer enough to provoke the crisis, but it has, in fact, contributed to the stabilisation of capitalist development. It is now one of the objective mechanisms through which capitalist initiative now controls and makes use of the class relation that drives it. We must break this process before it becomes yet another heavy historical tradition for the workers' movement to shoulder. It is necessary to move on to another process, albeit without losing the basic positive elements of this one. Obviously, non-collabora-tion must be one of our starting points, and mass passivity at the level of production is the material fact from which we must begin. But at a certain point, all this must be reversed into its opposite. When it comes to the point of saying 'no', the refusal must also become political, and therefore active, subjective and organised. It must once again become an antagonism – this time, at a higher level. It is impossible to think of initiating a revolutionary process without this. This is not a matter of instilling in the mass of workers the consciousness that they must fight against capital and for something that will transcend it in a new dimen-sion of human society. What is generally known as 'class consciousness' is, for us, nothing other than the moment of organisation, the function of the party, the problem of tactics – the channels which must carry the strategic plan through to a point of practical breakthrough. And at the level of pure strategy, there is no doubt that this point is provided by the very advanced moment in which this hypothesis of struggle becomes a reality: the working-class refusal to present demands to capital, the total rejection of the whole trade-union terrain, the refusal to limit the class relation within a formal, legal, contractual form. This is the same as forcing capital to present the objective needs of its own production directly and negating the working-class mediation of development. It blocks the mechanism's working-class articulation. Ultimately, this means depriving capital of its content, of the class relation that is its basis. For a period, class relations must be managed by the working class, through its party – just as up till now it has been managed by the capitalist class, through its state.

It is here that the balance of domination between the two classes is reversed, no longer just in theory, but also in practice. In fact, the revolutionary process sees the working class increasingly become what it actually is: a ruling class on its own – specifically political – terrain and a conquering power which, in destroying the present, takes revenge for a whole past (and not merely its own) of subordination and exploitation. This is the sense of the hypothesis which poses, as the highest point of this process, capital's own *demands* and the working class's *refusal*. This presupposes the previous emergence and growth of an organised political force of the working class able to constitute an autonomous power of decision in relation to the whole of society, a no man's land which capitalist order cannot reach and from which the new barbarians of the proletariat can depart at any moment. Thus, the final act of the revolution requires the existence of the workers' state already within capitalist society. That is, the workers must already have a power of their own, which then decides that capital must come to an end. But this workers' state is no prefiguration of the future, because the future, from the working-class point of view, does not exist; there is only a block on the present, the impossibility for the present to continue functioning under its current organisation and thus an instance of its possible reorganisation under an inverted notion of power. An autonomous working-class political power is the only weapon that can bar the functioning of capital's economic mechanisms. In this sense alone, today's party is tomorrow's workers' state.

This brings us back to the concept, which we attributed to Marx, of communism as the party. This party replaces the model for the construction of the future society with a practical organ for the destruction of the present one, and it closes here within all the revolutionary needs of the working class. Added to this, now, is the strategic inversion that sees the working-class articulation of capital being demanded by the capitalists and rejected by the workers – that is, the most concrete shift hitherto conceivable for the working-class revolution. As a discovery, this for good reason remains linked to the Leninist initiative of the Bolshevik October. The party here took responsibility for the tactical moment, on the class's behalf; for this reason, the class won. The workers' state born on this basis was not meant to go beyond the tasks that the party takes on within capitalist society. But Lenin's tactic became Stalin's strategy: this was the medium through which the Soviet experience failed, from the working-class point of view. The lesson for us today, though, is that we need to hold these two moments of revolutionary activity – *class strategy* and *party tactics* – together in theory and never rigorously separate them in practice.

13

Tactics = Organisation

'If we do not take power now, history will not pardon us': thus wrote Lenin to the party's central committee in September 1917. He invited them to rely on the 'turning point' in the revolution that was then mounting: 'the Party must recognise [that] ... the entire course of events has objectively placed insurrection on the order of the day ... it is impossible to remain loyal to Marxism, to remain loyal to the revolution unless insurrection is treated as an art.'[1] One month later, in a report to this same central committee he went further still: 'The Party could not be guided by the temper of the masses because it was changeable and incalculable; the Party must be guided by an objective analysis and an appraisal of the revolution.' Hence at the basis of action is 'the political analysis of the revolution.'[2] Moreover, among others even the representatives of the Vyborg district realised that the uprising 'must come from above'. Lenin imposed on everyone the directive to launch the final offensive, setting the touchpaper on the armed insurrection – imposing it on the party, on the soviets, on the masses and on the workers. It was a fundamentally important turning point: this imposition of the final act of the revolution dates the shift in the working-class point of view, which

---

1   'Marxism and Insurrection. A Letter to the Central Committee of the R.S.D.L.P.(B.)', 13–14 September 1917, text from marxists.org.

2   'Meeting of the Central Committee of the R.S.D.L.P.(B.), October 16 (29), 1917', text from marxists.org.

took back for itself and for its own class the aggressive marker of a now-dominant power. That moment demonstrated for all time that the working class can impose practically everything on capital. The upheaval of October 1917 and the strategic overturning of the working class's theoretical point of view are thus one and the same. Lenin's 19 November 1917 telegram to the presidium of the soviet of worker and soldier deputies in Moscow, in the form of a basic political-practical indication, in reality brought a decisive leap in the development of theoretical Marxism: 'All power is in the hands of the Soviets. Confirmations are unnecessary. Your dismissal of the one and appointment of the other is law'.[3] On this basis, the collapse of the institutions of capital's power presented itself as anything but a historical tragedy, instead becoming – as it had to – a piece of comedy, behind which it was possible to make out the mocking collective laughter of a working-class audience. It was the night between 5 and 6 (18 and 19) January 1918; the Constituent Assembly had rejected the Bolshevik declaration on the rights of the oppressed and exploited people; a sailor named Zheleznyakov entered and announced to President Chernov that he had received the order – seemingly directly from Lenin – to put an end to the session 'because the guard is tired'. So, it is not enough to say: the working-class point of view was completed with Lenin. No, with Lenin, the working-class point of view was overturned, in the sense that tactics always overturn strategies precisely in order to apply them and in the sense that, at a certain point, the party must impose on the class what the class itself is. Lenin and the laws of tactics are one and the same – which is to say, the *laws of the working class movement* took the place of *the law*, as mentioned in Marx. The law, indeed, is pure strategy, but not because Marx somehow set out in search of the law of movement of capital. Indeed, we have demonstrated that this law is always evident, in reality, as a working-class articulation of capitalist society. *Laws* in the plural mark only the working class's conquest, in the world of tactics, of a developed readiness to defeat the capitalists politically on the terrain of practice. Lenin thus materially practised the overturning of the relation between working class and capital that, in Marx, had been only a methodological discovery – the scientific, partial foundation of a working-class point of

---

3 'Telegram to the Presidium of the Moscow Soviet of Workers' and Soldiers' Deputies', 19 November 1917, text from marxists.org.

view on capital. Since Lenin, the working class can impose practically anything on capital – on one formidable condition: that it is armed from the outside with the intervention of tactics, with the party's leadership. Without Lenin, no one would have been capable of understanding what was the right moment, the right day, the right hour to unleash the final offensive and seize power: the class alone never manages to do this, and the party managed it only when Lenin was actually in the party. What are we doing here? Suddenly rediscovering pure subjectivism, after building up such a mass of analyses of the working class? No.

All that we have said thus far has tended to keep these two moments united. There is no revolutionary process without revolutionary will. And when there is, it has to do precisely with those passages that we have said cannot be called 'revolution', because they are excursions that capitalists take within the terms of the governance of their own interests. Gramsci was wrong to speak of the 'revolution against *Capital*'. When he did so, he delivered Marx into the reformist hands of the Second International. *Capital* was no 'bourgeois tome' in Russia, but the Bolsheviks' book. It was the book of the young Lenin who had set out from Russia. But Gramsci was right to see the person of Lenin within 'our Marx'. His May 1918 eulogy of voluntarism was indeed written in reference to Lenin: 'Will, in a Marxist sense, means awareness of ends, which in turn means exact knowledge of one's own power and the means to express it in action. It therefore means, in the first place, that the class become distinct and individuated, compactly organized and disciplined to its own specific ends, without wavering or being deflected.'[4] The Leninist inversion of praxis, along this path, brought down both the political power of capital and the tradition of official Marxism. The new strategic thesis – first the working class, then capital – was imposed by the facts themselves. But here we encounter a problem of considerable importance: Could we not say that, on the basis of the Soviet experience, the test of Leninism in practice has proven a failure? And does this not imply that the thesis as to the inversion of the relation between working class and capital has itself proven untrue in practice?

Let's go back and say that research on these problems is still lagging far behind. A mass of concrete studies should first set out the terrain for

---

4 Antonio Gramsci, 'Our Marx', in *The Antonio Gramsci Reader. Selected Writings 1916–1935*, edited by David Forgacs, New York: New York University Press, 2000, 36.

a definitive solution. This does not deny the possibility of adopting temporary rules of theoretical conduct in the meantime. These rules would all revolve around one immediate political need: extracting the revolutionary moment of October 1917 from the failure of the first working class power in the Soviet Union. We ought to, as far as the historical record allows, unravel the great political contradiction between the Leninist revolution and the building of socialism, between the revolutionary political process and the economic management of society. At this level, as usual, Lenin's strategy was not expressed in full. Lenin always and only expressed himself through tactical moves. It is by connecting all his political turns to one another, in their perfect continuity, that it becomes possible to reconstruct the formidable long-term vision that guided him. It is clear that when he stepped back and introduced the New Economic Policy, when he kickstarted the economic mechanism by capitalist means, he conceived all of this as a temporary tactical retreat, with which it would be necessary to violently settle accounts immediately afterward. Yet, at the foundation of his programme, there had to be something more: the idea of a capitalist management of the economic machine under the conscious political guidance of the workers' state. And all this for a sizeable historical period: without the mystifications of 'actually existing socialism' or, in other words, without the compulsion for the working class to manage capital. Here, too, the expected course of events had to be inverted: it was necessary to use the force of the power that had been conquered to bend economic development to serve as a crude instrument of the demands of the working class's political growth. The workers' state, with its party, first of all had to directly manage this growth, only secondarily checking that the general social interest was always effectively subordinated to it. The resumption of the revolution thus remained the order of the day. A chain of revolutionary leaps, with the active intervention of the working-class mass, should continually correct the many and inevitable deviations from the line. Once a high point of political development had been reached, it would again become necessary to smash the state machine, and the breaking of the party machine itself would become a revolutionary task. From this would result the final recovery of a directly working-class, mass, associated management of the whole new society. Workers around the world would have put their heads together and defended in their own countries not the homeland of socialism but a revolutionary process *in actu*. This would not have demanded that they sacrifice their own struggles, but that they relaunch them upon every turning point, upon every leap forward in this process. It would thus have united, concentrated and guided the international development of the class struggle. Far from being abandoned, the revolution in Europe would have been proposed anew at each fresh higher level reached in the unfolding of the revolutionary process in Russia. It is not important to know how far this strategic design existed in full in Lenin's head. We can admit easily enough that with this we are already going beyond Lenin – and that is only right. The development of Leninism is the immediate programme of working-class science.

Yet when we seek a practical, Leninist test of the strategic overturning of the relation between capital and the working class, we need to seek it in the right way, on the terrain of tactics. And thus, at the moment of the Treaty of Brest-Litovsk, when Lenin imposed peace all by himself in order to save the revolution, the new strategy did not collapse but proceeded in the only way that was then possible, tactically inverted into its opposite and concretely applied precisely in this way. This a difficult art, in which we should train ourselves at length in coming years in order to become its virtuoso interpreters: tactics and strategy must be united in our minds, while at the level of things, in facts, we must take care to keep them divided and – as circumstances demand – in mutual contradiction. The error of all the leftist positions in the history of the workers' movement is that they did not take account of this. It is an unpardonable error. The intellectual illusion of a 'scientific politics' is the shortest path to practical defeat for the working class. They should align with the opposite principle, for what is right theoretically may be mistaken politically. Theory is understanding and foresight, and thus knowledge – even if one-sided – of the process's objective tendency. Politics is the will to invert this process, and thus is a global rejection of objectivity; it is subjective action so that this objectivity is blocked and unable to triumph. Theory is anticipation. Politics is intervention. And it must intervene not into what is expected, but into what precedes it; here lies the need for the twists and turns of tactics. In this sense, theory and politics always contradict one another. Their identity and non-contradiction is the same thing as opportunism, reformism, passive obedience to the objective tendency, known and grasped only through science, which then ends up in an unconscious working-class mediation of the capitalist point of view. Working-class science, conceived as if it were itself immediately class struggle – in other words, if it is not divided from the practical moment and subordinated to it, if it wants to fulfil all the tasks of politics – risks functioning only as a science. Yet as science alone it is nothing other than the theoretical articulation that capital needs in order to construct its own point of view. Hence the practical danger detected with such concern by those who devote themselves to developing theory on the working-class side. This danger involves handing the weapons of knowledge proper to one's own camp over to the class enemy, without at the same time managing to provide weapons of another kind – of struggle, of organisation – to the class in whose ranks one fights. So a refusal to study the working class is not enough. It is necessary to proceed to organise the struggle – and this not in order to 'check' research hypotheses in practice, but to deny capital the use of these arms, to make them directly working-class offensive weapons. The greatest theorist of the proletariat is, again, Lenin, the Bolshevik organiser of the workers of St Petersburg and all Russia. Furthermore, the theorist on the working-class side and the revolutionary politician are one and the same: materially, they must coincide in a single person. So, something fundamental changes in the working-class point of view when it sets itself to examining its own class at a theoretical level. The working class is no longer the object of analysis as capital still fundamentally is, the latter functioning as an enemy-object: something confronting us which we must simultaneously both understand and combat. The subversive reconstruction of the workers' direct movements can be achieved only from within their struggle, from the point of view of their organisational needs. The discourse on labour-power is erected from within the working class. Only thus are those who elaborate this discourse directly involved in the class struggle. A sort of 'indeterminacy principle' grasps working-class science when it unfolds at the social level.

To look at society from the working-class point of view 'upsets' not only social science in general, but likewise one's particular consciousness of one's own class. There falls away not only a certain determinism in the development of the object, but also the subjective pretension to make the working-class point of view an 'exact science'. The tactical integration of research that we first found in Marx thus returns to the foreground. But what, in Marx's case, amounted to a conscious use of some of the subjective results of bourgeois science is for us, today, a continual and relentless critique of all the findings at which we have arrived. And this explains why as soon as we attempt to analyse the working class, there comes out – as an apparent deviation from our theme – this whole discourse on ourselves, on the simultaneously both practical and theoretical experiences of the past, and on the present state of the movement in struggle and in organisation. A direct discourse on the working class is thus today, first of all, a self-critique of the organised workers' movement. Only thanks to a tactical turn through this self-destructive movement does the work of strategically constructing the working-class point of view, the very task which must occupy us in coming years, become possible. But we cannot stop at this. The tasks of practice are likewise urgent, direct and complex. We need to know how best to move therein; not in some timeless 'correct' way, but in the way that is most useful to our own class in the present moment. Thus, there are two things we still need to learn. First, that at the level of the class as such, the tactical moment is still missing. This is an important point. The class is only strategy, and strategy lives in a wholly objective form at this level. A strategic perspective, like the strategy of refusal, presents itself as materially embodied in the class movements of the working-class social mass. It can begin to live subjectively – in a conscious way or, in other words, in practical form – only when it arrives at that moment of political organisation which it still now seems best to define with the word 'party'. It is precisely *and only* when we arrive at this organised strategic subjectivity that the moment of tactics comes alive: namely, the concrete, subversive, practical application of what had been anticipated in theory. Here, the working class begins to function as a revolutionary process. If the class is strategy, then, for us, class consciousness is precisely the moment of tactics, the moment of organisation, the party moment. Such is our interpretation of the Leninist thesis on the political consciousness and tactical overturning of strategy that must be brought to the workers from the outside, through the party organisation, as necessary. All the practical passages in the revolutionary process, the chain of the crisis in which capital's development is halted and the organisational leaps with which the class growth of the working masses is to be measured, are to be reconstructed from the outside. Linking all these with the iron continuity of a destructive political will – this is the party's task. Here, though, do we not perhaps run the risk of overvaluing tactics? Does this not go back to placing the party beyond and thus above the class? We have said that theory and politics are always in contradiction. Can we say the same of strategy and tactics, of class and party? Sadly, we can. And it is precisely this that makes the working-class revolution – as communism was for Brecht – the simplest thing so hard to achieve. The intensity of this contradiction changes in various moments and particular passages. Once the revolutionary process is underway, the contradiction between strategy and tactics is clearly minimal. Indeed, this moment presupposes that the organisational problem has already been resolved. Not even at that point do class and party coincide; they maintain a normal division of revolutionary labour, proceeding in unison toward the same goal. But look instead at today, when the initiation of the revolutionary process is still a theoretical programme, when the task is still to find the way to begin to practise it: the contradiction between strategy and tactics is here at its maximal level of development; theory and politics do not share terrain; the class is without the party and the party is without the class. Capital has managed to control and guide the whole objective functioning of its mechanism. And without any mediating organisation, the working-class side does not manage to make its own power function subjectively as a block to the system, as a rejection and subversion. In these conditions, the importance of tactics is heightened and foregrounded – as in Lenin's experience, when he had to impose the party question on the workers and their movement. As always, the problem of organisation needs resolving before everything else, or rather, as the precondition of everything else. A great deal of human coherence and compelling thought will be needed if we are to avoid being led astray by the day-to-day necessities of immediate political life and to keep our gaze on a distant theoretical horizon. This far-sightedness does not, however, exempt us from the need to recognise the problem today and the point of greatest difficulty that needs overcoming right away. So, we have to have the courage to say that the conquest of political power that Marx put on the order of the day of the class struggle presents itself still in our time, in its primitive or preliminary form, as the conquest of political organisation. This is the urgent task for the whole moment. This is the abyss that needs leaping across. Many experiences have already fallen down it. Ours will not. And if, at a given point in history, the working class does manage to achieve this, then the rest of the matter will be settled. For workers who are politically organised to say no to everything, we imagine that dismantling the machine of capital will be child's play. We really think that the revolutionary process is as straightforward as the Nevsky Prospekt. The tactical turns come first, today, when the task is to find the right alleyway that will bring us to some point on the main highway. To do this, we first need to skilfully chart our way. Thus, theoretical research into the concepts of labour, labour-power and the working class itself simply becomes an exercise along the path of the practical discovery of the means of achieving organisation. The tactic of research flips into research-as-tactic. Almost all the political turning points imposed by the practice of struggle lie therein. The working-class point of view does not prefigure the future or recount the past, but only contributes to the destruction of the present. Working-class science is but a means for the organisation of this destruction … and that's just fine.

14

The Struggle Against Work!

To finish, let's go back to the start: to the double, divided and self-counterposed nature of labour. But now we are speaking not of the labour contained in the commodity, but the working class contained within capital. The *zwieschlächtige Natur* of the working class consists in its simultaneous existence as both concrete and abstract labour, labour and labour-power, use-value and productive labour, capital and non-capital – that is, both capital and working class. It is here we find that the division is already a counterposition. And counterposition is always struggle. But struggle is not yet organisation. It is not enough for labour and labour-power to be objectively divided within the working class: in fact, this is precisely how they present themselves as united within capital. They must be divided through a subjective action: only in this way do they become the means for building an alternative form of power. It is true that *Trennung*, separation, division, is the normal relation in this society. But it is also true that precisely capital's strength is its ability to hold together what is divided – a strength that has underpinned its history and will be the basis of what remains of its future. Capital can live exclusively by keeping the working class within and against it, and on this basis it imposes the laws of its own development on society. It is thus necessary to find the point where it would be possible to impede this unity, where it becomes possible to block the mechanism of synthesis, forcibly separating the opposite poles to the point of rupture and *beyond.* And this point lies within the working class, just as the working class is within capital. This point is precisely the separation of the working class from itself, *from work*, and thus from capital. It is the separation of the political force from the economic strategy. And we need to speak of more than just division and separation: what is needed is struggle, opposition, counterposition. To fight against capital, the working class must fight against itself *qua* capital. This is the height of contradiction not for the workers but for the capitalists, and it is necessary to expand and organise this contradiction. The capitalist system will no longer function and the plan of capital will begin to retreat, not as a development of society but as a revolutionary process. A working-class struggle against work, the worker's struggle against her own condition as a wage-labourer, labour-power's refusal to become labour, the working-class's mass rejection of the use of its labour-power: such are the terms in which the initial division-counterposition that Marx's analysis first discovered within the nature of labour are here reproposed strategically, after the tactic of research. The *Doppelcharakter* of the labour represented in commodities is thus discovered to be a *dual nature of the working class* – dual and at the same time divided, divided and at the same time counterposed to itself, counterposed to itself and at the same time in struggle with itself. We should understand that the bases of the vast political complexity of all the great problems of organisation, and of their solution in the rediscovery of an organic relation between class and party, all lie in this critical relation internal to the working-class itself. And this relation becomes an even deeper unresolved problem as the working class grows into a dominant force. Both the well-honed weapons of theory and the blunter material weapons of daily practice should henceforth be aimed at precisely this point. And here, too, there is not much more that needs inventing.

Contemporary forms of working-class struggles in the heartlands of advanced capitalism all bear, in the rich content of their own spontaneity, the slogan of the struggle against work as the only possible means of striking a blow against capital. Again, the party presents itself as the organisation of what already exists within the class, but which the class alone cannot succeed in organising. No worker today is prepared to recognise the existence of work outside capital. Work equals exploitation: this is the logical prerequisite and historical result of capitalist civilisation. From here, there is no point of return. The worker has no interest in the 'dignity of work'; she can leave the 'pride of the producer' entirely for the boss. Indeed, only the boss now remains to eulogise work. True, in the organised workers' movement, there is still a place for such ideology, but not in the working class itself. Today, the working class need only look at itself to understand capital. It need only combat itself in order to destroy capital. It has to recognise itself as a political power and negate itself as a productive force. For proof of this, we need only look at the moment of struggle itself: during the strike, the 'producer' is immediately identified as the class enemy. Labour standing counterposed to the working class, as an enemy – such is the point of departure not only for antagonism, but also for its organisation. If the alienation of the worker has any meaning, its essence is highly revolutionary. *The organisation of alienation*: this is the obligatory path that the party must impose on working-class spontaneity. The goal is, again, refusal, but at a higher level – it becomes active and collective, a political refusal on a mass scale, organised and planned. Hence, the immediate task of working-class organisation is now to *overcome passivity*. This is possible on one condition: that this passivity is recognised as an elementary, spontaneous form of refusal by the working class. For mass passivity always follows a political defeat of the workers, to be blamed on their official organisations, or after a leap forward in capitalist development – that is, in the appropriation of socially productive forces. Everyone knows that, over the past few decades, these two objective preconditions of working-class passivity have combined. Indeed, they have ever more become the absolute despotic power of capital. While capital was conquering the whole of society at the international level and becoming socialised, the idea of giving working-class movements the political role of managing the national social interest risked a historic suicide. The result was an interruption of the revolutionary process that had advanced through stages from 1848 and 1871 to 1917. From 1917 onward, the annals of the revolution carried the mark of *working-class defeat*. What intervened at this point to block the further progress of the revolution? What prevented the process from reaching its intended end goal? The deeper we look, the more we see that passivity has been the most powerful barrier in blocking all future revolutionary possibilities. The truth is that the working class's massive refusal to consider itself an active participant in capitalist society already represents a decision to opt out, a stance against the social interest. Hence, what appears as integration of the working class into the system does not in fact represent a renunciation of the struggle against capital; rather, it indicates a refusal to develop and stabilise capital beyond certain given political limits, beyond a fixed defensive cordon, from which aggressive sallies can then be launched. If the working class had to find a single response to both capitalist production and the official workers' movement, the only possible one was a specific form of entirely working-class self-organisation, based on a spontaneous passivity. An organisation, in other words, without organisation, meaning a working-class organisation not subject to bourgeois institutionalisation. The result was one of those organisational miracles that are possible only from the working-class point of view, like Lenin's 'bourgeois state without a bourgeoisie': an organisation no longer seen as an intermediate form of the workers' state, but as a preliminary form of the working-class party. Today the basic planks of the party must be laid across a political void in terms of both practical experience and theoretical research. But this does not alter the fact that colossal foundations have already been laid on the decisive terrain of direct class struggle, marking out where the offensive must begin and where it must reach. *Passive* non-collaboration in the development of capitalism and *active* political refusal of its power are the beginning and end point of this breakthrough. The opening of the revolutionary process lies entirely beyond this point; on this side lie all the present problems of building organisation for the revolution. *We need the tactics of organisation in order to arrive at the strategy of refusal.* And it is here, in the middle, that we need continually to point against the class enemy the only subversive weapon capable of reducing him to a subaltern force: namely, the threat of denying him the mediation of the working class in the social relation of capitalist production. The working class must no longer shoulder the requirements of capital, even in the form of its own demands; it must force the class of capitalists to present its own objective needs and then subjectively refuse them; compel the bosses to ask, so that the workers can answer with an active, organised 'no'. This, today, is the only possible route to overcoming working-class passivity, overturning the spontaneous form this passivity presently takes while furthering its present political content of negation and revolt. The workers' first organised 'no' to the capitalists' first demands will then explode as a declaration of total war, a historic call to the decisive struggle, the modern form of the old revolutionary slogan, 'Workers of the world, unite!' None of this will be possible without the greatest degree of violence – this, we know from experience. In all the upheavals of the past, the *type* of productive activity was left intact. It has always exclusively been a question of the distribution of productive activity, redistributing labour to new groups of people. Only the communist revolution, as Marx said, or, as we can today begin to say, simply the revolution, the only plausible present-day minimum programme for the working class, challenges for the first time the whole of productive activity that has hitherto existed. This challenge will abolish work. And in so doing it will abolish class domination. The abolition of work by the working class and the violent destruction of capital are one and the same. What, then, of labour as 'the prime necessity of human existence' (Marx)? Perhaps it would be better to transport it from the future prospect of communism to the present history of capitalism – let the capitalists do it rather than the workers. Does this mean that if confronted with Marx, the working-class point of view would arrive at a kind of parricide? This is a question we cannot yet answer. The continuation of the research presented here will be decisive for the solution of this and all the other problems it raises. There are no pre-given solutions. Once again, everything remains to be done. To this end, we have to keep our eye on the most obscure aspect of the whole process – until, that is, we have reached the point at which we can distinguish *what has happened within the working class since Marx*.

1965

Postscript of Problems

The Progressive Era

The developments of the working class after Marx can be approached historically in two ways. The first is chronological. It reconstructs the great cycles of the working-class struggle from the 1870s onward, followed by the whole string of facts that make for *history* – the history of labour in industry, of industry in capital, of capital in politics and in political events – along with the great theorisations, like what was once called the history of thought, first in sociology (the last systematic form assumed by economics) and later in the birth of a new scientific discipline: that theory of technology as the science of labour, the enemy of the worker. Traditional historiography periodises it between 1870 and 1914. To be generous and to avoid upsetting the mental habits of the average intellectual, it may even be possible to enclose this era's first great block of facts within 'their' history and from this move toward us and the new working-class struggles which make for the real political event in our history, one that is still at its origins. And there is another way: to pass through great historical events by pausing on macroscopic sets of facts yet untouched by the critical consciousness of working-class thought and therefore excluded from a class understanding that moves to use their results politically. The more relevant of these events identify one fundamental aspect of capitalist society. They provide a kind of cross-section that proceeds from a series of struggles to a set of political-institutional, then scientific and then organisational answers.

When such a rare fruit can be identified under suitably propitious circumstances, which is to say when we find the node that cuts horizontally through all these lines running from bottom to top, we find that we have a historical model, a privileged period for research, and a promised land of facts, thoughts and actions that we should explore. What can be learned is far superior to any passive chronological account of indifferent past events. The alternative is between a narrative that itself incorporates an interpretation – which is the old pretence of historical objectivism – and the opposite, an interpretation that incorporates a narrative (which is to say, the new course of political research from the working-class point of view). The choice is between *history* and *politics*: two legitimate horizons, but which each stand for a different class.

There is a risk to be run here, which is at the same time an adventure of the mind worth celebrating: the task of combining and seeing simultaneously different things that the specialists have convinced us that we ought to see separately. The neo-synthetic conceptual apparatus of the working-class point of view struggles to avoid this temptation. It is incredible, for example, that the history of labour and the history of struggles have been and continue to have different enthusiasts. Incredible, too, that economic theory is separated from political thought as if they really were two doctrines, two departments or two different academic disciplines. It is incredible that industrial sociology – the only sociology really worth considering, once separated from the macroscopic problems of the socialisation brought about by capitalist industrialisation – is instead reduced to the microanalysis of particular factories. It is not hard to connect Haymarket Square with the Knights of Labor, the cannon of Homestead, Pennsylvania (1892), the strike in the company town of Pullman (1894), the recent birth of the AFL, and Lawrence, Massachusetts (1912) and Paterson, New Jersey (1914) with the Wobblies' call, 'the union makes us strong'. Struggles and organisation so greatly resembled one another that even the blind could see their unity. In his *The Age of Reform* Richard Hofstadter relates the American progressivism of the 1890s–1920s to the somewhat eccentric pseudo-conservatism of our own time: 'The relations of capital and labor, the condition of the masses in the slums, the exploitation of the labor of women and children, the necessity of establishing certain minimal standards of social decency – these problems filled them with concern both because they felt a sincere interest in the welfare of the victims of industrialism and because they feared that to neglect them would invite social disintegration and ultimate catastrophe'.

The hardly long history of capitalist initiative began when, unlike President Hayes's handling of the 1887 railroad strikes or President Cleveland's handling of the Pullman affair, in 1902 Theodore Roosevelt broke the great strike of anthracite workers not by sending in federal troops but by means of a well-conceived arbitration. Likewise, in the same year, he launched legal action against J. Pierpont Morgan's Northern Security Company in order to show public opinion that the country was run by Washington and not by Wall Street. This history was no longer just political progressivism for the sake of social conservation – something as old as human society itself – but a new political way of managing social relations and the private ownership of the means of production, a new form of the clash and reconciliation between the general interest and individual capitalists' profit, between the government of the res publica and production for capital. 'To realize the importance of the change in the United States itself one need only think of the climate of opinion in which the Pullman strike and the Homestead strike were fought out and compare it with the atmosphere in which labor organisation has taken place since the Progressive era. There has of course been violence and bloodshed, but in the twentieth century a massive labor movement has been built with far less cost in these respects than it cost the American working class merely to man the machines of American industry in the period from 1865 to 1900'.

In its two faces of working-class violence and capitalist reformism, the Progressive Era is the first great historical event that needs unwrapping in this manner. Here, the relationship between workers' struggles and organisation and capital's initiative set out a model that would later reach greater heights through still-more extensive experiences, but only after long pauses which would continually throw the problem back into the fog of the past. Obviously, whoever wants to find the revolution in action ought not go to the United States; however, American class struggles are more serious than those in Italy precisely in that they obtain more but with less ideology. More on this later. For now, we shall bear in mind Mr Dooley's 1906 *Dissertations*. Mr Dooley (Finley Peter Dunne) has been defined as one of the sharpest commentators of that era, who understood its character very well when he said: 'Th' noise ye hear is not th' first gun in a revolution. It's on'y th' people in the United States beatin' a carpet'.

The Marshall Era

What presented itself in the United States as the relation between working-class struggle and capital's politics instead presented itself in Britain during the same period as the relation between the movement of struggles and the capitalist answer in the realm of science. Capital's answer in America always sought to develop its discourse at the institutional level, on the terrain of state-level political initiative, in the rare and precious occasions in which states subjectively overcame the most modern intelligence objectified in the system of production. Contrary to what is often believed, Britain offers a developed theoretical synthesis of the class struggle from the capitalist point of view. The fact that Hegel lived in Germany does not mean that we should always see it as the site of capital's maximum self-consciousness. If economics is the science *par excellence* of the relations of production, exchange and consumption of commodities as capital (and therefore of labour, and working-class struggles as the development of capital), then no higher elaboration of this science can be found than in British economic thought. When Marshall claimed: 'it is all in Smith', he forced those who came after him to say: 'it is all in Marshall'. As Schumpeter put it, his great accomplishment 'is the classical achievement of the period, that is the work that embodies, more perfectly than any other, the classical situation that emerged around 1900'. This classical situation was more than the discovery of the theory of partial equilibria, proper both to him and the British capitalism of his time. It was greater than individual moments as isolated objects of research that eventually together formed a new system of economic thought. The same goes for the notion of elasticity of demand, the introduction of temporal (short- and long-term) factors in economic analysis, the definition of a situation of perfect competition and at the same time the concept of an enterprise's 'special market', and all the other things he took from others but which really seemed new to him and others because he rearranged them in his own way, from Jevons's marginal utility to Walras' general equilibrium, von Thuenen's principle of substitution, Cournot's demand curves, and Dupuit's consumer rent. In what may be the finest of his *Essays in Biography* – the one devoted to Marshall – Keynes wrote something that doubtless goes for not only his object of biography but the author himself:

> But it was an essential truth to which he held firmly, that those individuals who are endowed with a special genius for the subject and have a powerful economic intuition will often be more right in their conclusions and implicit presuppositions than in their explanations and explicit statements. That is to say, their intuitions will be in advance of their analysis and terminology.[1]

The classical situation of Britain at the end of the nineteenth century owed to the way in which intuitions before analysis, and concepts before words, directly linked with the element of class: the datum, the moment and the level of the class struggle. Still today, we consider a classic model a historical condition in which the struggle was connected to politics, theory and organisation. Britain in 1889 was not an isolated and unexpected thunderbolt; it came about after at least two decades of continuous individual clashes which, although backward, were very conscious, active and unionised – struggles that saw miners, railroad, maritime, gas, textile and steel workers all take to the field. After 1880, real wages steadily rose, the price curve fell, employment levels were generally stable and union density rose, except for a drop around 1893. The situation of the British working class must not be sought in the usual investigations reporting on the workers' miserable conditions, such as Charles Booth's then-famous *Life and Labor of the People in London*, which followed rather than anticipated or provoked the dockers' strike. Cole wrote: 'The appeals that had roused the workers in the thirties and forties would have made no impression on their successors in the latter part of the century. Though there were still, even in 1900 many thousands of hopelessly exploited "bottom dogs" … these were not typical of the organised or organisable working class. In the great industries, the workers had ceased to be a ragged and starving mob, easily roused, either by a Feargus O'Connor or a James Rayner Stephens, or by

---

1 John Maynard Keynes, 'Alfred Marshall, 1842–1924', *The Economic Journal* 34 (135), September 1924, 311–372, 355.

someone of the many "Messiahs" who sprang up in the early years of the century'. No longer were there mass uprisings and sudden revolts produced by desperation and hunger: the strikes were ordered, prepared and planned, directed, and organised. If socialist propaganda was to achieve results, it had to appeal to reason and no longer just excite the instincts. If 'O'Connor had been hot as hell, Sidney Webb was always as cool as a cucumber'. In 1889, the dockers demanded a wage of six pence per hour, overtime, the abolition of subcontracts and piecework, and a minimum daily employment of four hours. They were guided by Ben Tillet – a docker at the port of London, along with Tom Mann and John Burns, both mechanics. They were all exponents of the 'new unionism', which fought against craft unions, the unionism of specialised workers and mutual aid societies, in favour of a mass organisation of the whole working class, a type of struggle founded on class solidarity, and a series of objectives able to challenge the capitalist system. The dockers' triumph was the triumph of the new unionists. The 1890s saw very few struggles, but those that occured were very advanced: from the Lancashire cotton-spinners' fight against wage reductions to the 400,000 miners who fought against the sliding scale and for a kind of guaranteed minimum wage, to the railworkers' fight over scheduling and the machinists' fight for a forty-eight-hour week. The organisation of unskilled workers developed despite 'the sceptical comments among the old leaders'. Dockers, gas workers and miners built unions without craft divides. A new era was beginning in the already historic relation between *workers* and *labour*. Here, it was not the relationship between labour and capital that marked a step forward; rather, this relation stagnated at the political level, and at the theoretical level it was unable to find the space for a new consciousness able to elaborate and then express it. One can hardly term the good-old Fabians virtuoso interpreters of this era. The situation made evident the problem to be resolved regarding the internal compo-sition of the working class, even before facing the problem of funda-mentally attacking the capitalist class. However, this will almost always be the case in Britain. We ought not go there to seek out strategies for overthrowing the powers that be, models of alternative political organi-sation or non-utopian elaborations of working-class thought. And, above all, from capital's point of view, one should not seek in Britain the global impulse for great initiatives. The political moment at the state level has no margin of independence in imposing its own pattern on social relations. As V.L. Allen would say, the government is never more than a conciliator and an arbitrator; in other words, from the Victorian Conciliation Act of 1896 to the Prices and Incomes Act of seventy years later (which Harold Wilson's crew had to leave up to formal decision), there is a very British history of an absence of capitalist labour policy. This has also meant that the political level has lacked autonomy from capital's immediate need –which has thus far led to a strategic defeat of the workers. Hence, the dynamic support role in the real long-term management of power is taken on by scientific elaboration, by the theoretical consciousness of the labour problem translated into terms of bourgeois conceptualisation. The autonomy of politics from short-term capitalist development here presents itself as the autonomy of science: science not as technology but as theory, not as an analysis of labour, but as an economics of capital. We should not go looking through the high points of economic thought for a direct discourse on working-class struggles: the higher the level of elaboration, the more abstract the movement of categories and the more difficult it becomes to recognise that struggles are indeed present in this thought – not because such thought is removed from reality, but because it is close to it in a complex way, not passively reflecting the class relation but serving it to us well-seasoned and thus elaborated in a dish of tasty concepts. We should learn to read the scientific language of capital beyond these concepts, looking behind the logic of the discipline and of doctrines, reading between the lines and in the spaces of 'their' treatises, which systematise 'their' knowledge. We must not take what they say as read. Rather, the cultural hieroglyphics need deciphering: the scientific jargon must be translated into our own illustrious class vernacular. Faced with the capitalist side's great scientific discoveries, we must time and again take stock of their attitudes toward reality – not to reflect on these, but elaborate them in order to understand, and to understand what we are really facing.

In his inaugural address in Cambridge in 1885, Marshall said: 'Among the bad results of the narrowness of the work of English economists early in the nineteenth century perhaps the most unfortunate was the opportunity which it gave to socialists to quote and misapply economic dogma'. As the 1919 preface to his *Industry and Trade* testifies, socialists' works both repulsed and attracted him because they seemed lacking in any contact with reality. At that moment he everywhere saw 'admirable developments in the working-class capabilities' and recalled how some ten years earlier he had believed that the proposals generally bunched under the name 'socialism' were the most important object worth studying. Those were the years between 1885 and 1900, in which his home was visited on weekends by working-class leaders such as Thomas Burt, Ben Tillet, Tom Mann and others – the new unionists. They were the victorious dockers' leaders of 1889, the year when, after twenty years of work, Marshall finished what Keynes called a 'universe of knowledge': his *Principles of Economics*. Here, as in every subsequent classic product of economic thought, everything that happens within the working class presents itself as happening within capital. Rightly, from Marshall's point of view, bourgeois science assigns workers, and therefore the working-class struggle, no autonomy at all. History is always the history of capital; like labour or wages, like complex living machinery or simple natural energy, as a function of the system or as a contradiction of production, the working class always plays a subaltern role, not enjoying a light of its own but reflecting, in its own movements, the movement of the cycle of capital. This is exactly opposite of the truth from our own point of view, in which every discovery of an objective social science can and must be translated into the language of struggles. The most abstract theoretical problem will have the most concrete of class meanings. In September 1862, after having sent to the British Association his *Notice of a General Mathematical Theory of Political Economy* with his first ideas on the concept of marginal utility, Jevons wrote his brother: 'I am very curious, indeed, to know what effect my theory will have both upon my friends and the world in general. I shall watch it like an artilleryman watches the flight of a shell or shot to see whether its effects equal his intentions'. If the predictions are those of Jevons' 1871 *Theory*, the effects are found precisely in Marshall's *Principles*. Following the trace of his conceptual shell during this period in the history of the working class's class struggle is precisely *our* problem. Unless we are mistaken, this is precisely the historical node that needs unravelling, because this is the classic question of the relationship between struggles and science: working-class struggles and the science of capital. This relationship would subsequently have a long history, which is yet to reach its conclusion. If we have understood properly, in the underground of that era there should be found a strong current that brings this relationship to a first expression-model. We need to dig deeper to find it. The very way in which the problem is posed also offers a methodological indication that is also valuable for us, today, on this as on other objects of our research. As Keynes put it, 'Jevons saw the kettle boil and cried out with the delighted voice of a child; Marshall too had seen the kettle boil and sat down silently to build an empire'.

Historical Social Democracy

In his 1900 work *Demokratie und Kaisertum*, Friedrich Naumann defined the Bismarckian Empire as a republic of labour. The social monarchy of the two Wilhelms deserved this paradoxical name. Just as the profoundly Germanic tradition of the *Machtstaat* turned out to be the most fragile among all political institutions of modern capital, so too did the *bête noire* of reactionary Junkerism turn out to be the road most open to the development of a certain type of democratic working-class movement. Without Bismarck, German social democracy may never have existed in its classic form: 'without Mohammed Charlemagne would have been inconceivable'. On the other hand, from his uncomfortable perspective of agrarian socialism, Rudolf Meyer was right to say that, without social democracy, German industry would not have developed. All of these logical passages are rich in historical meaning. The theme of the political organisation of the working-class finds its happiest hunting ground in German-speaking *Mitteleuropa*, the terrain for what was once such a successful experiment. It is here that the relation between struggle and organisation is most worth measuring – if for no other reason than to grasp the starting point of a long historical arc. Today, this arc ought not be retraced through the small steps of practice, but rather subjected to the brief and dismissive glance of working-class theory, which in its present strategic indications goes well beyond what went before and has come after. But we should add right away that, in Germany at least, there was nothing so important as the impact exerted by classical social democracy's model of politics, from Lassalle's *Offenes Antwortschreiben* in 1863 to the year of united struggles in 1913, in which 5,672,034 working days were lost to strikes. Faced with this first historical form of the political party of the working class, all other organisational experiences have been forced to present themselves as answers, alternatives or as a kind of reversed image of what was not wanted: a negative repetition of what was considered a wrong-headed passivity. The revolutionary syndicalism of the turn of the twentieth century, the Luxembourgist historical left, the various council experiments from Bavaria to Piedmont and the first minoritarian groups ever to exist (the newborn communist parties) were essentially answers to the demand for a party, a demand that social democracy had imposed on the working-class vanguard. The Bolshevik model did not escape this organisational destiny of being first of all anti–social democratic – a model that exploded Lenin's head as soon as he, outside of Russia, came into contact with the experiences of the European working-class movement. Thus, Germany offered the classical *political* terrain for the working-class struggle, which then became the necessary reference point for every answer to the organisational question. Strangely enough, by adapting the young Marx to capital's old age, the working-class party proved to be the heir not of German philosophy but of classical German social democracy.

This fact also has another aspect, what we might call its historiographical side. The German working-class movement, along with the whole class struggle in Germany, seems to have an only-political history, a simple development of the organisational level, always a matter of leadership, a history of party congresses. From Mehring onward, Marxist historiography has easily fallen prey to this false outlook. In no country like in Germany is the number of struggles so difficult to ascertain. This is not because the struggles were few, but because they rarely come into view. Submerged as they have been in the organisational consequences they immediately provoked, they have rarely reached the surface. There was good reason, then, why, in this context, the union so struggled to grow, competing and often struggling with the party, strangely following chronologically behind the latter's development. There is good reason, then, why the average militant intellectual in Italy is familiar with the politically insipid name of one or other of the Liebknechts, while no one remembers the name of Karl Legien – the 'German Samuel Gompers', as Perlman used to call him – who, in the thirty years up to his death in 1921, remained at the head of the union and thus its struggles – in other words, workers' strikes. Before the Kashubian Junker von Puttkamer began to apply the Bismarckian laws against them with the sure hand of the policeman, the socialists had had enough time to divide, between the pro-Eisenach ideologists like Bebel and the followers of that philo-Prussian *Realpolitiker* von Schweitzer, who was both a worker and a baron. But they had also managed to reunite by singing in chorus the verses of that Gotha programme, which could have met with who-knows-what fate had it not fallen under the sharp claws of the old man in London. This was a time of unusually violent struggles close to riots, but which were almost synonymous with defeat. The strikes were local, isolated, badly organised and worse led, and managed only to unite the bosses' front. And yet the *Erwachungstreiks* of the late 1860s had their effect: between 1871 and 1872, struggles grew, from the engineering workers of Chemnitz to the Cramer-Klett mechanics in Nuremburg and the 16,000 Ruhr miners who took to the offensive, calling for an eight-hour day and a 25 per cent wage rise. In 1873, a violent crisis struck the German economy, and the workers doggedly defended themselves against unemployment and wage reductions with 'increasing lawlessness and lack of discipline', as one Reichstag bill put it. Theodor York, the president of the woodworkers' federation, took the opportunity to launch the antilocalist and unionist idea of centralising the organisation. But we are talking about Germany and thus the centralisation sought at the union level was instead found at the political level. The Gotha congress claimed that it was 'the workers' duty to keep politics away from the unions', but also that it was their duty to join the party, 'because only this could improve the workers' political and economic conditions'. Gradilone has rightly concluded that 'the date 1875 remains a landmark not only because it marked the birth of the first workers' party in Europe, but also because it indirectly influenced the onset of similar parties across the continent ... all of them more or less having arisen through the direct or indirect influence of the creation of the German party'. We should credit social democracy for having objectively derived the political form of the party from the content of the struggles, for having raised the relation between struggle and organisation to the level of state practice and thus for having used the struggles to grow as an alternative power: a negative institutional power, a temporary antistate preparing to become the government. Paradoxically enough, it was Lenin who gave social democracy a theory of the party. Before that there was only everyday political practice. Only within the Bolshevik group, from the outlook of the editors of *Iskra*, can we find a fundamental systematisation of the function of the historical party of the working class. Even the most classic *Aufgaben* of social democracy indicate only the party's strategic programme and tactical path, but not the dynamic laws of its apparatus. What was not posed was the wholly Leninist question, 'what type of organisation do we need?' By counter-posing one type of organisation to another, Lenin elaborated the theory of both. He needed to do this because his discourse was truly wholly political. He did not (nor did he want to) start from struggles. His logic was based on a concept of political rationality absolutely independent of everything. It was even independent of class interest, which, if anything, was common to both. His party was not the antistate: even before taking power, it was the only true state of the true society. We ought not look to the working-class struggle before Lenin as the origin of his theory of the party. This does not diminish the immensely insightful significance of the Leninist experience, but, rather, magnifies it. Although not moved by the impulse of the working-class struggle, Lenin completely grasped the laws of its political action. Thus, the classical bourgeois notion of the autonomy of politics is reconstituted from a working-class point of view. Different, on this terrain, is the historical destiny of social democracy. Its party form invented nothing: in its everyday practice, it has only ever reflected a very high theoretical level of the working-class attack on the system. Instead, behind German social democracy, just as behind British economics and American capitalist initiative, there stands the begin-ning of a long typology which has, over time, defined the character of the conflict between workers' wages and capital's profit in increasingly sharp terms. Not by chance, that is where the working-class history of capital took its first steps. This can now be demonstrated by invoking real struggles.

Let's open the third volume of Kuczynski's monumental *Geschichte der Lage der Arbeiter in Deutschland von 1789 bis zur Gegenwart* (the first part of a work whose second part concerns the working-class condition in Britain, the United States and France). Stripped of its paleo-Marxist conceptualisation and terminology, this work is a mine of detail on the class's development. The key year is 1889, the year of the birth of the Second International: that legitimate daughter of German capital and social democracy. On either side of the Channel, the British dockers and German miners were both on strike. After the struggle of 25,000 Berlin bricklayers and carpenters on the platform 'from ten to nine working hours, from fifty to sixty pfennigs in wages', there was the explosive struggle of the miners, that age-old vanguard: 13,000 in the

Saar, 10,000 in Saxony, 18,000 in Silesia and 90,000 in Westphalia. When they all stopped working, the army was sent in against them, leaving five workers dead and nine wounded. Engels and Luxemburg wrote about it, the problem gripped the Reichstag, and the leaders of the movement, Schroeder, Bunte and Spiegel, even went to see the Kaiser. Quick as a thunderbolt came the consequences the following year, 1890: on 20 February, the SPD's [Social Democratic Party's] candidates scored a million and a half votes, 20 per cent of the total, 660,000 more than they had received in 1887. On 20 March, Bismarck was dismissed: on 1 October, the special laws against the socialists were abolished. In Mehring's words, there had begun 'a new period in the history of the German Reich and in the history of German Social Democracy'. Today, we need to introduce this new form of historical periodisation into our theoretical elaboration and find new dates, new temporal bearings from which to begin the social response based either on large collective institutions or great individual thought. According to Walter Galenson, between 1890 and 1913, in Germany, the close interaction between the history of the party and the history of struggles brought the foundations posed by earlier experiences to a classic conclusion. From November 1890 to September 1891, there were around thirty strikes with 40,000 workers in struggle, beginning with the printers – the 'Englishmen' of the German union movement, with their legal victory on working hours. Between 1892 and 1894, there were 320 small, scattered and short strikes involving 20,000 workers. In 1895 and especially 1896, there was another great wave in Berlin, in the Saar, and in the Ruhr. The percentage of conflicts with outcomes favorable for the workers rose from 56.5 per cent to 74.7 per cent. Working-class victory was in the air. The dockers' strike in Hamburg in 1896 brought the idea of the antistrike law back into fashion, with the *Zuchthausvorlage* of 1899, which was felled in parliament. The 1903 Crimmitschau strike, however, had a different outcome. For five months, 8,000 textile workers struck for higher wages. The result was the development, born of necessity, of a powerful associative movement among the bosses; it was the start of the long process which led, after World War I, to the creation of the mass anti-working class (and thus counterrevolutionary) *Vereinigung der deutschen Arbeitgeberverbände*. The years between 1903 and 1907 saw a rise in the intensity of the struggle that matched its quantitative extension: the high point was in 1905, when the striking workers reached half a million and 7,362,802 working days were lost. Even in 1910, there were 370,000 striking workers and 9 million working days lost. This continued albeit at a decreasing level until 1913. These data are drawn from Walter Galenson, writing on the period from the 1890s to 1917. From this, we understand what confuses generalist historians of contemporary Germany like Vermeil, when from 1890 to 1912, the SPD vote rose from 1,427,000 to 4,250,000 and its seats from 35 to 110. According to Zwing, from 1891 to 1913 the number of union federations fell from 63 to 49, while membership soared from 277,659 to 2,573,718. Following a period of guerrilla warfare, after the Mannheim Act, peace and harmony spread between party and union. These developments were full of contradictions – flames that light up and die out – allowing us to see the forces that guided the process but also the negative outcome that fatally lay in store. In general, we have seen – wanted to see – in the Second International only its level of theoretical debate, as if everything had been written in *Neue Zeit,* everything said in the *Bernstein-Debatte,* andtherewasnothinglefttocommentonafterthe*Zusammenbruchstheorie* dispute between argumentative intellectuals. We have wanted to see classical German social democracy as a historical episode in the theory of the workers' movement. But the real theory – high science – lay not within the socialist camp but outside and against it. And this altogether theoretical science – scientific theory – had as its content, object and problem the reality of politics. The new theory of a new politics suddenly arose both in the great bourgeois thought and in subversive working-class praxis. Lenin was closer to Max Weber's *Politik als Beruf* than to the German working-class struggles, upon which classical social democracy was based like some giant with feet of clay.

During the Weimar period, when he still spoke to party cadres at Berlin's *Volkshochschule,* the Social Democrat Theodor Geiger wrote: 'We call '*die Mass*' that social group which has a revolutionary and destructive goal'. A year earlier, Lukács brought to light the essence of the 'social-democratic tactic': given that the revolution still remained distant and its true preconditions did not yet exist, the proletariat must make compromises with the bourgeoisie. He aptly observed that 'the more the subjective and objective preconditions of social revolution are present, the more "purely" will the proletariat be able to fulfill its class aims. So the reverse of practical compromise is often great radicalism – absolute "purity" in principle in relation to the "ultimate goal". This is the true, classical, historical social democracy. It is not true that the revolutionary goal was abandoned therein. Whoever says so is confusing it with some revisionist formula of Bernstein's. The beauty of that social democracy was precisely the fact that its tactics addressed both sides of the coin and of the party's possible policies: a daily practice of Menshevik activities and an ideology of pure subversive principles. This is why we would argue that, historically, it represents an organisational solution of the working-class struggle on the political level for which it would be difficult to find any equal. The Bolshevik model and the whole communist movement that followed did not go as far or, in truth, ended up at something qualitatively different. Let's put that another way. During this period, the classical form of the social-democratic party in Germany passively reflected a level of working-class spontaneity that, through its struggles, incorporated all the instances of ambiguity, contradiction and duplicity[2] that inhibit the demand for better capitalist working conditions and the 'socialist' refusal of these conditions as a whole, in the world beyond capital. The situation was not so backward as to prevent cyclical explosions of economic struggles, nor was it so advanced as to forbid alternative proposals for the formal management of power. It remains a fact that, from the very beginning, the contact between working-class struggle and the social-democratic party was so direct, the relation so close, as to deny even the mediation of the trade-union level. Trade unionism was altogether absent from the German working-class tradition, and hence the whole discussion on political perspectives in turn displayed a remarkable absence of conceptual mediations and surprise raids on the enemy camp. This other aspect of German social democracy's organisational miracle was an ambient intellectual mediocrity, an approximative approach to science and a theoretical poverty, which could only produce failure: that scholastic treatment of Marxist truth, which, ever since Lenin, we have had to waste time combatting. In the meantime, capital's high science was growing, and is growing, by itself, unrivalled and free from attack. This is the real illusion to which the social-democratic tactical horizon always remained

---

2 *Doppiezza:* a term typically used to characterize Palmiro Togliatti's PCI [Italian Communist Party], referring to the separation between its tactical compromises and formal revolutionary end goal, or more precisely, the invocation of this latter as a means of justifying the former, thus keeping different souls in the same party.

prisoner: a kind of optimistic vision of the historical process which pushes forward through its own gradual unfolding rather than through a violent confrontation with the opposite side, thus ultimately finding a reassuring and comfortable judgement from a just and good God. As an example of the high science of capital, Max Weber would rightly pose the alternative question: '(a) whether the intrinsic value of ethical conduct – the "pure will" or the "conscience" as it used to be called – is sufficient for its justification, following the maxim of the Christian moralists: "The Christian acts rightly and leaves the consequences of his actions to God"; or (b) whether the responsibility for the predictable consequences of the action is to be taken into consideration'. That was how the antithesis between *Gesinnungethik* and *Verantwortungsethik* was later posed in the essay 'The Meaning of "Ethical Neutrality" in Sociology and Economics': 'All radical-revolutionary political attitudes, particularly revolutionary "syndicalism", have their point of departure in the first postulate; all *Realpolitik* in the latter'. But barely a year later, in his lecture on 'Politics as a Vocation', Weber said that the two ethics are not absolutely antithetical, but instead complement each other. In fact, 'only in unison' do they 'constitute a genuine man – a man who can have the "calling for politics [*Beruf zur Politik*]"'. The politician – in other words, one who holds 'in one's hands a nerve fiber of historically important events' – must possess three highly decisive qualities: passion 'in the sense of matter-of-factness [*Sachlichkeit*], of passionate devotion to a "cause" [*Sache*]'; responsibility toward precisely this cause as 'the guiding star of action'; and far-sightedness as 'his ability to let realities work upon him with inner concentration and calmness. Hence his distance to things and men'. It is on this basis that, as Gerhard Maser puts it, Weber's sociology of power becomes a 'sociology of potential'. To the extent that the aspiration for power is the indispensable tool of political work, the instinct for power [*Machtinstinkt*] is in fact one of the politician's normal qualities. In the meetings of the Heidelberg workers' and soldiers' council in which Max Weber participated in 1918, he could have proposed, indeed elaborated, the proletarian laws of a politics and power. 'He would have dismissed as irrelevant the old problematic of the best possible form of government. For him, the struggle for power or domination between classes and individuals was the essence of things, or, if you will, the constant of politics'. No, we are not talking about Lenin, but still of Weber, 'Machiavelli's heir ... and Nietzsche's contemporary', as Raymond Aron correctly

defined him in the aforementioned context. But the politician Weber is
talking about is Lenin. Are the burning passion and the cold far-sightedness of which he speaks not to be found in that 'right mix of blood and
judgement' that Lukács attributes to his Lenin, in the afterword to the
Italian edition? And isn't that sense of responsibility the same as Lenin's
'constant preparedness', the mark of his figure as the 'very embodiment of
continually *being prepared*'? The truth is that the Weberian conception of
a purely and entirely political action could perhaps have been completely
applied only from the working-class point of view. This does not ever
imply the need to remain the passive victims of even the highest levels of
working-class spontaneity, as occurred in classical social democracy's
serious-minded opportunism. Rather, it means the need to actively mediate, in a complex way, the whole real complexity of concrete situations.
And in these situations, the working-class struggle never alone serves to
push things in a single direction, but it is always interwoven with capital's
political responses, with the latest results of bourgeois science and with
the levels attained by the organisations of the workers' movement. In this
sense, the working-class struggle stands behind social democracy much
more than it does behind Leninism. Yet, Leninism is politically the more
advanced of the two, because it foresees, or rather prescribes, that their
historical nexus – the relation between struggles and social democracy
– is the practical premise for the defeat of the workers in the open field. It
can foresee and prescribe because it knows the arcane laws of political
action and applies them without the illusions of moral ideals. Lenin
certainly had not read Weber's 1895 *Freiburg Address*. Yet he acted *as if* he
had known and interpreted its words in his daily praxis: 'For the dream
of peace and human happiness, on top of the door of the unknown future
is written: "leave all hope"'. This is Lenin's greatness. Even when he was
not in direct contact with great bourgeois thought, he was still able to
come to terms with it, because he had directly unearthed it in reality, or,
in other words, recognised it in its objective functioning. He had understood very early a maxim that we today are forced to relearn at great
difficulty – the one in Weber's *Address* which we ought to have the courage to take up as a party programme: 'Our descendants will hold us
responsible in front of history not for the type of economic organisation
which we will leave them in inheritance but, rather, for the space for
movement which we will have conquered and passed on'.

Class Struggles in the United States

Let's begin with a working hypothesis that already carries a powerful political charge. The proposal is as follows: the working-class struggle reached its highest level of development between 1933 and 1947, and specifically in the United States. There were advanced, successful and mass working-class struggles, or directly working-class mass struggles – and yet they were simple struggles over collective bargaining. We can take any revolutionary experience from old Europe, compare it with this particular cycle of American working-class struggles, and we will thus know our limitations, the expressions of our backwardness and our defeats. The biggest advantage is that we will know how far we are lagging behind subjectively; the catch is that we will understand the true absurdity of our pretence of being the vanguard without a movement, generals without an army, priests of the subversive gospel without any political knowledge. Today, we must invert the narrative of those who see European workers as running behind in backward situations which are nonetheless more revolutionary. If victory in the class struggle is measured in terms of what (and how much) has been gained, then European workers will find the most advanced model for their present needs in the way of winning – or, if you will, the way of defeating the enemy – by studying the forms adopted by American workers in the 1930s.

There was already a strong base for this fight. A wave of struggle had developed already during the war years, transforming the war between nations not into a civil war, but into a class struggle, in its own particular way. Because of a lack of scientific courage, or for fear of knowing how things really are, the behaviour of the American workers during the two great wars is a chapter of contemporary history that remains to be written. To say that the workers profited from the war involving *everyone* in order to advance their own *partial* interest is a bitter truth – one that we would wish history had never produced. The working-class struggle within the capitalist war is a great political fact of our era; with good reason, we are here going to find it outside of European confines in the American heart of the international capitalist system. In 1914 and 1915, the number of strikes was 1,204 and 1,593 respectively; in 1916 the number jumped to 3,789, and in 1917 to 4,450, with 600,000 and 230,000 striking workers respectively. Aside from the fabulous year of 1937, we have to wait till 1941 to again find 4,288 strikes in one year, involving 2,360,000 workers, or 8.4 per cent of the total occupied workforce, just as in 1916 – a percentage not reached again until 1945, except for the other fabulous year of 1919. In the years 1943, 1944 and 1945, there was an impressive growth in strike numbers – 3,752, then 4,956, then 4,750; the number of workers in struggle rose from 1,980,000 to 2,120,000 and then 3,470,000. The intensity of the working-class struggle during the war would only once be topped, in the immediate postwar period, during the first conversion of war industries into peace and civil welfare industries. It might seem that the workers ought to have abstained from creating difficulties in such a humane endeavour. But let's see: in 1946, there were 4,985 strikes involving 4,600,000 workers, 16.5 per cent of the entire employed workforce. In 1919, there were 3,630 strikes, with 4,160,000 strikers, or 20.2 per cent of all the workers employed at the time (see Appendix C in R. Ozanne, *Wages in Practice and Theory*). From the workers' viewpoint, the war was an excellent opportunity for making great gains, while peace was an opportunity to ask for more. And indeed, the National War Labor Board, which was 'new-deal-ist' even before the New Deal, could find no better way to derail labour conflicts than to let the workers win. The right to organise, collective bargaining through union representatives, recognition of union-shop and open-shop contracts on the same footing, equal pay for women, a minimum living wage guaranteed for all – such were the conquests of the first war period. Consolidating their organisation by exploiting the national needs of the class enemy, by 1918, the unions had over 4 million members. And in the postwar period, the confrontation shifted to the terrain of wages. When we mention the year 1919, the revolutionary militant thinks of the civil war in Bolshevik Russia, the Bavarian Soviet Republic, the Third International and Bela Kun, just as the Italian militant thinks of Turin, *l'Ordine Nuovo*, the councils and then the factory occupations. But the struggle in Seattle is unknown to them. We hear no mention of its shipbuilders, led by James A. Duncan, who drew 60,000 workers into a five-day general strike. Yet the action in Seattle began a key year for the class struggle in America, which was probably more important to the positive outcome of the world revolution than all the 'Eurasian' events put together. There was the Boston policemen's strike, organised in the Boston Social Club union, which wanted to affiliate to the American Federation of Labor. Here there are notes of France in

May '68, although this past experience was a little more serious, given that it took place half a century earlier and in any case the policemen's programme carried no mention of 'le football aux footballeurs'. But there were also strikes by mechanics and railroad workers, textile workers and longshoremen, strikes in the food and clothing industries. A decisive clash came on the terrain of the production of materials that were then fundamental to every other type of production: steel and coal. There were 350,000 steel workers demanding a collective contract with a wage increase and an eight-hour working day. The United States Steel Corporation answered that it had no intention of 'discussing business with them'. The days of the wartime New Deal were already over. The local, state and federal authorities and military forces were on the side of the bosses. After an anti-working-class witch-hunt, the isolation of their organisations among public opinion and about twenty deaths, the workers faced defeat. Foster R. Dulles has written that 'if the steel workers had won, the entire history of the labor movement during the following decade would have followed a completely different course'. As the steel workers retreated, 425,000 miners entered the field. Here, the workers' organisation was better, and therefore their demands were stronger: a 60 per cent wage increase and a thirty-six-hour working week. They got half of what they were asking for in wages, but no reduction in hours. Wilson, the idealist and neurotic twenty-eighth president of the United States, deployed a court injunction to stop the strike. John L. Lewis, the United Mine Workers president soon famous for quite another kind of initiative, reinforced the injunction from the level of the workers' own organisation. The miners listened to neither of the two presidents and kept up the struggle until they obtained the minimum they could under those conditions. One could read in the period newspapers, which said that 'no organised minority has the right to throw the country into chaos ... A labor autocracy is as dangerous as a capitalist autocracy'. These were the methodological rules that capital was beginning to draw from its tough clash with the workers: the social philosophy which was to triumph in the happy decade that followed. The American 1920s, 'the age of wonderful idiocies', social peace, great prosperity, welfare capitalism and high wages gained not through struggles or through concessions coming from capital's political initiative, but given as if by the individual capitalist's economic choice. For the first time in history, 'golden chains' were forged, union density collapsed, a new form of company unions came into being, the open shop won, and the scientific organisation of labor proceeded with giants' steps. It is said that the Great Crash came suddenly to awaken everyone from the 'American dream'. One of the reasons capital did not understand that it was running along the edge of the abyss was the working-class mass's impressive lack of struggles after the defeat of the 400,000 railroad workers in 1922 – a silence which lasted even beyond 1929. Working-class struggles are an irreplaceable instrument of capital's own self-consciousness: without them, it does not recognise its own adversary and thus does not know itself. And when the contradiction explodes – a contradiction among parts internal to the mechanism of capitalist development – again the workers do not actively intervene through struggle, either to accelerate the crisis or to somehow resolve it. They know that there is nothing to gain as a particular class if the general development has nothing more to concede. It goes without saying that the workers did not want the crisis. Much less obvious, and indeed rather scandalous, is the argument that the crisis was not the product of working-class struggles but of working-class passivity: of the massive refusal to go on strike, with demands, propositions, struggle and organisation. We do not mean, mind you, that the cause of *that* crisis is to be located in the working-class attitude toward capital. Rather, we mean that this attitude was the only one which could have shown that there was a crisis to be faced: the only one which, when expressed in struggle, could have allowed the possibility of foreseeing it. It is easy to understand, though, the flattening out of strike levels in a decade in which great opportunities seemed to be around the corner. But why was there such working-class passivity in the heart of the crisis? Why was there no attempt to seek a revolutionary solution in what was an objectively revolutionary situation and could hardly have been more so? Why was there no 1917 in 1929? Workers make no demands and do not try to impose them in struggle in only two cases: when they can secure them without asking and when they know that they cannot achieve them. Thus, the absence of great struggles from 1922 to 1933 had two different causes in the two periods between 1922 and 1929 and between 1929 and 1933. In the first period, the objective margins of capitalist profit spontaneously overflowed onto the territory occupied by the workers. During the second period, there were no margins for either of the two sides: it was unthinkable for workers' wages to take a share of capital's profits, and the boundaries between classes themselves disappeared: there was only one crisis for all. For what should we fight when it is impossible to fight to win concessions? To take power? We must never confuse the two. The American working class is not the Russian Bolshevik party. We must recognise the reality even when it causes us problems. When Roosevelt got stuck into resolving the crisis, the American workers, again arraigned in battle formation, drew a classic assessment of the immediately prior developments of their political history: they had struggled aggressively during the war and they won, they defended themselves violently after the war and were defeated, they benefitted without scruples from the 'golden glitter' of the happy decade and they had reacted neither in their own defence nor against their adversary during the crisis. It seems like an abstract ballet, lacking any meaningful content. But the logic of these movements was impeccable, like the self-enclosed form of a mathematical formula. We should take this to heart. Today the American workers are the hidden face of the international working class. To decipher the face of this class sphinx, which contemporary history places before us, we must first complete a full tour of the working class around the planet. The American night seems dark because we look at the day with our eyes closed.

Paragraph 7a of the National Industrial Recovery Act, with the right for workers 'to organise and bargain collectively through representatives of their own choosing' and with an injunction to owners forbidding them any 'interference, restraint, or coercion' with minimum wages and maximum allowed working time, was approved in June 1933 along with the rest of the law. The number of strikes in the second half of that year was equal to the entire previous year: the number of striking workers was three and a half times as many as in all of 1932. In 1934, there were 1,856 strikes with 1,500,000 workers involved: more than 7 per cent of all employed workers. The number of conflicts had not risen, but now they involved the big industries: the steel workers, the auto workers, the West Coast dockers, the northwestern woodworkers and in the front rank with the loudest voice, almost 500,000 textile workers with demands for a thirty-hour working week, a thirteen-dollar minimum wage, the abolition of the 'stretch-out' – as 'speed-ups' were called in the textile industry – and the recognition of the United Textile Workers. After the Clayton Act of 1914 and the Norris-LaGuardia Act of 1932, paragraph 7a fell away under the combined pressure of the individual capitalist and his still-bourgeois legal system – although the workers had already used it for all it was worth: that is, to create wriggle room for the new demands now raised to the level of organisation. The call 'to organise the unorganised', to enter together with the unions into the big mass-production industries, became possible only at the point when collective capitalist consciousness opened the factory to a modern working-class power which would counterbalance the backward and antiquated power of the owners. The year 1935 saw the birth and success of both the Wagner Act and the Committee of Industrial Organization (CIO) – further proof that there is an inextricable knot between capital's political initiative and workers' advanced organisation, which cannot be untied even if we wanted to do so. A National Labor Relations Board made sure that owners did not employ 'unfair labor practices', and that they did not oppose collective bargaining with 'disloyal procedure'; it issued 'cease and desist' orders only to the industrialists' side and never to labour's side; it got rid of the bosses' union, the yellow unions and craft-union divides and, for the first time, put the union in the hands of the common worker. It was not, therefore, an organ of political media-tion between two opposed and equal sides: Franklin Delano was not Theodore Roosevelt. Rather, it was an administrative organ with judicial functions: a kind of injunction exactly opposite to everything that came before it in the American tradition – an injunction by capital to the capi-talists to leave space for the autonomy of working-class organisations. What is more, within the working-class side, there was a shift in favour of rising sectors of production. The new mass worker was identified within the steel, automobile, rubber and radio industries. This explains why the CIO had already overtaken the AFL's membership by late 1937 even though it had been going only for two years, while the latter had been around for half a century, and why the 'appropriate bargaining units' established in 1935 mostly favoured the new industrial unionism, supporting a vertical form of organisation. If capital's advanced choices favoured the most advanced working-class organisation, the latter in turn intervened within the capitalist side, such that the new choices won out over old resistances. The Fair Labor Standards Act of 1938 – the logical sequel to the National Labor Relations Act – set a minimum wage of twenty-five cents per hour, to go up to forty cents within seven years, a maximum working week of forty-four hours by 1939, forty-two hours by 1941, and forty hours after that. But between the Wagner Act, or, rather, between its constitutional recognition, and this logical sequel, there needed to be 1937. That year saw a then-unprecedented number of strikes, at 4,740, an expansive movement not concentrated at the main centres but branching out across the vital nodes of production with new forms of struggle and tools of pressure whose effectiveness had never been seen before. It all began with the foundation of the Steel Workers' Organizing Committee; with the success of this organisational move alone, Big Steel, the impenetrable fortress of the United States Steel Corportation, was forced to surrender: there was a 10 per cent wage increase, an eight-hour working day, and a forty-hour working week. Then it was Little Steel's turn: 75,000 workers were forced to wage a very tough struggle against the smaller steel-producing companies, including the 'Memorial Day Massacre' in Chicago, which was a temporary defeat for the workers and only healed four years later by the intervention of the political ally pulling the levers of government. But the high point of the confrontation took place in the auto industry, namely between the country's most powerful union, the United Auto Workers (UAW), and capital's strongest corporations – General Motors, Chrysler and Ford. The sit-down strike made its appearance and for forty-four days, production at General Motors was blocked in Flint, Cleveland, Detroit and everywhere else. There was a court injunction to evacuate the factories, but it was ignored; the police attempted to storm the factories, but they were pushed back. 'Solidarity forever' was the slogan that united workers inside with the population outside. Then came the workers' victory: collective bargaining with the UAW as a recognised counterpart. This American form of factory occupation now exploded, and soon it was Chrysler's turn to capitulate. Only Ford would resist four more years before its first collective contract, but it then had to concede even more: nothing less than the accursed closed shop. The quantitative extension of strikes, typical of the events of 1937, grew to include rubber, glass, textile, optical and electrical workers. Roosevelt and his eggheads partly followed events with concern and partly used the movement in their battle within capital. The 1938 law on 'fair working conditions' was an advanced political response that only those struggles could have obtained. The working-class struggle could increasingly turn the state's hand in its favour, as soon as it understood that this hand was forced to be pliable precisely because of its own needs. We get to the war with a relation of forces violently shifted in favour of the working class.

Something that had never happened before now proved possible: the resolution of the crisis gave power to the workers by taking it away from the capitalists. The shift that followed, the demand that now imposed itself, was also logical and coherent. This was no longer the antiquated socialist call for struggle against the war, but the most modern and subversive class demand that was then conceivable: for the working class to be able to share in war profits. In 1941, even before Pearl Harbor, the struggle once more focused on wages; it was a struggle fought by auto workers, shipbuilders, teamsters, builders, textile workers and that nerve centre of war production, the captive mines tied to the steel industry, with Lewis still in the lead and 250,000 men behind. In a year, the average wage soared by 20 per cent. During World War II, the American miners wrote a special chapter in the history of the class struggle that deserves careful study. The War Labor Board could do nothing to stop them, and Roosevelt himself had to put on the ugly mask of the workers' enemy. In 1943, they turned their massive organised power to the thousands of spontaneous strikes against the government that had exploded all over the country, and they did so without the unions. Thus came another crescendo of struggles that marked the last two years of the war and the immediate postwar period. The year 1946 was like another 1919. There are almost 5,000 strikes, with almost 5,000,000 workers in struggle: 16.5 per cent of employed workers, and 120 million working days lost. Practically every industry was gripped by labour conflict. The National Wage Stabilization Board could not dam the movement. One working-class demand came above all others: peace wages equal to war wages. And there were slogans that would reappear a quarter of a century later in the streets of Europe: 'no contract, no work', '52 for 40', and the American form of workers' control, 'open the books'. Again, the high points were struggles involving General Motors's workers, the steel workers, the miners, and especially the railroad workers. The increase in the cost of living, owing to the war, was followed by a mad rush in the rise of nominal wages, which almost caught up with it. This was the beginning of the contemporary history of the class relation between prices and wages, the unfolding of that deadly illness which our capital has learned to live with and which the economist's diagnoses call the inflation process driven by the cost of labour. Thus began a certain development dynamic, a movement of struggles which would decide the destiny of modern capital: who would run it and who would be able to use it. In the United States, 1947 began under the sign of the 'great labor scare' which had shaken the country throughout the previous year. Incredible stuff. But the Taft-Hartley Act essentially proposed to put the capitalists' contractual power back on an equal footing with that of the workers. This says it all, for what had been going on in America since 1933. The equalisation of the two contending classes' contractual standing – that classic demand for equal rights usually advanced by the weaker force against the decisive one – was advanced for the first time by the capitalists, as something to be conquered or reconquered within their state. This was an emblematic moment in a history which is still relevant today. For it is not true that one class always dominates and another is always dominated. Rather, from time to time, in an ever-changing relation of forces, the power of the one surpasses the power of the other, even independently of institutional forms of power and of the formal structural designation given to a society's functioning, be it capitalist or socialist, according to the ancient language which dates back to the origins of our science. This episode is historically rich insofar as it brought together fundamental facts of the past – decisive elements that the class struggle had hitherto accumulated in only disorderly fashion. This episode is politically charged with a future not yet even scratched by a workers' movement that succeeded in reaching that point but could proceed no further. A fact in the history of capital, which was at the same time an act of working-class politics: the fourteen years running from 1933 to 1947 in the United States. All that we had found separated in different periods and in different countries before this era can here be found united in a single complex tangle of facts and thoughts: the relation between struggles and capital's political initiative, between struggles and science, between struggles and working-class organisation. In other words, the Progressive Era, the Age of Marshall and the era of social democracy here merged and recognised each other as distinct parts of a single whole. And they did so precisely during these years in the United States, in which we see the conclusion of a classical phase of the class struggle running from the immediate post-Marx phase to the moment before our actual possibilities of movement. In looking at these events, we can learn once and for all the path that starts out from working-class struggles to address the various levels of social development – the state, science, organisation. After this, the working-class struggle will always add itself to these levels taken as a whole, and this amalgamation will now be our real starting point for both analysis and class action. But let us elaborate with greater depth and clarity these concepts, which do not just *seem* to be obscure.

Marx in Detroit

Fundamentally, capital has only taken a great initiative once, and not by chance it did so after its greatest systemic crisis and amid the most advanced working-class struggles in its history. Perhaps it is truly excessive to claim, like Rexford G. Tugwell, that, on 4 March 1933, the alternative was between an orderly revolution, 'a peaceful and rapid abandonment of the methods followed in the past' and a violent revolution against the capitalist structure. Perhaps it is closer to reality to say that there was only one path left open, a very original but compulsory path which, when compared to the miserly institutional happenings of contemporary society, today necessarily assumes the aspect of a genuine 'capitalist revolution': a revolution, that is, not *against* capital's structures, but *of* these structures by a political initiative that invested them – which tried to invest them – from above with a new strategy. H.G. Wells wrote of Franklin Delano Roosevelt that he was 'continuously revolutionary in the new way without ever provoking a stark revolutionary crisis'. And C.G. Jung simply defined him as 'a force'. On his march from Hyde Park along the Hudson to the White House in Washington, as Arthur M. Schlesinger Jr tells us, the 'happy warrior' imposed the chosen terrain for his battle. It needs no further demonstration that the interest of the most modern part of capital in a given moment passed through Roosevelt. The whole historiography on the matter provides evidence aplenty that the opposing drives within his class were politically mediated through his own person, in between the more fierce and moderate new dealers. The arc of development of this revolution-of-capital begins in 1933, rises until 1938 and then begins to fall again. It is something that needs further investigation, looking into its meaning for the working class, America and Europe: What is the relationship between the class struggles in America and the economic neonationalism of a progressive stamp, the exchange between the historic isolationism of American working-class struggles and the Keynesian national self-sufficiency attached to the first New Deal? This question deserves a

critical examination. And, in general, there are many problems that
need to be subjected to research that sets out from history and passes
through theory to arrive at politics. These problems range from the fact
that the revolutionary form of capitalist initiative here had a working-
class content and indeed acquired this form precisely by virtue of this
content, to the fact that through their struggles the workers succeeded
in pitting capital against the capitalist, the state which was formally 'of
all' against the real interest of the few; thus, working-class conquest of its
own organisational terrain resulted in denying the class adversary
portions of its own terrain. It is a fact that a national labour policy
arrived rather late as part of the New Deal itself. In the famous hundred
days between the Emergency Banking Act, the Agricultural Adjustment
Act, and the Tennessee Valley Authority Act, there was little talk of
either industry or workers. Paragraph 7, it is true, was the spark, but it
took the great struggles of '33 and '34, it took Minneapolis and San
Francisco, Toledo and the company town of Kohler, the textile workers
in Georgia and the armed clash in Rhode Island for the flame of capital's
first law on labour to light up in 1935, with the workers no longer in the
juridical role of the subaltern class. The law was deemed 'unjust' because
it imposed obligations on employers and not on workers. The response
from Senator Wagner: 'No one would assail a traffic law because it regulates the speed at which automobiles run and not the speed at which
people walk.' Roosevelt and the men of the New Deal had understood
this much, with whatever degree of clarity: an economically advanced
society cannot remain politically backward. If it does, then ultimately
there will come crisis, blockages in the cogs of the system, and a generically non-capitalist revolutionary situation. William E. Leuchtenburg
has written that the New Dealers were convinced that the Depression
owed not to a simple economic collapse but to a failure of the political
system, and thus sought new political tools; the reformers of the 1930s
abandoned the old Emersonian hope in reforming man and sought
simply to transform the institutions. In this sense, the Roosevelt experiment was 'revolutionary' in the traditional bourgeois sense of an adapta-
tion of the state machine to society's developmental needs, bringing
institutions up to date with economic growth. However, there was one
important difference: namely, that the dominant presence of ideology as
an internal nexus of political practice fell away. The new dealers
concerned themselves with promoting purchasing power as an impulse

to development, they called welfare projects measures for conserving the workforce, they spoke to the unemployed about jobs, they spoke to farmers about markets, they spoke to industrialists about international trade and to bankers about national finance. It was the conservatives who wielded the weapon of moral indignation against the injustices that now piled on top of injustices. What Roosevelt called a brave and tenacious spirit of experiment ought not be confused with the Jeffersonian and Jacksonian US progressive tradition picked up by Theodore Roosevelt and by Wilson. Here, there was a political jump, a pragmatic transition that deliberately went beyond cynicism, an anti-ideological effort, an aggressive charge of antihumanitarian taste, behind which we can detect and recognise the working-class hand that indirectly pulled the strings. Thurman Arnold was responsible for the antitrust programme, and his polemic was directed precisely against the progressivism of all the laws from the Sherman Act onward, which, in what Andrew Shonfield called 'the form of a national religion', targeted the 'illegalities' of the industrialists' organisations rather than focusing on achieving economic objectives. The *Folklore of Capitalism* was precisely the simple ideological struggle against the power of the industrial empire.

The class struggle within the New Deal had forced capital to show its hand. After the crisis had driven it to modernise politically, the working-class struggle on an advanced terrain compelled it, too, to show its true class face openly. This was no mean result, if indeed we want to strike the real adversary and not its ideological counterpart. For Thurman Arnold, writing in his *The Symbols of Government*, the leaders of the industrialists' organisation, ignorant of juridical, humanitarian and economic principles, built on their own errors, through an opportunistic activity that experimented on human material with little regard for social justice. Yet all this led to levels of production capacity that their fathers could never have dreamed of. The great capitalist initiative was a working-class victory even for the sole fact that it allowed a raw understanding of the enemy at the highest point of its historical development. Hence to condemn it is useless; rather, the advantage for us comes from turning it to our purposes.

In summer 1933, an article by Keynes in the *Daily Mail* led with the title 'President Roosevelt is magnificently right'. The thunderbolt had arrived from America: there would be no stabilisation of the dollar's

gold value. And Keynes commented: 'It is a long time since a statesman
has cut through the cobwebs as boldly as the president of the United
States', with what he termed 'a challenge to us to decide whether we
propose to tread the old, unfortunate ways or to explore new paths: new
to statesman and to bankers but not new to thought'. He was arguing
with himself. His long fight against the gold standard, this decadent
principle that belonged to the concepts of the pre-war period, this
'Bourbon residue', had finally found an authoritative voice that was also
prepared to listen. The 'return to gold' in Britain had offered the keyhole,
allowing him to foresee and indeed prophesy two great misadventures
for capital: 1926 in Britain and the global 1929 crash. The decision to
revalue the sterling by 10 per cent meant reducing the worker's pay 'by
two shillings to the pound'. The 'economic consequences of Winston
Churchill' was published during the political strike which spread from
the miners across the British working class, barely a year after these
prophesies of Keynes's: 'The working classes cannot be expected to
understand, better than Cabinet Ministers, what is happening. Those
who are attacked first are faced with a depression of their standard of
life, because the cost of living will not fall until all the others have been
successfully attacked too; and, therefore, they are justified in defending
themselves ... they are bound to resist so long as they can; and it must
be war, until those who are economically weakest are beaten to the
ground.' The other prophesy, of far more terrifying consequences, would
materialise just a few years later: 'The gold standard, with its dependence on pure chance, its faith in "automatic adjustments," and its general
regardlessness of social detail, is an essential emblem and idol of those
who sit in the top tier of the machine. I think that they are immensely
rash in their regardlessness, in their vague optimism and comfortable
belief that nothing really serious ever happens. Nine times out of ten,
nothing really serious does happen ... But we run a risk of the tenth time
(and are stupid into the bargain) if we continue to apply the principles of an
Economics which was worked out on the hypotheses of laissez-faire and
free competition to a society which is rapidly abandoning these hypotheses.' He wrote these words in 1925; the application of the old principles
continued, and the 'tenth case' proved a reality: it seemed like a great
depression, and it was indeed a great crisis: 'We were not previously
deceived. But today we have involved ourselves in a colossal muddle,
having blundered in the control of a delicate machine, the working of

which we do not understand. The result is that our possibilities of wealth may run to waste for a time – perhaps for a long time.' The high science of capital showed as much courage faced with the danger as did the great political initiative that took form on American soil. Keynes was in the United States in June '31 and returned there in June '34. In the meantime, on 31 December 1933, the *New York Times* published his open letter to Roosevelt. Here, the president appeared as the depository, the 'Trustee' responsible for a 'reasoned experiment within the framework of the existing social system'. If he did not succeed, national progress would remain bottlenecked and the revolution and the orthodoxy would be left to fight among themselves. 'But if he did succeed, new and bolder methods will be tried everywhere, and we may date the first chapter of a new economic era from your accession to office.'[3] The two met in person, face to face. Keynes described the shape of the president's hands in minute detail. And Roosevelt would write to Felix Frankfurter: 'I had a grand talk with K and liked him immensely.' One of the two must have said, as Napoleon said of Goethe, *voilà un homme!* Harrod tells us that there is contradictory evidence as to what direct influence Keynes's theories had on Roosevelt's actions. It seems more likely that Keynes's influence on American events passed through somewhat different channels, through 'men in siderooms' who were prepared to listen. But this is not the point in discussion. There is no longer any reason to doubt that Keynes and his theories did indeed reach America by one channel or another. But what needs backing up is the other thesis: that America, the political situation of the US economy, the class struggle in the United States, weighted on the formation of the central core of Keynesian thought to a much greater extent than is generally acknowledged, much more than those who see a danger to science in this hypothesis would explicitly want to let on. Paul A. Samuelson has written, referring precisely to Keynes, that 'Science, like capital, grows by accretion and each scientist's offering at the altar blooms forever'.[4] Everywhere and for all time. Science, like capital, has no borders. We always know whose brain it is that gives birth to a discovery, as its 'mother', but the real father involved in the conception remains unknown and mysterious,

---

3 'An Open Letter to President Roosevelt', *New York Times*, 31 December 1933.
4 *Collected Scientific Papers of Paul A. Samuelson*, Cambridge, MA: MIT Press, 1991, 323.

even to she who bears the new creature. It has many seeds because the historical plot of facts is itself complex. Lord Keynes, whom E.A.G. Robinson called 'from head to toe a product of Cambridge', in line with the common perception of him, was, in reality, an American economist. Some have asked us if there would have been a *General Theory* without Keynes. And we could easily say no. But that is not the right question. The preface to the original edition of the *General Theory* is dated 13 December 1935. A fabulous year, this, which had already given rise to the Wagner Act and the CIO. And, over the previous decade, the elements of the 'Keynesian revolution' had ripened and flowered. In 1924, Keynes, intervening in the pages of the *Nation* in a debate started by Lloyd George regarding the use of a programme of public works as a remedy for unemployment, had already shown the way that lay open to a new conception of economic policy. With the *End of Laissez-Faire*, published two years later, he again used his brilliant intuition to hone concepts that would be fundamentally important for the future: 'We need a new set of convictions which spring naturally from a candid examination of our own inner feelings in relation to the outside facts.' Yet 'Europe lacks the means, America the will, to make a move'. From his articles on the Lancashire cotton industry in late 1926 to his spring 1929 pamphlet, *Can Lloyd George Do It?*, and then *The Means to Prosperity* in 1933, he continued to reflect out loud on his own concerns while also looking to find whether something was moving elsewhere. Only when the will to move decisively appeared on the American horizon did the mechanism of a programmatic exposition of theory set in motion; only then did science begin to pick open its own discoveries in a logical order, and only then did a whole anticlassical conceptualisation of economics become established in black and white and become objective in a text that was itself a classic. The serious question, then, is whether there could have been a *General Theory* without the great capitalist initiative and everything that stood behind it – the crisis, the struggles, America, the land of both crisis and struggles. Keynes asked how it was possible to set moving again when the batteries weren't working. Was it possible to have a new theory of political economy without the first practical moves by the most modern capital, on the terrain of the most advanced working class? Who came first, Roosevelt or Keynes? Could the new ideas have enjoyed such success so quickly without the destructive lesson of facts, which had swept away the most die-hard dogma of classical theory? 'The difficulty lies not so much in developing new ideas as in escaping from old ones.' The *Treatise on Money* was the product of a refined expert on monetary questions and the last (just as Malthus was the 'first') of the Cambridge economist, just as Marshall's *Principles* saw Victorian Britain express itself in all its scientific splendour. But the horizon behind the *General Theory* was wider: the great British science of the past could not have produced this, because it arrived precisely as a product *opposed* to that past science; the recent history of contemporary Britain was already beside the point for whoever had the ambition of producing *another* science. So here we are beyond isolated fruit and amid a vast ocean of influences coming from afar. We could call it a product of capital's global situation, if this were not a generic way of saying a product of the class situation in the 1930s United States. Only in this way could the relationship between struggles and science be recomposed at a high level of elaboration. We need not go off on a banal search to find in Keynes the explicit terms of the working-class question. In *How to Pay for the War*, he wrote 'I have not attempted to deal directly with the problem of wages. It is wiser, I expect, to deal with it indirectly.'[5] In the age of Marshall, capital's high science could still ideologically hum along with the fine but unrecognised qualities of the toiling classes. By this point, that was no longer possible. So here we are at the level of the discourse on bone and meat,[6] stem and leaf, however we want to translate the lifelike phrases of *A Short View of Russia* regarding the 'rough proletarian' counterposed to the bourgeois and the intellectual, which are indeed … 'qualities in life'. He had once written that if there was no harder condition than a state of continual doubt, the ability to maintain it can be a sign of political skill. He had no doubts as to his own social position and did not want to display any. But unlike what is generally thought, he was a great politician, one greater than many who have made careers in politics. He personally applied in practice the motto that he had in 1933 addressed to the reformers who were then getting to work: 'When a doctrinaire proceeds to action, he must, so to speak, forget his doctrine.' If Keynes, the theorist of the New Deal, had had to practically direct the 'capitalist revolution', he would have been an American Lenin.

---

5 John Maynard Keynes, *How to Pay for the War*, London: Macmillan, 1940, 55.
6 A reference to Manlio Rossi-Doria's distinction between the poorer South of Italy (bone) and the wealthier Po Valley (meat).

The CIO posters during the first great waves of affiliation to industrial unionism proclaimed that 'President Roosevelt wants you to join the union'. Roosevelt's own efforts to restore the unity of the unions after the historical split of 1935 are well known. The 'great initiative' needed a single interlocutor at the working-class level, precisely in order to allow it room to manoeuvre within capital. But, before that, it needed a *new* interlocutor. Without the New Deal, there would have been no CIO, or it would have existed only with great delay. But it was urgently necessary for the success of the new capitalist policy that the working-class organi-sation update its own tools and most importantly extend its grip over the ultimate, decisive and most challenging levels of the new working class in the growing mass-production industries. However, the inverse is also true. The immediate, impressive success of the CIO can be explained only with reference to the general political atmosphere that had taken hold in the United States, amid the weakness of the individual capitalists and the insufficiencies of the old working-class organisation. The new men of the CIO knew as much, and for this reason they used the presi-dent's name in their unionisation drive. The slogan of 'organising the unorganised' suited both modern capital and the new union. There exist certain moments of elective affinity between the two class protagonists of modern history, when each of them, in their own field, is internally divided and they must each simultaneously resolve problems of strategic positioning and organisational restructuring. Then we see how the most advanced part of capital extends a hand to the most advanced part of the working class and – differently from what we might think from a sectar-ian standpoint – the working class does not refuse the embrace, does not reject the unnatural arrangement, but gladly exploits it in order to win itself what it can. There exist moments, then, in which the interests of the two opposed classes come to coincide, though not in the traditional sense of a formal political interest, when they were both fighting to win democ-racy. Rather, the content of this common interest now assumes a certain material depth: calling no longer for one's own rights but for the duties to be imposed on others. When John L. Lewis spoke of how labour requested and laid claim to a role in setting industrial policy, he meant to say that it wanted a place at the board meeting, where decisions are taken that influence the amount of food that a worker's family can eat, the time that his children can spend at school, the type and quantity of the clothes that they can wear and the entertainment that they can afford. The cry went out: 30 million workers wanted the foundation of a labour democracy, yes, but they also laid claim to 'their share in its concrete fruits'. It was through the opening of this path, through these words, that the mass of unskilled, immigrant, black and women workers flocked to the new industrial unionism. Pelling writes that in 1933 the AFL seemed like little but an association of undertakers, a group of mutual aid societies among artisans, led by old men whose only concern was to keep up good relations with the employers – the classic picture of any old organisation. Schlesinger instead provided the portrait (again, a typical one) of any new organisation: 'In the wake of the CIO drive an almost evangelical fervor began to sweep over large sections of American labor. The awakening of 1936 had, indeed, many of the elements of a revival. Organizers labored endless hours and braved unknown perils, like missionaries; workers crowded labor halls to hear the new gospel; new locals sprang out of communion and dedication to pass on the good news. And they sang their sardonic, wistful hymns; it was, to a great extent, a singing movement.'[7] As the tune of *Mammy's Little Baby Loves a Union Shop* rang out across America, at the end of 1937, the CIO could count some 3.7 million members, as against the AFL's 3.4 million: they included 600,000 miners, 400,000 auto workers, 375,000 steel workers, 300,000 textile workers, 250,000 clothing workers, 100,000 workers in agriculture and food processing; there was an organisation for each industry, running from top to bottom, without any distinction of skills or categories. This was the objective political charge contained within the trade union's form as an organisational weapon. When Hillmann, like Dubinsky, an 'American-style socialist', said, 'Our program was not a program for labor alone', he did not give the correct political sense of the operation the new organisation was mounting. When Lewis, acting through the CIO leadership, participated in the formation of the American Labor Party in New York and a Labor Non-Partisan League supporting Roosevelt electorally, this was not the real political outcome that could, through a more coherent approach, have been derived from the struggles taking place in America. But when the Steel Workers' Organizing Committee was recognised as a party to collective bargaining for all companies controlled by the US Steel Corporation; when the sit-down strike forced the great giants of the auto industry (except Ford) to their knees; when the new

7   Arthur M. Schlesinger, *The Coming of the New Deal*, Boston: Mariner, 1963, 416.

figure of the mass worker, of the nonspecialised worker, of the out-of-work worker became established on the ultimate terrain of organisation and thus came to relate to the rest of society in an alternative guise – then, and only then, could it be said that the political direction had been found for the recomposition of the working-class interest *into a class*. In this sense, the history of the CIO – precisely as an experience of the political organisation of American workers – is rich in lessons, however ambiguous its content and brief its extension through time. By 1938, when the Committee for Industrial Organization changed its name to the Congress of Industrial Organization, the heroic period, the time of the offensive, the era of the radical break with tradition, was all already in the past. It was no accident that, in the same year, after the Fair Labor Standards Act, the New Deal began to tank, losing the galloping pace of its innovating thrust now that it had practically already fulfilled its historical function. The ambiguity of a political solution that did not go beyond trade-union proposals was not particular to the CIO alone, but affected the whole terrain of working-class organisation in the United States. If we head off in search of the party on that country's soil, we will find nothing more than 'groups' of intellectuals tending to their own backyards. But if we turn our gaze to the results, we see that no political party of the working class has ever achieved as much as the new industrial unionism did within the framework of the New Deal. American workers are still drawing the annuities from those historic conquests. This will scandalise the high priests of the revolution: the best-paid working class in the world won once, and it has allowed itself the caprice of enjoying the fruits of victory.

At this point, we can argue that the early CIO was the most advanced working-class political-organisational experience thus far possible on American soil. To succeed where the Knights of Labor and Eugene V. Debs, the American Railway Union and the IWW, De Leon and the Communists had failed was no easy task. The first industrial unionism met with success and imposed a level of organisation which was, in that moment, perfectly adequate to a class in struggle within the bounds of a specific situation. An organisation ought to be judged not for the results it has bequeathed over the course of its long-term historical development, but for the political function it fulfilled in the given moment in which it emerged. The relationship between struggles and organisation within the upward phase of the New Deal could only be posed in political terms. The new union was a political fact for three reasons: because it came out of a terrain of real and advanced working-class struggles, because it responded to a new working class's need for new organisation, and because it crossed paths with a great initiative undertaken by capital. We should not remain prisoners of the names given to things. A party can call itself the 'political organisation of the working class' in its statutes and, in reality, be an association of undertakers, a mutual aid society, like the AFL was in 1933. A union can limit its programmes within the narrow field of the immediate working-class interest, and yet, for this very reason, play the function of a party in a given moment – that is, fulfil the political task ·of mounting a confrontation with the system. The working class is freer and more uninhibited on the terrain of organisation than in any other field. It knows that organisation alone is never enough for victory and that it also needs help from capital; it knows that organisation must hold firm to a specific layer of workers in industry, who are then the very workers who trigger the struggle in a given moment; it knows that these struggles must begin from the working-class condition within the factory and then mount an offensive on the grounds of the social distribution of the nation's wealth. In this sense, the US workers' tradition of organisation is the most political of anywhere in the world, because the charge of their struggles is the closest to the economic defeat of the adversary, the closest not to the conquest of power aimed at building another society over the void, but to the wage boom which can render capital and the capitalists subaltern within this society itself. Adolph Strasser once said that 'We have no ultimate ends. We are going on from day to day. We are fighting only for immediate objects.' Samuel Gompers later said 'More and ever more of the product of our labor." For John Lewis, 'Let the workers organize. Let the toilers assemble. Let their crystallized voice proclaim their injustices and demand their privileges.' For those who know how to see it, there is a path running through all these statements. The American workers' organisational experience, from the International Cigar Makers' Union to the AFL and CIO, should not be written off (as has happened thus far); rather, it should force us more seriously to confront a problem of our own. Behind this choice of a particular organisation may be concealed today's response to the eternal question of what the working class is, in general.

Once we have put things in this way, here we find that the Marxist approach, or the orthodox Marxist approach, to the question of the working class proves seriously inadequate. Sometimes we suddenly become aware of our primitive articulation of language, archaic terms that link our thoughts to conditions of expression which are too basic to be able to capture the complexity of the modern social relation. Looking deeper and further back, there rules a whole conceptual apparatus which has not marched with the times, has not renovated itself and transformed even as the levels of struggle have expanded without interruption. It has not updated, as a real theory should, in tandem with the rhythm of politics, but it has stopped at describing our class's prehistoric conditions. This occurs even now that we could say that our class's history has already run almost its whole course. What's more, to read the class struggles in America today with Marx in hand is so difficult as to seem effectively impossible. What needs doing is an interesting job, indeed: a labour of developing a new history, or a new theory, by writing a chapter on the (mis)fortunes of Marx in America. What happened in the United States is the opposite of what happened here in Italy. There, capital's political initiative, its science and (on the other side) working-class organisation have always seen Marx indirectly, through the mediation of the class struggle. Here, conversely, we have always seen the class struggle through the mediation of Marxism. The American situation was objectively Marxian. For at least half a century, up till the aftermath of World War II, it was possible to see Marx in the things going on there; that is, in the struggles and in the responses that the questions posed by struggle provoked. We would do better not to delve into Marx's books looking for an interpretation of the American workers' struggles but rather to seek a more perfect interpretation of the most advanced Marxist texts precisely by reading these struggles. An 'American' reading of *Capital* and the *Grundrisse* is an attractive prospect for whoever has the taste or the knack for critical discovery. Marx, instead, had to mediate an advanced strategic perspective for capital with reference to the backward situations in the countries of Europe, looking at them nation by nation. Marx himself thus needed ideological readings, tactical applications such as could link – as in Italy – the advanced points of the system with the holes in which it is marked by backwardness. For this reason, there has been a creative development of Marxism only where working-class organisation has bridged that gap of practical activity, of politics, in the relation between what proceeds under its own steam and what follows only when it is forced to do so. Marx and the party then seem to have had the same function and the same fate. The US working class has done without either. But it has not done without an organisational tool of its own, or the need for a science of its own. There is a whole American history of organisations that are not parties and yet are true working-class organisations. It is almost as if there were a non-Marxist yet truly working-class current of thought. A strong working class is not as jealous of its own autonomy as the semi-subaltern layers that seek a revolutionary outcome to their own desperate situation. A strong working class is able to use the capitalist organisation of industrial labour as its own form of organisation; it is able to capture the findings of capital's intellectuals, sympathetic to the workers, as the form of its own science. In this regard, John Roger Commons' reflection in his 1913 book *Labor and Administration* is worth citing in full. Two years earlier, Taylor had published his *Principles of Scientific Management* and, in 1912, he had made his deposition to the US Congress's special commission. Commons was enthused because worker psychology was finally being analysed with experiments as accurate as those used in the chemical testing of different types of carbon: 'a new engineering profession springs up with industrial psychology as its underlying science. Wonderful and interesting are these advances in harnessing the forces of human nature to the production of wealth.' The pioneers in this field could be compared to the great inventors of the turbine and the dynamo, because they sought to reduce costs and multiply efficiency: 'But in doing so they are doing exactly the thing that forces labor to become *class*-conscious. While a man retains individuality, he is more or less proof against class feeling. He is *self*-conscious ... But when his individuality is scientifically measured off in aliquot parts and each part is threatened with substitution by identical parts of other men, then his sense of superiority is gone. He and his fellow-workmen compete with each other, not as whole men, but as units of output. The less-gifted man becomes a menace to the more gifted as much as the one to the other. Both are then ripe to recognize their solidarity, and to agree not to compete. And this is the essential thing in class conflict.'[8] This was not yet at the level of the true institutionalism of the Wisconsin school. But

---

8   John Commons, *Labor and Administration*, Toronto: Macmillan, 1913, 74–5.

here we have already grasped a precise awareness of the political consequences that the scientific organisation of work produces in the class
struggle within capital. There is a long line of thought and of practical
experimentation that runs from German *Sozialpolitik* to the American
technique of industrial government. It would be worth following the
path from Karl Knies's 'old' historical school to Gustav Schmoller's
'young' one, to its American transplant by Richard T. Ely, through
Veblen's rich and penetrating work, up to the institutionalists' own
'Wisconsin theory': Adams, Commons, Selig Perlman and maybe even
Tannenbaum. Within this line of investigation into the working class,
research into labour breaks apart. Task management and, more generally, industrial engineering – industrial production techniques as the
scientific organisation of labour – are the other side of the realistic
discourse on the pragmatic approach to the moment of working-class
struggle or, as they put it, to the moment of conflict, as the basis of the
various forms of class organisation. This allows us better to understand
the 'look and see' principle, the re-elaboration of Veblen's concepts of
'efficiency' and 'scarcity', and their possible compatibility through the
corrective of 'collective action'. *Avant la lettre new dealers*, as Giugni put
it, the institutionalists were ready not only to accept, but also to theorise
Roosevelt's programme. In his article 'The Principles of Collective
Bargaining', published in 1936, Perlman argued that collective bargaining 'is much less concerned with algebraic formulae summing up basic
economic trends than with the problems of building discipline in organization and of training leaders'.[9] 'Job consciousness', or the 'communism
of economic opportunities', the natural economic pessimism of groups
of workers, and the absolute gap between the working-class mentality
and the political-ideological mentality are not just brilliant definitions
produced by brilliant minds. They are precious factual observations
regarding the historical condition of a concrete working class in the land
of capital-in-general. All of us have committed the original sin of having
considered the working class 'an abstract mass in the grip of abstract
forces'. The polemical rejection which has crushed the figure of the
Marxist intellectual in the egg and which has always prevented him
from intervening in the real struggles of the American workers'

---

9   Selig Perlman, 'The Principle of Collective Bargaining', *The Annals of the American
Academy of Political and Social Science*, March 1936, 154.

movement is one of the very rare traditions which we will have to make our own in the immediate future. If even after falsifying the data it is impossible to present the worker as the 'knight of the ideal', the scholar of labour cannot dress himself up as the teacher of revolutionary morality. Perlman has written that Commons was completely free of the most insidious kind of snobbery: to condescendingly lend one's superior brain to the cause of the weak.

Sichtbar Machen

Sichtbar machen: making things visible: saying things clearly in order to be understood, perhaps at the risk of not interpreting very sharply things that are necessarily obscure. Despite the difficult title, this section is the easiest of all. We must free ourselves of the temptation to talk about problems in dogmatic terms. Today, it is better to emphasise the critical terms of the situation and to begin by pinning down the open problematic framework for our research. It is pointless to look for the easiest paths or for shortcuts. Rather, we should start from the points that are hardest for us to understand and then explain simple things by way of the more complex. As we have mentioned, for a contemporary Marxist research has a point of no return. It is this modern sphinx, this obscure enigma, this social thing-in-itself that we know exists but which remains unknowable: the *American working class*. Here we must fix our sights on a more distant horizon, in order to try and see that there is a form of more restricted Eurocentrism which ought to be condemned: one that refers only to European revolutionary experiences whenever we seek or cite models of correct behaviour in the struggle. We ought to explode the legend that the history of the working class had its epicentre in Europe and in Russia. This is a nineteenth-century vision which has persisted to this day thanks to those last splendid rays of the nineteenth-century labour movement in Western Europe represented by the years immediately following World War I and the early 1920s. We talk about two major trends in the labour movement: social democracy and communism. Yet, when we compare them to the American labour movement, we find that, in spite of their apparent irreducible diversity, both of them turn out to be united in a single bloc. To reconnect the situation of the British or German working class to that of the Italian or

French working class, we need only set all of them in counterposition to the situation of the American working class. These are the two major trends in the history of working-class struggles and the only further particular points of view possible within the general working-class point of view. This is not a matter of establishing a hierarchy of nobility, nor of compiling a list of preferences for one or the other; rather, the important thing is to see how they play respectively in our context of class struggle, how they help us understand reality, and how they advance, suggest or rule out particular organisational tools in the factory and means of intervention on the terrain of state power. From this point of view, the traditional disadvantages of the American class situation become opportunities for us. What is different in American working-class struggles is precisely what remains to be done on the old continent. No, we do not want to reiterate the Marxian concept of the most advanced point explaining and prefiguring the most backward one. That would be all too easy a way of getting around the problem, and we have, in any case, already indicated elsewhere how this explanation conceals the danger of political opportunism and turns out to be a manifestation of that passive waiting for events, which disarms the working class politically while leaving it lagging behind history. If we want to start out from the working-class struggles in America, we need to find other explanations. Marxist analysis has not left us even a schematic set of narratives of the major struggles, nor a model of how to judge major events; and yet while this seems to be a serious handicap to research, on closer analysis it turns out to be perhaps the most favourable condition for its development. We have not ourselves hidden reality under ideological veils; these ones would be the most difficult to tear away, since while it is easy to criticise the ideology of the adversary, it is difficult and sometimes, for a series of circumstantial reasons, impossible to criticise our own ideologies. The facts of the history of the European working class are literally submerged under the ideas of Marxist intellectuals. But the facts of the history of the American working class are still raw and exposed, without anyone ever having thought them through. The less critique of ideology needed, the easier it is for scientific discoveries to make progress. The smaller the contribution of leftist culture, the more the wholly *class* import of a given social reality comes forward. Today, working-class struggles need a new *unit of measurement* because the old one, ours, is no longer adequate or useful. A new *standard of judgement* has to be applied to the facts of the working class in a given situation. It must be a standard that revolves around the present in motion, a standard thus contained within that political type of industrial reality which marks the steps, the path, and the development of contemporary society. We must avoid measuring the present against the past, working-class struggles against proletarian uprisings and refuse to compare today's reality with the 'glories' that immediately preceded it, to which we are so sentimentally bound. Equally, we should avoid judging the present by the yardstick of the future, and likewise refuse modern management's invitation to turn working-class struggles into a kind of social cybernetics – a psycho-industrial automatism in service of collective profit. Today we must steer clear of these two easy temptations: historical tradition and technological futurism.

In Part IV of his *Economics*, Samuelson opens the chapter on competitive wages and collective bargaining with a quote from the New Testament: 'The labourer is worth of his hire', and concludes with a section on the unresolved problems of labour, strikes, rising costs and structural unemployment. For Samuelson, 'Science like capital grows through a series of contribution, through which the supply that each scholar brings to its altar blooms eternally.' He goes on to say that, in the postwar years, in some countries, there has been an attempt to introduce a new element to collective bargaining and macroeconomic policy in order to maintain the general increase in wages and in other monetary income at a rate compatible with the increase in productivity and with stable prices. But in controlling the various types of wage dynamics, the mixed economy has stabilised only at a level of *imperfect planning*. If an income policy could be found that prevented the inflation of sales prices due to rising costs, the ice block of structural unemployment could be dissolved by an increased aggregate demand strengthened by retraining and relocation programmes. Yet the danger is that each point in the economic cycle seems to have a disruptive tendency. This is nothing new in capitalist development. Every downturn of the cycle is provoked, preceded or followed by a determinate high development of working-class struggles. Such a downturn is represented by a particular moment of the class struggle, and it is difficult to figure out why a certain development took place, *how* it developed and above all, *which* of the two classes can be said to have ultimately won. The economist tells us that every point of the economic cycle has many tendencies which develop it and *one* that upsets it. In the best of cases, the entrepreneur turns to the economist in order to know which is the one. What once seemed absolutely right has become only relative and *economic*. What is closer to the class truth that coincides with a particular class interest: the workers' universal claim to a fair wage or the distribution of income in a given country according to the 'Lorenz curve'? This must first be decided at its highest level of development: capital has already replaced the rough approximations of professional ideologists with the precision work of computers. The 'Phillips Curve' for the United States is decidedly 'bad', because it intersects with the axis of price stability only at a high level of unemployment. The cost push has become an institutional problem because capitalist control of wages is still yet to come. Nobel laureate Samuelson, with his high science, 'After looking at Dutch, Swedish, British, Italian, German, Canadian, and American experience, I leave all this as an open question.'

And yet it would be all too comfortable to define every problem that capital finds in the path of its development as irresolvable. We should not immediately say: you cannot resolve it, only we can do that for you. A problem for capital is, first of all, a terrain for working-class struggle. Its economic terrain is our political terrain. While capital looks for a solution, we are only interested in increasing our organised strength. We know that each of capital's economic problems can ultimately be resolved. We also know that what appears here as an irresolvable contradiction may already have been overcome elsewhere or may have become *another* contradiction. From the working-class point of view, the premise for a powerful and effective class struggle moving in the sense of a positive violence is the *specific knowledge of the specific contradiction* for capital at a given moment and in a given situation. A working-class victory forces the backward owner to take revenge in various ways, in a quantitative assault on that new part of income that labour has conquered. Sometimes this happens for want of economic margins and, at others, on account of a lack of political intelligence. This is not the real point where the working-class victory is turned into a defeat; such a crude answer by the bosses only promotes the repetition of a cycle of struggles at the same level as the earlier one, with a higher charge of spontaneity and therefore a lesser need for organisation. Following this path, the movement of the struggles is easier, mobilisation is simultaneously both great and simple, and the moment of generalisation is immediate. But the new contents and new forms of the working-class assault do not grow; if the massive obstacle to a frontal confrontation on a backward terrain is not first subjectively swept aside by the contending class forces, then there will be no new working-class struggles. In other instances, however, the bosses' answer may itself be defined as advanced. After a partial defeat, even following a simple contractual battle, capital is violently driven to come to terms with itself – in other words, to reconsider precisely the quality of its development, to readdress the issues in its relation with its class adversary. It does so not in a direct form, but through the mediation of a type of general initiative involving the reorganisation of the productive process, the restructuring of the market, rationalisation within the factory and the planning of society. It seeks help from technology and politics, new ways of using labour and new forms of exercising authority. And here is the truly great danger of working-class defeat: even if the workers have 'won the battle' over the contract, they can, for this very reason, 'lose the war' of the class struggle over a sometimes long historical period. This is why America has so much to teach. There they risk defeat if the level of organisation fails quickly to advance the contents of the new struggles, if the conscious-ness of the movement – which is to say, the already organised structure of the class – fails immediately to grasp the meaning of the coming capi-talist initiative. Those who arrive too late will lose out. Mind, the task here is not to hurry along preparations for an answer to the boss's move: rather, it is above all a matter of foreseeing this move, in some cases of suggesting it, and in all cases anticipating it with the forms of working-class organisation, in order to render this move not only unproductive for capitalist goals, but productive for the working class's. For our part, the only answer needed is one responding to the working-class demand for new organisation at each fresh level of confrontation. Capital's move, its present initiative, both on the level of production in the heavens of formal policy, must itself be the *answer*, the attempt always to resist the different forms assumed by the working class's attack. And the reorgani-sation of this attack goes on under the radar – given its historical nature and political direction, it must be *unpredictable* from an organisational perspective.

Lenin used to say: there is spontaneity and then there is spontaneity. Today we say: there is organisation and then there is organisation. But even before all this, there is struggle and then there is struggle. A complete

typology of working-class struggles, with relevant marginal notes, is a
manual for the perfect trade unionist – something we do not wish to put
into circulation. In the recent context of the class conflict in the Western
world, the working-class struggle has isolated certain fundamental *types*.
These recur and reproduce themselves by continually heading back from
the most advanced to the most backward points, elevating the meaning
of the contents and the dimensions of the forces set in motion. There is
the great contemporary fact of the struggle over the contract. For us, it is
a lived reality. It is a new type of landmark, which has already become
common parlance in the street. Yet even prior to that, it had forcibly
introduced itself into the normal existence of the average worker, into the
calculations of the economist, into the projects of the politician and into
the mechanisms of society's material functioning. When, after a long and
uncertain path, capital stumbled upon the idea of collective bargaining
with its workforce, guaranteed by state laws, one era of the class struggle
ended and another began. Collective bargaining must serve, and *does
serve*, to discriminate between different historical levels of capitalism's
development. It does so more than turning points like the birth of finance
capital, the various 'stages' of imperialism, the so-called 'ages' of monopolies, at least in the theories of the miserly epigones. Here, we have an
example of that *working-class history of capital* which is its true history,
and compared to which everything else is just ideological legend, the
dreams of visionaries, the unconscious ability to mislead or the unwanted
will to err on the part of weak subaltern intellectuals. 'A New Way of
settling Labor Disputes', according to the title of one article by Commons
from way back, is what forces capital to make a qualitative leap toward its
mature existence. The dynamic of class relations finds in the collective
contract a form of periodic stabilisation. The price of labour is fixed and
applies across a certain period of time, a new system of industrial juris-
prudence is born and a new mechanism for the representation of workers' interests begins operating. According to the path laid out by Dunlop,
collective bargaining is followed by an industrial relations system with
three actors: managers for the company, unions for the workers and various means of institutional mediation for the government. But the changing, critical and contradictory reality of the struggle over the contract
cannot be captured in the schema of a Parsonian-type abstract subsys-
tem. And this is the point. The contract is first of all a *struggle for the
contract*. The collective dimension of the bargaining process has revealed

anew the collective nature of the struggle. As we move from the single company to the entire sector and category, the number of participants grows and the mass struggle – and these masses are exclusively working-class – comes to the fore. This is no small detail. For too long – and even today – working-class struggles and mass struggles have been considered mutually exclusive. As a generic 'people', the working masses could *include* the active minority of vanguard groups but failed to *identify with* their actions, dissolving their specific demands in a set of formal political ones, thus moving the centre of the confrontation from the factory to the streets – a fight not against the enduring state but against the government of the moment. The *Massenstreik* – even if it is not Sorel's myth of the general strike, but, in Luxemburg's sense, a struggle that precedes and makes the organisation – always ends up as the feat of what is not a specifically *class* movement. That is, until the working-class struggle itself assumes mass dimensions and until the concrete concept of the *working-class masses in struggle* emerges from social relations rather than merely in the sacred texts of ideology. Here, the concept of the mass does not lie in the quantitative aggregation of many individual units under the 'same' condition for exploitation – if that were so, then the term 'class', in the usual statistical meaning lumped on it by the Marxist tradition, would suffice. Rather, here we are talking about a process of the massification of the working class. This is the process of the workers' growth as a class and of the internal homogenisation of industrial labour-power.

In this process, if, for us, *politics* is the working-class struggle that surges to ever-higher qualitative levels, and *history* is the capital which, on this basis, updates its technological and productive structures, its organisation of work, its instruments for controlling and manipulating society, and which substitutes obsolete parts of its power mechanism upon the objective suggestion of its class adversary – then politics always precedes history. There is no possible process of class-massification unless a mass level of struggle has first been reached. In other words, there is no true *class* growth of the workers without mass *working-class* struggle. Collective bargaining stands precisely between the massification of the struggle and that of the class. We do not start with the class, but arrive at it. Or, better, we reach a new level of class composition. We begin with struggle. At the beginning, the struggle will have the same characteristics that will subsequently become attached to the class itself. That is not to say that before the mass working-class struggle there was no working class. Rather, it was a different working class, at a lower level of development, with a clearly less dense internal composition, and with a shallower and certainly less complex pattern of organisational possibility. Not only would we be mistaken to formulate a concept of 'class' that applies across all eras of human history. Whoever seeks to even define the class once and for all within the development of capitalist society is also making an error. Workers and capital are not only classes standing opposed to each other, but ever-changing economic realities, social formations and political organisations. There are methodological problems that need heeding in the body of the investigation. But again, this is not the thing most worth emphasising. We should proceed in the aforementioned direction, going from the struggle to the class, and from the mass struggle to the massification of the class, but through the new reality, the new discovery, the new capitalist concept of the collective contract. The working-class struggle had already taken on mass characteristics when capital forced it to transform into a struggle over the contract. Collective bargaining is a form of control. It is an attempt to institutionalise not the working-class struggle in general, but that specific form of struggle that encompasses, binds and unifies the immediate material interests of a compact core of categories of workers within the corresponding sector of capitalist production. When, through the content of its demands, its forms of mobilisation and its models of organisation, it takes on mass characteristics, the working-class struggle runs the risk of losing its specifically working-class character. The original proletarian struggles, along with certain kinds of working-class struggles from the nineteenth century into the twentieth, have not only run this risk, but fallen victim to it. When the working-class struggle begins to assume mass characteristics while remaining firmly based on the working class – that is, when the mass struggle becomes a working-class struggle without ceasing to be massified – it marks the beginning of a new period in politics and therefore of a new history. To use words richer in meaning, this is the none-too-distant starting point for a possible new working-class politics and thus of a first real new economics for capital.

This new politics of the working-class was articulated in the American labour struggles of the 1930s. Even if they are more limited in quantitative terms, the Italian struggles of the 1960s are the adequate reflection of this red sun coming from the West, without adding too many shadows. Here, we face very important theoretical problems. We are not yet sufficiently mature to be able to prefigure the solution to a long and slow critical-historical investigation. Can one, for instance, abandon an 'objective' definition of the working class? Is it possible to define as 'working class' all those who subjectively struggle in working-class forms against capital, from within the social production process? Is it possible to finally separate the concept of the working class from the concept of productive labour? And, in such a case, would it still remain connected to wages? The problem is how to find new definitions of the 'working class' without abandoning the domain of objective analysis and without falling back in ideological traps. To reduce the objective materiality of the working class into purely subjective forms of anticapitalist struggles is another ideological error of the new ultra-leftism. Not only this, but to broaden the sociological boundaries of the working class in order to embrace all those struggling against capitalism from within, such as to reach the quantitative majority of the social workforce or even of the active population, is a grave concession to democratic traditions. On the other hand, to restrict these boundaries too far, to the point of making only 'the few that count' workers, can lead to the dangerous theorisation of the 'active minority'. We should steer clear of these extremes. The analysis of the outer limits of the class must be an observation of the facts. The consequences will come later. The working class does not end where capital begins.

The line of argument in this book tended to see workers and capital within capital. The discourse added by this postscript tends to see workers and capital within the working class. Thus, the more recent tendency is to consciously complicate the domain of investigation, in the hope that this will open the way to the simplest solution. Certainly, advanced capitalism today offers us a spectacle and gives us all the instruments to participate in this play of autonomies that move beyond simply formal: namely, the autonomies between the political sphere and the economic world, between science and the short-term interests of capitalist production, between working-class organisation and the class precisely as capital. The oversimplifications of economism – base and superstructure – apply to the first phases of capitalism, which resemble precapitalist societies too much to be seriously considered politically. And the voluntarism of pure politics – revolution at all costs – lies, if it was ever possible, even further back, as a still-utopian, millenarian socialism: a modern medieval heresy, admitted by the Pope as a class church. Mature capitalism is a complex, stratified and contradictory society. Such a society has more than one centre claiming to be the source of power and struggling for supremacy against the others, but this is never resolved, because it never can be within this society. This is what the immediate past tells us. It is worth studying only in order to find out what there is to study afterward, in other words, *today*. In fact, we must not confuse the two levels.

Historically, yesterday's American political situation is our own present. We should know that we are living through events that have already been lived elsewhere but have no preconstituted outcomes or sure conclusions. Here in Italy, we are really at the fork in the road between capital being raised as a power above everything and everyone, and an opening toward infinite possibilities for the working class. This is, let us say, the plan for political action. It was no accident that we first addressed this element here. Then there is the other level. Today's United States is the theoretical problem for the future of all. We have already mentioned this. It is worth reiterating. Today, there is a kind of sensation, an idea felt more than thought, of having reached the final limit of a classic era of the class struggle. In spite of all that we have said, America's working-class struggles perhaps had to be translated into European language just so that the working-class point of view could fully become conscious of them. And this becoming-conscious will surely destroy a tradition from the past. Building further requires leaving behind our present of classical working-class struggles and entering, with the anticipation of research, into a postclassical epoch of our own. And if the history of capital is any guide, this might bring out the spark of a working-class 'general theory'. 'They' will be forced to head toward new forms of 'industrial government'. 'We' must reject the temptation to go off and write *Die Froehliche Klassenkampf*. We must instead devote ourselves to inventing, in the interests of practice itself, never-yet-seen techniques allowing the working class to make political use of the capitalist economic machine. And we must do so with a long-term strategic perspective, which is nonetheless always a temporary one.

December 1970

Our *Operaismo*[1]

The Italian *operaismo* of the 1960s starts with the birth of *Quaderni Rossi* and stops with the death of *Classe Operaia*. End of story. Thus goes the argument. Or, alternatively – *si le grain ne meurt* – *operaismo* is repro- duced in other ways, reincarnated, transformed, corrupted and ... lost. This text originally sprang from the urge to clarify the intellectual distinction between *operaismo* – 'workerism' as the inadequate but unavoidable English translation – and post-*operaismo*, or the *autonomia* movements of the late 1970s and after. Then the sweet pleasures of remembrance did the rest. Whether this 'rest' is in good taste or of any use today will be for its readers to judge. This is my truth, based on what I believed back then and which I only see more clearly today. I don't want to provide a canonical interpretation of that project, but this is one of the possible readings, one-sided enough to support the good old idea of partisan research, that indigestible theoretical practice of 'point of view' that formed us.

I say we, because I believe I can speak for a handful of people insepa- rably linked by a bond of political friendship, who shared a common knot of problems as 'lived thought'. For us, the classic political friend/ enemy distinction was not just a concept of the enemy, but a theory and

1 Extract from *Noi operaisti,* published by DeriveApprodi in 2009. Originally translated by Eleanor Chiari and published in *New Left Review,* 73, January–February 2012.

a practice of the friend as well. We became and have remained friends because we discovered, politically, a common enemy in front of us; this had consequences that determined the intellectual decisions of the time and the horizons that followed. I shall try to speak simply, eschewing literary language. Yet it needs to be said that 1960s *operaismo* forged its own 'high style' of writing – chiselled, lucid, confrontational, in which we thought we grasped the rhythm of the factory workers in struggle against the bosses. Each historical passage chooses its own form of symbolic representation.

Semi-literate partisans facing Nazi execution squads produced the *Lettere di condannati a morte della Resistenza*, a work of art.[2] In the same way, the boys who stood outside the gates of the Mirafiori factory in Turin in the early morning went home at night to read the young Lukács's *Soul and Form*. Strong thought requires strong writing. A sense of the grandeur of the conflict awoke in us a passion for the Nietzschean style: to speak in a noble register, in the name of those beneath.

I have never forgotten the lesson we learned at the factory gates, when we arrived with our pretentious leaflets, inviting workers to join the anticapitalist struggle. The answer, always the same, coming from the hands that accepted our bits of paper. They would laugh and say, 'What is it? Money?' A 'rough pagan race' indeed. This was not the bourgeois mandate, *enrichissez-vous*; it was the word, wages, presented as an objectively antagonistic reply to the word, profit. *Operaismo* reworked Marx's brilliant phrase – the proletariat attaining its own emancipation will free all humanity – to read: the working class, by following its own, partial interests creates a general crisis in the relations of capital. *Operaismo* marked a way of thinking politically. Thought and history encountered each other in a direct, immediate and frontal clash. The result had to be exposed to analysis, reflection, criticism and judgement. What had been said and written on it came later.

The biographical account that follows retains an element of ambiguity between personal and generational registers. But I should say at the outset that my *operaismo* was of a Communist kind. This was not the case for the most part, even in the early days; party members were never a majority within Italian workerism, nor dominant in *Quaderni Rossi* or

---

2 Piero Malvezzi and Giovanni Pirelli, eds, *Lettere di condannati a morte della Resistenza italiana, 8 settembre 1943–25 aprile 1945*, Turin: Einaudi, 1952.

Classe Operaia; the combination was perhaps my personal issue. Here, I will describe the *Lehrjahre* – the formative apprenticeship years – of the *operaisti*, a limited but significant generational faction. A clumsy historian of events, as well as ideas, I will try to explain the complex, early stabs at the *operaisti* argument and some of what came after.

Rupture of '56

One key date emerges as a strategic locus for us all: 1956. Several things made that year 'unforgettable', but I would stress the transition – in effect, an epistemological rupture – from a party truth to a class truth. The time span from the Soviet Twentieth Party Congress to the Hungarian events constituted a sequence of leaps in the awareness of a young generation of intellectuals. I sensed, even before I consciously thought it, that the twentieth century ended there. We awoke from the dogmatic slumber of historicity. In Italy, the rule of the proper noun, as substantive or adjective, materialist or idealist – the De Sanctis–Labriola–Croce–Gramsci line – had exercised an unparalleled cultural hegemony in politics. Thanks to Togliatti's charisma, a powerful group of PCI leaders had formed around it in the postwar period and now set about putting it to work. At the Istituto Gramsci, you could encounter party members from the Directorate and the Secretariat. They didn't write books, or get improbable ghostwriters to do so for them. They read books. And, between each initiative, they discussed what they thought of them.

At a certain point, a strange-looking character arrived from Sicily. He had been teaching in Messina and was tall, wiry, with a hooked nose and hawkish face. He spoke in difficult language and his writing was even harder to understand. But Della Volpe took apart, piece by piece, the cultural line of the Italian Communists, paying no heed to orthodox allegiances.[3] To be honest: we freed ourselves from the PCI's Gramscian 'national-popular', but a certain intellectual aristocratism still clung to us. Understanding was more important than persuasion; toiling over the concept created difficulties with the word. Today, the

---

3 See also Galvano Della Volpe, 'The Marxist Critique of Rousseau', *New Left Review* I, 59, Jan–Feb 1970, and 'Settling Accounts with the Russian Formalists', *New Left Review* I, 113–114, Jan–April 1979.

opposite is true – ease of discourse means dispensing with thought. The approach we took then seems all the more valuable now, when the triumph of mediatised vulgarity over political language is complete. Ours was a school of ascetic intellectual rigour, which came at the cost of a slightly self-referential isolation. Science against ideology – that was the paradigm. Marx *contra* Hegel, like Galileo against the Scholastics or Aristotle against the Platonists. Then, broadly speaking, we outgrew this schema as far as content was concerned, while retaining its lessons with regard to method. On reflection, it was precisely on this basis that, from 1956 onward, while others – the majority – were rediscovering the value of bourgeois freedoms, we few were given the chance to discover, one step at a time, by trial and error, the horizons of communist liberty.

I remain unsure about the choice of political tactics at that point – not what was 'correct', but what would have been most useful. It's true that, at times, little depends on your own decisions and much on circumstances, openings, encounters. But there was another path open to us in 1956: that of political growth within the mass-membership PCI, whose leadership had embarked upon a period of 'renewal in continuity'. What would this second path have entailed? A long march through the organisation; a cultural sacrifice on the altar of praxis; the exercise of that Renaissance political category, 'honest dissimulation'. In my personal formation, Togliatti was a master politician par excellence. I ask myself if it would have been possible to be a Togliattian, but with a different culture – and answer yes. Politics has an autonomy of its own, even from the cultural framework that sustains and at times legitimates it. We let ourselves get carried away by the fascinating pleasure of alternative thinking. But the lingering doubt remains that the other path may have been the right one: saying a little less and doing a little more. The theoretical discovery of the 'autonomy of the political' took place within the practical experience of *operaismo*; it was only its historical-conceptual elaboration that came later – and with it, the realisation of having failed to reach a synthesis of 'inside and against'.

Some years ago, I wrote: 'We young communist intellectuals were right to be on the side of the Hungarian insurgents. But – this is the paradox of the revolution in the West – the socialist State was not wrong in bringing the contest to an end with tanks'.[4] This is the kind of sentence that even one's closest friends, precisely because they wish you well, pretend not to have read. Yet resolving this Oedipal enigma of the twentieth-century labour movement was exactly the task that confronted us. It is easy to choose between right and wrong; what's hard is when you have to choose between two rights, both of them internal to your side. The dilemma is whether to pursue the passion of belonging or the calculus of possibilities. The two rights of 1956 were also the two wrongs, dividing those who saw only the possible development of what would be called 'socialism with a human face' from those whose sole yardstick was immediate control over emplacements, in the crossfire between the two opposing blocs.

Yet one of the most significant critical analyses of the Soviet system came from within *operaismo*. Rita Di Leo's *Operai e sistema sovietico* demonstrated that starting from the point of view of the workers made it possible to comprehend a great deal more than the capitalist factory.[5] The workers' political experiment par excellence was here brought critically into play. It remained an extremely isolated analysis: truth and fact coincided too closely for it to be welcomed by the two dominant, opposing ideologies.

It was in the early 1960s that an *operaista* group began to form spontaneously. Not in the way that 'groups' became institutionalised in the early 1970s. Ours was an original, completely informal way of coming together, politically and culturally. It is strange how, over time, a sort of mutual affection has remained, even among those comrades who did not make the same journey from *Quaderni Rossi* to *Classe Operaia*. I still feel a deep sympathy, recalling the human qualities of people such as Bianca Beccalli, Dario and Liliana Lanzardo, Mario Miegge, Giovanni Mottura, Vittorio Rieser, Edda Saccomani, Michele Salvati and more. *Quaderni Rossi* was a beautiful title for a journal, with an evocative simplicity, eloquent in itself. 'Notebooks' expressed the will for research, analysis and study. The red of the cover was the sign of a decision, a commitment to be this. To start the writing, and therefore the reading, on the front cover – black on red – was a brilliant idea on Panzieri's part.

---

4   Tronti, *La politica al tramonto*, Turin: Einaudi, 1998.
5   Rita Di Leo, *Operai e sistema sovietico*, Bari: Laterza, 1970.

Raniero – he died in 1964, in his early forties – was one of those fated to spend too little time on this earth. Enough, though, to leave a trace. Remembering him today, thinking about him again, I feel nostalgia for a lost political humanity. He was not by nature a romantic hero, but became one by force of circumstance. He wanted to go from being an organiser of *operaismo* to being the organiser of workers' culture. But he couldn't really organise anything. There lay the charm of his limitations, so similar to our own – to mine in particular – which made us feel close to him. Panzieri's Marx was that of Luxemburg, not Lenin. Like Rosa, he read *Capital* and imagined the revolution … unlike Lenin, who read *Capital* in order to organise the revolution. He was not, and could never have been, a Communist. His tradition was that of revolutionary syndicalism, with a dose of the anarchic socialism that the old PSI historically bore within itself. But 'workers' control' was a magic word that woke us from that other dogmatic slumber – the Socialists' 'party of all the people'.

To walk with Raniero at night through the streets of Rome or Milan – not the hated Turin – was to realise Benjamin's idea of 'losing oneself' in the streets of a city. There is an art, too, to losing oneself in the polis – that of politics; we put all our efforts into mastering that art. More than once we got lost and found ourselves on the boundary that divides one side from another, without ever crossing it. We preferred enlightened bosses, but only the better to fight the war that interested us. We were not enamoured of progressive democracy, but used it as a more advanced field of struggle. Intuitively, we recognised the reformists of the left as serious functionaries of the capitalist general intellect (reigning today at the Euro-global level). We valued the movementist impulse as a passion rather than as a fact. It was an event of the political imagination which we thought about constantly – and practised, a far more serious matter.

Quaderni Rossi turned on the lights inside the factory, focused the lens and took a photograph, in which the relations of production stood out with startling clarity. Whatever has been said about ex-workerist intellectuals, there is always a consensus that the analyses of its workers' enquiries were 'lucid'. *Operaismo* opened up a new way of engaging in sociology: Weberian methodology mixed with the politics of Marxist analysis. In that sense, looking back between *Quaderni Rossi* and *Classe Operaia*, or between Vittorio Rieser and Romano Alquati, there was less disagreement than we thought at the time. The debt of Italian sociology to *operaismo* is now widely recognised, but the latter also offered a context in which to envisage new ways of history. Umberto Coldagelli and Gaspare De Caro opened a critical path with their 'Marxist research hypotheses on contemporary history', in *Quaderni Rossi* 3. Coldagelli began his long venture into the political and institutional history of France; Sergio Bologna began research on Germany, Nazism and the working class.

Paths Through Purgatory

Our disagreement with Panzieri and the sociologists of *Quaderni Rossi* arose over the idea and practice of politics; nothing else. The primacy of politics was present from the start in *Classe Operaia*, launched in 1963 as 'the political newspaper of the workers in struggle'. The slogan of my editorial, 'Lenin in England', in the first issue – 'first the workers, then capital'; that is, it is workers' struggles that drive the course of capitalist development – that was politics: will, decision, organisation, conflict. The movement from analysing workers' conditions, as *Quaderni Rossi* continued to do, to intervening in the claims they advanced for their class interests was what gave the leap from the journal to the newspaper its meaning. And, if *Quaderni Rossi* effected an innovation in content, *Classe Operaia* was also a revolution in forms. The choice of graphics was a matter of high-level craftsmanship; poets and writers, from Babel to Brecht, Mayakovsky to Eluard, crowded its pages; it pioneered comic-strip political satire – the victorious dragon chasing a fleeing Saint George, in a reversal of bondsman and lord. We saw *Classe Operaia* as the *Politecnico* – the legendary postwar cultural weekly – of the factory workers.

Inscribed on the paper's red masthead were Marx's words: 'But the revolution is thorough. It is still on its journey through purgatory. It goes about its business methodically'. *Die Revolution ist gründig.* Togliatti's translation/interpretation: it goes to the bottom of things. Not bad. That *aber* at the beginning was crucial; a significant doubt. Today we no longer know if it is still working methodically, or perhaps precariously, or whether it has in fact retired. Long, slow periods of restoration are prone – more than other epochs – to will-o'-the-wisps of revolutionary illusion; between 1848 and 1871, Marx saw several of them. From our small corner, we saw others, and this would later be one of the selection criteria for those who took the *operaista* experience onto the field of struggle. Today, the famous split within *Quaderni Rossi* may seem, at first glance, to have been due to the incompatibility of figures such as Panzieri and Romano Alquati. They came together on the basis of a shared research project but could not coexist. In Alquati, intellectual disarray was raised to the level of genius. He saw not so much what is, as what was coming into being. He told us that it was only as an adult, when he was finally able to buy himself some spectacles, that he realised fields were green. Alquati would invent and thus intuit; he would say he was always a step ahead. But it was he who showed us how the young Fiat workers were waging their struggle.

In other words, we brought together a fine old madhouse. During our meetings, we would spend half the time talking, the rest laughing. And apart from a few rank-and-file PCI militants, I've never yet met people of higher human worth than those I associated with first at *Quaderni Rossi* and then at *Classe Operaia*: such selfless public interventions, free of all personal ambition; such a straightforward sense of commitment; and not least, such a disenchanted, self-ironizing way of sharing collective work. The comrades from *Quaderni Rossi* are better known, and they have been pardoned by the inimical times that followed, welcomed into the Parnassus of the well intentioned. The *Classe Operaia* comrades are less cited and more often denounced; I remember them with infinite nostalgia. These young men and women did not theorise 'a new way of doing politics'. They practised it.

Our Workerism

What, then, is *operaismo*? An experience of intellectual formation, with years of novicehood and pilgrimage; an episode in the history of the workers' movement, oscillating between forms of the struggle and organisational solutions; an attempt to break with Marxist orthodoxy, in Italy and beyond, on the relations between workers and capital; an attempted cultural revolution in the West. In this last sense, *operaismo* was also a specifically twentieth-century event. It emerged at the exact moment of transition when the tragic greatness of the century turned on itself, moving from a permanent state of exception to new 'normal', epochless time. Looking back on the 1960s, we can see that those years had a transitional function. The maximum disorder renewed the existing order. Everything changed so that everything essential could stay the same

The factory worker that we encountered was a twentieth-century figure. We never used the term 'proletariat': 'our' workers were not like those of Engels's Manchester but more like the ones in Detroit. We didn't bring *The Condition of the Working Class in England in 1844* with us to the factories, we brought the struggle of the workers against work in the *Grundrisse*. We were not moved by an ethical revolt against factory workers' exploitation, but by political admiration for the practices of insubordination that they invented. Our *operaismo* should be given credit for not falling into the trap of Third Worldism, of the countryside against the city, of the long farmers' marches. We were never Chinese and the Cultural Revolution of the East left us cold, estranged, more than a little sceptical and indeed strongly critical of it. Red was, and is, our favourite colour; but we know that when guards or brigades take it up, only the worst aspects of human history can come from it.

But we welcomed the fact that twentieth-century workers had disrupted the 'long and glorious' history of the lower classes with their desperate rebellions, their millennial heresies, their recurrent and generous attempts – always painfully repressed – at breaking their chains. In the great factories, the conflict was almost equal. We won and we lost, day by day, in a permanent trench war. We were excited by the forms of struggle but also by its timing, the moments seized, the conditions imposed, the objectives pursued and the means to pursue them: asking for nothing more than was possible, nothing less than what could be obtained. It was another penetrating discovery to find that, during the long phase of seeming quiescence at Fiat – from 1955 (the internal commission election defeat) to the return of general contractual struggles in 1962 – there had not been worker passivity but another kind of wild-cat struggle: the *salto della scocca* ('skipping a chassis'), sabotage on the assembly line, the insubordinate use of Taylorist production schedules.

Yes, these workers were the children of the antifascist workers of 1943, who had rescued warehouses and machinery from Nazi destruction. But they were also heirs to the factory occupations of the

revolutionary years, 1919–20, when the red flag waved over the factories, testimony to the will to do as in Russia. In the forced concentration
of industrial labour in Italy between the 1950s and the '60s, the needs of
breakneck capitalist development created an unprecedented crucible of
historical experiences, daily needs, union dissatisfaction and political
demands; this was what the *operaisti* were trying – naively, no doubt – to
interpret. Blessed naivety which made us – Fortini said well – 'as wise as
doves'. *Operaismo* was our university; we graduated in class struggle –
entitling us not to teach, but to live. The workers' view became a political
means of seeing the world and a human way of operating within it, by
always staying on the same side. The fact is that the whole history of the
first half of the twentieth century converged on the figure of the mass
worker; only the worker-subject who emerged in that time, between
1914 and 1945, and grew up after it, could rise to the height of that
history.

Yet with the 1960s, we were already entering the declining half of the
century; only the miserable course of the decades that followed, through
to the end of the century and beyond, could make it seem a miraculous
season of new beginnings. The qualitative difference between unrest
and revolution requires deeper investigation. To criticise power is one
thing, to put it in crisis is another. The 1960s emancipation of the individual led to the restoration of the old balance of forces, now burnished
with some new reforms. We were the sacrificial victims in this process,
which was not an anomaly but a normal feature of politics. To understand this is not enough to overturn it, but it is a necessary precondition.
The whole discussion on the 'autonomy of the political' – which originated in *operaismo* and spread from there – was about this. Workers'
struggles determine the course of capitalist development, but capitalist
development will use those struggles for its own ends if no organised
revolutionary process opens up that is capable of changing that balance
of forces. It is easy to see this in the case of social struggles in which the
entire systemic apparatus of domination repositions itself, reforms,
democratises and stabilises itself anew.

A paradox: the most culturally backward struggles – for 'emancipation' – had social consequences that were favourable to labour, forcing
capital to make concessions: the welfare state, constitutional reforms,
the role of unions and parties. Yet the more culturally advanced struggles – for liberation – ushered in a vengeful capitalist resurgence, the

pensée unique of a single possible social form, and the subordination of everything human to a universal theory and practice of bourgeois life. Maybe, as conservatives and liberals would chorus, the first struggles were right and the second ones wrong? I believe we need to look for another explanation. In the struggles for emancipation, the organised workers' movement played a central, active part. In the struggles for liberation, it was the crisis of that movement which played an active role – and, paradoxically, the struggles exacerbated that crisis. Did *operaismo* also function in this way? I leave the question open.

Operaismo and the PCI

Yet there was a simple fact which could not be eliminated by an act of political will. Many of those who made up the 'alternative subjectivity' of the 1960s had been formed outside, and were to some extent oriented against, the official, institutional forms of the labour movement and its parties. Thus, in 1962, the Fiat workers' dispute over a new contract became the opportunity for an extraordinary public agitation, which made itself felt at national level. This, we learned, was how the political centrality of the working class operated, in practice: putting back on the country's agenda, each time it erupted, Brecht's proposal to the Paris antifascist conference of 1935: 'Comrades, let us talk about property relations!' But the PCI did not acquit itself of its allotted function of translating the great workers' struggles of the early '60s into high politics. Contrary to what is commonly supposed, the 'party of the working class' was more willing to listen to the sixty-eight students than to the sixty-nine Italian workers. (Here, too, there is proof ex post facto: in the years that followed, the party's leadership was replenished far more from the ranks of the students than from those of the workers.) At the same time, a leftist anticommunism developed which requires historical analysis. Here, it was fundamentally anti-PCI, composed of intellectual forces that still exist today (despite the disappearance of their antagonist), who grew up under the sign of a movement, a generation, an outlook; a mode of feeling, intimacy and communication rather than of being, thought and struggle. The vanguards of those days have now been joined by an army of repentants.

This phenomenon intensified after Togliatti's death in 1964, not just because of a real decline in the party's capacity for mediation, but also because of the profound transformations that were taking place within Italian society. It was only with the late 1950s and early '60s that modern capitalism really took off in Italy, and the ancient little world of civil society, embedded in the memory of the nineteenth century, finally came to an end. The small-minded 'Italietta' of the Risorgimento still weighed on those of us born in the 1930s; we would learn more from studying that decade than from experiencing all those that followed. We were vaccinated against the vetero-italica disease. The whole of Italian history up to that point had been a minor story of the twentieth century. Those of us attempting to think in modern, disenchanted ways felt its weight on our shoulders – from the limitations of the Italian language to the blindness of its culture. As we discovered, reading Locke and Montesquieu and examining the Westminster model, the entire pre-fascist era was, after all, a caricature of Western liberal systems. And the two 'red Viennas', so different from one another – 1919–20 and 1945–46 – were magical moments that could only have emerged from the ashes of the great wars.

The quiet strength of the PCI was to place itself within this minor history of *longue durée*, scaling back its objectives, calling a halt to any impulsiveness, organising a 'what is to be done?' that never went beyond the possible, being careful never to reach for the unfeasible. The PCI's 'national-popular' was a *bête noire* for us workerists, at a level of culture even before politics; this was something we understood early on. In 1964, our comrade Alberto Asor Rosa, at the age of thirty, wrote *Scrittori e popolo*[6]: it was an essay on – and against – populist literature in Italy. His book marked the beginnings of a crisis in an aspect of Italian political culture that had remained hegemonic to that point. Yet, without that popular – not populist – politics, we could never have had reason to sing, *Avanti, avanti, il gran partito noi siamo dei lavoratori* … The real strength of the PCI was its conscious strategy of rooting itself, lucidly, culturally, in the people who had emerged from this history.

It is commonplace to say that the PCI was the real Italian social democracy. It was not. Rather, it was the Italian version of a communist party. The Italian road to socialism had been a long one, stretching far

6 Alberto Asor Rosa, *Scrittori e popolo*, Rome: Einaudi, 1965.

into the distance: behind us was the history of a nation, the reality of a people, the tradition of a culture. Gramsci's life and work synthesised these things and bequeathed their hegemonic intellectual legacy to the totalizing political action of Togliatti. Thus, reformism was, in an original sense, the political form that the revolutionary process took in that context. This cycle concluded with the dissolution of the myth of capitalist backwardness, which had long persisted in the PCI, even during the rise of capitalist development in Italy. The most orthodox Togliatti faction, the Amendola group, cultivated this myth beyond any justifiable point and made it the social basis for a cultural common sense. This is where the split occurred between the party and young emerging intellectual forces, who found support in parts of the union sector, especially in the North, and in the restive ranks of the party.[7]

In fact, the northern Italian workers' struggles of the early '60s were closer to those of New Deal America than to those of the southern Italian farm workers in the 1950s. The Apulian labourer who became a mass worker in Turin was the symbol of the end of 'Italietta' history. Togliatti had a firm grasp of the superstructural and political aspects of the early centre-left but was unable to see the social, material causes that had brought them about and the central role of the great factory. *Quaderni Rossi* and *Classe Operaia* saw more clearly than the PCI journals, *Società* and *Rinascita*, the factory-society-politics nexus as the strategic location in which capitalist transformations took place. One need only turn the pages of the *operaisti* journals: correspondence from factories, onsite analysis of the restructuring of the production process, assessments of management strategies, critique of demands, evaluation of contracts, interventions in struggles, international issues, as well as editorials on the key political questions of the time.

Culture of Crisis

The hypothesis that the chain had to be broken not where capital was weakest but where the working class was strongest set the *operaista* agenda. Even now, I am not sure whether a relish for intellectual adventure and the exercise of political responsibility can be truly compatible;

---

7 For the PCI's internal debate, see *New Left Review* I, 13–14, Jan–Apr 1962.

yet they coexisted for us, in the political friendships born on that basis. If not much else came out of it, at least we found a way of surviving, with an enjoyable *hominis dignitate*, in a hostile world. In this sense, our *operaismo* was essentially a form of cultural revolution, which produced significant intellectual figures rather than determining historical events. More than a way of doing politics, it defined a way of doing political culture. This was a serious, high culture: specialisation without academicisation, aiming at a practice with strategic consistency and historical depth. It was a matter of restoring, or perhaps implanting, a postproletarian aristocracy of the people against the existing drift of a bourgeois populism. We saw a subject without form – or rather, with a traditional, historical form which was in crisis. Our new social subject, the mass worker, was no longer contained in the old political form. A subject that is born of crisis is a critical subject. A passionate love affair would later develop between *operaismo* and nineteenth-century Central European thought: a love that was not disappointed, and that I would say was returned, given the work produced within that framework. It is enough to skim through magazines such as *Angelus Novus*, *Contropiano* and, later – to a certain extent – *Laboratorio politico*, to be convinced that for us, communication has never been separate from thought.

Much ink has been spilled in controversies over anti-Hegelianism in Italian *operaismo*. Hegelianism was to be found, first and foremost, in that ideology of the workers as a 'universal class', saturated with Kantian ethics in the era of the Second International, and with dialectical materialism in that of the Third. That image of the proletariat – which, 'by freeing itself frees all of humanity', present in the nineteenth-century Marx – was shattered by Munch's scream, after which followed the great breakdown of all forms in the early twentieth century. Here we are speaking of artistic avant-gardes, but also of scientific and philosophical ones, and the revolution of all other collective human forms, social, economic, political, under the tragic impact – 1914! – of the first great European, and global, civil war. The tide of human progress – the *belle époque* – crashed against the wall of the worst massacre ever witnessed. But where there is danger, deliverance also grows. Out of that inferno came the principle of hope: the most advanced revolutionary experiment ever launched. It was the Bolsheviks, alone and cursed, who made the leap; all that followed, in the course of their experiment, cannot cancel the gratitude which humanity owes for that heroic effort. One need not be a communist to understand this. And whoever does not understand it – or does not want to do so – is missing a part of the soul they need in order to exist and to act politically in this world. We had the good fortune to set out with this thought. We added the *virtù* of the 'worker's perspective', and so began the intellectual adventure recounted here.

Critique of 1968

Two good twists of fate were that we lived 1956 while we were still young and 1968 when we no longer were. This allowed us to grasp the political kernel lying beneath the ideological crust of those dates. We could respond to 1956 without the constraint of the historic shackles that weighed upon the previous generation; we could seize the possibilities it opened up. It was a time when history and politics were in full flow, imposing themselves on everyday life; we had no choice but to engage with events, to question ourselves, make decisions, choose between two sides. I never accepted the notions of good and evil used by the Church to tame the faithful. But I understood, through hard experience, that evil means those long, dismal periods when nothing happens; good manifests itself when you are forced to take a stand; it's the fall into sin that awakens you to freedom. Similarly, nihilism is not produced by dark periods of barbarism but by false glimmers of civilisation – against which it is not the worst response.

There was no room for narcissistic gambolling or analysing the unconscious in 1956 – at least, not in that troubled land which was the international communist movement. The political calamity triggered a great cultural crisis. Little by little, as dramatic events unfolded – the Twentieth Party Congress of the CPSU (Communist Party of the Soviet Union), Khrushchev's secret speech, the Hungarian revolt and its destruction – everything was accounted for. Togliatti's mandarins trod warily between the contradictions of the Soviet system, vulgarizing the Gramscian edict against Croce: less dialectic of opposites, more dialectic of differences. We were young and free-spirited: naive as it may appear, we wanted clarity rather than confusion, yet we were offered a delicate chiaroscuro. It was the first 'no' – agonizing but emphatic – that we gave to the party leaders. Not having lived through the war against fascism, we did not feel that iron bond with the socialist motherland: it had not become the focus of our lives. For our elders, antifascism had been a political and moral imperative, capable of leaving its stamp on one's existence forever; a commitment of great human intensity, from which no thinking heart could escape in the climate of those times. Born in the 1930s, we were too young for the antifascist resistance, and never feared in the postwar era that fascism would return. As militants, we experienced the Cold War as a 'clash of civilisations', not a conflict over spheres of influence. From that point on, there was no room in our thinking for 'magnificent and progressive destinies'. Communism was no longer the final stop on a railway line that led humanity inexorably towards progress. Following Marx, it would be the self-criticism of the present; following Lenin, it would be the organisation of a force capable of breaking the weakest link in history's chain.

This reiteration of 1956 is not excessive. Without that leap, *operaismo* would never have existed: we would not have had Panzieri's 'Theses on Workers' Control', nor would we have come together as intellectuals of the crisis.[8] The year 1968 would still have happened – it sprang from other roots, from the modernizing imperatives of capitalist society – but perhaps it would have assumed a different form, with more flower children and fewer apprentice revolutionaries. We witnessed 1968 as adults, which was another stroke of luck, for to experience that year in one's youth turned out, in the long run, to be a great misfortune (as Marx had said it was to be a wage-labourer). The appearance took hold and the real substance was lost. The appearance – that is, what the movement expressed symbolically – was its antiauthoritarian character. In its own way, this worked. The substance was its character as revolt. This did not last, though: in individuals it was extinguished and absorbed, in groups it was diverted and bastardised.

Those of us who had lived through the struggles of the factory workers in the early 1960s looked on the student protests with sympathetic detachment. We had not predicted a clash of generations, though in the factories we had met the new layer of workers – especially young migrants from the South – who were active and creative, always in the lead (certainly compared to the older workers, who were exhausted by

---

8 Raniero Panzieri, 'Sette tesi sulla questione del controllo operaio', *Mondo Operaio*, February 1958.

past defeats). But in the factories, the bond between fathers and sons still held together; it was among the middle classes that it had snapped. This was an interesting phenomenon, but not decisive for changing the structural balance of forces between the classes. At Valle Giulia in March '68, we were with the students against the police – not like Pasolini. But at the same time, we knew it was a struggle behind enemy lines, to determine who would be in charge of modernisation. The old ruling class, the wartime generation, was exhausted. A new elite was pressing forward into the light; a new ruling class for the globalised capitalism that lay in the future. The Cold War had long become a hindrance; the crisis of politics, parties and 'the public' was upon us. The poison of 'anti-politics' was first injected into the veins of society by the movements of '68. The maturation of civil society and the conquest of new rights transformed collective consciousness. But first and foremost, these transformations were beneficial for Italian capitalism and its pursuit of modernity. The reprivatisation of the whole system of social relations began with this period, and it has not yet come to a close.

Paradoxical Outcomes

The remarkable youth of 1968 did not understand – nor did we, though we would grasp it soon enough – this truth: to demolish authority did not automatically mean the liberation of human diversity; it could mean, and this is what happened, freedom specifically for the animal spirits of capitalism, which had been stamping restlessly inside the iron cage of the social contract that the system had seen as an unavoidable cure for the years of revolution, crisis and war. The year 1968 was a classic example of the heterogenesis of ends. The slogan *ce n'est qu'un début* could only be successful for a very brief period, against the backdrop of an eruption across the Western world which constituted the strength of the movement. To chant *la lutte continue* was already an acknowledgment of defeat.

In the long run, the game was lost. The radicalisation of discourse on the autonomy of the political from the early 1970s was born from this failure of the insurrectionary movements, from the workers' struggles to the youth revolt, which had spanned the decade of the 1960s. What was lacking was the decisive intervention of an organised force, which could only have come from the existing workers' movement, and therefore the Communists. A concerted initiative could have pushed the reluctant European social-democratic parties toward undertaking a historic reconstruction, for which the moment was ripe. We should have pushed for a new 'politics from above' inside the rank-and-file movements, to counter the implicit drift toward antipolitics and thus to disrupt the social and political balance of forces rather than restabilizing it. At that moment, another world was possible. Later, and for a long time, it would not be. The opportunity was not taken, the fleeting moment passed and the dead reconquered the living. Real processes defeated imaginary subjects. In some respects, things went better in the United States than in Europe. There, the American Goliath was humiliated by the Vietnamese David. Here, we passed from the Paris rebellion to the invasion of Prague, from *Quaderni Rossi* to the *nouveaux philosophes*, from Woodstock to Piazza Fontana, and from the flower children to the *anni di piombo*. 'The times they are a' changing': ten years after 1968, the times really had changed. The Trilateral Commission dictated the tenets of the new world order and its civic religion.

In Italy, the era of classical *operaismo* was finished. *Classe Operaia* took the controversial decision to declare its project exhausted. 'Don't subscribe', it told its readers with characteristic irony in the final issue, published in 1967, 'we're going now'. What role might the 'political newspaper of the workers in struggle' have played if it had still been alive during the events of 1968, with its compact, prestigious core of activists? Could it have influenced the movement, offered a lead, given it a political orientation? I don't think so. The decision to close it down was taken to avoid the looming risk of turning into a 'groupuscule', with all the usual deformations: minoritarianism, self-referentiality, hierarchisation, 'dual layers', unconsciously imitating the practices of the 'dual state' and so on. At best, small groups were fatally led to repeat the vices of larger organisations. There was thus no continuity between political *operaismo* and the potentially antipolitical movements of 1968. Of course, we smiled when we heard people chanting 'student power', but I remember vividly the moment when a student march on the Corso in Rome unexpectedly raised the cry of 'workers' power'. In fact, if *operaismo* was diffident about 1968, 1968 discovered *operaismo*, and long before the 'hot autumn' of 1969. 'Students and workers, united in the struggle' was a thrilling, mobilising slogan, helping to form a generous generation of militants, and it is still quietly present in the pores of civil society.

Classe Operaia shut down just as the Eleventh Party Congress of the PCI was opening. There was never a more striking coincidence of opposites. I was then on leave from the party, but party membership – conscription by one's own free will – was taken for granted: this was so before the *operaista* experience and remained the case as long as *il partito* existed. But we did not involve ourselves in the bitter struggles at the top for the leadership that came after Togliatti. We were against Amendola without being for Ingrao. We did not like the idea of a single left-wing party for Italy, which would mean the explicit social-democratisation of the PCI. But, above all, we fought the party's right on the question of its analysis of Italian capitalism. We put forward, in true Marxist style, the concept of neocapitalism, which we saw as a more advanced – and therefore more productive – terrain of struggle, while the other side had an outdated view of the Italian economy, compounded by an equally backward Soviet orthodoxy. The international context, too, had been altered by the beginning of the Cold War détente and 'peaceful coexistence' between the two systems. Capital would need a new levy of political professionals, armed with a different cultural tradition – yet to be constructed – and with new intellectual tools. This would be a figure brought up to date for neocapitalism, a combined specialist-cum-politician, able to operate skilfully within the contingencies of the disorder to come.

The Italian 'hot autumn' of 1969 was a spontaneous movement: this was also its limitation, its ephemeral character eventuating in its structuring role, within the medium-to-long term, of modernisation without revolution. *Operaismo* was, at least in Italy, one of the founding premises of 1968; but at the same time, it made a substantive criticism of '68 in advance. In its turn, 1969 corrected a great deal and caused much more alarm. That was the real *annus mirabilis*. The year 1968 was born in Berkeley and baptized in Paris. It arrived in Italy still young and yet already mature, poised between workers and the PCI, exactly where we had positioned ourselves. *Operaismo* pushed 1968 beyond its premises. In 1969, the issue wasn't antiauthoritarianism but anticapitalism.

Workers and capital found themselves physically face to face with one another. With the *autunno caldo*, wages exerted a direct effect on profits;

the balance of power shifted in favour of the workers and to the disadvantage of the bosses. The idea of *lotta operaia* took on a general social dimension, and this was clear in the two consequences that derived from it. First, a leap in national social consciousness and a political opening for consensus around the greatest opposition party, which still saw itself formally as the party of the working class. Second, the violent reaction of the system, which used all its defensive strategies, from legal concessions to state terrorism, from the secret service to the social compromise. The system's aggressive response to the jolt administered by the *autunno caldo* swept the movement away – or, in what amounted to the same thing, made it change course. It was this second path that predominated, and from it another history would flow.

All of this was already inscribed in the unresolved contradiction between struggles and organisation – new struggles, therefore new organisation – which had blocked the path of *operaismo* in its early phase. All attempts to connect with internal developments within the PCI in the mid-1960s went awry. The exceptional 'human material', which played such a major part in the experiment that was *operaismo* was not made for, was not organically adapted to a political game in which one's hypotheses had to be tested on different terrain from that which one has chosen oneself. The idea of 'inside and against' – that sophisticated, perhaps overly complex principle that was expressed in its classic form as political *operaismo* – was unable to take root in flesh-and-blood individuals; it remained the statement of a method, indispensable for understanding but ineffective as a basis for action.

Leaden Times

The true difference between our *operaismo* and the formal workerism of the PCI lay in the concept of the political centrality of workers. We carried on this discussion right up till 1977, when we convened a conference on 'workerism and worker centrality' with Napolitano and Tortorella, in a leaden Padua, subjected to the non-pacifist forays of the so-called *autonomi*.[9] I do not here take 1977 as a date of key significance – a choice rather

---

9 For the conference proceedings see Tronti, et al., *Operaismo e centralità operaia*, Rome: Riuniti, 1978.

than an oversight. I agree that, compared to 1968, 1977 has more political weight and marks a more decisive social shift; much of the negative relation between new generations and politics was solved there, on that battlefield. But I'd like to say that the Italian workerism of the early 1960s did not lead in this direction. Viewed from the present, *Classe Operaia* was closer to *Quaderni Rossi* than it was to Negri's Potere Operaio, or to all those who went on to participate in *autonomia operaia*. The precise dividing line was as follows: these initial two projects, first the magazine and then the daily newspaper, took themselves to be critically inside the workers' movement, while the later endeavours – grounded more in self-organisation – placed themselves dangerously against that movement. Toni Negri's intelligence is manifest in the theory of the transition from 'mass worker' to *operaio sociale*,[10] but, by that point, the practical damage had already been done and a violent waste of precious human resources had passed hopelessly to the wrong side.

Negri played a key role in the experience of *Classe Operaia*; he was essential to the birth of the paper, and then to editorial work and distribution. With his feet planted firmly in the strategic location of Porto Marghera, he sensed developments and gave shape to his position. The experience of the Fordist–Taylorist worker – and the later criticism of this figure – lies at the root of all his later research. 'Workers Without Allies', cried the title of *Classe Operaia* in March 1964, which had an editorial by Negri. That was a mistake. The system of alliances – employees, middle classes, Red Emilia – that the official workers' movement had built on the basis of an advanced precapitalism certainly needed to be criticised and opposed. But a new system of alliances was coming into view within developed capitalism, with the new professionals emerging from the context of mass production, the consequent expansion of the market and spread of consumerism, and the civil transformations and cultural shifts under way in the country. These were all ways in which the workers of 1962 anticipated the modernisation of 1968 and the dawning postmodernity of 1977.

What followed was the paradoxical story of a general defeat, punctuated by illusory small-scale victories. Thus it went until the end of the 1980s, when we were all forced to understand where history had ended

---

10 Antonio Negri, *Dall'operaio massa all'operaio sociale: intervista sull'operaismo*, Milan: Multhipla Edizioni, 1979.

up going. The leadership of the PCI suffered, in a subordinate mode, the same fate as the ruling classes of the country. Modernisation required a passing of the baton from the generations of war and resistance to the generations of peace and development. The movements of 1968 supplied new personnel for this handover. What happened in the party was what happened in the circles of power: a new political class was not born; rather, in its place, a new administrative class emerged, always managerial, at the levels of both government and opposition. The whole Berlinguer leadership – as much with the historic compromise as with its alternative – proved to be nothing more than a tumultuous period of defence, which lined up *il popolo comunista* to contain and slow the neobourgeois flood. But, at that point, there was little else that could be done. In the last act of the tragedy, the Communist Party was rechristened as the Democratic Party of the Left. This was followed by the farce, when even the word 'party' disappeared, under pressure from antipolitical populism. There were no more barriers. Just the flood.

From the 1980s onwards, neoliberal capitalist restoration sapped the workers' capacity for opposition. With the breaking of the weakest link in the anticapitalist chain – the Soviet state – there was no longer any way to block the returning hegemonic power from taking absolute command. The newly declared dominance of capital was not just economic but social, political and cultural. It was at once theoretical and ideological, a combination of intellectual and mass common sense. Yet it's worth stressing one final fact: for as long as the postcapitalist horizon remained open, the struggle to introduce elements of social justice within capitalism achieved some success. Once the revolutionary project was defeated, the reformist programme became impossible, too. In this sense, the latest form of neoliberal capitalism may prove ironically similar to the final forms of state socialism: incapable of reform.

Index

political power, 48–9, 60, 61, 96, 196, 204,
205, 230, 236, 239, 241, 246, 247,
248, 249, 251, 252, 256, 257, 261,
265, 270, 274
political stabilisation, 98
political struggle, 43, 66, 69, 75, 76, 90,
91, 95, 189, 190, 249, 256
Politik als Beruf (Weber), 290
popular sovereignty, 49, 57, 91
post-*operaismo*, 327
Potere Operaio, 347
Poverty of Philosophy (Marx), 143, 188
power
demand for, 258
labour-power. *See* labour-power
political power. *See* political power
social power. *See* social power
workers' power, 10, 146, 194, 344
working-class labour-power, 58, 168,
182
working-class political power, 241, 261
working-class power. *See* working-class
power
Prices and Incomes Act, 282–3
Principles (Marshall), 284, 309
Principles (Ricardo), 114, 118, 121, 125
'The Principles of Collective Bargaining'
(Perlman), 316
Principles of Economics (Keynes), 284
Principles of Scientific Management
(Taylor), 315
private capital, 47, 81
private property, 45, 47, 48, 56, 107, 108,
109, 110, 139–40, 141, 184–5, 186
process of valorisation. *See* valorisation
process
production
as aim of society in general, 241
and distribution, exchange, and
consumption, 17, 26, 29, 32, 107
as end, 29
as means for consumption, 16
means of, 12, 13, 19, 20, 29, 39, 40, 47,
50, 53, 54, 122, 123, 128, 129, 130,
131, 170, 171, 207, 234, 279
natural laws of, 27
price of, 42
shut down of, 78

production process, 17, 18, 20, 21, 22, 23,
29, 34, 38, 40, 52, 54, 56, 62, 91, 120,
126, 133, 135, 154, 155, 156, 170,
178, 202, 203, 205, 206, 207, 218,
220, 221, 229, 230, 245, 246, 325,
339
production relation, 18, 27, 29, 34, 56, 71,
122, 135, 136, 176, 181, 206, 207,
219, 226, 229, 230, 233
productive capital (*produktives
Kapital*), 37, 38, 46, 126, 129, 130,
131, 174
productive consumption, 16, 37, 40, 74,
130, 159
productive labour, 25, 72, 96, 106, 119,
154, 159, 160–83, 211, 217, 219, 243,
245, 272, 325
productive worker, 138, 161, 162, 165
profit
absolute mass of, 53
according to Marx, 41
as appropriation of someone else's
surplus-value, 47
average profit, 41, 42, 46, 55
rates of, 19, 20, 46–7, 53, 58, 126
superprofit, 46
surplus-value as same as, 41
Progressive Era, 277–80
proletarian, 180, 182
proletarianisation, 28
proletarian revolutions, 250–1
proletariat, 151, 156, 180, 181, 182,
184–98, 233, 239, 248, 268
Proudhon, Pierre-Joseph, 40–1, 108, 140,
143, 188, 212
PSI (Italian Socialist Party), 84
Pullman Strike (1894), 278, 279
Putilov Works, 88

Q
Quaderni Rossi, 327, 328, 331, 332, 333,
334, 339, 344, 347

R
Raniero, 331, 332
'red Vienna,' 338
reductio ad unum, 29
refusal, strategy of, 241–62, 275

relative surplus-value, 17, 19, 21, 23,
    25–6, 31, 53, 131, 136, 168, 208
Renner, Karl, 233
revolutionary class, 6, 32, 34
revolutionary crisis, 243, 303
revolutionary culture, 254
revolutionary movement, 10, 66, 150,
    187, 228, 232
revolutionary theory, 7, 9–10. *See also*
    theory of revolution
revolutions
    bourgeois revolution, 43, 189, 250, 251,
        254, 255
    February revolution/February republic,
        148, 149, 150
    October Revolution, 11, 113
    proletarian revolutions, 250–1
    Russian Revolution, 258
    socialist revolution, 33, 57
    workers' revolution, 100, 150
    working-class revolution. *See* working-
        class revolution
Ricardo, David, 4, 103, 106, 112, 114,
    118–22, 125, 126–7, 128, 144, 152,
    163, 225, 228
Rieser, Vittorio, 331, 332
Rinascita, 339
Risorgimento, 338
Robinson, E. A. G., 308
Rollin, Ledru, 191
Roosevelt, Franklin Delano, 299, 300,
    301, 303, 304, 305, 307, 308, 310,
    311, 316
Roosevelt, Theodore, 279, 299, 305
Rosa, Alberto Asor, 332, 338
ruling class, 48, 55, 63, 65, 81, 142, 188,
    201, 239, 261, 343, 347
Russian Revolution, 258

S
Saccomani, Edda, 331
Saint Simon, 140
Salvati, Michele, 331
Samuelson, Paul, 319
Schlesinger, Arthur M., Jr., 303
Schlesinger, Rudolf, 3
Schmoller, Gustav, 316
Schumpeter, Joseph, 112, 212, 237, 280

'scientific politics,' 267
Scittori e popolo (Rosa), 338
Seattle, Washington strike (1919), 295
Second Conference of the Communist
    League, 189
Second International, 265, 288, 290, 340
sectarianism, 51, 63, 113
self-consciousness, 43, 115, 117, 141, 280,
    297
self-valorisation/self-valorization, 14,
    126, 216
Sherman Act, 305
Shonfield, Andrew, 305
shop-floor actions, 87
A Short View of Russia (Keynes), 309
Sichtbar Machen, 317–26
simple labour, 58, 103, 104, 105, 110
Sismondi, Jean Charles Léonard de, 103
skilled labour, 110
Smith, Adam, 105, 106, 109, 118, 119,
    120, 121, 144, 160, 161, 164, 167,
    241
social capital, 14, 28, 36, 37, 38, 39, 40, 41,
    42, 44, 45, 46, 47, 48, 49, 50, 52,
    53–4, 55, 56, 60, 61, 62, 67, 90, 137,
    222, 231, 242
social character, 44, 56, 104, 105, 131
social class, 49, 54, 63, 90, 95, 137, 178,
    179, 233, 237, 238, 239, 243, 245
Social-Democracy/social democracy, 193,
    194, 251–2, 285–93, 302, 317, 338
Social Democratic Party (SPD), 289, 290
Social-Democrats, 43–4
socialism, 33, 60, 141, 142, 143, 145, 146,
    170, 204, 229, 230, 231, 244, 247,
    266, 283, 331
Socialist Party (PSI), 84, 85
socialist principle, 185
socialist reformism, 70
socialist revolution, 33, 57
social labour, 13, 14, 19, 25, 37, 46, 54, 55,
    103, 104, 105, 110, 132, 145, 177,
    178
social power, 30, 45, 48, 180, 197, 219,
    241, 248
social product, 39, 40
social production, 23, 26, 27, 44, 48, 50,
    51, 56, 122, 136, 172, 325